PRAGUE

PRAGUE

༄

Belonging in the Modern City

CHAD BRYANT

HARVARD UNIVERSITY PRESS

CAMBRIDGE, MASSACHUSETTS

LONDON, ENGLAND

2021

First printing

LIBRARY OF CONGRESS CATALOGING-IN-PUBLICATION DATA

Names: Bryant, Chad Carl, author.
Title: Prague : belonging in the modern city / Chad Bryant.
Description: Cambridge, Massachusetts : Harvard University Press,
2021. | Includes bibliographical references and index.
Identifiers: LCCN 2020042436 | ISBN 9780674048652 (cloth)
Subjects: LCSH: Belonging (Social psychology)—Czech Republic—
Prague—Case studies. | Alienation (Social psychology)—Czech
Republic—Prague—Case studies. | Minorities—Czech Republic—
Prague—Case studies. | Nationalism—Czech Republic—Prague—
Case studies. | Toleration—Czech Republic—Prague—Case studies. |
Prague (Czech Republic)—Social conditions—Case studies.
Classification: LCC HM1131 .B79 2021 | DDC 302.5/44094371/2—dc23
LC record available at https://lccn.loc.gov/2020042436

For Lukas, Dominik, and Milada

CONTENTS

CENTRAL
EUROPE

North
Sea

DENMARK

Copenhagen

SWEDEN

Baltic Sea

LITHUANIA

Vilnius

Kaliningrad

RUSSIA

BELARUS

Amsterdam

NETHERLANDS

Berlin

POLAND

Warsaw

GERMANY

Lviv

Brussels

BELGIUM

UKRAINE

LUXEMBOURG

Prague

CZECH

Bohemia

Moravia

REPUBLIC

SLOVAKIA

FRANCE

Munich

Vienna

Bratislava

AUSTRIA

Budapest

HUNGARY

LICHTENSTEIN

SWITZERLAND

ROMANIA

SLOVENIA

Milan

CROATIA

BOSNIA
HERZEG.

SERBIA

BULGARIA

MONACO

SAN MARINO

ITALY

Adriatic Sea

MONTENEGRO

KOSOVO

NORTH
MACEDONIA

Rome

ALBANIA

N

0   100 km

0   100 miles

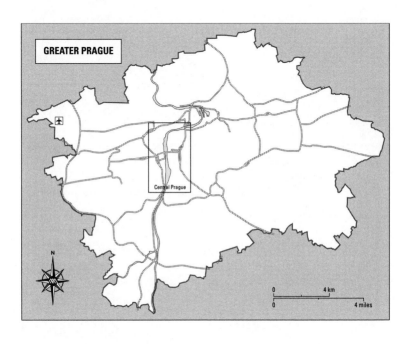

GREATER PRAGUE

Central Prague

N

0   4 km

0   4 miles

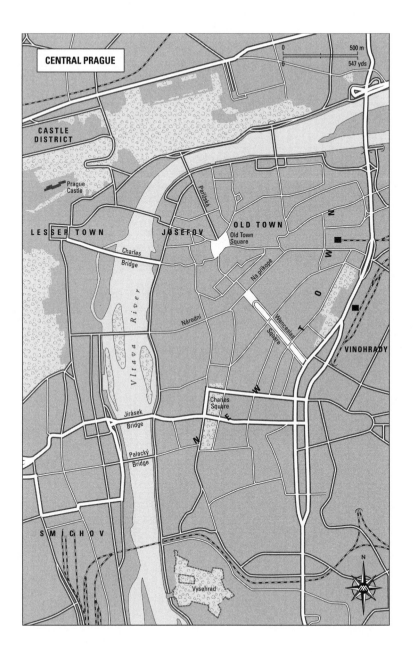

CENTRAL PRAGUE

0
500 m
0
547 yds

CASTLE
DISTRICT

Prague
Castle

LESSER TOWN

JOSEFOV

OLD TOWN

Old Town
Square

Charles
Bridge

Vltava River

Na příkopě

Partyzská

Národní

Wenceslas Square

Charles
Square

VINOHRADY

Jirásek
Bridge

N E W   T O W N

Palacký
Bridge

SMÍCHOV

Vyšehrad

N

INTRODUCTION

☙❧

Belonging and Imagination

PRAGUE'S BEST PLAYGROUND lies within the walls of the ancient fortress of Vyšehrad. A beautiful linden tree greets visitors at the entrance. The zip line is fast. Trees spread their branches gracefully above the wooden play equipment. There are plenty of places to play hide-and-seek. Ice cream is for sale around the corner. What makes the Vyšehrad playground so special, however, are its carved wooden totems, each representing a character from Alois Jirásek's *Old Czech Legends* (1894). Behind an evergreen, on the right side of the path leading to the zip line, is Father Čech, who, with his flowing beard and determined countenance, led his Slavic tribe, Moses-like, from the other side of the Carpathians to this spot. Over by the sandpit is Čech's son and successor, Krok. On the other side of the path to the zip line, facing the sandpit, is Libuše, undoubtedly the most recognizable figure in the playground. Libuše briefly ruled over the Czechs after Krok died without a male heir. She then, reluctantly, sought out and married the predestined king, a peasant named Přemysl who used an iron plow as a dining table. Libuše was also a prophetess. She foretold that male rule would result in higher taxes and greater servitude. She foretold where Czechs could find precious metals in the hills and mountains of Bohemia. She foretold wars. Most famously, she cast her eyes northwest of Vyšehrad to a steep cliff across the Vltava River, where Prague Castle now stands, and declared: "I see before me a great city, whose glory shall reach the heavens!"[1]

Now picture yourself leaving the playground for Vyšehrad's northwestern wall, high above the city. As you scan the panorama, Libuše's vision would seem to be confirmed. Prague has become a great city. With a population of 1.3 million people, it is a dynamic center for the arts, business, and technology. More than 7 million tourists visit Prague each year to see the city's architectural treasures, which, unlike those of so many other European cities, were largely spared the ravages of World War II. As the Prague City Tourism Group declares in its pocket guide, the city, a UNESCO World Heritage Site since 1992, is a charming collage of architectural styles, from Romanesque to Cubist, with modern amenities and an efficient transportation system.[2] This particular vision of Prague, which today elicits justifiable pride in most Czechs, is a relatively new creation, however. Around 1900, Czech city leaders obliterated much of Prague's right bank. Modern, French-inspired apartment buildings and broad avenues replaced "slum" housing, part of a larger effort to reimagine Prague as a modern European city.[3] After World War I, when Prague became the capital of the newly established Czechoslovakia, its new president, Tomáš Masaryk, took up residence in Prague Castle, just as a long line of Bohemian kings had done many years ago. From his perch atop this left-bank hill, Masaryk also oversaw the renovation of the then dilapidated Castle, determined to make it a powerful symbol of his new republic. Decades later, mass-produced concrete apartment complexes appeared on the landscape, part of a larger, Communist-era effort to transform Prague into a socialist city. Below the Castle, near the left bank, stands Nový Smíchov, one of Europe's largest shopping centers. Opened in 2001, it inhabits a space previously dominated by a Communist-era factory, which had, among other things, manufactured streetcars for the Eastern bloc.[4]

These visions do have one thing in common. Just like Jirásek's story of Libuše, they have all been coded Czech in ways meant to legitimize political power in the name of the nation. They have thus complemented more overt symbols of Czechness that are embedded in the cityscape. Since the nineteenth century, street names, plaques, and monuments have been named for national heroes, whose bodies have often found their final resting place in the cemetery behind Vyšehrad's imposing Saint Peter and Saint Paul Basilica. On the Vltava River, south of the Castle, is Palacký Bridge, completed in 1878 and named in honor of František Palacký, the nineteenth-century historian and "father of the nation." Legionnaires' Bridge, two bridges farther north, is named in honor of prisoners of war turned national liberators during World War I. In between is the concrete and iron Jirásek Bridge, opened to the public in 1931, well after Jirásek and his Libuše story had entered the national canon. Most tourists today fly into Václav Havel Airport, named after the country's most famous Communist dissident and its first post-Communist president.

Now picture a contemporary Praguer atop Vyšehrad. She takes in these visual cues, which inspire her to conjure up episodes from Czech national history that have played out in Prague's buildings, streets, and surroundings. (She might pause to wonder, too, why most of these monuments are to men.) Linden trees remind her of poetry and stories celebrating the nation's official tree. Just below Libuše's overlook on Vyšehrad, along the right bank of the Vltava, a streetcar clanks along, filled with more Praguers who might conjure these same visions. Most likely, however, they are doing other things: reading the local newspaper (in Czech), conversing about the fate of the national soccer team (in Czech), or bemoaning the current state of politics (again, in Czech). Most Praguers might also imagine children reading Jirásek in classrooms across the city. If it is late December, they might picture thousands of bathtubs filled with carp, part of the traditional Christmas meal. They might even visualize a map of railroad tracks crisscrossing the country, with many of its lines connecting to Prague and two running under the Iron Bridge below Vyšehrad.

Other perspectives would reveal less harmonious visions and more human complexity. Rather than visualizing a glorious, eternal Czech city, as Jirásek had done, someone gazing on Prague in the early nineteenth century would have seen a peripheral city in the multilingual Habsburg monarchy. At that time many considered Prague to be a "German" city. The German language and German speakers predominated in the civil service, the university, and early industry. Imagine Karel Vladislav Zap, a self-described Czech, strolling on Žofín Island with his wife, Honorata, and friends. The son of a humble craftsman, he strove for the kind of respectable, middle-class life that had traditionally been reserved for German-speaking elites. Skip ahead to the turn of the century, after Czech speakers have taken control of city hall and installed Czech-language signs throughout Prague. Imagine Egon Erwin Kisch, a German-speaking Jew from a solidly middle-class background, who remembered well the antisemitic riots that followed a recent row about installing more Czechs in the Habsburg civil service. As Kisch wandered the streets, he wondered, as had his friend and rival Franz Kafka, if there was a place for him in the city any longer. Not long thereafter, following four horrific years of war, the Habsburg monarchy had fallen. Prague had become the capital of the newly created Czechoslovakia. Imagine Vojtěch Berger, a World War I veteran and carpenter, who often marched in protest against the government. At the war's end, middle-class political leaders dashed his hopes for a genuine revolution. The political party to which he belonged, the Communist Party, was hounded by police.

Jumping ahead again, to the 1970s, imagine Hana Frejková, an actress, coming home to her apartment on the outskirts of Communist Prague. Soon after the Communist regime had come to power following the Nazi occupation, it arrested and executed her father on trumped-up charges of his having been a Zionist enemy of both the nation and of the Communist struggle. The same regime then expelled eight-year-old Hana and her mother, a native German speaker, from the city. They were able to return to Prague but, despite professional success, Hana was filled with unease. In 1989 Communist rule collapsed and, a few years later, Czechoslovakia dissolved into the Czech Republic and Slovakia. Imagine Duong Nguyen, a young graduate of one of Prague's new private universities, as she returned from her study-abroad year in France. As a struggling Czech government dabbled publicly in xenophobia, a landlord on Charles Square rejected Nguyen's lease application, calling her a "foreigner." Nguyen's parents had emigrated from Vietnam but she had grown up in the Czech Republic, spoke fluent Czech, and had Czech friends.

All of these Praguers, in their own ways, experienced a sense of marginalization in the city that they called home. Their stories follow the rise of nationalism while exposing tensions between homogenizing national imaginations and the persistence of urban diversity.[5] Each individual—an aspiring Czech-language guidebook writer; a clever, German-speaking journalist; a Bolshevik carpenter; an actress of mixed heritage living in the shadow of Communist terror; and a Czech-speaking Vietnamese blogger—has produced a rich set of artifacts: letters and published books, articles and essays, a diary, a memoir, and online content. In these writings, all five authors have puzzled through their respective relationships with the city, national imaginations, and their fellow Praguers. None of these authors appears in the traditional canon of writings about Czech Prague. In fact, their very existence and their writings complicate that canon. They also reveal, through their lives and writings, alternative ways of imagining the city. They challenge us to ask what it means to belong.

Like most cities, and especially capital cities, Prague has been a site where the tension between national imaginations and the persistence of diversity has been intense and salient. Lewis Mumford once wrote that cities are magnets and containers.[6] They are magnets because they attract goods, ideas, and, most importantly, people. They are containers in that generations of inhabitants store thoughts and memories in them, often within cityscapes. Cities are also containers in that they are condensed spaces in which interactions among people and institutions are multiple and intense. Within these spaces, urban and political elites work to make the nation imaginable while coding the city national. Yet cities, as magnets, draw extraordinarily diverse people and populations into the container. Urban interactions and economic forces create further difference. Difference is inevitable, a defining characteristic of the city. Prague has not been an exception to this general rule, not even after the Holocaust and Czechoslovakia's violent expulsion of the city's Germans following World War II.

Cities, especially well-planned cities in open societies, inherently possess the ability to mitigate these tensions, to offer a sense of well-being and security to those marginalized by overbearing national imaginations. Cities intrinsically possess extraordinary possibilities for community making and for creating various individual notions of place. Generations of scholars and popular writers dating back to the nineteenth century have argued that city dwellers, ripped from the comfort of traditional rural communities, are destined for alienation and thus for producing social discord. More recent scholarship, however, has demonstrated that population density, resources, and the variety of spaces that cities can provide are particularly conducive to the creation of subcultures.[7] What better place than the city for odd hobbyists and political nonconformists to find each other in greater numbers, and to be less oppressed by the gaze of majoritarian cultures? Other urban sociologists have shown how cities create the conditions for multiple social networks and a variety of acquaintances. These "weak ties," in their multitude, can substitute for "strong ties" that bind smaller population settlements.[8] Similarly, the visual richness of the city allows for individualized interpretations of the cityscape and multiple interactions with the built environment. Cities are good for what humanist geographers call "emplacement," in which "lived bodies belong to places and help constitute them" while "places belong to lived bodies and depend upon them."[9] Community and place can, of course, reinforce each other. Proper sidewalks and safe streets, as Jane Jacobs has argued, allow for different urban characters to intermingle in a "sidewalk ballet" that creates a sense of security, place, and community.[10]

Cities thus abound with potential for what we might call everyday "practices of belonging." In the early nineteenth century, modern urbanites in Prague and elsewhere reinvented salon gatherings to create respectable, face-to-face communities. They strolled newly created paths and parks, marking the ground beneath their feet and the city laid out before them as their own. Later in the century, they met in cafés and nightclubs that were less respectable, more modern, and more exciting. They wandered the nighttime streets of the Old Town, experiencing moments of oneness with the mishmash of sights and the brief human encounters made possible by streetlights and sidewalks. They joined clubs and associations, united by common hobbies, talents, and political causes. For brief moments they took over streets and public spaces, bodies pressed together in protest. Under Communist rule, Praguers gathered for work. Some enjoyed collective pride in their efforts, or pride in the skills and artisanship that they shared with others. They met in spaces, such as theaters, that enjoyed a degree of autonomy from a regime determined to coordinate and surveil. More recently, Praguers, like so many people around the world, have met and gathered in virtual spaces. They have created online connections that, while rife with the potential for abuse and hate, have also formed a basis for face-to-face communities and organizations throughout the city.

For those alienated by national imaginations, for those inhabiting an environment thick with symbolic reminders of their otherness, everyday practices of belonging are all the more necessary, and perhaps more revealing. Historically minded scholars and writers have tended to impose certain characteristics on Prague and its past, to imagine it as magical, surreal, or multicultural—depictions often crafted in opposition to totalizing national visions.[11] This book toggles between the heights of Vyšehrad and ground-level practices of belonging in the city. The purpose here is to critique those totalizing visions while recasting Prague as a particular city characterized by extraordinary differences and immense changes over time. The aim is to recapture various struggles against marginalization and alienation on their own terms, within their particular contexts, described in each character's own time-bound words. What follows, then, is part urban biography, part individual biography. It is also a story of belonging and imagination set in Prague, but its significance extends far beyond this magnificent capital city.

Belonging is typically understood as the sense of comfort, acceptance, and certitude found in a particular place or group of people. It is a term, however, that can be elusive. Some scholars suggest that it often acts as a synonym for notions of identity or citizenship. Others have pegged belonging to a fundamental human motivation.[12] Our pursuit of belonging, evolutionary biologists have argued, is part of what makes us human. We are, after all, social animals.[13] In his hierarchy of fundamental human needs, the noted psychologist Abraham Maslow ranked "belongingness" just below having enough food and feeling safe. His successors have set out to demonstrate that the need to belong, "to create at least a minimum quantity of lasting, positive, and significant interpersonal relationships," constitutes a "powerful, fundamental, and extremely pervasive motivation" behind human behavior.[14] Still other scholars have turned to phenomenology, which they claim helps refocus our attention on the individual subject, arguing that belonging is an everyday mode of being that is rarely the object of conscious thought, unless it is absent or lacking.[15]

Echoing scholars of emotions, we should resist seeing *belonging*— whether as a psychological motivation or mode of being—as innate and universal.[16] In English, our contemporary meaning of the word emerged only in the nineteenth century, simultaneously with mass migration to cities and the melting away of many traditional structures of community.[17] There is no exact equivalent of the word in either Czech or German, although there are clusters of words referring to its various elements. Both languages have equivalents to the English-language phrase "to feel at home" in a place or among some people. The Czech phrase *u nás* might be translated as "among us," "at our place," "at home," "in our culture," "in our house," "in our town," or "in our country," depending on context. In fact, *u nás* neatly combines notions of community and place with broader notions of belonging, thus capturing a central theme of this book.

We might also think about how *belonging* points to a common set of problems and struggles that characterized the rise of modern Europe. As Montserrat Guibernau has argued, a distinctive feature of modern societies is the individual's freedom—and burden—to choose to belong to a community and thus "transcend his or her limited existence" as "an antidote to alienation and aloneness."[18] How Praguers chose to forge face-to-face communities, and how they understood those communities, took many different forms both within the city and across time. Similarly, the ways in which people made sense of place and their reasons for doing so were extraordinarily numerous across time and space. Indeed, Praguers and others have engaged in an ongoing struggle to create and re-create community, to create and re-create a sense of place, amid relentless institutional and political changes that have characterized the uncertain swirl of modern history and of a world in which "all that is solid melts into air."[19]

The idea of the nation promised to address this dilemma. The nation, Benedict Anderson tells us, is "imagined because the members of even the smallest nation will never know their fellow members, meet them, or even hear of them, yet in the minds of each lives the image of their communion."[20] The nation, in its modern sense, first came into existence in the eighteenth century, when it needed to be imagined, when it could be imagined. As Anderson has argued, the rise of the state and then industrialization, combined with increased mobility, eroded traditional communities. These same forces, along with ideas emerging from the Enlightenment, also dealt a fatal blow to the medieval Christian natural order of things. Europeans' place within society and within the cosmos had become uncertain. Into this breach emerged the nation, a new form of kinship tie, a particular, bounded community that anchored individuals within the flow of history and gave them and their conationals a shared past, present, and future. The nation, which Anderson defines as an "imagined political community," has served additional purposes in the modern era. Now everyone, it seems, is a member of a nation, which, instead of God or tradition, legitimizes political power. Nations and the states that allegedly represent them compose the new order of things on this earth. Nationalist passions have mobilized the nation's loyal adherents to take part in unspeakable violence and the murder of millions.

Post–World War II scholars, horrified by the violence that nationalism had wrought, have generally agreed that the modern nation is a construct, something that is invented or created. Yet few scholars have probed Anderson's most innovative keyword, *imagination*. It is not a coincidence that imagination, the "power to convert absence into presence, actuality into possibility, what-is into something-other-than-it-is," became a celebrated human faculty in Europe around the same time that the modern nation was first conjured into existence.[21] Thomas Aquinas, echoing most pre-Enlightenment philosophers, warned that imagination, in making "everything other than it is," threatened the natural order that defined Europeans' place within society and within the cosmos. St. Augustine had warned that imagination, or, in Latin, *fantasia*, invited irrational passions. A more positive assessment of imagination emerged in the eighteenth and nineteenth centuries. As the Enlightenment gave way to Romanticism, Immanuel Kant and early nineteenth-century German idealists argued that imagination, which transformed the real into the ideal, and absence into presence, was crucial for human knowledge and individual consciousness. Nor was imagination just the plaything of philosophers. As Anderson knew quite well, the eighteenth and nineteenth centuries witnessed the rise of the novel, a genre capable of transporting readers to other times and places, allowing them to inhabit the minds of fictional characters. Expanded literacy and print cultures multiplied the possibilities for imagination and for imagining nations.

Capital cities such as Prague were loci for imagining nations as political communities, places where the nation became imaginable. National imaginations did not emerge organically. Much of the hard work of making the nation imaginable took place in capital cities. For the most part, middle-class activists and political elites based in Prague codified the language. They and their publishers inserted national imaginations into popular print and into required readings in school. They wrote histories and national poetry that endowed the nation and its members with a shared sense of destiny and a common set of characteristics. They spoke of nations as naturally existing entities, even as their homogenizing, totalizing efforts created these nations. From Prague, they produced maps and manipulated census counts to imagine the geographical boundaries of the nation, to combine a sense of place with a sense of community. Prague, as a physical space, has been a locus of national imagination in other ways as well. Great events in national history are imagined onto the cityscape, which acts as a mecca, museum, and stage for the nation.[22] Monuments, statues, plaques, government buildings, street names, and urban layouts demand awe, respect, and obedience to political power situated in capital cities such as Prague.[23] Together, these efforts, while often justifying the order of things, possess extraordinary power to exclude those not imagined into the nation.

These efforts have not been uniform. As Cynthia Paces observes, Prague's Czech elites have engaged in protracted and often heated struggles over the form and content of the imagined nation. For much of the modern era, except while under Nazi and Communist rule, various political party elites have mobilized their followers using particular imaginations of the Czech nation. In interwar Prague, the (pro-Catholic) Czechoslovak People's Party mobilized its loyalists around their revered patron, St. Wenceslas, whose bronze likeness has long overlooked St. Wenceslas Square. During that same era, Masaryk and Czech liberals typically followed a long tradition of linking Czech nationalism with Protestantism. They revered the proto-Protestant martyr and hero Jan Hus, whose own bronze likeness stares into the distance on Old Town Square, just yards from city hall.[24] In 1905 tens of thousands of Czech Social Democrats filled the streets and squares of Prague demanding universal suffrage. Their leaders had shrewdly appropriated Hus and reimagined him as a populist hero who invoked a uniquely working-class notion of Czech nationalism.[25] These attempts were not entirely successful either. As both Tara Zahra and Pieter Judson have shown, liberal activists based in Prague and else-where often complained of the "nationally indifferent" individuals who adopted various national labels or refused to mobilize behind national projects.[26] For some, such as Praguers happily singing the national anthem at a hockey game, everyday practices of belonging and national imaginations mix easily. Those alienated by national imagi-nations, however, must bear an especially heavy burden of creating alternative communities and notions of place. During times of extreme violence, national imaginations could justify their expulsion and murder.[27]

We might think of imagination in another way, too, as distinct from the national imaginations of the past. The book's five main characters, through their writings and their actions in the world, contributed to and embedded themselves within imaginative storyworlds that they often shared with others. Thanks to imagination, and to the stories that our characters told, they could picture themselves belonging to various communities while claiming Prague as their home. This book invites readers to perform their own acts of imagination, to see in their mind's eye the grand sweep of Prague's history and to inhabit, albeit imperfectly, the lives of five relatively unknown Praguers. The historical profession, whose modern incarnation arose around the same time as modern nation-making and the novel, has long relied on imagination. A common "romantic impulse" to withdraw and escape, C. V. Wedgewood wrote, "[the] desire to remove from one age into another, to imagine and to share in the thoughts and feelings of a time remote from the present," is a central element of historical inquiry.[28] Imagination is also crucial for understanding the past. In the "natural" and "hard sciences," most would agree that one's knowledge of various objects relies on perception, on a relationship between the observer and the observed. The additional challenge for historians is that our objects of study have passed and are gone. Thus, as R. G. Collingwood maintains, historians must imagine worlds, people, and events beyond our immediate perceptions, and they must reenact events and thoughts as well as the actions that connect the two. History, however, is not fiction. Unlike the imagination fired by the novel, Collingwood continues, history requires evidence—artifacts that are analyzed and critiqued before being used to conjure up visions and thoughts.[29] Good history also relies on the careful work of predecessors and on convincing documentation—hence the copious citations at the back of the book.

Perhaps more than ever, our present needs historical imagination. Imagination allows us to connect ethical concerns and abstract concepts to individual lives. It enables us to inhabit, albeit imperfectly, the lives of others. Imagination allows us to think about a better future and better cities, visions that draw inspiration from our understanding of the past. Imagination also creates the words that allow rational human beings in a rational society to pursue their own interests while improving the world around them. Or, as Richard Rorty has suggested, "reason can only follow paths that the imagination has first broken. No words, no reasoning. No imagination, no new words. No such words, no moral or intellectual progress."[30] Imaginations can, of course, serve the powerful, as this book will make clear. They can also give life to conspiracies and lies that threaten both our polity and the most vulnerable in our society. They can legitimate and produce evil. Yet there is another pressing concern. We imagine less and less. We have little time to imagine, to contemplate what others think and feel, to see in our mind's eye, however imperfectly, the past and future. We are bombarded by fleeting, flashing images on our screens, symptomatic of a now flourishing culture of technologically produced stimuli so ably described by Walter Benjamin many decades ago.[31] We are at risk of losing something essential to ourselves and of losing our imaginative ability to change things for the better.

What follows, then, is both a critique of national imagination and an invitation to engage in historical imagination. In this endeavor, Prague presents a number of advantages. It has been the object of first-rate scholarship in a variety of languages, which allows us to faithfully understand the city's national imaginations while re-creating the worlds inhabited by the book's five characters. Each of our five Praguers has produced great amounts of written materials, their voices waiting to be heard and interpreted. Finally, almost all of the built structures, streets, and monuments described in the book can still be found and viewed in Prague today. Few cities in the world have the ability to evoke visions of the past as Prague does. The challenge is to imagine the past in a way that provokes a sense of empathy and historical understanding, while inspiring hopeful visions of the future.

1

GERMAN CITY

༄

IN 1847 KAREL VLADISLAV ZAP published *A Guide to Prague: A Necessary and Useful Book for Everyone Who Wants to Become Familiar with Memorable Sites in the Bohemian Capital City,* which at first glance might seem unremarkable. Dozens of similar books about Prague, then a city on the peripheries of the Habsburg monarchy, had already been published. In fact, Zap shamelessly plagiarized entire passages from his predecessors—an accepted practice at the time. One thing, however, distinguished Zap's guide. Unlike his predecessors, he wrote his book in Czech, not German. There were good reasons to publish books about the city in German. Prague, an increasingly important hub of trade and commerce in central Europe, had become a popular destination for a German-reading public throughout the region. Many readers, and their local guides, imagined Prague as a "German" city. Long ago, when the city had been the seat, albeit briefly, of the Holy Roman Empire, travelers and German-speaking locals drew upon romantic idioms to sentimentalize Prague's past. There were other reasons to think of Prague as a "German" city. Since the eighteenth century, German had been the administrative language of the Habsburg monarchy—a choice made by Habsburg monarchs for practical, not national, reasons.

In Zap's time there were no Czech-language universities. German-language schooling predominated. German-speaking educated elites—civil servants, traders, burgeoning industrialists—dominated the city's social and cultural life.

So why did Zap write in Czech? When his guide was published, Prague's Czech-speaking middle-class elites, Zap included, made up a tiny, loose-knit community. They had good reason not to feel at home in Prague. Because many had migrated to the city from the country-side, the urban landscape was foreign to them. They lived in worlds largely distinct from those of the nobility, and they felt little in common with the poorer, Czech-speaking inhabitants of the city. They were typically first-generation university graduates, if that, and they inhabited the lower levels of middle-class society, several rungs below German-speaking elites. By Zap's time, however, many in this community were making concerted efforts to speak Czech, not German, with each other. They established and consumed Czech-language newspapers and journals. At a time when other middle-class elites considered Prague to be a "German," or "Habsburg," city, they claimed Prague as their own. They declared Prague to be a Czech city and the capital of a newly imagined nation. These are the readers to whom Zap appealed.

What follows is, in part, the story of Zap's intense and sometimes selfish determination to earn a respectable place within this community of Czech speakers. It is also the story of the efforts of Zap and other Czech speakers to create for themselves a sense of belonging in the city—and then to brashly declare Prague to be their city. They did this through writing and reading in Czech. They attended Czech-language theater and spoke Czech during salon discussions, thus simultaneously claiming middle-class and Czech national status. Zap's guide as well as his personal story also pointed to another middle-class sociability practice: strolling. Similar to their German-speaking counterparts, Czech speakers strolled in, around, and beyond the city. Strolling, a form of leisure walking characterized by surprisingly strict rules and customs, confirmed their middle-class credentials. Strolling also created community by endowing locales with common meanings and no-tions of place. Strolling the historic cityscape, as Zap wrote, enabled readers to imagine Prague as a Czech city, the capital of the nation, and the wellspring of national imagination. Zap's guide offers a view of the future, a time when writing about Prague in Czech seemed both obvious and unremarkable.

———

As many travelers and locals observed, early nineteenth-century Prague at first appeared to be a closed, traditional city that exuded an enticing sense of the past. Prague's fortifications, although of dubious military value in an age of modern cannon fire, remained some of the most impressive and extensive in Europe. Massive walls, whose perim-eter took four hours to walk, surrounded the entire city. Soldiers and militia manned guard towers atop the walls. Bridges spanned deep moats that further protected several of the city's gates.[1] Within the walls, physical remnants of bygone eras dominated the cityscape. On the west bank of the Vltava River, atop the city's highest hill, stood the still uncompleted St. Vitus Cathedral, an imposing example of medieval Gothic architecture and the final resting place of many of Bohemia's kings. Surrounding St. Vitus was the Prague Castle, a reminder of Prague's brief moment as capital of the Habsburg monarchy before the Thirty Years' War (1618–1648). Below the Castle lay the Lesser Town, home to many of the Baroque churches erected by Habsburg rulers following that war's end. On the other side of the river was the Old Town, whose jagged roads and town hall recalled the earliest days of urban construction as well as municipal independence. Squeezed be-tween the Vltava's eastward curve and the northwestern border of the Old Town was the Jewish Town, with its synagogues, cemetery, and crowded housing. (For centuries, walls also surrounded the Jewish Town, which could only be reached by passing through one of its manned gates.) The New Town, a vast expanse of medieval-era boulevards and squares, radiated out from the Old Town's other borders. Along with St. Vitus Cathedral and an impressive stone bridge connecting the Old Town to the Lesser Town, the New Town stood as a stark reminder of the architectural ambitions of Charles IV, Bohemia's fourteenth-century king and Holy Roman emperor.

Prague's walls, although remnants of an earlier era, also served various purposes for a city long wary of the world beyond. During the day, guards halted incomers at the city gates as a clerk took note of each entrant's name, social standing, and occupation. Visitors had to declare where they would be lodging and to hand in their passports. A solicitor collected a toll from those entering the city. Anyone bringing goods to the city also paid a customs tax. The gates closed at night, although those riding in carriages could pass through by obtaining special permission from the police and by paying an extra fee of one kreuzer.[2] At night, when the gates closed, residents were appointed to stand on the city's walls and scan the dark cityscape for flames in a city where memories of the devastating fire of 1689 still loomed large. Prague's walls also served as a visual reminder of the city's past as well as the persistence of an urban social order defined by corporate rights and privileges. Well into the nineteenth century, Prague's greater and lesser nobility enjoyed various privileges in the Bohemian kingdom, including serf labor and exemption from military conscription. Burghers and guild members, such as barrel makers, candle makers, and brewers had particular rights and privileges in the city, such as access to municipal charities.[3] The vast majority of Prague's population—day laborers, wood haulers, domestic servants, those without work, and others—had few or no rights in the city. Most of Prague's 7,000 Jews lived in the Jewish Town and were largely subject to the laws—and whims—of the city magistrate.

By the early nineteenth century, however, an array of forces had begun to penetrate Prague's walls and thus to transform the traditional social order and the cityscape. In 1774 the Habsburg ruler Joseph II decreed that the city's four non-Jewish districts—the Old Town, the

New Town, the Lesser Town, and the Castle District—would hence-forth be fused into one administrative unit, thereby ending a long tra-dition of divided, locally autonomous rule in the city. By 1808, the bur-gomaster and municipal council were no longer elected but appointed by the Habsburg governor of Bohemia, whose office and administra-tion were located in Prague. Ruling elites, a burgeoning city adminis-tration, and much of the police force were now civil servants with sala-ries and duties established in Vienna, the Habsburg capital. The result was a professionalization of the city administration, but to the detri-ment of municipal independence and self-sufficiency. A series of im-perial decrees led up to the 1811 citizenship law, which eroded protec-tions and privileges previously enjoyed by the nobility, such as the right to dispense justice to their serfs.[4] From 1782, Habsburg rulers granted certain privileges to Jews, including the ability to practice trades and to own land. Gradually, beginning in 1800, Jews were permitted to open shops and to live in houses just beyond the boundaries of the Jewish Town, but they could not purchase property. The last gates sur-rounding the Jewish Town came down in 1823, although some wires demarcating the district stretched across the borders until 1885.[5] Mean-while, other reforms linked Prague more intricately to the outside world, and thus to outside economic forces well beyond the city's walls. The monarchy's administrators in Prague built an impressive road system that led out from Prague toward the major trading centers of German-speaking Europe and beyond.[6] By the 1830s Prague had be-come a major trading center. Manufacturers produced sugar, porcelain, paper, beer, textiles, and, after 1843, railroad cars.[7] The railroad reached Prague in 1845, connecting it to Vienna. The construction of a line to Dresden was well under way. In 1847 the steamship *Bohemia* started carrying passengers between Prague and Dresden.[8]

Prague's emergence as both an economic and administrative center acted as a magnet that drew increasing numbers of outsiders to the city and thus transformed the character of the population. The city's first census in 1770 counted a little more than 70,000 people. By 1846 this

Old Town Square, 1835. Lithograph by Vincenc Morstadt. Reproduced from a copy of
Václav Hlavsa, *Praha v obrazech Vincence Morstadt* (Prague: Orbis, 1973), in the author's
personal collection.

population had expanded well beyond 100,000 inhabitants, and this
did not include working-class residents who crowded into the newly
built suburbs in Karlín and Smíchov located just outside the city walls.
By 1843, four in every ten people living within Prague's walls had not
been born in the city.[9] Italians and Wlachs worked as tradesmen and
chandlers. Swiss, Dutch, and French émigrés taught foreign languages,
fencing, and dance.[10] Most of these newcomers, however, arrived from
Czech-speaking towns and villages throughout Bohemia.

Some aspects of Prague's population remained constant. The number
of master journeymen, key members of the guild system, remained at
roughly 2,000 throughout the period. A remarkably high concentration of nobles, 683 according to the 1846 census, still considered Prague
their home. Indeed, many of these nobles found positions within the
burgeoning Habsburg bureaucracy. Most positions would be filled,

however, by first-generation university graduates born into the lower classes and the peasantry—more than 2,000 literate, politically engaged elites who, along with an unemployed intelligentsia, joined Prague's emergent middling classes. Tradesmen and shopkeepers formed another portion of this growing social group. The number of fruit sellers increased from 36 in 1834 to 240 in 1847. The number of butchers and butter sellers rose from 21 to 114 and 55 to 141, respectively, in the same period.[11] Still more elites could be found among the owners of factories, warehouses, and inventories that were often located just outside the city walls. As the century progressed, Prague's tradesmen, shopkeepers, civil servants, and industrialists gained rights as burghers and hence access to corporatist resources, such as charity services.

Although these emergent middling classes enriched the Habsburg tax coffers, they also posed a threat to the Habsburg regime. Despite not being drawn toward revolutionary action, many nevertheless quietly shared liberal beliefs that took shape after the French Revolution.[12] Habsburg rulers therefore coupled their centralization efforts with a wave of repression designed to prevent the further influx of ideas born of the French Revolution—an event that had led, they believed, to the devastating Napoleonic Wars and had caused many Europeans to question monarchical rule. The Habsburg army became a visible presence, not just in the city's newly built barracks but also along its fortifications.[13] A special office in Prague censored letters that arrived from abroad. A related system of censorship stripped local publications of serious political content, even if the censors did allow space for the arts, science, and relatively apolitical reportage. Libraries provided police with lists of borrowed books. Books on the Censorship Court Bureau's index were either banned or restricted in various ways. Habsburg spies monitored conversations.[14] Liberal reformist ideas still entered the city in the form of pamphlets smuggled in from abroad. By the 1840s, liberal publications printed abroad could occasionally be found in reading clubs and cafés throughout the city. Traces of liberal thought crept into officially sanctioned publications as well, especially by the 1840s. Radical political societies met out of earshot of the Habsburg secret police.

Prague was still a Habsburg city. Soldiers guarded the city's walls and marched through its streets. The railroad station, just steps from one of the city's largest military barracks, connected Prague to Vienna and was a monument to Habsburg economic power. The monarchy was one of Prague's largest employers, and Habsburg bureaucracy exerted a strong influence over people's daily lives. Even churches in the so-called thousand-tiered city exuded Habsburg power. Prague's Baroque churches still resonated as Counter-Reformation efforts to reestablish Catholic, Habsburg rule using a combination of awe and sensuality. Monuments to Counter-Reformation heroes, including the predominant symbol of Catholic rule and piety, St. John Nepomuk, lined Charles Bridge. Still, conservative, repressive Habsburg Prague had its limits. The city's emerging middling classes only rarely challenged Habsburg rule, but nevertheless claimed their own spaces within the city. They gathered in recently constructed theaters and reading rooms. They attended concerts and founded various associations that met throughout the city. They also carved out a private sphere in the home, which they decorated in their own Biedermeier style. At home, Prague's emerging middling classes entertained guests. Prominent members of society hosted salons and other discussions, even if they remained wary of raising politically sensitive topics.

Prague was also a German city in many ways. In the eighteenth century, Habsburg rulers, as part of their larger centralization efforts, had made German the common language of their rule. It became the language of the bureaucracy and of most educational institutions, including universities. German speakers thus predominated within the highest levels of Prague's civil service, the arts, commerce, and early industry. (The same was true of Budapest, Zagreb, and, of course, Vienna.) As the language of high culture, German offered access to social capital within the city and made it possible for people to connect with other middle-class German speakers throughout central Europe. History and geography only reinforced Prague's "Germanness." The king of Bohemia had long enjoyed rights as an elector within the Holy Roman Empire. During the glorious reign of Charles IV in the fourteenth century, the imperial seat lay in Prague. Following the empire's dissolution during the Napoleonic Wars, Bohemia became a member of the loosely organized German Confederation. Maps from the period placed Prague squarely within a German-dominated central Europe. The roads from Berlin to Vienna and from Nuremberg to Breslau went through Prague.[15]

Many middle-class German speakers thus considered Prague to be within German central Europe and viewed it as a "German" city, even if the majority of its inhabitants primarily spoke Czech at home. This may be one reason that, by the 1840s, Prague had become an increasingly popular destination for travelers from the German lands, travelers whose itineraries also typically included Dresden or the spas of Karlsbad.[16] Both travelers and locals formed a reading public for German-language travelogues and other writings about Prague that, according to Peter Demetz, became a "virtual literary genre of German Biedermeier writing" after the Napoleonic Wars.[17] These publications further enhanced visions of Prague as a German city. Their descriptions of Prague often drew comparisons with other cities in German central Europe. They imagined the city through the lens of German romantic sensibilities.

Their descriptions often began from a distance high above the city. Prague's topography lent itself to panoramas, an increasingly common visual perspective in which a landscape or city was viewed from an elevated point, often with a circular vista.[18] As one Baedeker guidebook declared, Berlin, Munich, and Vienna lay on plains that provided few high points from which to view the city. In Prague, however, hills ran along the western boundary of the city, crossed the Vltava at Vyšehrad, and then continued onto Vítkov Hill, creating what another traveler called a "natural amphitheater."[19] Locals also celebrated

Prague's panoramic views. One well-regarded historian and Prague en-
thusiast wrote, "Indeed there are few cities that make a greater first
impression than the ancient capital of Prague, which spreads out as a
wide oval, ringed by hills, at times built upon hills, and divided by the
Vltava, which flows slowly through the valley below."[20] In 1826 the artist
Antonín Langweil, formerly a civil servant, began work on a large-scale
papier-mâché model of Prague inspired by Symphorien Caron's model
of Paris, which had been exhibited in Prague in the spring of that
year. Other artists, including Vincenc Morstadt, the city's most well-
regarded lithographer, sold panoramas of Prague in local bookstores.

German-speaking observers also wrote that Prague's panorama
blended nature and timeless architecture to create a majestic collage
that in turn evoked romantic notions of the past. Prague's panorama,
one German traveler wrote in 1808, "recalls the romantic legends and
tells of old and new eras—it makes a great and lasting impression."[21]
"Bohemia is a land wonderfully separated by nature and the rest of the
world," wrote another traveler, J. G. Kohl. "In the middle of this magic
circle rise the hills of Prague, where every great event by which the
country has been agitated has set its mark, either in the shape of edi-
fices and enduring monuments or of gloomy ruins and widespread
desolation."[22] In the Romantic era, nature, Mack Walker once wrote,
was considered closer to God, more virtuous than things man-made.
Nature represented changelessness and a sense of certainty as central
Europeans entered a modern world of constant change and upheaval.[23]
Prague, however, combined nature and the urban to suggest a similar
sense of changelessness and certainty in spite of, or perhaps because
of, the many changes under way in the city. "On the right bank of the
Vltava, a wide space extends outward while on the left bank the land
itself rises like a terrace toward the hilltops," one traveler wrote. "We
see a wide river with boats and islands, an ancient, great bridge decorated with colossal statues, a multitude of churches and monasteries
with shining spires, magnificent cupolas, and tremendous palaces that
suggest eternity itself!"[24] It would be a mistake to think of Prague as a

center of early nineteenth-century German nationalism. Prague was a Romantic city par excellence, one described in German and often assumed to have a German character. Prague's Germanness, in many ways, was a given.

————

Karl Zapp was born in 1812 in the New Town. He attended a college-track high school (*gymnazium*) before enrolling in Prague's Charles-Ferdinand University, where he studied philosophy and law. Zapp's father most likely believed that a university degree would offer the young man access to Prague's German-speaking middling classes. At university, however, Zapp befriended a number of Czech speakers, several of whom, including the folklorist Karel Jaromír Erben and the Romantic poet Karel Hynek Mácha, later became influential figures among the Czech-speaking intelligentsia. These three young men shared humble backgrounds. Zapp's father had been a member of the boilermakers' guild; Mácha's father had been the foreman in a Prague mill; and Erben, whose father had been a shoemaker and fruit grower in a small village northwest of the city, was among the many recent Czech-speaking arrivals to Prague. They also shared the experience of being impoverished students. Together they survived an 1831 cholera outbreak that, as Zapp described to his father, had taken the lives of several of his classmates. (Zapp also became ill but fortunately recovered.)[25] Zapp grew up in a German-speaking household and continued to correspond with his father in German throughout his life, but once at university he proudly proclaimed himself to be a Czech and a Slav. Karl Zapp Czechified his name to Karel Zap, later adding a classic Slavic middle name, Wladislav, which he modified to Vladislav.[26]

For financial reasons Zap never finished his degree, but he did manage to find work as an accountant for the tobacco and tax revenue office in the Habsburg bureaucracy. Zap was determined, however, to become a respected member of the Czech-speaking intelligentsia and

Karel Vladislav Zap, circa 1865, from his personal archival collection. Památník národního písemnictví.

to write works that appealed to Prague's Czech-speaking middling classes. It was a goal that sometimes consumed his life, one that he would eventually realize by carving out a niche for himself as a specialist in the topography of Prague. In 1835 he published *A Description of the Royal City of Prague for Foreigners and Locals*, the first book of its kind published in Czech. It was reviewed positively in several highly respected Czech-language publications.[27] A year later, much to the surprise of his compatriots in Prague, Zap accepted an administrative posting in far-off Habsburg Galicia where, over the next eight years, he reviewed books, translated works from Polish to Czech, and offered Czech readers in Prague a unique perspective on Polish literature.[28] He also composed ethnographic descriptions of peasant life, which he published in a three-volume work. These descriptions found an eager audience among Czech-speaking elites in Prague, only a tiny fraction of whom had traveled to Galicia. His often critical judgments of the Polish nobility sparked lively controversy in Prague surrounding the main tenets of pan-Slavism—a movement that imagined shared historical and cultural bonds among the Slavic-speaking peoples of Eastern Europe.[29] In 1845 Zap returned to Prague and founded *Pautník* (The Traveler, or Pilgrim), an almanac whose stated purpose was to familiarize the reader "with all sorts of lands, nations, cities, with their memorable sites . . . and with [descriptions] of national and community life, and their lessons for [those here at] home and beyond our borders."[30] That same year he published a short guide to Prague's historical sites, which included lithographs.[31] In 1847 he published *A Guide to Prague,* a revised and updated version of his 1835 book; a second edition appeared just before the tumultuous spring days of 1848. A German-language translation appeared that same year.[32]

National imagination and nationalism in Prague existed primarily among the city's Czech-speaking emergent middling classes. Most were first-generation university graduates who occupied the lower rungs of middle-class society. Many were newcomers to the city, drawn to Prague by the promise of commercial success or employment in the Habsburg bureaucracy. They drew on intellectual traditions and national imaginings first crafted in the eighteenth century by early national "awakeners," who in turn had been largely funded by Bohemian nobles hoping to push back against Habsburg centralization. The early awakeners codified the Czech language in dictionaries and grammars while seeking to revive Czech as a literary language and a culture of European import. Their geographical imaginations departed from those of many German speakers as well. The word *český,* both then and now, can be translated as either "Czech" or "Bohemian." Loyalty to

Bohemia as a territorial unit often mingled with loyalty to an imagined community of Czech speakers that extended into Moravia and Silesia. Furthermore, nationalist-minded intelligentsia who engaged in patriotic activity often belonged to a community of similarly inclined intellectuals that stretched from Prague to Pressburg (now Bratislava)—a community with various and overlapping notions of Czech, Slovak, and Czechoslovak identities.[33] Slovaks such as Ľudovít Štúr, for example, often published in *Kwěty*, which, until 1848, called itself a "national journal of amusements for Bohemians, Moravians, Slovaks, and Silesians."[34] This same community often shared notions of pan-Slavism that embraced various forms of Austro-Slavism within the Habsburg monarchy.[35]

Many of these intellectual currents and national imaginations would persist up to the time of the 1848 revolution, but the goals and composition of the Czech national movement would undergo radical changes in the 1830s. Rather than depending solely on noble patronage, those who took up the national cause began to speak to and for Prague's emergent middle-class Czech speakers. Just as important was the appearance of new political and cultural currents in Europe more generally. The Polish revolution, in particular, sparked ideas about pan-Slavism and inspired the patriotic intelligentsia to imagine a national renaissance that went beyond cultural production. Influenced by Giuseppe Mazzini and the German writers Moritz Hartmann and Alfred Meißner, they imagined a Europe of independent nations. They understood that nations had to be created through hard work and effort. Prague's post-1830 elites were not, however, revolutionaries. Habsburg spies and censorship repressed more radical ideas. Czech elites still lived in a society in which patriarchalism ran deep, meaning that they remained dependent on the upper echelons of society for their cultural and economic advancement. In general, they imagined a Czech national community developing within the Habsburg monarchy rather than as an independent nation-state.

This generation set about creating Czech-loyal publishers, raising national awareness, broadening the national community, and eliminating the dialects that hindered communication among their conationals. Language, the Czech language, was to bind and define the nation. Language distinguished the emerging Czech-speaking middling classes from their German-speaking counterparts. Fostering a language of culture and learning was meant to assure the Czechs a place among the civilized nations of Europe.[36] Thus, self-appointed revivalists composed poems and other odes in Czech. They wrote plays to be performed in Czech. They translated great works of European literature into Czech, with an eye to elevating the status of their nation, its language, and its culture, and they commented on scientific discoveries of the day. Others, such as Erben, collected folktales as part of a wider literary effort that placed the nation's imagined soul in the Czech countryside and in the person of the Czech peasant. Still others wrote about the Czech past. The prominent historian František Palacký, the most powerful voice of his generation, was later remembered as the "father of the nation." In addition to his many duties, Palacký also edited the *Journal of the Czech / Bohemian Museum,* a highly influential Czech-language publication whose articles embodied the spectrum of efforts mentioned above.

Palacký and others also believed that the fate of the nation, as they imagined it, lay within their hands. A statement read to the first semi-annual meeting of the Burghers' Club in 1846 declared:

> The sentiment of nationality, which was reawakened in the nations of mid-Europe after the wars of our time, woke up us Czechs, too, albeit as the last ones, and civic life began—at first among modest enough numbers of learned practitioners of sciences and arts and the clergy. Thence it was transferred into the heart and core of the nation—the middle class.[37]

The statement's reference to class is telling. Prague's Czech-speaking middle-class elites, this "core of the nation," might have romanticized the Czech peasant, but they inhabited a world distinct and separate from Czech speakers beyond the city's walls. They often disdained the poorer Czech speakers in their midst. They mimicked sociability practices found among the nobility and their German-speaking peers, whether that meant gathering in salons, at the theater, or in reading clubs. They were middling elites who, similar to their German-speaking counterparts, struggled to find a sense of place and belonging within a city. This need to create a sense of belonging was all the more urgent for Czech speakers, however, not least because many were recent migrants to the city.

Czech patriots thus inhabited a relatively small and isolated community. Decades later Palacký quipped that if the roof had collapsed during one of their meetings, the national movement would have come to an abrupt end. One of Palacký's early compatriots, Jan Kollár, described their efforts as "playing a piano which still, it seems, has no strings in it." Outsiders commented that Czech elites inhabited a secret society with its own words, rituals, and Czechified names.[38] They insisted on greeting each other in Czech, a public display that struck their educated peers as odd, and perhaps unseemly. Two of their most prominent associations, the Sophie [Music] Academy and the Union for Advancement of Industry in Bohemia, had only 190 and 594 members, respectively, in the months before the 1848 revolution.[39] Between 1842 and 1848 the average number of subscribers to the *Journal of the Czech / Bohemian Museum* was only 1,843, of whom 556 lived in Prague.[40] Palacký, who as editor knew these numbers well, once complained that a Czech-language book would be fortunate to sell 600 copies.[41] These elites, however, would soon begin to claim Prague as a Czech city, as their city.

Much of Zap's success within the nascent national movement resulted from his keen ability to forge relationships with key personalities in the small world of the Czech-speaking intelligentsia. Contacts among the editors of important Czech-language publications gave him his start. In Galicia he was an energetic letter writer who maintained correspondence with leading Czech patriots in Prague. In 1841 Zap became the 410th dues-paying member of the Czech / Bohemian Foundation;[42] five years later he became a contributing member of the Bohemian Museum.[43] He entertained Czech-speaking elites and engaged in a variety of the middle-class sociability practices. (In his Lviv apartment Zap served coffee to guests in porcelain cups sent to him by his father.) His marriage to a young Polish noblewoman, Honorata z Wiśniowskich, further secured his place among the Czech-speaking middling classes. As was Czech custom, Honorata took on his last name while adding "ová" to the end, making her Zapová, and thus confirming Zap's status as the male head of the household and as a Czech patriot.[44] The well-known Czech writer Karel Havlíček Borovský spoke of this status and his impressions of Zapová after having visited the couple on his way to Russia in 1842:

> As you can well imagine, Mr. Zap has done a good job of teaching her Czech. She does not speak a word of German, only French—a capital quality for a Czech patriot, you know, and one which he boasted of right away. Polish women make friends very easily, so after the very first week I felt at home with the Zaps. . . . Polish women are very frank: they tell you everything on their minds.[45]

Zap, however, longed to return to Prague. Expressed in the Romantic idioms of his time, this longing reflected his increasing desperation and despondence as the years dragged on. In his letters home he fretted about his aging father's health and often professed a heartfelt desire to care for him. He longed to introduce his father to Honorata. He often asked about his two sisters and wondered why his brother rarely wrote him.[46] He had missed his brother's wedding, at which Erben stood in as best man, a grand affair with more than eighty well-regarded guests that ended with a ball.[47] He detested the cold winters in Lviv and found the city boring in comparison to Prague.[48] He also worried about his income, especially after the birth of his first daughter, Bronislava. "She is a beautiful child," Zap wrote his father, but one whose cries were "shrill to the ears."[49] When Bronislava, suddenly and tragically, died shortly after her birth, Zap blamed the cold drafts in his apartment.[50] Months later Zapová gave birth to twin girls, one of whom also died in infancy.[51] Zap constantly worried about the health of the lone surviving daughter. Weak and sickly, she was often visited by doctors, although Zap could not afford to pay them, despite an upgrade in status and a higher salary in 1843.[52] In faraway Lviv he found it difficult to obtain the books he needed for his work, and he described himself as professionally "paralyzed." Unable to defend himself in person against his critics, he worried about his personal reputation and the standing of his written work in Prague.[53] He also missed his hometown, as letter after letter to his father emphasized. "Maybe in the course of this summer my greatest wish will finally be fulfilled," he wrote in 1843, "maybe I will behold, once again, the spires of my hometown. I can think of no greater joy than that moment when I see [my hometown] again!"[54] "My life here is without enjoyment," he wrote the following year. Memories of Prague filled him with "melancholy and an unspeakable yearning."[55]

The main obstacle to his return was the need to find employment. He called in favors and made pleas to various officials for four long years. "Hopes of a return to my longed-for Prague seem to have been fulfilled," Zap wrote to Zapová in 1840 after receiving word that he might be offered an editorial position on a Czech newspaper.[56] This promise fell through, however, as did many other opportunities in the ensuing years. Finally, in 1845 Zap was reposted to the state's accounting office in Prague. His life, as he had predicted, improved immediately. In 1845, when his income was nearly double that of the previous year, he bought more clothes than at any other time in his life.[57] He became an editor and enjoyed numerous literary successes. He and his wife attended balls, where Zapová danced the mazurka.[58] They moved into a house in the New Town along the right bank of the river, not far from the Burghers' Club.[59] The couple spent many Sunday afternoons wandering around Prague and its surroundings with Czech notables. They were often joined by the eminent Prague historian Václav Vladivoj Tomek, with whom Zap had corresponded while in Lviv. Once Tomek joined them on an outing that began with a four-hour carriage ride to nearby Beroun. The party spent the next three days walking back toward Prague and visiting various sites, including a castle built by Charles IV.[60]

While Zap enjoyed professional success, status, and a sense of belonging among friends and acquaintances in Prague, Zapová often suffered from loneliness and a feeling of displacement. She had been wary of moving to Prague well before they relocated to the city, a concern that Zap had summarily dismissed: "So my beloved Honorata, do you prefer to be the wife of an office worker in Galicia, or the wife of an editor in Prague? But there is no question about this, it's just that I am going to make sure that you do not give in to an unpleasant feeling."[61] That unpleasant feeling, however, turned to dread after the couple's arrival in the city. "At first it seemed to me that I had come to Prague in order to sprinkle all of its stones with tears," Zapová told a friend. In 1846 yet another child died shortly after birth. A year later the Austrian authorities executed her beloved uncle, Teofil Wiśniowski, for participating in an armed plot to establish Polish independence in Galicia and Prussian-controlled Poland.[62] Zapová found the life of a Prague housewife unbecoming. The frankness that Borovský had found appealing did not sit well in the Czech salons. Polish salons exuded an aristocratic air that was countered by direct, often exaggerated speech. Unlike women in Galicia, women in Prague salons were not expected to take part in "serious" conversations on political, scientific, and literary matters. As one of Zapová's friends later recalled, she was "expected to talk about childrearing, about the children's physical and mental well-being, spicing up the conversation a bit by turning to the mischief of the servants, and then simply [to speaking about] clothes, again to clothes."[63]

Zap did little to help his wife, perhaps further evidence of his blind concern about status. Shortly after arriving in Prague, Zapová confided in one of Zap's good friends, Ludvík Ritter, about her social difficulties. Ritter then wrote to Zap, urging him to intercede on her behalf: "As you know, Poles can bother and annoy each other, yet more often than not [they] reconcile, but among us, simply put, an enemy always remains an enemy." Zap seemed unmoved. Ritter then scolded Zap in a subsequent letter, using language rare among correspondents: "In Prague, when your wife is harmed, then you, the man, must stand up for her."[64] There is no evidence that Zap did anything of the sort. For her part, Zapová reluctantly adapted to Czech manners while fashioning herself as an exotic curiosity. Her circle of friends slowly expanded, and she resumed writing. Much of her writing, while embracing the tragic sentimentalism of the era, suggested that she still did not feel at home in Prague. As she lamented in the nostalgic, homesick portrait of her upbringing in Galicia that she wrote for Havlíček's *Česká včela*, "I had a splendid view from my room in my parents' house; such a reminder of youth would be loved and cherished by anyone; but all the more dear and sweet for anyone far away from fatherland, home, and family."[65]

Zap was not an extraordinarily talented writer. His published works and letters, in contrast to the honest elegance of Zapová's, are bland, at times formulaic. Sometimes it was clear that entire phrases had been copied from the work of his predecessors, although, to be fair, this was a common practice at the time. In addition to what we would now call networking, his success depended largely on finding blank spaces in the Czech-language publishing world and then establishing himself as an expert on those areas, whether it was Galicia or Prague's history and built environment. Yet his insights and observations fit squarely within many of the main currents of contemporary thought. One such theme that runs through much of his writing and his life is the topic of walking.

The generation of Zap's grandfather, and most likely the generation that followed, would not have taken walks in ways that Zap and his compatriots did. Throughout much of the eighteenth century, respectable Europeans thought little of walking. Only "footpads"—paupers, beggars, vagabonds, and the poor more generally—went on foot. Anyone who could afford to do so rode, either by carriage or on horseback. Before the Napoleonic Wars the nobility might have strolled in private gardens or left the city to hunt bears, deer, and Hungarian ox, but few urban elites ventured beyond Prague's gates for pleasure. Writing in 1825, one local noted the numerous dangers found beyond the city walls, especially in the forests where robbers and wild animals lurked. Riffraff loomed in nearby grounds outside the city walls where Prague's dead were buried.[66]

In the late eighteenth century, however, this attitude had begun to change, especially after improvements to the road system and the decline of highway robbery. Walking also became celebrated as a way of observing the world that drew upon rational, Enlightenment notions about knowledge. Throughout Europe, amateur botanists, entomologists, and zoologists scattered throughout the countryside. In England, especially, amateur geologists inspected rock formations exposed by the construction of the first train lines. Yet adherents of walking also questioned those notions; many of them communed with nature and the past in search of an understanding that could not be obtained by counting, categorizing, and codifying. WIlliam Wordsworth walked the countryside, as Rebecca Solnit writes, because of "a Romantic taste for landscape, for wild places, for simplicity, for nature as an ideal, for walking in the landscape as the consummation of a relationship with such places and an expression of the desire for simplicity, purity, solitude."[67] Walking in nature also helped to define the middling classes. One notable Romantic walker from the German lands was Johann Wolfgang von Goethe, whose poetry and prose, according to Wolfgang Kaschuba, imagined nature to be an "object as well as a medium of human knowledge" and self-discovery. Goethe's writing, Kaschuba continues, was also suggestive of an aesthetic education embraced by a rising middle class seeking to distinguish themselves from both laborers and privileged nobles.[68]

For Zap and so many others in Habsburg central Europe, walking was an activity that possessed many of these meanings and purposes. Walking was also a way to discover the essence of the nation and the Slavic soul found in the countryside and among the peasantry. In writing his reports from Galicia, Zap walked and sometimes rode by carriage around Lviv and across the poorer eastern reaches of the region. He sought a pan-Slavic essence that bound Czechs to the native Ruthenian peasantry he encountered. Czechs and Ruthenians, he claimed, originated from the Carpathian region. Their shared essence had survived despite a thousand-year spiritual struggle against the German and Western worlds. He observed evidence of this common, deep-rooted essence in the countryside and in the customs, songs, and lives of the peasantry.[69] Zap was hardly alone in this respect. Fellow pan-Slavs throughout the region had traveled across eastern Europe before 1848 engaging in ethnographic work and aesthetic celebrations of the countryside and its people. As Wendy Bracewell has argued, their writings often implied a peculiarly Romantic criticism of the "modern, bourgeois, secular, and industrialized civilization" that was emerging in the West.[70] Zap's university friend Erben walked the Bohemian countryside in search of folk songs, fairy tales, and poetry. Mácha traipsed across much of Bohemia in search of inspirational landscapes and historical ruins. During one journey, he walked almost the entire distance to Venice and back.[71]

These forms of walking drew inspiration from similar practices in Germany, such as Jacob Grimm's collecting of fairy tales. They also drew intellectual inspiration from Johann Gottfried Herder's sense that a nation's soul rested in the countryside and in its simple inhabitants, a soul that became animated through language.[72] "Our travels were pleasant; and I felt the advantages of traveling by foot," the Slovak Romantic writer Jozef Miloslav Hurban reflected as he wandered the Moravian countryside on his way to Prague. "The humming of the mountains distracted us from the enticements of nature's beauty and the delights of Slavic visions, until we took comfort along a valley leading to the melancholy Svitava River."[73] Only walking could allow for such inspirations and insights. Traveling by carriage, Zap wrote, might get one quickly and safely to your destination, but only by walking can one "count on a complete depiction of the country's local sites as you journey on your way."[74] A ride on the train, which finally connected Prague to Vienna in 1845, proved even less appealing than the carriage, others wrote. Hurtling through space, while invigorating, could also prove disconcerting. "Countryside, cities, and towns fly by and disappear, as if transformed by someone with magical powers," Hurban wrote of his 1840 train ride across the Danube from Vienna to Brno.[75]

Observations made while walking informed much of Zap's writing about Prague. German-language central European notions about the city greatly influenced his work as well. Zap's hometown offered unrivaled panoramic views, as he indicated in his 1835 work on Prague. From atop Petřín Hill he advised readers to gaze

> at the entire region from the dignified royal castle on the left-hand side, toward the black, rocky hillside of Vyšehrad, [at] house after house, palace after palace, [at] church spires and domes, and to those comforting, blessed surroundings in the distance, [where] the eye is drawn to forests, knolls, and the peaks of the high, distinctly seen Krkonoše Mountains, sixteen Viennese miles [approximately 121 kilometers] from this spot. How enchanting, how magical this view is!

Prague, unlike other central European cities, he declared, also exuded a sense of the past that existed in harmony with its natural surroundings, and he added that "the view of our royal Prague is beyond compare."[76] Other Czech patriots shared his sense of enchantment. In Morstadt's panoramic lithographs, Palacký wrote, "Nature and art, present and past, appear to vie with one another so as to give the city a beautiful sense of diversity within the whole, as well as a magnificent grandness."[77] The front matter in Zap's 1847 guide includes a lithograph depicting a panorama of Prague as seen from Petřín Hill, similar to the kind made famous by Morstadt.

Zap's view of the city differed from that of his German-language peers, however, and over time this difference became more pronounced in his writings. Zap's Prague was a Slavic city, a Czech city. "I see before me a great city, whose glory shall reach the heavens!" Zap declared, repeating Libuše's famous prophesy, in the opening to his 1847 guide. (No matter that she had allegedly stood on the hilltop at Vyšehrad.) From atop Petřín Hill, Zap invites the reader to gaze across the city. The text pauses at various points on the panorama to recall the historical events and legends embedded in the landscape. "Prague is the fruit of Czech history, the fruit of the thousand-year spiritual and bodily activities of the whole nation, and every single era, every age that the Czech nation has lived through, suffered through, and has become intertwined with . . . her stones and metal."[78] Prague is "our Rome, where our history has been concentrated and monuments [to that history] have been built," which in turn serve as "immediate witnesses, the surest proof" of the Czech past, he wrote.[79] Whereas German travelers had seen an indistinct, enchanting past, Zap saw a Czech past that was firmly embedded in the cityscape.

In claiming Prague as a locus of the national past and container of the Czech national spirit, Zap contributed to a larger shift in the national imagination. Before the 1830s the national spirit was located squarely in the countryside and among the peasantry. These sentiments, in addition to drawing on Herderian ideas about the nation, had a hint of childhood nostalgia in them. They suggested a longed-for past, a sense of belonging that often eluded Prague's recent arrivals from the countryside. Josef Kajetán Týl's play *Fidlovačka* (a spring folk festival) is best remembered for a song embraced by patriots then and now as the Czech national anthem:

> Where is my home? Where is my home?
> Water roars across the meadows,
> Pinewoods rustle among crags,
> The garden is glorious with spring blossom,
> Paradise on earth it is to see.
> And this is that beautiful land,
> The Czech land, my home,
> The Czech land, my home.
> Where is my home? Where is my home?
> If, in the heavenly land, you have met
> Tender souls in agile frames,
> Of clear mind, vigorous and prospering,
> And with a strength that frustrates all defiance,
> That is the glorious race of Czechs,
> Among the Czechs is my home,
> Among the Czechs, my home.

As Vladimír Macura has pointed out, however, the song was sung by a blind man who had never actually seen these images. The pursuit of belonging found in "Where Is My Home?" thus suggests something both comforting and elusive, nostalgia for a place and sense of communion that might never have existed and never will.[80]

The Czech-speaking middling classes lived in Prague, where they worked, socialized, and had families. Prague had become their home, and therefore those who had created Czech culture eventually made Prague home to the nation as well. In the 1830s and 1840s, Czech playwrights, poets, and other fiction writers began to make Prague an object of sentimental praise. Prague, like the Czech nation itself, was described in various feminine forms such as maiden, mother, or widow.

Authors endowed spaces with historic meanings that recalled a distinctively Czech past. They imagined the city as a collection of signs
rather than as a living, organic entity with urban characteristics. Together, these signs contributed to an overwhelming sense of past, even
to the extent, as Macura writes, that readers were meant to perceive
"the present only to the extent to which it is a reflection of the past."
These signifiers recalled a "past glory" tinged with a nostalgia typical
of the Romantic era. They had, however, a purpose in the present.
Czech-language literati now attempted to make Prague a Czech space,
a sanctum and mecca for national loyalists.[81]

Zap and others also urged Czech speakers to see the city as their
own, to imagine Prague as their national capital. First, however, they
had to know the city, Zap maintained. Prague's Czechs, Zap wrote in
1835, sorely lacked a book about their city. In the preceding fifty years
many domestic and foreign books had been written about Prague,
some short, others extensive, some good, some bad, he proclaimed.
In these books the Czechs are hardly mentioned, Zap wrote, adding:
"It appears to me, however, that the audience for which these books
are written, their countrymen, that is, the nation . . . with which their
writing is associated, is hardly noted."[82] "Prague was for me an unknown
world," Zap's future friend, the historian of Prague Václav Vladivoj
Tomek, wrote before his arrival to the city from Hradec Králové in
1833.[83] And yet, in his writings on Prague, Zap not only called these
new arrivals "Praguers," he suggested that the city belonged to them
and their imagined nation.

In providing this knowledge Zap once again returned to and adapted
German-language writings about the city. Most important for him
were German-language "topographies" of the city such as Jaroslav
Schaller's *Description of the Royal Capital and Residence Prague,* which
Zap singled out for praise.[84] Written primarily for the local nobility,
who, in the late eighteenth century, had begun to embrace Bohemian
history as part of an effort to push back Habsburg efforts at centralization, Schaller's four-volume topography provided an outline of the city's

history, topographical features, and local organizations. It provided much statistical information about the city and its inhabitants drawn from the monarchy's first imperial census. The bulk of the book, however, concerned itself with Prague's "most noteworthy" structures, which Schaller described with the help of primary sources that he used to trace out the origins and history of each site. After the Napoleonic Wars, Schaller and his successors adapted the genre slightly to appeal to travelers from Germany. They included basic information, such as carriage arrival and departure times, and information about inns and hotels. They also included suggested walks and, similar to guidebook writers such as Karl Baedeker, reinforced notions about "what ought to be seen." Zap's own books on Prague, similar to those of his German-language competitors, not only mirrored the organization found in Schaller's books but often contained much of the same information, albeit updated based on the latest census. Many copied prose directly from Schaller, who, in his later works, also borrowed words and phrases from others. The walks found in these publications and those written by Zap bore a remarkable similarity to each other, which suggested an emerging consensus about what constituted "must-see" sights.

Zap and others maintained that walking was central not only to observing the city but also to appreciating the city and its history. Zap thus placed special emphasis on walking in his guide. Each district of Prague, and its noteworthy structures, received its own chapter. In contrast to his German-language predecessors, however, Zap organized each chapter's sites based on the order in which someone might see them while walking, not according to type or alphabetically. As a result, the reader, whether on the street or at home, was meant to visualize sites as points linked by series of lines running through the city, not as abstract, atomized structures stripped from the cityscape around them. Zap's reader, whether following a walk through a district or across town, was supposed to imagine stopping in front of a notable building to consider its history and significance, and then, based on detailed directions found in the guide, walking to the next site. In addition, each district offered a variety of sensual experiences for the pedestrian. Few cities, Zap wrote, could offer the contrast of "ambling [in the Old Town] through dark, crooked, narrow streets full of shops, life, and hubbub, a place too narrow for two carriages to pass each other side by side, then suddenly stepping into the wide, open spaces [of the New Town], where the eye takes in the beautiful houses that decorate the wide, straight streets." In the Castle District, the "widowed seat of the Bohemian crown," every step on the streets echoed through the empty, forlorn district. Outside St. Vitus Cathedral, the final resting place of Bohemian kings, Zap wrote that only those with a "heightened sense of religiosity and national feeling" should enter.[85]

He wrote that the city had become more walkable, and he boasted that Prague had 210 streets, 32 alleyways, and 60 squares. The city magistrate had recently added marble cobblestones to some streets and constructed marble-plated sidewalks, replete with run-off canals. This was a marked improvement over the hard and angular cobblestones that proved especially tiring to walk on. The marble sidewalks' only disadvantage, Zap noted, was that they became especially slippery after rain. City hall had signed a contract with a private firm to construct even more marble sidewalks and streets in the city. Unfortunately, Zap noted, much of the city remained in darkness at night, but that, too, was improving. Gas lamps had been introduced in pockets of the city in the 1830s, and city hall had recently signed a contract with another private firm to extend gas lighting in the city. A factory in the working-class suburb of Karlín was busy making cast-iron lamps, which the city installed along the main streets of the Old Town and the New Town. "In the near future," Zap wrote enthusiastically, "this new enlightenment will become part of life [in the city]." One day soon, he predicted, the entire city would be illuminated.[86]

In other ways, Zap was urging his readers to take part in a European—and particularly English—moment in the history of urban experience. As had early nineteenth-century Londoners, Zap praised the act of walking the city streets and of taking pleasure in Prague's newly paved streets and sensual experiences.[87] The bulk of his book consists of what Hayden Lorimer has called a "walk as a product of places," or "a cultural activity that is made distinctive and meaningful by the physical features and material textures of a place."[88] Yet Zap's was also a peculiarly east-central European, and perhaps Czech, project. Zap's guide in hand, Czech elites and others could further the national cause—and participate in the national community—by walking through a city that had been endowed with powerful new meanings. Just as others had codified the language and established a common narrative for the nation, Zap codified Prague's memory landscape, which his readers were meant to confirm over and over again as they wandered through the city. Zap claimed Prague, in its entirety and its individual parts, for the Czech nation. But he expected his readers to follow his paths through the city, his guide in hand. Middle-class Czech speakers could then claim the city as their own, create a sense of place, and feel at home while claiming the city for the nation.

————

Zap also walked to create a sense of belonging among his fellow Czech speakers. In addition to walking across Galicia to complete his controversial ethnography of the region, he walked with friends in and around Lviv. He preferred walking in Prague, however, even in the winter. In a letter written shortly after their marriage, he described for Zapová how the people of Prague could now walk on marble squares and streets. Yellow sand was thrown over the walkways in Prague, but in L'vov one must trudge through the mud and endure the freezing cold, Zap moaned.[89] One of the first things that he and Honorata did upon returning to Prague was to take a Sunday afternoon stroll with his friend Tomek and others, a practice that they continued on a weekly basis for the next few years. Zap was known for taking out-of-towners on strolls throughout the city and its environs, and he no doubt offered ruminations on the history of these places as they walked.[90] In his books on Prague, he dedicated fifteen pages in 1835 and nineteen pages in 1847 to places to take a stroll, understood broadly as a leisurely walk with companions. Many of these prescribed strolls encouraged people to venture beyond the city to historically important sites and villages. Other suggestions encouraged strolling through gardens. One path's description advised strolling along the top of the New Town fortification. Seeing the city while on foot, as Zap knew well, was crucial to imagining Prague as the capital, sanctum, and mecca of the nation. Strolling, as Zap also knew quite well, was a fundamental practice of sociability. It mimicked a noble practice but also served to distinguish the middling classes from the nobility. Zap and others might have sought to define the nation and their city in opposition to the Germans, but on a walking path Czech and German speakers were largely indistinguishable, unless one overheard the language of conversation. Strolling was also an early nineteenth-century European phenomenon that, in Prague, owed much to the nobility and Habsburg officials.

In Prague, strolling and a host of other middle-class practices of sociability slowly began to take hold in the decades following the end of the Napoleonic Wars. In 1812 Sebastian Willibald Schiessler, a young army officer and Prague native who would later gain renown for this charity work in the city, complained, "The noble is somewhat sociable with his own. . . . The same cannot be said of the other classes."[91] The Praguer, according to the civic patriot A. W. Griesel in 1825, was "typically closed and monosyllabic; this is quite striking when compared to most inhabitants of other larger cities." Private relationships, he continued, existed only within very tight circles of friends. Dancing was the only event that allowed people to come together, but this camaraderie lasted only as long as the music played.[92] More than a decade later, thanks in part to the burgeoning of Prague's middling classes and a loosening of Habsburg repression, Prague's middling classes not only danced at balls but also attended the theater, conversed in reading clubs and various societies, and met in private salons. These practices often mimicked those of the nobility, and thus counted among efforts to claim middle-class status alongside, or just below, the noble classes.

The middling classes also sought to distinguish themselves from the nobility by embracing a peculiarly central European Biedermeier culture in which, as Virgil Nemoianu writes, "everyday life [became] the locus for applying Romantic ideals in a rational, moderate fashion—under Enlightenment auspices, as it were."[93] This meant embracing Romanticism in the arts, such as in the music of Franz Liszt, Hector Berlioz, and Frédéric Chopin, not to mention in the compositions of an array of locally trained composers. Essayists and short-story writers filled the pages of local publications with sentimental tales of romance, domestic drama, and excursions into nature. Women of the middling classes wore fashionable dresses and bonnets in public; men wore hats and tailcoats.[94] Home life and interior design expressed frugality, modesty, a love of the family, and a deep concern for domesticity that paralleled a public life of grace and moderate enjoyment.

Prague's Czech-speaking middling classes enjoyed the same practices of sociability as their German-speaking counterparts, such as going to the theater, participating in salons, and dressing the part. The boundaries between the two communities were porous as well. Many middle-class Praguers spoke both Czech and German. They attended theater performances and read newspapers in both languages. As Czech patriots knew, language was often the only marker distinguishing them from their German-speaking counterparts. Good Czech-language skills, many claimed, defined the good and authentic Czech. The philologist Josef Jungmann, for example, enjoyed mocking a fictional Czech pretender whose proper sociability practices could not mask his laughable Czech. (The translation to English is by David Cooper.)

> Der is no kafehaus in Prag ver I was not at home, no hall ver I haf not tanzed, theatr and church ver I haf not entertaint myself. I haf der smokt gut tabak, played gut billiard, cached

(drank) and feched (fenced) and done everything der das
vas chic vor a man of kultur [*od kultůr*], better dan many a
kavalier.[95]

At the same time, Czech practices of sociability mimicked those of
their German-speaking counterparts, which further enhanced their
credentials as respected members of society. As Zap knew well, walking
in Prague while imagining the city and its historical structures as "Czech"
was not just a claim on the city. Walking, and especially strolling, was
a way for Czech speakers to claim their rightful place among the city's
middling classes.

Strolling, and the history of strolling, can be found throughout Zap's
two books about Prague, and in German-language topographies and
travel accounts. At the end of the Napoleonic Wars, strolling remained
a pursuit restricted to Prague's nobility, who, since the seventeenth
century, had strolled through private gardens walled off from the outside world. As one civic patriot bemoaned in 1820, the middling classes
simply did not stroll. Few saw strolling as a worthwhile or necessary
pursuit. At the time, few green spaces in the city were open to the
public. Footpaths leading from the city had become overgrown. Only
people with access to carriages visited gardens and sites of note beyond
the city walls.[96] In the coming decades, however, Prague's rising elites
would take up the practice of strolling and ambling. "Strolling has become quite popular in recent times," one traveler noted on arriving in
Prague in 1835.[97] The middling classes sought to escape an increasingly
dirty and polluted city. They celebrated fresh air. Unlike peasants, urbanites living enclosed within the city walls imagined the natural
world, whether a garden or path through the woods, as an escape. They
were inspired by Jean-Jacques Rousseau, who saw the escape to nature as a journey of self-discovery and self-fulfillment.[98] Praguers ventured to nearby villages, to sites of historical significance such as Troja
and Hvězda, and to the wild forests of Divoká Šárka.[99] Many walks with
companions ended, as they do today, at a pub.[100]

Praguers enjoying a stroll near Prague Castle, 1836. Lithograph by Vincenc Morstadt. Reproduced from a copy of Václav Hlavsa, *Praha v obrazech Vincence Morstadt* (Prague: Orbis, 1973), in the author's personal collection.

The nobility also provided opportunities for middle-class elites to stroll. Count Waldstein-Wartenberg, for example, allowed certain Praguers to enter his garden in the Lesser Town on Thursdays and Saturdays.[101] Over time, an increasing number of nobles generously opened their gardens to certain members of the middling classes. Some of the wealthiest middle-class elites constructed gardens of their own, typically just outside the city walls. One industrialist created a garden next to his paper mill on the banks of the Vltava.[102] Wealthy elites tended to build English gardens, which suggested liberal values, as opposed to the traditional baroque-style gardens of the nobility, which suggested conservative absolutism. Joseph Malabaila Canal's much-celebrated English garden, which opened to the public in 1817, had paths that went among trees before leading the stroller to family monuments and a garden pavilion. Specialists and students from Charles-Ferdinand University visited the garden to observe its 700 types of fruit trees and other botanical rarities. The garden's sugar refinery, allegedly the first in the city, suggested middle-class values of commerce, technology, and economic productivity.[103] Unlike the nobility, who strolled primarily during the week, middle-class elites strolled on Sunday afternoons and holidays, thus underscoring the merits of labor and the workweek, as opposed to the endless pleasure and luxury gained from heredity.

Thanks to Habsburg officials, Prague's middling elites could also stroll in a growing number of publicly available green spaces. In 1804 Emperor Francis I opened the Royal Game Preserve to the public following his coronation there. Located north of the city's walls, the park, also known as Tree Garden (Baumgarten / Stromovka), featured English gardens that attracted promenaders from across the city, especially on Sunday evenings in the summer. According to one English travel writer, this popular park was Prague's equivalent of Vienna's Prater, which he equated to London's Hyde Park.[104] Other strollers ambled up to nearby Petřín Hill, and not just because it afforded some of the best views of the city. It was a place for community and human connection. As one local topographer wrote:

> [This] hill is, especially in the afternoon and early evening
> hours, filled with individual walkers, students, and painters,
> and soon-to-be lovers, who think little of this world because
> they find themselves between heaven and earth. Joyful groups
> of children amble here and there on the lively green . . . which
> is ringed by fruit trees, vineyards, and grain fields.[105]

In the early 1820s, Bohemia's highest government official, Count Karl Chotek, opened a section of the city's fortifications to promenaders. By 1842, Praguers could stroll almost the entire perimeter of the city's walls, which had become a garden path of sorts lined with trees and other plants. Many writers, Zap included, declared that the views afforded by Prague's fortifications were among the best in the city. Near

Strollers on a landscaped fortification above Horse Square, 1835. Lithograph by Vincenc
Morstadt. Reproduced from a copy of Václav Hlavsa, *Praha v obrazech Vincence Morstadt*
(Prague: Orbis, 1973), in the author's personal collection.

the Castle, just steps from the Royal Gardens, Chotek transformed a
storage space for lumber into the city's first officially designated public
park, called "The People's Garden."[106]

Islands on the Vltava River also became popular destinations,
as Washington Irving described in a letter to his friend Emily Foster
in 1823:

> There are really delightful walks in the vicinity of [Prague]. . . .
> There are several islands in the Muldau [Moldau in German,
> Vltava in Czech] that are laid out in walks; one that particular
> delights me is called, I think, der Grosser Venedig [Greater
> Venice Island]. It is covered with trees, and has the most
> beautiful shady avenues and rambling footpaths, that wind
> among groves and thickets along the banks of the Muldau.

I spend hours there in the morning, before the Germans come
to poison the air with themselves and their tobacco pipes;
as the pure air is too insipid for a German. . . . I don't know a
better punishment for the German delinquents, than to deprive
them of their pipes, and banish them to Buenos Ayres—
they'd die of the purity of the air.[107]

(Due to a fear of fires, smoking in the streets was banned in Prague;
offenders would have their pipes immediately confiscated by local police. Czech speakers, no doubt, enjoyed pipes as well.)[108] Czech-
speaking middling elites descended upon Dyer's Island, named after
the leather dyer who owned the island, which was later renamed Žofín,
after Archduchess Sophie. Pedestrians accessed the island via a small
wooden footbridge, which lay just steps from Zap's family's residence
in the New Town. On the island, strollers meandered along numerous
poplar-lined paths. Visitors could enjoy warm or cold baths, listen to
occasional outdoor concerts, or play billiards in the saloon. Vendors
offered pony rides for children. Shooter's Island, just up the river, was
more wooded, and it had a reputable dance hall.[109]

Romantic poets might have written of men, book in hand, wandering through a melancholic, natural setting, but strolling was the
pastime of middle-class families and small groups of men and women.
It was thus a sociability practice that also created personal connections
within the bounds of accepted respectability. Strollers conversed, and
flirted, according to a set of rules laid out in advice books. Strangers
were supposed to stay more than two meters apart from each other.
The most intimate friends and family members went arm in arm. A
certain ease, combined, paradoxically, with an upright stance and stiff-
ness of the limbs, distinguished this leisurely walk. Gothic ruins, Chinese bridges, monuments, memorials, and garden gnomes provided
material for conversation. Sociability also meant seeing and being seen.
Men wore specially designed walking hats and often carried tobacco
pouches. Women often wore gloves as well as restrictive, often ex-

tremely uncomfortable corsets. Children brought rolling toys, dolls, and butterfly nets. Men typically carried walking sticks, and women carried umbrellas, items that recalled the noble practice of strolling with a dueling sword.[110]

———

By the 1840s, strolling had become one of the most beloved pastimes of Prague's Czech- and German-speaking middling classes. Strolling was not the only practice of walking-as-belonging in early nineteenth-century Prague. Nor was walking an exclusively middle-class social and cultural practice. Members of the lower classes continued to walk beyond Bohemia, and sometimes to Prague, on religious pilgrimages. During Corpus Christi celebrations, banners hung from buildings decorated with symbols of spring such as flowers and green birch branches. Trumpeters and other musicians took to the streets as the city militia marched through the city.[111] On the afternoon of November 2, All Soul's Day, the city's residents proceeded to graveyards outside the city's walls to pay respect to the dead.[112] Some members of the lower classes also took up strolling, albeit in ways that reinforced their inferior status vis-à-vis the middling and noble classes. By the 1840s, for example, the lower classes were largely limited to strolling on Greater Venice, well after Irving's pipe smokers had abandoned the island. Bleach from nearby textile factories washed up on the island. Newly built railway tracks cut through previously pristine forests. Paths on the island had fallen into disrepair.[113]

Strolling was just one way, then, in which members of the middling classes claimed certain spaces while excluding the lower classes. Members of the lower classes, of course, could not purchase tickets to balls and were not invited to salons. "Brilliance and luxury, poverty and meagerness alternate before your eyes [in Prague] as in all cities large in size," one traveler remarked.[114] The number of working poor—especially industrial laborers—grew substantially in the first half of the nineteenth century. At the end of the 1820s, between 2,000 and 3,000 industrial workers inhabited Prague and its surrounding industrial districts. By 1850, that number had doubled.[115] Most industrial workers, including those hired to complete the construction of Prague's railroad lines and station, lived in the newly constructed suburb of Karlín. Topographers and guidebook writers such as Zap cautioned readers against visiting Karlín where, he wrote, it was impossible to find "a clean cobblestone" on the ground in a neighborhood whose slipshod architecture was "piled up in a chaotic mess." Just as disturbing was the fact that Karlín had not a single church, making it, he claimed, the only community in Bohemia of its size that had no place of worship. Tropes of dirt, disorder, and a lack of religiosity featured prominently among middle-class depictions of the laboring classes across Europe in the nineteenth century. For Zap, Karlín also represented a loss, the disappearance of a portion of Romantic Prague as envisioned by middle-class travelers, guidebook writers, and topographers. Karlín, he wrote, had once been a pristine, untainted space just outside the city walls with no more than three pubs, a military hospital, vegetable gardens, and fields.[116] In the course of just one summer, 4,000 workers tore down ten houses, a garden, a courtyard, and an army barracks to make room for the railroad station, which was situated just inside the New Town walls near Karlín. The massive customs house serving incoming passengers had been a Franciscan monastery.[117]

Physical indications of the laboring classes' presence might sometimes have been glimpsed on the cityscape and then disparaged, but the laboring classes themselves remained largely invisible in Czech- and German-language guides about Prague. The laboring classes did not appear in listings of professions, census numbers, and the city's history. They briefly appeared on the page when discussing middle-class charity work and the humane, reforming aspects of the local prison system. Many in the middling classes considered laborers and the poor distasteful, and feared them as well. By the 1840s, steam-powered machines had begun to replace human labor, thus forcing many industrial workers into the streets and into desperate poverty. Bad harvests contributed to a rise in prices for basic foodstuffs. In June 1844 several factories around Prague slashed wages, sometimes in half. Small groups of workers, including many cotton printers, turned to violence and destroyed factory machines before attacking Jewish shops inside the border of the city walls. Several weeks later railroad workers, soon joined by masons, attempted to force their way through the city's gate near Karlín. The Habsburg army attacked the demonstrators, who retaliated by throwing bricks, rocks, and other building materials at the soldiers. Five civilians died before the army defeated the protesters and arrested their leaders. Hunger and other deprivations, one anonymous pamphleteer wrote, made "those classes into wild animals" who were driven by a desire to fill their empty stomachs. "Fear and terror lurk in every corner" in a city where people eyed each other with suspicion, another anonymous pamphleteer wrote. So tense was the atmosphere, he continued, that the sight of something like a simple cabbage knife caused nervous police to draw their bayonets.[118]

Zap also wanted Prague's Jews to remain invisible. Just as he ignored the 1844 uprising, he made no mention of the looting of Jewish homes and trading stalls that accompanied the demonstrations. His books make no mention of Jewish traders setting up shop beyond the walls of the Jewish Town. His books barely mention the Jewish Town, which is striking because the town and especially its Jewish cemetery figured prominently in the writings of German-speaking travelers and guidebook writers.[119] He lamented the fact that Prague's Jewish population had grown rapidly in the 1830s and 1840s, that poorer Christians had begun to move into the Jewish Town, and that wealthier Jews had taken up residence outside the Jewish Town. Zap approvingly cited an 1846 decree requiring the forcible relocation of all Jews who had illegally moved past the permitted zone just beyond the Jewish Town, yet he complained that this permitted zone encompassed nearly half of the Old Town.[120] When Jews appeared elsewhere in his writing they were often paired with Germans, who then became associated with "cosmopolitanism," by which he meant a sinister rootlessness and foreignness. Both Jews and Germans, he wrote in the history section of his 1847 guide, had a pernicious influence on the city's Slavic character following the arrival of the first waves of Germans to the city in the ninth century. From that time, he wrote, the city had alternated between its purely Slavic essence and "cosmopolitanism." Until recently, he concluded, cosmopolitanism had been ascendant, aided in part by Habsburg administrative reforms. "German civil servants, professionals, and speculators," many of whom had recently spoken only Czech, "swarmed the street corners and nooks" of the city, he wrote.[121] (No matter that Zap had grown up speaking German in Prague.) The railroad threatened to open the city to further influences and links to the German world. Czech national awakeners may have revived Prague's Slavic essence. But, Zap concluded, "the spiritual and moral strength of the nation must now move forward in step" in order to counter these cosmopolitan influences.[122]

———

On March 15, 1848—around the time that the second edition of Zap's guide appeared in print—the afternoon train from Vienna brought startling news to Prague. Klemens von Metternich, the Austrian chancellor and despised symbol of Habsburg conservatism, had fled the imperial capital. The Viennese authorities had ended censorship and called for the formation of a constitutional government. On hearing the news, jubilant crowds took to the streets in Prague, drinking champagne and participating in nighttime demonstrations. Various political organizations emerged. Most German- and Czech-speaking elites, however, kept a careful distance from their more radical counterparts among the students and working classes.[92] During the summer Zap became a member of the preparatory committee of the Slavic Congress, which was intended to be a public display of Slavic unity against liberal German efforts to include Bohemia within a unified Germany. Another purpose was to lay the groundwork for future political participation within the Habsburg monarchy. The congress convened on June 2 in a building located amid the poplar trees on Žofín Island.[123]

Ten days later fighting broke out between Prague's radical student groups and Habsburg soldiers commanded by Field Marshall Alfred Windischgrätz, a determined arch conservative. Apparently Zap was not in Prague at the time. Zapová and their children were not as fortunate. She described one day's scene in a letter to her husband. A group of armed millers took up a position just in front of their house near Žofín. Habsburg cannons were positioned on the other side the river. Infantrymen occupied Shooter's Island. Gunfire broke out, and bullets hit their house. "You would hardly recognize your beloved Prague," Zapová signed off, "such horrible devastation."[124] After six days of street fighting Windischgrätz ordered his artillery battalion, perched atop Petřín Hill, to bombard the city. The rebels capitulated soon thereafter. Hordes of people—20,000 by one estimate—fled Prague. Among them was Zapová, who took refuge in a friend's house.[125] In the ensuing years, Prague and the Habsburg monarchy entered a new period of political repression and neo-absolutism. In 1850 Zap was summoned to appear before a military court, but he escaped punishment. Zapová succumbed to illness in 1856.[126]

Zap continued to edit and write in Czech, as did Zapová until her untimely death. Zap also continued to pursue his all-consuming goal: to become a well-regarded member of the Czech-speaking national movement. He continued to stroll and gather with fellow Czech-speaking urban elites. He remarried. Prague's other self-appointed nation-builders continued their work—codifying the language, writing histories, collecting stories, and performing plays. As Zap reached old age, Czech-speaking members of the middling classes had grown in number. Their political power increased, thanks in part to Habsburg reforms, some of which had been demanded in 1848. A new generation of middle-class Praguers walked and strolled. Many of the early nineteenth century's most popular walks, such as those along the paths of Žofín, remained the first choice of Praguers on Sunday afternoons. One of Prague's first streetcar lines ended at Baumgarten / Stromovka, previously known as the Royal Game Preserve. Praguers traveled by train to enjoy walks beyond the city center. One guidebook writer, however, complained that the pathways had fallen into disrepair. People littered. A visit to a pub took priority over the enjoyment of nature.[127] In 1900 another local guidebook writer suggested, "For those of you with spare time we recommend visiting Petřín for a breathtaking view, one without comparison in all of Europe." He added that the view was best in the afternoon, when smoke from the city's factories had burned off.[128] Prague was becoming Czech and modern, in ways that Zap and his small circle of compatriots, steeped as they were in Romantic visions, could hardly have imagined.

2

CZECH CITY

ତ୍ୟୁ

I N   T H E   S U M M E R   O F   1910, Egon Erwin Kisch published the first of his many "Prague Forays" columns in the city's highly respected German-language newspaper, *Bohemia.* Kisch, a rising star in German literature, began this foray at the western edge of the working-class district of Smíchov, at the gates of a private park named Klamovka. Once the noble gardens of the Clam-Gallas family, the site included several "must-sees," he wrote. There was a statue of Clam-Gallas's warhorse, Cassil, drinking from a trough. Another marker noted the place where Prinz Wilhelm von Auersberg lost his life at age twenty-four in a duel one day in May. Kisch then guided the reader to the park's dilapidated dance hall, once popular among Czech-speaking maids and "boys and girls of the people." There, in the middle of the park, locals danced the quadrille and a six-step waltz, called *na šest,* whose "defining characteristics were drawn-out, slow steps, done with eyes closed in feigned or real ecstasy." Kisch then told the story of a shabbily dressed artillery reservist, of dancing past military curfew, and of love lost. The story, he wrote, does not have a punchline; there is no big reveal, no flourish, except perhaps that the soldier's partner told the story many times thereafter, and that he no longer dances with her.[1]

Few, if any, of *Bohemia*'s German-speaking middle-class readers
would have ever visited Klamovka, let alone known of its existence.
Perhaps that was the point. The story, with its familiar romantic echoes
of decay and nostalgia, also stood in stark contrast with new, powerful
imaginations of Prague. At the turn of the twentieth century, Prague
was still a Habsburg city and, in some ways, a German city. Habsburg
army barracks and civil servants remained. Most of the city's wealthiest citizens were German speakers. By the time Kisch wrote his story,
however, Prague had become an undeniably Czech city that reflected
Czech middle-class imaginations of their nation. Over the course of
the nineteenth century, members of the Czech-speaking middle class
had grown in number and political power. Once content to imagine
their nation onto the existing cityscape, Czech elites were now determined to transform the built environment. They erected monuments
to national heroes and constructed ostentatious architectural reminders
of the Czech past and present Czech wealth. Czech urban and political
elites worked tirelessly to modernize their city, their de facto national
capital, as they sought a rightful place among the civilized nations of
Europe. Many Czech politicians rose to power thanks to vicious antisemitism. In 1892, when no German speakers remained on the city
council, municipal leaders tore down German-language street signs.
Czech-language street signs replaced bilingual ones.[2]

Another transformation had taken place as well. According to
the 1900 census, nearly half of the city's German-speaking population listed "Jewish" as their confession.[3] Earlier in the century, as
emancipation unfolded, many Prague Jews as well as Jewish migrants
to the city had adopted German language and culture as a means of
integration. Many had successfully entered the middling classes,
found apartments just beyond the old ghetto, and embraced a middle-
class liberalism that promised them a respected, secure place in
Habsburg society. By the turn of the century, however, their sons
and daughters confronted an array of alienating forces. Kisch was
one such son. A reporter by trade, Kisch's weekly "Prague Forays"

column offered readers a subtle counterimagination of his hometown. Instead of Czech national treasures, he celebrated local customs and lesser-known institutions that spoke to a gentler time. He composed "little novels" about the city's forgotten, down-and-out characters whom Czech national elites had tried to make invisible. Instead of focusing on Czech urban renovation and technological innovation, Kisch's vignettes described the tragic but dignified characters found in the forgotten corners of the city.

Kisch also struggled to find a sense of belonging in the modernizing city. Indeed, the experience of dislocation inspired several of Prague's German Jewish writers, among them Franz Kafka, to experiment with literary forms that puzzled through questions of belonging and alienation. Kisch, Kafka, and other German Jewish literati also practiced belonging, most notably in cafés where they were celebrated regulars. In addition, Kisch stepped outside the boundaries of his German Jewish milieu, carousing late into the night in cabarets and less-than-respectable pubs. In these locales, as during his daytime and nighttime forays throughout Prague, Kisch observed life in this fast-modernizing city. He chatted with Praguers, usually in Czech, far beyond the city center where he lived. He played with modern notions of belonging that embraced change, uncertainty, strangers, and human difference. He probed the limits of class and national boundaries while imagining a city that he, at least, could call home.

———————

In the second half of the nineteenth century, the Czech national movement became a mass effort based largely in Prague and led by middle-class urban elites. Since the 1860s, Emperor Francis Joseph had gradually acquiesced to a number of liberal demands that created the conditions for popular national movements across the monarchy. Pieter Judson has convincingly argued that the ensuing reforms were not just an acknowledgment of the increasing power of nationalism throughout

Europe; Habsburg leaders also sought to embed self-described nations into the monarchy's various institutions and administrative practices, which, in turn, informed nationalist efforts.[4] Freedom of assembly, although limited by police surveillance and bureaucratic oversight, allowed the emergence of national clubs and associations across the monarchy. Throughout the Bohemian lands, many of these organizations mobilized their compatriots behind national causes such as the construction of schools, economic boycotts, and language usage. Drawing upon liberal notions of progress, competing Czech and German national elites in urban centers such as Prague often focused their efforts on so-called language frontiers and mixed cities such as Budějovice / Budweis. In doing so, they aimed to modernize the countryside while also seeking to eliminate local "national indifference," which they broadly understood as a backward unwillingness to mobilize behind the national cause or even to choose a side.[5]

From 1861 to 1914, no more than 6 percent of Prague's population was eligible to vote in municipal elections, meaning that the vast majority of Praguers, including those whom nationalists hoped to mobilize, could not choose their local political leaders. Czech middle-class elites, whose ranks expanded rapidly in the second half of the century, thus obtained a firm hold on political power in the city. These gains came at the expense of their German counterparts.[6] By 1882 only five German-speaking aldermen remained on the ninety-seat city council. The last German-speaking alderman left office three years later.[7] Limited representative government and expanding voting rights at the federal level then spurred further national mobilization efforts. In 1907 all men in the Bohemian lands gained the right to vote in the election of members of the lower house of parliament, or Reichsrat. This accelerated the development of mass politics and political parties that often claimed to represent the interests of their respective nations. (Women obtained the right to vote after World War I, and they could join political associations only as of 1912.)[8] Nationalist parties published their own newspapers, which benefited from loosened political censorship and expanded literacy.[9] From their base in Prague, Czech-language publications thrived, which created imagined communities of readers who shared a common sense of history and present concerns. *Golden Prague,* a newspaper founded when Czechs gained unrivaled dominance in city hall, boasted in 1904 that it had published 2,171 Czech poems and 395 Czech prose works.[10] Habsburg universities continued to turn out Czech-speaking members of the middling classes. In 1910 more than 40 percent of the students at the Czech half of Charles-Ferdinand University in Prague, which obtained independence from its German counterpart in 1882, were the offspring of peasant farmers, estate managers, self-employed craftsmen, and owners of small- to medium-sized businesses.[11] Access to higher education also enabled some Czechs to join the ranks of the city's most powerful economic elites. In 1884 Czechs assumed control over Prague's official chamber of commerce and industry. By the turn of the century, a Czech banking sector based in Prague established financial independence from its German counterparts in Vienna.[12]

Prague was thus a central node of Czech economic success and Czech middle-class nationalism. It was home to nationalist organizations and publishing houses as well as "professional nationalists."[13] Prague continued to play a central role in the national imagination Local patriots celebrated the city's historic structures as memory containers for the nation. Funerals provided opportunities to praise deceased nation builders and to claim public spaces for gravesites.[14] In the last quarter of the century, however, middle-class Czech elites began to remake the cityscape in their own image. The neo-Renaissance National Theater, located at the end of Ferdinand Street, opened its doors in 1881. Eight weeks later a devastating fire consumed the building, but, thanks to public donations, the theater reopened in 1883 with a performance of Bedřich Smetana's opera *Libuše*.[15] Further along Ferdinand Street, as throughout the city, newly built art nouveau structures housed Czech-owned insurance companies, businesses, and banks. The massive, neoclassical National Museum, completed in 1890, towered over Wenceslas Square. Twenty years later, the art nouveau Municipal House, located in the heart of German-speaking Prague, opened its doors to the public. Partly funded by city hall, it included a grand concert hall, six restaurants, meeting rooms, and shops, all adorned with Czech nationalist symbols and scenes from a mythical Slavic past. Prague's Czech elites also staked their claim to the city by erecting markers and totems celebrating national heroes, engaging in what Zdeněk Hojda and Jiří Pokorný have described as an era of "monument fever." Palacký Bridge, which linked the New Town to Smíchov, opened in 1878, two years after the death of the "father of the nation." Statues from Alois Jirásek's *Old Czech Legends* adorned the bridge. Decades later, city leaders unveiled a towering monument to Palacký on the New Town side of the bridge. In 1901 the first of many Czech heroes was buried in a mass crypt on Vyšehrad, part of a larger monument whose inscription read, "Though dead, they still speak."[16]

These efforts, as Marek Nekula has argued, sought to "code" Prague in national terms, to create a symbolic universe that paid homage to the nation while claiming the city's built environment for the Czechs. They were not totalizing. The city still contained powerful symbols of Habsburg rule, such as the Lesser Town's monument to Marshal Josef Radetzky, a hero of the 1848 counterrevolution. Habsburg army barracks stood opposite the Municipal House on Francis Joseph Square. An impressive new train station also bore the emperor's name.[17] Nor were Czech reconfigurations of the cityscape homogeneous and singular. They reflected a number of artistic styles, from neoclassical historicism to art nouveau to modernism that, as Cynthia Paces has demonstrated, reflected generational rifts within Prague's artistic community.[18] Nor were these efforts focused solely on a parochial national past. By the turn of the century, Czech artists, benefiting from contacts in Paris, had established Prague as the second home of European cubism. The city became a showcase of innovations in architectural cubism.[19]

Czech urban elites also cast their eyes abroad, to the progressive future, as they sought to establish Prague's credentials as a modern, technologically advanced European city.[20] A prominent example was the Jubilee Exhibition, which opened in the newly erected iron-and-glass Palace of Industry next to Stromovka Park in 1891. The centerpiece of the exhibition was a dancing, electrically illuminated fountain just behind the exhibition hall. Designed by František Křižík, a successful industrialist once praised by Thomas Alva Edison, it used steam power to shoot water high into the air. Křižík's fountain, promoters boasted, propelled water higher than similar fountains that had been featured at previous jubilees in Vienna and Paris. Exhibition promoters also encouraged participants to visit a modified version of the Eiffel Tower constructed atop Petřín Hill, which could now be reached by a newly built funicular. Electric lights shone on landmarks across the city. Organizers proclaimed the event an extraordinary success. The

Main entrance gate to the Industrial Palace, 1891, site of that year's Jubilee Exhibition. Archiv hlavního města Prahy.

Křižík Fountain. Drawing by Jan Vilímek, printed in *Zlatá Praha,* June 12, 1891. Wikimedia Commons.

Czechs must be counted among "modern nations, of enlightened nations, of the first nations of the world!" one official publication proclaimed. Approximately 2.5 million paying visitors attended the event, another publication proclaimed, 750,000 more than a recent jubilee in Budapest.[21]

The jubilee marked a turning point in the electrification of the city in general. In 1898, after an extended legal battle, the city purchased a privately owned streetcar system and began to replace the horse-drawn cars with electric-powered ones. Prague's first electric streetcar went into service in time for the 1891 jubilee, thus beginning a network that came to include several enterprises and some Prague suburbs, including Žižkov and Vinohrady. By 1908 Prague's streetcars ran along tracks totaling 51,844 meters in length, powered by a newly built electrical plant not far from Stromovka. Modern street lighting, also powered by electricity, allowed middle-class Praguers to walk more safely at night while also creating conditions for a flourishing nightlife. (Locals referred to night streetcars as "theater trams.")[22] Electrical lighting replaced gas lamps in middle-class apartments throughout the city.

Prague's new streetcar system complemented other efforts to modernize the city's transportation system. Many of the bridges that span the Vltava today—including Palacký Bridge, Čech Bridge, and Mánes Bridge—were completed between 1860 and the end of World War I. (Crossing bridges required the payment of a toll, which was one reason that most Praguers chose to walk across the frozen Vltava in the winter.)[23] Several railway stations, including Francis Joseph Train Station, opened to the public. City leaders and their allies also expanded their influence outward from the city to incorporate the burgeoning suburbs of Vyšehrad (1883), Holešovice (1884), and Libeň (1901).[24] Adjacent, working-class suburbs such as Smíchov and Žižkov, as well as the eminently middle-class suburb of Vinohrady, became little more than extensions of Prague, even if they managed to retain municipal independence until 1921. Most of the city's walls came down as well. Earlier in the century, tradesmen, shopkeepers, and industrialists had called for the destruction of the city's walls, arguing that they hindered the flow of human traffic. Strollers and a vocal group of preservationists protested, but to little avail. Demolition of the city's walls began in 1875, a process that lasted until 1907 because of financial wrangling with the imperial government over ownership and the costs of the work. (Several remnants remain to this day, most notably behind Prague Castle and near Petřín Hill.) Czech and German medical experts, pointing to Prague's polluted, noxious air quality, demanded that newly available land be used for public parks. In the end, however, the city sold most of the property to builders.[25]

Czech urban elites could undertake these extraordinary projects because Habsburg leaders had devolved much governing power to the municipal level. This devolution of political power gave civic leaders the primary responsibility for caring for their inhabitants, whose numbers had skyrocketed in the decades before World War I, thanks to industrialization and the increased difficulty of making a living from the land. From 1890 to 1910 Prague's population had tripled;[26] by 1900 nearly three in five "citizen residents" of Prague and its inner suburbs were migrants, most of them from the Czech-speaking regions of Bohemia.[27] As the 1891 jubilee opened, according to Claire Nolte, only some Praguers had access to clean drinking water.[28] Industrial and human waste flowed into the Vltava. The city lacked a modern sewerage system.[29] Despite the efforts of health inspectors and medical experts, overcrowded apartments and poor hygiene continued to threaten the population with tuberculosis and other diseases. Besides diminishing their quality of life, these problems presented a challenge to urban elites' own conception of their city. Similar to their counterparts across Europe, they turned to scientifically informed notions of economic growth, crime, health, and hygiene to remake entire sections of the city. In this respect, their crowning achievement was the razing and reconstruction of the former Jewish Town, renamed Josefov in 1850 when it was formally integrated into the city proper.

Over the course of the century, Jews who could afford to leave Josefov typically did so and were often replaced by some of the city's poorest inhabitants. (In 1843, 95 percent of Josefov's population was Jewish; by 1900 that number had plummeted to 24 percent.)[30] Subletting in Josefov had led to vastly overcrowded housing and despicable living conditions. Primitive sewer lines that ran under Josefov, which was relatively flat and only slightly higher than the Vltava, often became clogged. Human waste filled house basements. Josefov thus became an embarrassing eyesore in the middle of "golden, Slavic Prague," and one that, for some Czech nationalists, evoked backwardness as well as various xenophobic and orientalist tropes.[31] As *Golden Prague* declared in 1887, Josefov was a "repulsive labyrinth of twisting, narrow streets filled with devilish odors . . . animated figures and scenes, which look as if they were carried to Prague straight from the Orient, from somewhere in Baghdad."[32] Josefov also remained a site for literary and popular imagination about Jews, as well as antisemitic tropes. Conspiracy theorists fabricated reports about plans for Jewish world domination hatched in Josefov.[33]

Nationally minded urban elites, assisted by experts and informed by the liberal language of scientific and technological progress, thus set their sights on Josefov and its surrounding neighborhood. Their original 1887 plan, partly inspired by massive urban renewal efforts in Paris earlier in the century, was extraordinarily ambitious, and destructive. It reached beyond the borders of Josefov, threatening Old Town landmarks such as the Estates Theater, the Clam-Gallas Palace, and the St. Agnes Convent. Within Josefov, planners with little knowledge of or regard for Jewish tradition took aim at the Old Jewish Cemetery. Preservationists, members of the Jewish Community, and local notables, including the former mayor Tomáš Černý, protested. The Old Town landmarks, six of Josefov's nine synagogues, and most of the Old Jewish Cemetery were ultimately spared. The slum clearance, or *asanace,* proceeded apace, however. Jewish leaders raced to preserve artifacts, and their efforts eventually led to the creation of Prague's Jewish Museum. By 1912, when the *asanace* was completed, 260 stone structures had been demolished and apartments for the well-to-do were constructed. The curved, haphazard, labyrinthine streets that *Golden Prague* regarded as "oriental" were replaced with wider, straighter streets, with Nicholas Boulevard running along Josefov's eastern border. Underneath Nicholas Boulevard ran an enormous, stone sewer tunnel that continued under the Vltava to a waste station in Bubeneč. City authorities did not provide original residents with compensation, only a deadline for evacuation.[34]

––––––––––

Egon Kisch—he added the "Erwin" later in life—was born in 1885 and was thus a teenager when the *asanace* had begun. The second oldest of five boys, he grew up in a spacious apartment on Melantrich Street, near Old Town Square and the area of ongoing urban renewal around Josefov. Kisch's father was a successful clothes seller before his death in 1901 at the age of sixty. Thereafter, Kisch's mother cared for the children and the apartment alone. In addition to enjoying a middle-class upbringing, Kisch inhabited a decidedly Prague German milieu. Fellow German speakers predominated in his immediate neighborhood. Middle-class Prague Germans' most important meeting place, the three-story Casino, stood just minutes away on Am Graben / Na příkopě, whose name referred to the moat that once separated the Old and New Towns.[35] Also nearby was Kisch's dear Aunt Lotti, who admired Goethe and hosted guests in an apartment filled with Biedermeier-era furniture.[36] In 1903 he enrolled in Prague's German Technical University, and the following summer he took a course at the German half of Charles-Ferdinand University. Kisch also inhabited a decidedly German Jewish milieu in Prague. Similar to many of the city's German-speaking Jewish boys, Kisch attended the German Nikolander High School, which was a ten-minute walk from his childhood home. (When Kisch entered high school, roughly nine-tenths of Prague's Jewish kids, including many from Czech-speaking households, were attending German primary and secondary schools.) Jews predominated among the German speakers in Kisch's decidedly middle-class neighborhood; by 1879 nearly two-fifths of the members in the nearby German Casino were Jewish. In St. Gall / Havel, the parish district where Kisch grew up, Jews made up two-thirds of the neighborhood's German-speaking population in 1890 and 1910, respectively.[37] Kisch rarely referred to religious life or Jewish customs, save a few scattered references in letters to his brother Paul. He once mentioned to Paul that he had to rush off to a Passover celebration. In another letter he attempted to dissuade Paul, who had been toying with Austro-German nationalism, from being baptized.[38]

It was little coincidence that German-speaking Jews predominated in Kisch's district and in neighboring districts around Am Graben / Na příkopě. In the early nineteenth century, wealthier Jews could leave the Jewish Town and relocate in a restricted zone just outside of Prague's ghetto. In 1848 the monarchy removed all restrictions on movement and residence for Jews, and in 1867 Bohemia's Jews obtained full emancipation and could now enjoy the same legal and political rights as other Habsburg citizens. Over the course of the century, Jews from across Bohemia migrated to Prague. Prague Jews inhabited neighborhoods throughout the city and also lived in the flourishing suburb of Vinohrady. Still, the neighborhoods radiating immediately outward from Josefov remained the core of Prague's Jewish middling classes.

Not all of Prague's self-declared Jews considered themselves to be Germans—in the 1910 census nearly half listed Czech as their language of everyday use. Jewish entanglement with German language and culture, however, remained strong in the city.[39] Beginning in the late eighteenth century, imperial decrees demanded that official communications within the Jewish community be in German, not Hebrew or Yiddish. Prague's Jews were required to take on German last names. Men were permitted to attend schools and universities, where German-language instruction had long predominated. The Jewish Enlightenment (*Haskalah*), which influenced Prague's Jews and which they sometimes challenged, was a largely German-speaking movement. Until later in the nineteenth century, according to Hillel Kieval, many of Prague's Jews assumed that German language and culture "were to be the principal vehicles of social advancement and national integration."[40] It was in the German *Realschulen,* such as Kisch's Nikolander High School, that Habsburg efforts at integration combined with many of the ideas of the Jewish Enlightenment as well as social advancement.[41] Liberalism, and especially German liberalism, promised social and economic advancement and acceptance.

By the turn of the century an increasing number of Prague's Jews—many of them migrants to the city—embraced the Czech language, joined their own Czech-language associations, and sometimes supported Czech nationalist efforts. The adoption of Czech language and culture by their offspring seemed promising to some parents. Poorer Jews as well as poorer non-Jewish German speakers often felt ignored by the well-to-do, elite middle class. Yet the relationship of Prague's elite Jews to German language and culture remained deep. Indeed, non-Jewish German-speaking elites had good reason to ally with their Jewish counterparts as their collective influence and numbers dwindled. As a result, as Gary Cohen writes, there were few places in central Europe where urban Jews could publicly embrace their Jewishness and, with relative ease, remain prominent and respected members of the local German community.[42]

After his summer at Charles-Ferdinand University, Kisch enrolled as a one-year volunteer as part of his mandatory military service for the Habsburg army. This privileged choice, one often made by well-to-do members of the middling classes, allowed him to reduce his conscription to one year with the possibility of becoming an officer in the reserve army. Kisch, restless and resistant to military discipline, spent much of the year in the brig, emerging only as a corporal.[43] Back in civilian clothes, he dabbled in writing poetry and prose before eventually moving to Berlin. The experience proved to be transformative. He enrolled in a journalism academy led by Richard Wrede, a highly respected practitioner known for his emphasis on veracity and realism. At his brother's urging he also threw himself into the nightlife of one of Europe's most vibrant metropolises. Good reporting and living a full life required it, Paul had suggested.[44] Also on his brother's advice, Kisch participated in a number of extracurricular activities

Egon Erwin Kisch in military uniform, circa 1905. ČTK.

along with a group of fellow students, one of the whom was an actress, Kisch wrote excitedly.[45]

Still, Kisch told Paul, he felt alone and different in Berlin: "I am the
only Austrian and the only Jew," and none of his friends knew about the
latter.[46] Therefore, in the spring of 1906 Kisch returned to Prague, where
he enjoyed a short spell as a volunteer for the *Prager Presse* newspaper.

Less than two weeks later he accepted a position at the *Presse*'s rival, *Bohemia*. Kisch's beat was crime. He made daily visits to courts, police stations, town halls, and various hangouts where fellow crime reporters exchanged information.[47] He explored sections of the city that few urban elites dared to visit. He met with victims and others who inhabited worlds radically different from his own. After a year as a crime reporter, Kisch published his first feuilleton, an essay that took readers inside Prague's newly built high-security state prison, Pankrác.[48] Months later he sold two more crime-related feuilletons, "A Guest of the Police" and "Asylum for the Wayward."[49] He then contemplated pursuing a writing career in Vienna or Berlin, capitals of the German literary world, but he reconsidered. He wrote Paul that he thought himself to be talented but not a genius, and thus had to rely on those around him rather than striking out alone. "I know well that I must limit myself to Prague," he continued in a letter filled with self-mocking pity. Paul, who shared a similar sense of humor, offered a sympathetic reply. He, too, was a struggling writer, based in Vienna. They were clearly very close as well.[50]

Crime reporting, as Kisch knew well, held great appeal for Prague's middle-class readership and for the editorship of newspapers such as *Bohemia*. As in cities throughout Europe, stories of crime, and especially murder, played on popular insecurities linked to rapid population growth and modernization. The new science of criminology complemented a generalized fear and suspicion of urban lower classes. For the increasingly sensationalist mass press, violent crime was a favorite subject, further stoking middle-class fears and justifying police actions against the urban poor.[51] The famous London case of Jack the Ripper sparked a number of imitations throughout central Europe, including sensationalist reporting about the "Austrian Ripper," who in 1910 brutally murdered a prostitute in Vienna's well-known public park, the Prater. Works of fiction, such as Czech and German translations (in 1905 and 1907, respectively) of Arthur Conan Doyle's adventures of Sherlock Holmes, expressed similar sentiments.[52] These fears

Paul Kisch (middle, wearing a bowler hat) with friends in Vienna, 1911. From Egon Erwin Kisch's personal archival collection. Památník národního písemnictví.

were also highly exaggerated. Just fifteen Praguers were murdered in 1909, a number that dropped to eleven the following year. Most murders occurred outside the city center. A Prague inhabitant was 138 times more likely to die of pulmonary tuberculosis than of homocide.[53]

Aside from murder, there was much crime to report. As throughout Europe, an array of newly defined crimes and misdemeanors were pursued by a rapidly expanding police force, which did more than just protect public safety. They aimed to protect the social order while, especially in middle-class neighborhoods, removing the urban poor from sight. Police and other city officials had the right to remove from public spaces drunkards, beggars, and others charged with minor misdemeanors. If an offender lacked the right of domicile, a legal protection bound up with the town of his or her birth, the police could deport that person from the city. City authorities could place "idlers" in workhouses and the mentally ill in hospitals. City authorities were able to arrest and imprison Praguers who could not pay their rent. They could also seize a debtor's possessions, which were shipped to a warehouse in distant Braník.[54] These efforts complemented a social geography that kept Prague's urban poor out of sight of the respectable middling classes. Industrialization and the promise of work had attracted tens of thousands to the city. Many settled in the frightfully crowded, unhygienic apartments near industrial centers, including Smíchov, Žižkov, and Karlín, that ringed the city. Urban projects such as the *asanace* forced even more of the city's urban poor from the city center.

Kisch's early crime reporting contributed to popular fears and helped to justify officially sanctioned repression of the city's poor. As he turned to writing feuilletons, Kisch flipped the script. His feuilletons deployed an empathetic realism that brought the urban poor into view. In his first feuilleton, in 1907, Kisch wrote that outside the Pankrác prison new tenements and shops dotted the landscape in the growing suburb of Nusle. In the distance, bustle and noise from the brightly lit streets of Prague could still be heard. Behind the prison walls, however, there was no trace of that lively, outside world, "no hint of freedom."[55] Readers might take comfort in the fact, he noted ironically, that the prison complex, completed in 1889, had all of the modern facilities for reforming its inmates. It contained 7,236 German- and Czech-language books (high-quality fiction and nonfiction); a special wing for prisoners with tuberculosis; a gymnasium with "modern equipment"; a "beautiful prison chapel with artistic carvings made by the hands of prisoners"; a kitchen; a bakery; a washroom; a hospital; and, of course, cells. The focus of the essay, however, was a fifteen-year-old boy in the juvenile ward and a description of the deleterious effects of prison life. Along with his brother, he had robbed and killed a man. He had four more years to serve. When Kisch asked the boy if he would be an upstanding citizen upon release, he winced and demurred. The grimace on his face and the look of his eyes told a story of recidivism, Kisch concluded. Middle-class efforts to reform the boy had failed. "This is someone sure to commit a crime—one would think," he wrote.[56]

Several years after the Pankrác feuilleton, in 1910, Kisch's mentor at *Bohemia,* Paul Weigler, gave the young writer a weekly column. The column, "Prague Forays," ran for more than a year and, along with several books containing reprinted and original material, made Kisch a local celebrity.[57] Many of the themes that informed his first texts, such as empathetic realism and a keen desire to make the invisible urban poor visible, ran through these feuilletons, even if the tone had become more lyrical and less didactic. He pointed out to readers that just around the corner from a major thoroughfare for carriages delivering middle-class riders to Baumgarten / Stromovka for a Sunday stroll, stood a homeless shelter.[58] Another piece about the prison for petty criminals, nicknamed Fišpanka (according to legend its building once housed the Fischbein fish bone processing plant; the material was then used to make corsets, among other things), began by describing a walk to Podskalí, a district along the Vltava at the southern edge of New Town. Podskalí had one of the city's most important docks and was one of the poorest sections of the city, undergoing an *asanace* of its own. In the summer many of its inhabitants eked out a living retrieving logs that had floated downriver from forests and sawmills to the south; in the winter many cut ice from the Vltava to refrigerate storage cellars across the city.

> From Charles Square one branches off in the direction of Palacký Bridge and onto Moran Lane, which declines into Vaclár Lane and then left into an inhospitable area. Here one finds the darkest Podskalí, one-level houses with abandoned shop fronts, which now serve as living quarters . . . lumber-yards with crooked, rotten planks, all dilapidated, freight wagons under the open sky. An old man with an oily, glistening newsboy's cap, a cane leaning against his knee, sits in front of the building, and one can just imagine the life tragedies of this raftsman.[59]

A street in Podskalí, 1899. Archiv hlavního města Prahy.

Still other pieces took readers to unexpected corners of the city. The Old Town's soup kitchen was on Gemeindehofgasse / U Milosrdných, just west of the well-to-do apartments on Nicholas Boulevard. The New Town's soup kitchen was not far away on Petersgasse / Petrská Street, two blocks north of the State Train Station.[60] A red workhouse for beggars and vagabonds stood in front of a military hospital in the Castle District, on Loretto Street.[61] A wintertime visit to a "warming shelter" followed a street familiar to middle-class pedestrians next to a canal running past Kampa Island and under the Charles Bridge. Along the way, Kisch wrote, mist clung to gas lanterns that lined the route, foreshadowing a scene of Prague's down-and-out huddling for warmth just out of view.[62]

Other pieces, again recalling his Pankrác essay, offered sympathetic portraits that challenged haughty middle-class notions regarding the urban poor. Several essays upended common ideas about idleness and work. In one soup kitchen, street sweepers wearing caps with the city's coat of arms gathered for a warm meal.[63] Some of the inhabitants of the warming house earned money by shoveling snow or delivering ice from the frozen Vltava to storage cellars throughout the city.[64] In a homeless shelter, everyone addressed each other not by their names, but by their professions. When a former baker asked for the best route to Hamburg, he obtained directions from a coachman. The route included the best roads and offered suggestions as to where the most bountiful plum trees could be found.[65] As he had done in his Pankrác article, Kisch was quick to denounce recidivism and the deleterious effects of institutions that were praised for their reform efforts. Statistical evidence, he wrote, demonstrated that few if any of the three hundred alleged vagabonds and beggars dressed in mandatory brown clothes at the workhouse in the Castle District would actually be "reformed" through work.[66] He ended the piece with a scene in which the director asked a young man how much he had worked that day. The answer was barely audible, full of hate, Kisch observed, the kind of speech recently witnessed during a riot in the mental asylum of Bohnice.[67]

Character sketches, or what Kisch termed "little novels," poked fun at middle-class notions of respectability and labor while also celebrating the autonomy and individuality of his characters. "In the cheap nightclubs you often come across people who do not earn 'honorable' bourgeois livelihoods but nevertheless do not earn their money in some dishonest way," he wrote. "People born with some talent who aren't suited for the track of ordinary life. So they derail themselves, and the course of their lives runs along side roads."[68] One such character sketch featured Rudolf Nešvara, a.k.a. Antoušek, one of the city's official dogcatchers. The job paid little and was often dangerous and disturbing. (Dogs not reclaimed after three days were massacred in his newly built thermochemical extermination station.) Antoušek declared, however, that he would never give up his autonomy for factory work.[69] Determined autonomy and a rejection of regimented, dehumanizing factory work also characterized the men trapped in the poorhouse: "Quite a few of them have left home and property, and thus become poor, in order to wander about the world, many have left their wages in the hands of their employers, they slink out . . . of the yard, in the night and fog, and wander the streets and paths along fields, without money, into the distance."[70]

Kisch wrote later in life that his sympathy for the down-and-out, as well as his keen curiosity about their lives, had emerged from his time in the brig as a young army recruit. Contemporaries praised his gregariousness and charm, which no doubt contributed to his ability to converse with the characters he wrote about. His German school had mandatory lessons in Czech, but Kisch learned Czech slang on the street.[71] The popular feuilleton genre also suited his efforts. The feuilleton allowed Kisch to combine his journalistic background with self-reflection, merging wordplay and wit while tackling subjects that had often been left to high-minded reformers. The genre made him famous, just as it had done for central European literary lights such as Jan Neruda, Karel Čapek, Theodor Herzl, Joseph Roth, and Karel Kraus. German publishers produced two collections of his feuilletons before World War I, as did a Czech-language Social Democratic publisher, which praised Kisch for his ability to "find deep human feeling" portrayed with "a healthy sense of humor, irony, and understanding of common people's pain" that avoided sentimentality. "Few know Prague like this young writer," it continued, "who has attempted to become acquainted with and portray Prague life of all sorts, even its lowliest and most impoverished levels."[72]

German-language reviews, including one published in Berlin, echoed similar sentiments. In a review published in *Bohemia,* Hans Strobl praised Kisch for writing a "truly Prague book" characterized by misery and humor, and full of love for the city that he called home.[73] The review, which Kisch's brother called "splendid," further praised Kisch for his subtle critique of the "silhouette of the city" imagined by

Czech urban elites and middle-class society in general.[74] Strobl, a fervent nationalist who embraced Nazism later in life, intimated that Prague's Germans and German literature "knew" Prague better than their Czech rivals, a knowledge that constituted a rightful claim to the city. Kisch might well have agreed with this interpretation. Kisch wrote in a German nationalist publication that his feuilletons opposed Czech romantic notions by revealing a genuine knowledge of the city and its people. "For the Germans of Prague, however, this book is a noble testimonial, a powerful monument to the fact that they are rooted in this soil and are at home here [in Prague]," he wrote. It demonstrated that "they love their ancient, beautiful homeland and that they appreciate and understand [the city] better than the Czechs."[75] The piece also revealed shameless ambition. It was published anonymously as a book review. Everything had been arranged by his brother Paul, who had connections with the publisher.[76]

———

Kisch's anonymous review of his own work was most likely a one-time ploy to gain a wider readership. Indeed, nationalism figured only rarely in Kisch's feuilletons. When he did broach the topic, he returned to the 1860s and 1870s, often expressing nostalgia for a gentler time while also suggesting the origins of the national hatred of his day. In one feuilleton, for example, Kisch took readers on a tour of locales where student fraternities met as well as hidden corners where their members dueled. From these origins, he hinted, national rivalries and violence had only become amplified. (Kisch admitted that he was no stranger to dueling. He had drawn a sword three times, he wrote: once on Jewish Street in a conflict with a German nationalist who had attacked a Jew; once in a "noble German hotel" in the New Town with a gentleman who became a noted Czech political figure; and finally in a monastery with a Zionist doctor.)[77] In another essay, Kisch offered a nostalgic portrait of a medical complex in Nusle, near Pankrác, that had been nicknamed, ironically, the "poison hut" (*Gifthütte*). Before the university was divided into Czech and German sections, and before nationalist student groups had begun attacking each other in the streets, Czechs and Germans worked in the medical complex together. They danced together at the institute's ball, which was held at a nearby pub. Soon, however, "the poison of national hatred took root in the 'poison hut,'" he wrote. German doctors worked elsewhere and the Czechs who remained squabbled among themselves. The daughters of professors no longer danced at the pub. In their place, Kisch concluded, prostitutes from a local village now eked out a sad existence.[78]

Nostalgia and a tragic sense of loss were understandable elements of a reimagining of history, as was Kisch's decision to avoid direct discussion of contemporary nationalist hatreds. The past, liberal and nationalist, also lingered in the background of his writing, and for good reason. Kisch's parents' generation had enjoyed a golden age of German middle-class liberalism, both in Prague and in the Habsburg capital of Vienna. They had spearheaded liberal reforms that usurped power from the aristocratic classes while keeping the working classes at bay. Economic reforms and the embrace of laissez-faire capitalism further undermined corporatism and traditional privileges. German science and the arts thrived. Education reforms and German cultural influence, they promised, would raise the general level of civilization in the monarchy, while a deserving few from the masses would be allowed entry into the world of German-speaking liberals. Similar to their pre-1848 predecessors, some continued to look upon the Czech national movement with condescension. The Prague German writer Rainer Maria Rilke, for example, once referred to the Czech nation's rise as "the story of the child who grows up among adults."[79] Well into the twentieth century, many middle-class Germans still considered themselves to be part of German central Europe. They maintained close ties with German speakers in Vienna as well as in Berlin and other cities in Germany. They hosted prominent German-speaking theater troupes, professors, and authors from abroad.[80]

For many of Prague's German Jews, liberal reforms provided an unprecedented opportunity for integration and the granting of equal political rights. Many thrived, both economically and in terms of social standing. As mentioned above, these reforms, along with migration to Prague, also created the conditions for Prague's rival Czech middlling classes to usurp German liberal power in the city. German elites responded by spearheading a drive to create a vibrant German associational life, centered in the German Casino. By 1890, German groups made up almost a fifth of the city's registered associations—and in a city in which German speakers made up only 15 percent of the population. These efforts, as one German professor stated, aimed to create "a smaller city within the larger city."[81] For a brief period they also allowed Prague's German liberals to establish and dominate within various nationalist organizations, or "protection associations," that erected schools, staged protests, and mobilized German nationalism throughout Bohemia. As the decades progressed and as nationalist politics became more radicalized, Prague German leaders lost their grip on many of these associations in Bohemia. Other, more radical rival groups emerged. Furthermore, proud German liberals made little effort to include the city's German-speaking lower classes—workers, craftsmen, petty employees, and their families who made up 35 percent of the city's German-speaking population in 1900.[82] Many of these poorer German speakers, especially small retailers, clerks, and mechanics, simply began to identify themselves as Czechs and joined the larger Czech-speaking community.[83] Similarly, while the adoption of German culture and language once held out the promise of integration and advancement, an increasing number of the city's Jews, many of them from the countryside, began to embrace Czechness and joined Czech-language associations.[84]

Prague's German-speaking elite, Kisch later observed, made up a "prosperous stratum suspended in the air"—a stratum, one might add, with diminished ability to affect events on the ground.[85] The decline of German urban elites' influence in Prague paralleled the extension of suffrage and the concomitant rise of mass politics in the Austrian half of the Habsburg monarchy. Candidates from rival political parties representing the lower classes ran for office in the Reichsrat, marched on the streets, and published their own newspapers. Moreover, as Carl Schorske has written, fin-de-siècle politics was played "in a sharper key," engaging in a "mode of political behavior more abrasive, more creative, and more self-satisfying than the deliberative style of the liberals."[86] Several Czech parties, exploiting economic frustrations and despair, engaged in overt antisemitism.[87] In 1899 a rising Czech nationalist politician, Karel Baxa, served as lead prosecutor in the sensationalist trial of a Jewish man falsely accused of blood libel. Antisemitism had become part of the fabric of Prague's political life, and beyond. Political antisemitism had even infected Europe's shining symbol of liberal progress, Paris, whose newspapers, along with their counterparts in Vienna, Budapest, and St. Petersburg, delighted in the drama of the Dreyfus affair. There was also an exclusionary logic to Herderian ideas inherited from the nineteenth century, now imbued with organic notions of race. If national language reflected the soul of a nation, which had deep roots in a particular portion of Europe, then a Czech- or German-speaking Jew was a pretender, or worse.[88]

Anti-German, antisemitic violence, typically running just below the surface, often burst into the open. In 1897, when Kisch was just twelve years old, riots over the use of the Czech language inflamed the city for days. German students dressed in national caps and sashes brawled with their Czech rivals during their traditional Sunday stroll along Am Graben / Na příkopě. At a meeting of city alderman, Prague's Czech mayor, Jan Podlipný, claimed incitement:

> I have heard complaints that the German students are conducting themselves provocatively in the streets and squares (Calls from assembled: For shame! Březnovský: Jewish rabble!), that they themselves were purportedly incited by the professors (Calls: The knife to the professors!), that with their

uniforms they provoked our peaceful people in a daring, indeed impudent manner, and in Czech Prague, on this Slavic soil, they dare to sing the [German nationalist hymn] Wacht am Rhein![89]

Urged on by nationalist leaders and the political press, with the exception of the Social Democratic press, Czech demonstrators took to the streets, shattering the windows of the German Casino and the New German Theater, and damaging numerous hotels and businesses in the heart of the city. They also attacked Jewish stores and property, irrespective of the owner's self-proclaimed nationality. Outside the city center, rioters attacked synagogues in Vinohrady and Žižkov attended by Czech-speaking Jews.[90] Waves of riots swept over the city again in 1904–1905 and in 1908. German and Czech students continued to clash right up until the outbreak of World War I.

Yet a look at the everyday lives of middle-class citizens suggests that Prague was not a constant nationalist battleground. German-speaking elites hired Czech clerks and house servants. Czech- and German-speaking elites attended each other's theater performances and lived in the same apartment buildings. Despite their differences, they often held fast to core liberal values.[91] The decidedly "Czech" Ferdinand Street and the "German" Am Graben / Na příkopě, both popular boulevards where locals gathered for demonstrations or evening strolls, met at the northern end of Wenceslas Square, but the square itself bustled with shoppers of different national loyalties and social backgrounds.[92] In Prague, as in capitals throughout central Europe, turn-of-the century artists experimented with various forms of modernism that challenged the liberalism of their fathers while seeking to make sense of an uncertain, postliberal world. Here, too, Czech and German speakers, while often taking different paths, inspired each other's work.[93]

Still, a sense of isolation and alienation was palpable, especially among the German-speaking Jews of Kisch's generation born after 1880. Pavel Eisner wrote, "The life of the German Jew in Prague became fundamentally pathological because he belonged to a sociologically abnormal minority which hung like a mote in the air."[94] This same isolation and alienation, in turn, provided the raw materials for one of the century's most vibrant and original modernist movements. According to Scott Spector, for these German-language writers, including Kisch, questions of territoriality, both literally and metaphorically, often provided a framework within which they attempted to make sense of their lives amid liberal decline, popular nationalism, and antisemitism. Many wrote of inhabiting an "island" or of belonging to various, often claustrophobic circles surrounded by a Czech majority, miles away from the vibrant centers of German-language art and culture. Many belonged to the so-called Prague Circle, a metaphor coined by Max Brod that described a series of outwardly expanding circles of Prague writers and artists in which he was at the center. They engaged in a project of "radicalized rootlessness," Spector continues, that experimented with various literary forms as well as political notions of belonging, whether they be Zionism, pan-Germanism, or socialism.[95] One of the Prague Circle's most well-regarded members, Franz Kafka, explored themes of alienation and dislocation suggestive of the modern condition. His writings were often brooding and expressed feelings of entrapment and helplessness. Still, according to Noah Isenberg, "Kafka's yearnings for 'belonging' . . . can be considered as much an integral component of his modernist writings as are his portraits of 'non-belonging'" for which he is best known. Rather than abject despair and isolation, Kafka imagined himself existing somewhere between aloneness (*Einsamkeit*) and community (*Gemeinschaft*), as he explained in one diary entry.[96]

Kafka and members of the Prague Circle did not lead isolated lives. Many had regular jobs. Several of them, in the tradition of the Prague salon, regularly took part in philosophical discussions in the home of Bertha Franta.[97] Around the time that Kisch was writing his "Prague Forays," Kafka dabbled in Zionism and explored his Jewishness. He attended lectures by the existentialist philosopher Martin

Buber that were hosted by Prague's most prominent Zionist student organization, Bar Kochba. He also attended performances by a visiting Yiddish theater company. He marveled at how the performers, many of them hailing from distant Galicia, appeared to be "bound to each other by their Jewishness in a degree unknown to us." While watching the performance, Kafka continued, he did not feel alone, but "among them," if only for a brief moment.[98] Kafka's favorite gathering place, however, was Café Arco, which opened in 1907. Designed by the renowned architect Jan Kotěra, it was a thoroughly modern establishment divided into three sections: a main room with tables and chairs, a billiard room, and a reading room replete with newspapers and publications from across Europe. Prague's German-speaking literati, whom the Viennese satirist Karl Kraus mockingly referred to as "Arconauts," were among the café's most well-known regulars.[99] Here, they belonged.

The Arconauts gathered in their favorite café for long stretches of time. Artists of various sorts were especially attracted to the interactions—and caffeine—that cafés offered. Café Arco, similar to other cafés, also served frankfurters, cold food, bread, and desserts.[100] Café Slavia, located in the heart of Czech-speaking Prague, at the end of Ferdinand Street across from the National Theater, was a favorite spot of Czech modernists. In these cafés, however, national borders were porous. German speakers mingled with Czech-speaking counterparts in Café Slavia, and Czech speakers did the same in Café Arco. Café Unionka was known as a place where Czech- and German-speaking artists mixed freely.[101] It mattered little that Café Slavia and Café Unionka occupied buildings on Ferdinand Street, a decidedly "Czech" boulevard where Czech strollers and students predominated. Similarly, Café Arco was near the "German" boulevard Am Graben / Na příkopě. Café Savoy, also located on Ferdinand Street, hosted the Yiddish theater performances attended by Kafka.[102] Nor were cafés the sole preserve of artists. Other professions and social classes congregated in various cafés throughout the city. Café Arco attracted travelers from the nearby State Train Station and office workers walking home after work. Czech and German merchants often met in Café Corso.[103] Crime reporters, as Kisch knew well, gathered at various cafés throughout the city to exchange information.[104] Small-scale traders did the same in cafés that lined a street near Old Town Square.[105]

By 1900 the café had become a staple of middle-class urban life throughout Europe, especially in fellow Habsburg cities such Vienna and Budapest.[106] The café, as Jürgen Habermas has famously argued, was one of many institutions crucial for the emergence of a bourgeois "public sphere" in which participants discussed common problems and exchanged information. In cafés and in other public spaces, public opinion took form, as did plans for public action.[107] Similar to the salons that preceded them, cafés were also key sites of middle-class sociability, albeit with fin-de-siècle intonations. Middle-class norms of manners and polite language distinguished the café from working-class establishments such as the pub. Even in Café Arco, the hub of modernist critiques of bourgeois culture, the owner, Josef Suchánek, could not resist making tongue-in-cheek policies on proper café culture. For example, ripping out a section of a newspaper was "foul robbery" that could cause the offender to be banned from the premises. Anyone providing information about said crime could receive a reward of 100 crowns.[108] Café conversational styles also combined middle-class upbringing with rhetorical innovations. In artists' cafés such as Arco, the "bon mot," a conversational style that entertained the listener with clever word use and playful paradoxes, reigned supreme. Similar to the feuilleton, the bon mot style combined self-ridicule with light tones while addressing serious or deeply meaningful issues. *Stammgäste*, or regulars, had reserved tables where they would meet with friends and spend part—or all—of their day chatting, reading, writing, and drinking.[109]

Kisch was a regular at Café Arco, but Café Montmartre, located just around the corner from *Bohemia*'s editorial offices, was his preferred gathering spot. He often rushed there after leaving work around midnight.[110] Café Montmartre, where Czech and German speakers mixed freely, was less a café than a cabaret, where drinking and carousing combined with intimate, often experimental performances and readings.[111] ("Ah, finally," Kisch allegedly said after Josef Waltner informed him of his plans to open a cabaret in Prague.)[112] Named after the neighborhood in Paris where the cabaret was born, Café Montmartre offered live music that continued until the wee hours of the morning.[113] The clientele, as Kisch recalled, included professors, high-ranking civil servants, and even powerful state officials, but artists and the spirit of modernism predominated. Cubist and futurist art decorated the walls. The café album, he continued, was where the best young poets, "drunk with alcohol and erotic desires," joined artists in memorializing their beloved establishment.[114]

The cabaret deliberately thumbed its nose at many middle-class social mores, yet, similar to the café, it, too, was a site of middle-class sociability, if on its own terms. His friend Waltner fondly recalled Kisch's "grotesque dances" with a regular named Revolution, dances that Kisch had first learned as a high school student visiting a down-and-out music hall on the edges of the city. Montmartre was also a site of belonging. Notions of camaraderie and of the cabaret as an oasis run through the published version of Montmartre's album. Otakar Hanuš, a self-described "poor literati" who later became a noted screenwriter and publicist, ended his self-mocking poem "Chanson de Montmartre" with the words "In Montmartre we all meet up!" The word "friend" appears throughout the album, often in self-mocking, playful tones that betray a genuine sense of attachment to others. The celebrated Czech satirist Jaroslav Hašek's short story "My Montmartre Tragedy" featured dogs and falling asleep on the streetcar, as well as Waltner's heroic efforts to save the writer from himself. Kisch's melodramatic entry implored his cherished friends to tell his "dear Montmartre" how much he longed for it. The album concludes with Waltner thanking all who had supported him and expressing gratitude "for their advice

Kisch's Café Montmartre dance partner, Revolution, from Egon Erwin Kisch's personal
archival collection. Památník národního písemnictví.

as well as their frequent visits" to his establishment. Enemies have been
made, as have friends, he continued, "and to the latter, my heartfelt
thanks!"[115]

In the same album, Waltner also praised Kisch for patronizing
down-and-out drinking establishments throughout the city, where
he "gained, thanks to his modest and unobtrusive manner," an array of
additional friends.[116] The playful irony suggests a tension that runs

through Kisch's many feuilletons detailing visits to dives and other gathering places. Pubs, too, had their own Stammgäste and their own nicknames familiar to regulars. Similar to middle-class cafés, regulars and others used their stares to police class borders. Only rarely did Kisch succeed in becoming an unobtrusive observer able to cross class boundaries. Upon entering the Omnibus watering hole, he wrote, conversation immediately stopped as everyone looked at him. "But I greet a one-legged party girl by her nickname. The Czech greeting 'Hey there, Revolution' legitimizes me sufficiently, and conversation picks up again." Although he was accepted, Kisch's sense of class difference remained, despite his near fluent Czech and natural gregariousness. After having listened to a long and colorful conversation about the tragic murder and suicide of two regulars, and the regulars' collective plans to attend the funeral, Kisch paid up and began to leave:

> Remiška points to my beer mug, from which I had taken only
> a swallow from the least-used place, back near the handle.
>   "Can I finish it?"
>   "Sure."
> She thanks her benefactor.[117]

Indeed, throughout his feuilletons, Kisch confronted class barriers with mixed success as he ventured beyond territory familiar to Prague's German-speaking elites. At many dive pubs, or *spelunke,* the stares persisted, the experience at the Omnibus aside.[118] At a homeless shelter, where men shared stories of tramping across Europe, they mocked Kisch for his naiveté and scolded him for not observing the shelter's strict rules regarding dress and behavior.[119] When he asked some desperate souls in the Old Town where the local soup kitchen was, one responded curtly, "If you don't know where the soup kitchen is, then go ahead and get something to eat at the Blue Star Hotel. It's on Am Graben."[120] When he did manage to cross into the territory of the destitute, Kisch often congratulated himself, with a wink toward his readers. For example, once he managed to enter a warming house by wearing secondhand, dirty clothes as a disguise. One fellow, Kisch noted triumphantly, even invited the author to join him in finding a place to sleep for the night. Kisch politely refused.[121] At times, the mocking wink toward his readers was meant to serve as a reminder of their, and his, privilege and good fortune. After a night in a homeless shelter, for example, he went home and took a bath, something that "in the interest of my non-homeless acquaintances should be carefully noted."[122] Another essay offered his "gentle reader" a series of tips to avoid embarrassment should he decide to visit a soup kitchen.[123]

Brod found this aspect of Kisch's work particularly distasteful:

> But what a shame that in his many books what Kisch experienced, or pretended he experienced, in the criminal world, in the milieu of whores, and so on, is written with this reaction in mind: How the good citizens of Prague, the subscribers to the chauvinistic German paper *Bohemia* ... will be astonished at my wickedness! This sidelong glance at the impression he produces is really an unartistic element in Kisch's work.[124]

There is, of course, much to criticize in Kisch's feuilletons. Kisch, who allegedly was well known in bordellos throughout the city, sidestepped the business of prostitution. Although at times he expressed sympathy and familiarity with the so-called Magdelenes of Prague, he was largely ambivalent to the fates of women who sold their bodies for sex.[125] In his writing, women, especially younger women, were typically objects of pity. Only rarely did he develop them as characters. In tending toward the lyrical or lyrically tragic that appealed to his middle-class readers, Kisch prioritized subjective experience over calls for political change. For example, he offered no concrete suggestions for reform, including prison reform. Nor did he use his knowledge to call out legal injustices, to lay the foundations for change through appeals to the law. Before World War I, he paid little attention to the various working-class parties that emerged in his time, including the Social Democratic Party. Nor did he take note of the factory workers who participated in a vibrant Social Democratic culture with its own publications, libraries, theaters, and speeches.[126] Distrustful of philosophical theory, including that of Arthur Schopenhauer, who was so beloved by members of the Prague Circle, Kisch appeared to be equally uninterested in Marxist theory. He never wrote directly about the antisemitic politics or the rising German nationalist parties in his midst, even though he did express fears about them to Paul.[127]

———

Kisch's writing, according to Eisner, betrayed a lifelong effort to flee the ghetto. By this he meant Kisch's desire to break free of national and confessional isolation as well as his "passionate escape" from bourgeois life and values. Kisch's flight, Eisner continued, took him into a largely Czech-speaking world, and then beyond into the social peripheries of the city.[128] Kisch always returned, of course, to familiar, comfortable spaces, but he also reminded his readers of the near impenetrability of class difference and noted the distressing circumstances of others in their midst. The poor and working poor could not follow Kisch into his middle-class worlds. They would never have dared to walk into Café Arco or Café Montmartre. Kisch's escapes into the peripheries were revealing, trenchant, and entertaining, but always fleeting. Still, they were meaningful, and, if read from a more sympathetic perspective, well-intentioned efforts to create not just an alternative to middle-class Czech visions of Prague, but also an alternative, more inclusive notion of belonging and place in his hometown. Central to these efforts were new, modern practices of urban walking, which in various ways informed Kisch's writing.

Throughout the nineteenth century, improvements to urban infrastructure created the conditions for Europeans, more than ever before, to walk the city for pleasure and purpose. Sidewalks raised above street level began to appear in European cities in the late eighteenth century.[129] In Prague, marble sidewalks first appeared in the early nineteenth century. Cobblestones covered dirt streets that had turned to mud after rain.[130] Ferdinand Street and Am Graben / Na příkopě were among the first streets to receive sidewalks and cobblestones. By the end of the century, most of the streets in the city center enjoyed the same improvements.[131] City leaders, ever concerned about hygiene and safety, required property owners and shopkeepers to spray water on the sidewalks in front of their buildings to keep them clean in the summertime, and in the winter sidewalks had to be cleared of snow and ice.[132] Later in the century, the city employed impoverished residents to shovel snow from the streets. In the summer, a mechanized street cleaner traveled the city.[133] (As Kisch wrote, its powerful sprays brought "the bacteria of the streets in fruitful union with the bacteria of Prague's water.")[134] Gas and electric lamps reduced middle-class fears about walking at night in a city that, earlier in the century, had gone almost completely dark after sundown. Police presence was intended to assuage those fears further.

More than ever before, Praguers and city dwellers throughout Europe walked the streets for pleasure—to socialize, to seek out sex, and to visually consume urban scenes and spectacles described in sensationalist, often lurid, tones by the popular press. (One Parisian newspaper estimated that, in April 1895, roughly 10,000 people had visited a Paris mortuary to gawk at two drowned girls placed in a display window—a common practice at the time.)[135] Night walking permitted evening theater and musical performances and gave rise to a vibrant nightlife in the cafés, restaurants, and cabarets. By the late nineteenth century, the taboo on women walking the streets alone had been broken, as witnessed by the appearance of women shoppers on their way to newly built department stores.[136] Women social workers, such as those who worked in Josefov before the *asanace,* made the rounds of the poorer sections of the city on foot. Men and some women commuted to work on public transportation but also on foot. For those without means, walking to work was the only option.

Walking, and wandering, the city streets had also become a leitmotif in European literature. The spectacle of a busy Berlin street was described by a curious observer in E. T. A. Hoffmann's essay "My Cousin's Corner Window," which partly inspired Kisch to pen his own street-level observation in an essay titled "Characters of the Street."[137] Wandering the urban landscape was a common trope among a number of Prague writers before and after Kisch began penning his feuilletons.[138] At the beginning of Kafka's short story "The Sudden Walk," a man experiences the exhilaration of leaving his family home for the freedom of the street: "And when you walk into the long streets this way—then you have completely stepped out of your family for the evening, and they dissolve into non-existence, while you yourself, thoroughly strong, outlined in black, slapping the back of your thigh, raise yourself to your true form." The adventure that follows, which culminates with a walk toward Petřín Hill with an acquaintance, takes a number of disturbing turns, however, punctuated by the uneasy behavior of his companion and threatening dark spaces.[139] After the turn of the century, Andrei Bely's and James Joyce's characters walked St. Petersburg and Dublin, respectively, in novels that endowed these cities with memorable character traits of their own.[140] Other writers focused on the mesmerizing, sometimes disturbing effects of crowds in motion along city sidewalks. As evening descended, Edgar Allan Poe wrote from a London café in 1845, "a tumultuous sea of human heads" filled the pavement as "tides of human population rushed past the door." Soon, however, his eyes "descended to details, and regarded with minute interest the innumerable varieties of figure, dress, air, gait, visage, and expression of countenance" that revealed noblemen, merchants, attorneys, tradesmen, stockjobbers, "a tribe of clerks," pickpockets, gamblers, and "Jew-peddlers."[141] As one commentator noted in 1914:

> Berlin was storming homeward from its work. Solid masses
> crowded the pavements, a stream of trams and crowded
> motor-buses clamored along the street. The *Stadtbahn,* or city
> railway, thundered across its arches overhead. The *Unter-*
> *grund* [Underground] engulfed rivers of humanity in the side
> streets. Shop-girls, clerks, petty bureau-officials, tradespeople,
> typists—fresh eager faces, restless and nervous bodies.[142]

Crowds and the experiencing of crowds were central for the flâneur,
the most well-known urban pedestrian in nineteenth-century literature. Coined by Charles Baudelaire, the term "flâneur" first referred
to an aristocratic dandy of sorts who was both spectacle and observer
on the crowded streets of early nineteenth-century Paris. The flâneur,
Baudelaire wrote, was alone on the streets, but also experienced an
exhilarated sense of belonging among the crowds:

> For the perfect flâneur, for the passionate spectator, it is an
> immense joy to set up house in the heart of the multitude,
> amid the ebb and flow of the movement, in the midst of the
> fugitive and the infinite. To be away from home and yet to feel
> oneself everywhere at home; to see that world, to be at the centre
> of the world, and yet to remain hidden from the world—such
> are a few of the slightest pleasures of those independent, pas-
> sionate, impartial natures which the tongue can clumsily
> define.[143]

Crowds and a host of other stimuli became defining features of efforts
to understand the modern urban experience as the century progressed,
and not just among novelists. Medical experts fretted about shocks to
the system caused by crowds and other external stimuli. Some suggested that city dwellers, over time, developed a protective, psychological "shield" against these shocks.[144] Others, such as the Berlin so-
ciologist Georg Simmel, argued that the "intensification of nervous

stimuli" of the city led to the blasé, "matter-of-fact attitude" of a "metropolitan man" whose torn nerves, relentlessly attacked, could not regenerate within the urban environment.[145] These same excessive stimuli, Robert Alter suggests, gave rise to late nineteenth-century novels whose narratives were conducted "more and more through the moment-by-moment experience—sensory, visceral, and mental—of the main character or characters."[146] After World War I, Walter Benjamin immersed himself in Baudelaire's writings, arguing that the Parisian essayist was a pioneer in seeking to understand the shocks of the modern city. Imagining backward onto Baudelaire's Paris the bustle of twentieth-century Berlin, Benjamin argued that the flâneur, who "demanded elbow room" in the crowd while remaining a man of leisure, had a particular knack for embracing and absorbing the modern city's stimuli. The flâneur offered, for Benjamin, hope that the shocks and impressions of urban life (*Erlebnis*) could be translated into experience (*Erfahrung*) that was central to consciousness.[147]

Kisch's Prague, however, was not Paris or Berlin, the two major metropolises that had inspired Baudelaire and Benjamin. With half a million residents, Prague was still relatively small compared to these two capital cities and also to London, Vienna, and St. Petersburg, each of which counted more than 1.5 million inhabitants before World War I. In the European context, Prague's population size had more in common with that of medium-sized European cities such as Dresden, Dublin, Amsterdam, and Odessa.[148] Furthermore, Prague's total area was relatively large. Contemporary observers and artists commented on the speed of streetcars and the noise of the streets, but vast crowds in motion rarely appeared among their representations of Prague. Instead, Prague was better suited for the type of observant meandering and insightful encounters that characterized Kisch's feuilletons. It was a city best suited for someone willing to make thoughtful, curious forays into the city, a *Streifzügler*.

The title of Kisch's feuilleton series, "Prager Streifzüge" (Prague Forays), is suggestive in many ways. The original, German-language meaning of *Streifzug* (the singular form of the noun) referred to a brief military incursion. During the course of the nineteenth century, the word also came to mean a cursory venture into a body of knowledge, historical period, or subject. By the time Kisch had begun writing his feuilletons, the word had obtained yet another meaning: a sort of wandering, a movement that does not have a particular goal or destination in mind, but with a definite purpose, whether it be to enjoy an experience or understand something by way of inquiry.[149] In Kisch's time, the closest equivalent to *Streifzug* in Czech was the word *toulka*, which today leans more toward the sense of rambling or wandering without a particular purpose.[150] In English, the closest equivalent to the plural form *Streifzüge* is most likely the word "forays," not "wanderings," as several translators of Kisch's work have suggested.

For Kisch, *Prager Streifzüge* carried several complimentary meanings. It referred to the form and content of his feuilletons, which meandered through various topics, driven by a spirit of inquiry. In this respect, walking, with a vague purpose and an open-minded spirit of adventure, empathy, and observation, was key. His investigative forays made no claim to expertise. They contained no bold, definitive conclusions, even if they did create a sense of empathy while subtly, and often ironically, commenting on the social maladies of his day. *Streifzug* also described the physical movement through space enjoyed by Kisch and his readers, which provided him with the raw material and impressions to write the feuilleton. During one adventure, Kisch and a friend embarked on a pub crawl across the city, visiting eleven seedy dives and dance halls forbidden to Habsburg army conscripts. Officers, he wrote, had helpfully posted the list in army barracks. Here, the theme of walking was present throughout the narrative.[151] More typically, his feuilletons began with a walk that established context while locating the essay in a particular location on the city map. Kisch's visit to Fišpanka, for example, consciously took readers on foot from Charles Square into the depths of Podskalí. His essay about the dogcatcher Antoušek began with a long walk to the outskirts of the city.

His adventures to soup kitchens, warming houses, and shelters often began with walks originating near well-known locations. Other forays into the streets revealed a human carnival of charlatans, local characters, and friends.

"Prague Forays," and the walking that they entailed, also suggested an alternative way of experiencing the city and of creating a sense of place unique to Prague. One might even say that Kisch's forays, which admittedly predated Benjamin's essay on the flâneur, offered their own means of translating the many impressions offered up by urban life into a meaningful experience, or *Erfahrung*. Indeed, taking the raw materials of life and conveying them as subjective experience was a defining feature of the feuilleton genre. As Schorske writes:

> The *feuilleton* writer, an artist in vignettes, worked with those discrete details and episodes so appealing to the nineteenth century's taste for the concrete. But he sought to endow his material with color drawn from his imagination. The subjective response of the reporter or the critic to an experience, his feeling-tone, acquired clear primacy over the matter of his discourse. To render a state of feeling became the mode of formulating a judgment. Accordingly, in the *feuilleton* writer's style, the adjectives engulfed the nouns, the personal tint virtually obliterated the contours of the object of discourse.[152]

For Kisch, adventures into the streets, while based on careful observation, had as their primary purpose the conveyance of a number of emotions and feelings. They evoked discomfort at the sight of poverty and the poor; tensions from crossing class boundaries; and nostalgia for a time when nationalisms were less hateful. In this respect, Kisch's feuilletons, while generous in their attempts to give his characters their own words and allow them to give meaning to their own lives, were also self-consciously aware of the limits imposed by subjectivity, even as they reveled in the subjective.

Kisch's forays were, first and foremost, about Prague. (They also played with German dialects peculiar to Prague.) Taken together, imagined as a collage, they did more than reject visions of middle-class Czech visions of Prague. They suggested alternative notions of place, of Kisch's hometown, that were both sympathetic and nostalgic. Within the limits of his class subjectivity, they also sought to imagine a city that embraced, rather than obliterated, difference. These efforts might be bundled into essays swirling within three categories: urban institutions and practices that distinguished Prague from other cities in Europe; urban characters who inhabited the cityscape; and locales endowed with alternative memories of the past.

No city in Europe, Kisch claimed, had anything similar to the Café Candelabra, a precursor to the food truck where "hundreds of weary pilgrims across nighttime Prague are guaranteed an invigorating, warm drink as beneficence." Similar to the names of other drinking establishments throughout the city, "Café Candelabra" was a nickname given by regulars. Its official name, "The Hot Drink Ambulance," was written in gold letters on its front. Kisch also referred to it as the "Teamobile." Café Candelabra did not serve much tea, however. Grog was the signature drink, and customers could also purchase a warm dessert and two cigarettes for just twenty heller, better than any café in Prague, he wrote. Located in the Old Town, it attracted a cross-section of city residents, from middle-class revelers to the homeless, who could warm themselves for one-third the price of a flophouse room. The name of its inventor, Kisch exclaimed, "remains unlisted in the annals of world history! I must flush out my anger." He continued in a calmer tone, writing that every schoolchild knows that James Watt invented the steam engine, but the person who invented Café Candelabra "is not known to a single schoolchild, his name not in a single song, a single book of heroes."[153] Café Candelabra was not the only nighttime establishment that Prague could claim as its own. Although other European cities deployed a variety of means of getting drunks off the streets, only in Prague, Kisch claimed, could the observer find a *Gemeindetruhe*—a coffin-shaped wagon used to transport the hopelessly inebriated home or to the police station. The *Gemeindetruhe* also doubled as an ambulance that brought the poor to hospitals.[154]

Other institutions and practices, and the people associated with them, echoed traditions that inspired nostalgic visions of the city and its inhabitants. While Prague's street sprayer represented the latest technology, the tradition of spraying the streets harked back to the 1850s, when firemen did it on an ad hoc basis. The drivers of street sprayers were favorites among street kids. Urged on by their admirers, the drivers could, with a press of the button, spray with a little more strength, drenching wary and unwary pedestrians alike.[155] Other traditions and institutions would have remained generally unknown, save for Kisch's efforts. Antoušek the dogcatcher told Kisch that his family had been doing the same job for generations; he proudly showed Kisch an eighteenth-century proclamation from Empress Maria Theresa attesting to his family's dogcatching privilege. The hangman had become a civil servant in 1860, but dogcatchers continued to enjoyed corporatist employment, a remnant from the time of guilds.[156]

Some forays offered up visions of the city as a human comedy whose personalities, together, gave Prague its distinctive character. If someone were to hold a vote to determine the most well-known man in Prague, Kisch wrote, the winner would almost certainly not be a politician, a scholar, or an artist but instead one of the tragicomic eccentrics of the street.[157] "Lad Dance!" was a typesetter by day who, by popular request, danced for nighttime passersby. Sleeping Honzíček walked in his sleep through the streets of the Old Town.[158] Antonín Fiala, who wore an Inverness cape similar to that of Sherlock Holmes, was a weather prophet who had predicted the appearance of Halley's comet in 1910 with the same precision as Harvard's observatory.[159] Ferda de Podskal boasted that his flea circus could compete with the arrival of the Barnum & Bailey Circus. "I'll ruin the American barkers in no time," he proclaimed.[160] Detective Lederer knew every regular in every dive bar in

Antonín Fiala, the weather prophet, from Egon Erwin Kisch's personal archival collection. Památník národního písemnictví.

town, and they knew him.[161] When the well-known panhandler Wilhelm Muneles, also known as Wilhelm von Prag, was run over by a streetcar, police found a will bequeathing a remarkable sum of money to a hospital nurse who once cared for him. He also left money for a policeman who had arrested him in the past.[162]

In writing his forays, Kisch typically added further depth to the characters of the street, thus embedding them further into the reader's consciousness while evoking a sense of empathy. The most famous street character, he wrote, was the panhandler Haschile, known for his comical retorts. If someone failed to give him a decent amount of money, he would say, "I am no beggar. I'm a panhandler." Local shops sold a four-color postcard of Haschile, which often sold out. "If someone wants to send a postcard to a friend abroad, reminding him of home," Kisch wrote, "should he send a picture of the train station or Vyšehrad?" No, he concluded, Haschile was the best choice. Yet few knew, Kisch continued, that Haschile's real name was Jacob Weiss. Born in Prague, Weiss had worked as a messenger in the nearby town of Kolín until one day, at the age of twenty, he was arrested for the unauthorized sale of matches. Thereafter, he was arrested thirty times for begging. He had also been arrested for trespassing, drunkenness, despoiling a hallway, and slander. He was once falsely accused and arrested for arson. He was well known to various public authorities and to the staffs at psychiatric wards.[163] Ferda de Podskal was a baby when the 1853 flood destroyed his family's home. For the rest of his life he hated water. As a young boy, he organized a small zoo in his home. After his father died, he learned to cook while apprenticing with a goldsmith. He then walked westward to Germany, where he worked as a "cattle drover, swing pusher, and carousel operator."[164] Before organizing the flea circus he hawked macaroons in Josefov, falsely claiming that they were kosher. Detective Lederer, Kisch wrote, had a well-earned respect for political neutrality and a sense of decency. Always aware of his surroundings, he had a knack for spotting suspicious behavior. Once he arrested a gentleman in a coffeehouse who was obscenely "guzzling champagne and throwing money around." Further investigation showed that the man was running a phony telegraph office in Nusle.[165]

Kisch's Prague, and the forays that defined it, was often nighttime Prague, and for good reason. Prague's bustling nightlife stood in stark contrast to London's, Kisch wrote while visiting the British capital, where after sunset it was darker and police surveillance more intense. As a result, London's liveliness and rush disappeared at night.[166] Nighttime Prague also permitted the existence of many of the characters that inhabited Kisch's imagined cityscape. "At night," he wrote, "the philistinism of humanity is not so assertive." Only then, he wrote, did those with odd professions who "derailed" themselves feel comfortable in public places. "A whole assembly's worth of colleagues of such rare talents" could be found in Prague's nightclubs, he wrote: "silhouette cutters, market hawkers, chantant directors, fair acrobats, instant portrait artists, conjurers, weather forecasters, couplet singers, mind readers, harmonica virtuosos, eccentric dancers, and similar artists."[167] Nighttime also allowed other Praguers, if only for short periods, to enjoy a different existence. At Montmartre, he wrote, bourgeois women arrived to sing, dance, and leave the strictures of their daily lives. When the music ended, and the lights came on, they lost their refuge and were forced to return to their "happy marriages."[168] In working-class dance halls, factory girls found in the night a means of escape from their daily toils and the demands of their families, and had the chance to enjoy their youth.[169]

Kisch also led his readers to urban sites charged with their own human and localized memories—stories that created an alternative sense of place and belonging. He often recalled Josefov before the *asanace,* a world of panhandlers, hawkers, and sneaks among jagged streets and dilapidated buildings erased by what we would now term urban renewal. Kisch was far from alone in engaging in ex post facto nostalgia for the neighborhood, which spoke to a distant Jewish past and implicitly questioned the *asanace.* (Haschile had, in fact, been a central character in Gustav Meyrink's *The Golem,* a fantastical, drug-induced journey through the lost world of Josefov.)[170] Unlike many Czech- and German-speaking literati who plumbed old Josefov for artistic inspiration, however, Kisch's portrayals, again, were tinged with sympathetic nostalgia. Before the *asanace,* he wrote, Café Candelabra was still mobile. Afterward, it was forbidden from entering the bourgeois neighborhood that was emerging from the rubble. The authorities then required it to remain stationary in a less respectable section of the Old Town. Late-night brawls before closing time had become more common, Kisch wrote.[171] Other essays subtly sought to undermine antisemitic portrayals of the district as a haven for unseemly greed that undermined "Czech" Prague.[172] Shortly after the opening of the ghetto, Kisch wrote, traditions of self-help among secondhand traders expanded to include small-time Jewish and non-Jewish traders in the city center. Their loose organization still went by the original name, Chabrus.[173]

Few, if any, Praguers walked the city the way Kisch did, in part because Kisch was particularly suited for the forays depicted in his feuilletons. He was unusually outgoing and took particular pleasure in crossing social boundaries, even if self-reflectively constrained by his middle-class background and appearance. Indeed, his gregariousness struck others as one of his defining qualities, as friends and acquaintances would later remember. He seemed to feed off the energy of social interaction, regardless of the language or social standing of the interlocutor, and to be both charming and entertaining while also being empathic and attentive. Brod raved about his sense of humor, a characteristic that others consistently commented upon as well. Some remembered him as both hospitable (*gastfreundlich*) and popular.[174] Kisch, as those who knew him commented, was one of a kind.

In this respect, the Streifzügler, similar to the flâneur, was not a typical urban character. He—such adventures would have been especially difficult for women—would not be a fair representation of middle-class experience in the fin-de-siècle city. Yet Kisch's sentimental depictions of the city and his colorful, yet thoughtful encounters with Prague's down-and-out, reveal a struggle to forge a sense of place in a city increasingly imagined as "golden, Slavic Prague." He was also, perhaps, striving for an alternative way of belonging in the city, a way that tended toward the sentimental and was allergic to direct political action, but also embraced difference and did not shy away from encounters with difference. It was a sense of belonging that acknowledged privilege and the inescapability of subjective experience yet strove for empathy. Kisch, dismissive of abstractions, preferred the quotidian, the everyday occurrences that made each individual's life novel. In creating a relationship, albeit fleeting, with individuals with whom he and his readers shared a common urban space, he was forging a sense of belonging for himself, his subjects, and his readers. The kids in Pankrác were Praguers who were just as worthy of attention as the elite bankers on Nicholas Boulevard were, the characters of the street more deserving of regard than historical figures whose monuments dotted the city. Fleeting experiences, brief daily encounters, have become central to the urban experience. They are also, as Melinda Blau and Karen L. Fingerman argue, essential for a sense of community and well-being.[175] Kisch was among the first to celebrate such encounters, to see them as part of the urban fabric and as the building blocks necessary for the creation of a common sense of urban belonging.

Kisch's celebrity from "Prague Forays" extended well beyond his admirers at Montmarte. The issues of *Bohemia* in which his feuilletons appeared, he bragged to Paul, always sold out. "This muck is gathered up with great passion," he wrote.[176] He met and interviewed Thomas Edison and the famed Western adventure novelist Karl May,[177] and his responsibilities and standing at *Bohemia* continued to grow.[178] After publishing his first book of collected feuilletons from the "Prague Forays" series, Kisch wrote to Paul that he was constantly being accosted by passersby asking him for a free copy. Hopefully, some people will actually buy the book, he wrote.[179] He was the first investigative reporter to break the story of Colonel Alfred Redl, a Habsburg army officer who, under orders, committed suicide following accusations of passing sensitive information to the Russian government. Kisch published the story anonymously in a Berlin newspaper, and *Bohemia* ran it, again anonymously, in Prague. In 1913, perhaps lured by greater fame, he decamped to Berlin, where he joined the staff of the highly regarded *Berliner Tageblatt* newspaper. Kisch's fame spread well beyond the borders of Prague, aided in part by a work of fiction, *The Pimp*, released by a Berlin publisher in 1914.[180]

Kisch's identity as the author of the Redl story would become public years later, thus cementing his reputation as one of central Europe's most highly regarded reporters and literary talents. By that time, though, the world around Kisch had radically changed. In the summer of 1914, a young Serbian patriot shot and killed the heir to the Habsburg throne, Francis Ferdinand, and his wife while they were touring Habsburg-occupied Sarajevo. The assassination set in motion a series of events that plunged Europe into war. Kisch, still a corporal in the reserves, reported for duty in the garrison town of Písek, in southern Bohemia. Weeks later he was fighting on the Serbian front, jotting down notes that he would later publish as a war diary. He wandered war-torn villages, gathering observations for a book.[181] As the war finally came to an end on November 11, 1918, the Habsburg monarchy collapsed. Prague exploded into revolution. Riots and other forms of popular violence took aim at Germans and Jews. Kisch survived the war, but he, and Prague, would never be the same again.

3

REVOLUTION CITY

☙❧

ON SEPTEMBER 21, 1920, Vojtěch Berger and his wife joined a protest at the People's House, an organizational hub for the Social Democratic Party in downtown Prague. Berger, a lifelong Social Democrat, had faithfully participated in many such demonstrations in the past, but this one was different. Days earlier, leftists within the party had seized the building, which included the party newspaper's editorial offices. As one of the orators declaimed, however, leftist efforts to have the Social Democrats join Bolshevik Russia's Third International and to pursue a Marxist-style revolution faced an uphill battle. Rightists within the party controlled many of the printing presses and, at that very moment, were rallying their supporters on Žofín Island. Writing in his diary that evening, Berger made it clear where he stood. The rightists, he commented, had "relegated ideas of revolution to the archives and delivered masses of workers into the hands of capitalist and agrarian profiteers." After years of effort on behalf the party, Berger lamented angrily, "We have been betrayed. . . . They don't give a shit about us."[1]

The betrayal of which Berger spoke was the Social Democrats' decision to support the First Czechoslovak Republic, which arose amid the collapse of the Habsburg monarchy at the end of World War I. At the war's end, a radical leftist revolution had seemed possible. Hungry demonstrators filled the streets of Prague. In Russia, Bolsheviks were waging a civil war against forces of the Right. Radical leftists seized power, albeit briefly, in Munich and Budapest. For Berger, a hardscrabble carpenter traumatized by four years on the front line, leading Social Democrats in Prague had made a deal with the devil: in return for power and influence, they had quashed the moment of revolution. There is something to Berger's sentiment. The First Czechoslovak Republic enjoyed the support of the victorious Western powers in part because it promised to act as a bulwark against Bolshevik Russia and radical leftism. Its embrace of liberal democratic principles further ensured its loyalty to and dependence upon the former Allies. Many Czechoslovak leaders, however, interpreted their political ascendancy as a revolution of its own, just not a Bolshevik one. They fashioned Prague into a capital for a new country, dotting the city's landscape with peculiarly Czech expressions of liberal democratic progress. Memories of the vanquished Habsburg monarchy, now vilified as a reactionary "prison house of nations," disappeared from the landscape.

The First Czechoslovak Republic also tolerated the existence of the Communist Party, founded by splinter leftists months after the People's House protest. Berger became one of the party's first members. Throughout the interwar period, he continued to reject the republic, just as its leaders had apparently rejected him and his vague dreams of revolution. Among fellow Communists, however, Berger found a home. Under the umbrella of the Communists, he participated in various practices of belonging—participating in public demonstrations and taking part in associational life—which were also encouraged by rival parties across the political spectrum in interwar Czechoslovakia. Rather than revolution, these practices of belonging spoke to continuities with the prewar era, which had witnessed the emergence of mass politics and mass political parties within the Habsburg monarchy. These practices endured until the Nazi occupation (1939–1945), which set the stage for the Communists' seizure of power in 1948. Throughout those years Berger continued to write in his diary, in which he pasted newspaper clippings, theater tickets, pamphlet materials, and other everyday artifacts. His entries reflect a curmudgeonly personality, someone who interpreted the world with biting cynicism and a vague hope for the future. They also offer rare insights into one working-class man's thoughts and actions, as well as his search for belonging in a disturbing political age.[2]

————

Born in 1882, Vojtěch Berger grew up in the small Czech-speaking village of Todně. This village, and the ones around it, counted among the poorest in South Bohemia. Since his youth and for most of his life, Berger worked to get by, engaging in a seemingly endless struggle for food and basic security. At the age of ten, he worked as a herdsman. Similar to so many other rural poor throughout Europe, Berger then migrated to the city, desperate for work. At the age of nineteen, he followed his older brother, Franta, to Vienna, where they shared a cramped apartment. Berger took jobs wherever he could in the quickly modernizing Habsburg capital. He installed electrical lines along city streets and in middle-class homes. One winter he shoveled coal for a Viennese gasworks. At another time, desperate for basic subsistence, he earned pocket money chipping ice blocks for a local pub. He typically worked six days a week and was off only on Sundays. Sometimes he worked seven days a week.[3]

After gaining his footing, Berger began apprenticing to become a carpenter. In 1909 he earned his carpentry license, which provided him with a modicum of financial stability, along with a sense of belonging in the city. He spent the remaining years before World War I working as a freelance carpenter, typically working under a master carpenter for months at time on various construction or repair projects throughout the city. He faithfully attended meetings of the Czechoslovak Federation of Carpenters, a Prague-based self-help organization that provided insurance and unemployment aid to its members. (Berger eventually became treasurer of his local branch's relief fund and a member of its agitation commission.)[4] He counted many fellow members as friends and often joined them at the pub when not at work. Berger was also a dedicated reader of their weekly publication, *Carpentry Trade*. (His archival collection includes one volume of clippings from this newspaper.)[5] As so often happens, this particular path owed much to a relationship from his youth, as Berger remembered it. Back in Todně, one of his closest acquaintances—the son of the shepherd with whom Berger worked—was a carpenter. The two also read newspapers that his friend Zeman purchased each Sunday while in the nearby city of Budějovice. The newspapers captivated him, Berger later wrote, "even though I understood crap."[6] In Vienna, Berger developed a voracious newspaper-reading habit that extended well beyond his reading of *Carpentry Trade*. It was there, too, that he began to make sense of the world through reading while jotting down notes about his life.

Carpentry provided Berger with a sense of belonging—and a paycheck—but he felt most at home in the Social Democratic Party. Again, another influence proved crucial. Not long after Berger's arrival in Vienna, Franta encouraged his younger brother to join the party. "And so I was a Social Democrat," Berger reminisced, "for the moment only a paying one; otherwise I understood it as a goat does parsley"—meaning not at all.[7] Berger, however, soon became deeply immersed in the world of Austrian Social Democracy, largely through reading. In many ways he became an ideal party member, at least as envisioned by leaders such as Victor Adler, who sought to "revolutionize minds" through newspapers, plays, novels, bombastic oratory, and other transmitters of ideas. These texts provided a common vocabulary, drawn from Marx's younger days, that allowed party members to interpret their experiences within the flow of history.[8] The shared vocabulary of revolution offered hope for a more just society. It celebrated labor, the male breadwinner, and comradeship while fostering a shared sense of community and destiny. Berger appropriated many of these words and their meanings into his life and writing, especially the term "comrade." When talking about his work, he referred to himself as a carpenter, but when speaking about politics in general he became a proud member of the working class, or of the proletariat.

Berger also developed a sense of camaraderie and outrage in opposition to rival political parties that emerged within the Austrian half of the Habsburg monarchy at the turn of the century. He saved his most poisonous venom for the National Socialists, Czech national rivals for the socialist vote who were "actually in cahoots with the bourgeoisie. . . . They are a thorn in the ass of the country. They are *traitors* to the working class."[9] This oppositional sense of belonging naturally had a class element as well. He disparaged the bourgeoisie, broadly conceived, which he envisioned as both frightened and manipulative, as opposed to the brave and honest working classes. He held the "peasants" of Todně in contempt, considering them helplessly ignorant of "politics, trade unions, or the interests of the working class."[10] He had a particular distaste for the Catholic Church, born of unpleasant experiences with his overbearing religious mother in Todně, which was now informed by Social Democratic anticlericalism. Berger's entries on the subject of religion, as with other subjects, reflected his particular style and penchant for disdain. In one diary entry he described seeing priests praying at a nearby table as he shared a beer with friends in a local pub. "In one spot alcohol, in another fake prayers. Human idiocy remains unfathomable," he concluded.[11]

Berger also found a sense of community and purpose through action, engaging in a variety of public practices that emerged in tandem with the rise of mass politics. Berger was particularly drawn to mass demonstrations and political rallies organized by the Social Democratic Party. The "stormy year" of 1905, as Berger called it, included a number of invigorating public events.[12] Throughout the year, he faithfully attended emotional oratorical performances by party leaders. He reveled in speeches describing the (short-lived) autumn revolution that followed workers' demonstrations in Russia. He excitedly participated in the November 28 general strike and accompanying rallies that pressured the Austrian government into granting universal manhood suffrage for elections to the federal parliament.[13] Two years later he took part in the celebrations that followed the Social Democrats' remarkable victories in Vienna, Prague, and elsewhere in the monarchy—the peak of the party's success, when membership in the Bohemian lands alone was 100,000, the largest in the region.[14] He faithfully attended the party's annual May Day celebrations, when workers captured streets and public squares as part of an annual show of strength and solidarity. He collected pamphlets and leaflets that were handed out during the event.[15]

Berger also participated in the extraordinary associational life that swirled around the Social Democratic Party. Not long after becoming a party member he joined the party's United Workers Gymnastics Club, which, similar to its middle-class counterparts in the monarchy, organized local exercises and public performances of coordinated bodies in motion. Berger not only became an active and dedicated party member but also counted fellow Social Democratic gymnasts among his closest friends, first among them a fellow South Bohemian named Štepánek. Informal gatherings often had a decidedly Social Democratic imprint as well, such as Berger's Saturday evening get-togethers with fellow party members at a local pub. Gatherings and other practices related to the Czechoslovak Federation of Carpenters shared a Social Democratic imprint. Their membership lists and their public events often overlapped. Their leadership shared space with the Social Democrats in the People's House in Prague. Berger's personal life extended beyond the world of Social Democracy. He also belonged to a decidedly middle-class organization that advocated for Czech-language schools in Vienna.[16] In 1914 he was still living with his brother Franta, with whom he enjoyed going on walks throughout the city. His girlfriend Mařenka, another Czech speaker with roots

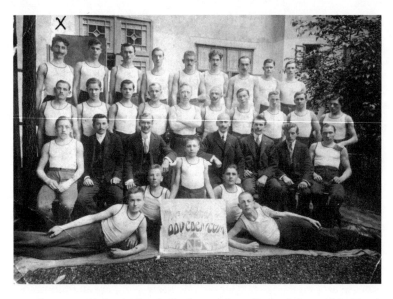

Vojtěch Berger, top left under the *x*, with other members of his local chapter of the United Workers Gymnastics Club. The image is from a postcard that he sent to a relative in Bohemia, dated just before Berger's deployment to the front. Archiv hlavního města Prahy.

in South Bohemia, knew little about the workers' movement and attended church, much to Berger's chagrin.[17]

The existence that Berger had carved out for himself in Vienna, however, would soon come to an end. On July 31, 1914, Berger woke up early and went to a café on the corner of Treustrasse and Wallensteinstrasse. A little more than a month earlier, Gavrilo Princip had assassinated Francis Ferdinand, heir to the Habsburg throne, and his wife, Sophie, in Sarajevo. Two days before entering the café that morning, Berger, along with countless citizens across the monarchy, had read newspaper accounts about the Habsburg declaration of war against Serbia. This morning he was reading the newspaper again while enjoying breakfast and a coffee. Across the room, the café owner, who had just received his call-up notice, was "crying like an old hag." "And these are the heroes who will defeat Serbia?" Berger wrote in his diary.

Soon thereafter, Berger, now thirty-two years old, learned that he, too, had been called up. He visited with friends in the carpentry union and in the Social Democratic gymnastics club. In the evening he strolled through a park with Mařenka. Once home, filled with thoughts about death, he wrote a note bequeathing his library to Franta. If Franta should also die, he wrote, the library was to go to Štepánek.[18] The next day Berger traveled home to South Bohemia on a train full of fellow reservists. Before being deployed he spent several days in Todně and, seeking an escape from his mother's crying, spent a drunken night on the floor of a Budějovice pub.[19] Three weeks after being mobilized, Berger joined other members of the ninety-first infantry regiment, based in Budějovice, as they boarded a train headed for the Serbian front.

Remarkably, Berger emerged from the war alive. Roughly 1.2 million of his fellow Habsburg soldiers and approximately 10 million soldiers worldwide were not so lucky.[20] Veterans of Berger's regiment, which also fought on the Russian and Italian fronts, later claimed that the ninety-first had the highest number of deaths in the Habsburg army.[21] Berger did, however, endure extraordinary hardship and loss. In 1914 he watched as fellow soldiers, facing fire for the first time, drowned while attempting to cross the Drina River. A Serbian sniper shot one of Berger's close friends in the chest as he was fetching water. By February of 1915 few members of his original platoon remained. Berger cried, but refused to pray, upon learning that Franta had been shot dead in Galicia. Letters and newspaper notices informed him of the deaths of carpenters and fellow Social Democrats from his Vienna days. "The war has brought some wonderful things and results: massacre, destitution, hunger, uncleanliness, sickness, and, last of all, lice," he wrote.[22] He suffered from loneliness and fear: "We've been amputated from the world, awaiting with uncertainty what the next day will bring."[23]

Berger tried his best to fight this sense of isolation. He befriended a handful of Social Democrats within his platoon. Despite being a negligent correspondent, he treasured letters from Štepánek and from his mother, sister, and other friends. (His relationship with Mařenka went through a rocky period. She fretted about his involvement with social democracy. He chided her for sending letters with so many grammar mistakes.) He also found a lifeline in Vienna's Czech-language Social Democratic daily, *Dělnické listy* (The Workers' Newspaper). One diary entry, dated several months after his deployment, excitedly detailed the contents of a care package that Štepánek had sent him: a pipe, tobacco, half a liter of rum, a decagram of tea, a quart of sugar, and soap. "And also my beloved *Dělnické listy* has arrived. I haven't read it since we were in Vienna."[24] He shared copies of *Dělnické listy* and its Prague-based counterpart, *Právo lidu* (Right of the People), with comrades in his platoon.

Berger was a skeptical reader, and for good reason. Forbidden from employing war correspondents and being subjected to military censorship made it difficult for newspapers to provide reliable news about the front. Berger was certain that *Dělnické listy* was underreporting casualties. He thus chose to focus on other sections of the newspaper, especially poems that spoke to his experiences of war and losing loved ones. One poem about dancing brought back memories of a dance hall and better times in Vienna. Another was about a frontline soldier who did not write letters.[25] He also relied on *Dělnické listy* and the newspaper of the Czechoslovak Federation of Carpenters to stay up to date on the lives of friends and comrades. He, in turn, sent updates about his movements and health to their editors, which they faithfully reprinted. At one point, he even appealed to *Dělnické listy* for help, asking if there existed a regulation stating that the death of one or more brothers on the front would allow the survivors to be released from duty. He received a kind response, noting that, sadly, no such law existed in Austria. The letter also included an address where he might pursue the matter further.[26]

Anger and disgust fill the pages of Berger's diary entries as well. He especially detested most professional officers, whose incompetence and arrogance had led to needless deaths. Only 10 percent of them were decent human beings, he wrote: "The rest are human beasts."[27] He became less tolerant of his German-speaking comrades in arms. He continued to appropriate the language of the Social Democratic Party to condemn capitalists, the bourgeoisie, and the Catholic Church, although in even harsher terms. He also turned his ire on the Social Democratic leadership, a falling out that had been years in the making. In this, as Jakub Beneš writes, Berger was far from alone. The revolution promised in the 1907 elections, of course, had never arrived. Losses in the 1911 election to competing nationalist / socialist parties had exposed divisions between the Social Democrats' Czech and German sections, making hopes for revolution even more distant.[28] Similar to their counterparts across Europe, the Social Democratic leadership had passively supported declarations of war. For Berger, this acquiescence was the last straw: "Those asses, the leaders of the workers' party, they are swindlers and bastards," he told Franta during a conversation in the summer of 1914.[29] As the war dragged on, he consistently referred to this betrayal, saying that the Social Democrats now counted among the nationalist, bourgeois parties. His language, peppered with words like "revenge," "mutilation," and "bloodthirsty," became disturbingly violent.

The experience of war and the language of revolution thus created the conditions for Berger the Social Democrat to become a leftist radical and a self-described Bolshevik. Ironically, however, this transformation might not have happened if not for Berger's reading of *Dělnické listy*. In 1917 the army's high command lost direct control over the censorship of newspapers in the monarchy. Prewar censorship rules and punishments became the norm.[30] Thanks to *Dělnické listy*, Berger learned about schisms within the Social Democratic Party in Germany. He read numerous articles about the Russian Revolution. Although it did not overtly approve of Bolshevism, the paper faithfully reprinted many of Lenin's speeches, which, along with other commentary, provided Berger and others with a new hope for revolution, and the language with which to express it.

Reading newspapers also fed Berger's radicalism and calls for violent revolution after the war's end. When the Habsburg army collapsed, he eventually retreated to Todně, where, after a brief stint in the newly created Czechoslovak army, he took up a few local carpentry jobs. Back home, overwhelmed by anger and disgust, he read voraciously, often going to nearby Budějovice and returning with piles of newspapers, including *Dělnické listy* and *Právo lidu*. His diary from that period included lengthy articles, with commentary, about political developments in Prague. He read about protests in Vienna, the Russian Civil War, the rise and fall of Communist governments in Budapest and Munich, and the Polish-Bolshevik war. Even as radical leftists fell to counterrevolutionary forces across Europe, Berger called for revolution in the Bohemian lands and beyond. "The bourgeoisie are bloodthirsty and are taking revenge on the working classes," he wrote, "but there will come a time when the workers will have their own celebration."[31]

War had also transformed Prague's inhabitants, as well as the social and political order that they inhabited. At first, centralized authoritarianism swept away prewar elements of liberal democracy and mass politics. The day before mobilization, Austria's minister-president suspended parliament, with barely a protest from its members, including the Social Democrats. An emergency decree stripped away protections previously guaranteed by law. Censors blacked out portions of newspapers before publication and rifled through private letters. An imperial decree declared that civilians could be tried in military courts for a range of crimes, from high treason to disturbing the peace. Many workers in factories that were crucial for war production essentially came under military law, which meant, among other things, that attempts to quit a job or evade work constituted acts of treason.[32]

The smooth, humming machine of war mobilization and authoritarian rule envisioned by military planners and others, however, would eventually give way to disorder and dissolution. As elsewhere, including Russia, major cities such as Prague experienced devastating food shortages, thanks in part to a complicated rationing system, poor transportation planning, and a priority placed on feeding frontline soldiers. (By June of 1918, each Praguer was allotted just a half a loaf of bread per week.) City officials expanded Prague's network of soup kitchens, which were now frequented by clerks, tradespeople, police, lawyers, journalists, and other self-described members of the middle class. Well-to-do Praguers ventured, illegally, to the countryside, where they traded jewelry and even furniture for foodstuffs. In the last years of the war, articles about food and food supplies dominated the front pages of workers' newspapers. Vicious resentment toward black marketeers, who profited from others' misery by selling scarce goods at inflated prices, grew by the day. The Habsburg authorities, who had assumed immense powers to produce and distribute food, also became the targets of popular ire. The heavy hand of the army in domestic matters, combined with an open disregard for the rule of law, only worsened the monarchy's crisis of legitimacy.[33]

In 1916, demonstrators, radicalized by war and deprivation, began taking to the streets. Local notions of morality and justice, as Rudolf Kučera observes, informed many of these actions, which the authorities incorrectly dismissed as irrational outbursts of anger and desperation.[34] The following year, the main outlines of the revolution in Russia were reported in Prague's newspapers, which further emboldened protesters. Hungry Praguers, women and men, workers and veterans from the front, children and the elderly, attacked public spaces. Deprivation and loss also inspired an increasing number of strikers. Radicalized young workers in Prague organized work stoppages at the Kolben electrotechnical plant and at other factories in the Karlín, Libeň, and Bubny districts that together constituted the city's "red ring." Strikes at the Ringhoffer train factory in Smíchov prompted the military to arrest eighteen leading agitators and expel them from the city. Other strikes, to the great alarm of government authorities, threatened the functioning of the railway system.[35] In January 1918, 50,000 people marched on Old Town Square calling for food, peace, and—at times—national self-determination. On May Day, roughly 100,000 marched from Wenceslas Square to Old Town Square. Many wore the Czech national colors of red and white, or just red buttons, before setting up camp on Shooter's Island, Žofín Island, and in other sections of the city. This was at a time when Prague's population was 300,000.[36]

The disintegration of the Habsburg monarchy, combined with Allied victories, thus created the conditions for revolution and a new political order. Not long after the war had begun, several prominent Czech political personalities had fled abroad. They were led by the well-respected philosopher and liberal progressive Tomáš Masaryk, who was among the first Czech nationalist political figures to abandon his Habsburg loyalties. In exile, Masaryk and others led lobbying efforts on behalf of the Czech and "Czechoslovak" nation in London, Paris, and Washington, DC. Masaryk also organized the highly acclaimed Czechoslovak Legionnaires, soldiers largely composed of Czech prisoners of war captured by the Russian army and now tasked with fighting the Bolsheviks as the Civil War raged in Russia. Other Czechoslovak Legionnaires joined the Allies on the Western front against the Habsburg monarchy, Germany, and the other Central Powers. When the time came, then, Masaryk was well-positioned to join exiles from other Habsburg regions in calling for the dismantling of the Habsburg monarchy. In its place, they told Allied leaders, liberal democratic nation-states loyal to the West could emerge. In May 1918 the Allies, led by Woodrow Wilson and his calls for national self-determination, definitively abandoned efforts to pursue a separate peace treaty with the Habsburg monarchy. They instead recognized Masaryk and his National Council as the legitimate governing body over a still undefined Czechoslovakia with undefined borders.

In the meantime, Habsburg soldiers had begun deserting the army en masse, further undermining the monarchy's hold on power. Following uprisings in Budapest and Vienna as well as in Germany, the threat of Bolshevik takeovers loomed large throughout central Europe, prompting Habsburg leaders to accept Allied demands for a ceasefire. In Prague, leaders of the Agrarian and Social Democratic Parties seized the Corn Institute, near Wenceslas Square, on October 28, 1918, which is still celebrated as Independence Day in the city. Crowds gathered on Old Town Square to hear speeches and sing the unofficial national anthem, "Where Is My Home?" In addition to seizing control over the purchase and distribution of food and gaining control of the streets, the revolutionaries soon received an official declaration from the governor of Bohemia granting the self-assembled National Committee political legitimacy. Masaryk arrived in Prague shortly thereafter and, four days before Christmas, was formally inaugurated as president.[37]

A liberal democratic republic, replete with a constitution and suffrage for women, eventually took form in Czechoslovakia. Until 1922, however, as Zdeněk Karník notes, the Prague government acted more like a "Czech national dictatorship" than a liberal democracy. As they did throughout the existence of the republic, Czech political leaders had a stranglehold on power, much to the disgust of German, Slovak, and other political leaders.[38] Often, the establishment of Czechoslovak authority relied upon the continuation of wartime violence. Hastily organized Czechoslovak soldiers fought border wars with Poland and the short-lived Communist government in Hungary. In the German-speaking town of Kaaden/Kadaň, the army responded to popular protests by shooting and killing fifty-five people and leaving roughly a thousand injured. Some Czechoslovak Legionnaires, radicalized by their experiences on the front and fueled by popular xenophobia, ravaged local populations who threatened the new order. While reclaiming the Subcarpathian city of Užhorod/Ungwar from the Hungarian army, soldiers dragged a priest from his home and, after several hours of torture, stabbed him to death on the street in front of local bystanders. Soldiers attacked priests as well as Jews throughout the region, pillaging homes and shops.[39]

Other forms of violence, beyond the control of political leaders, spilled out onto the streets across Czechoslovakia, including Prague. A week after the National Committee seized power, a group consisting largely of Žižkov factory workers surrounded the baroque Marian column on Old Town Square and pulled down what they considered to be an odious symbol of Habsburg rule and Catholic oppression.[40] Spurred on by right-wing political leaders as well as the presence of thousands of Jewish refugees from the monarchy's eastern regions, other crowds set upon Jewish synagogues and places of business.[41] In May 1919, Legionnaires took part in the looting of German and Jewish property throughout Prague. They threatened anyone who protested and sometimes even oversaw the distribution of the stolen goods.[42] Death also took other forms in postwar Czechoslovakia. Tens of thousands of people, many of them children, succumbed to the Spanish flu. Soldiers buried Prague's dead in mass graves.[43] Well after the war's end, inflation, shortages, and hunger provoked an increasing number of demonstrations and strikes that threatened the new republic's legitimacy.[44]

War, along with events in Prague, had also created a crisis within the Social Democratic Party. The party's leaders only begrudgingly lent support to the 1918 protests, often acting as a mediator between the protesters and the government authorities. Although the party had been the main organizational force behind worker protests preceding the war, it now played only a minor role—and sometimes even hindered—in the popular protests leading up to the Czechoslovak declaration of independence. Young worker secretaries, not party officials, organized most of the industrial strikes. As had Berger, many rank-and-file members and a contingent of political leaders remained disgusted with the party's 1914 support for the war effort. Radical leftists, inspired by the events in Russia, had hoped for a Bolshevik-style revolution in Prague. Instead, the Social Democratic Party, while obtaining concessions such as unemployment benefits, entered the newly formed Czechoslovak government with their National Socialist rivals and three bourgeois parties. Many on the radical Left not only despised the Social Democratic Party but also rejected the new government's claim to legitimacy. Many of the participants who pulled down the Marian column had been arrested during a 1917 workers' uprising and were then exiled to the front lines. The assembled crowd brashly ignored the personal plea of the Social Democratic leader, František Soukop, to spare the monument. "You are the National Committee; we are the nation!" the group's leader, Franta Sauer declared.[45] Similar to their Habsburg predecessors, the Czechoslovak government—Social Democrats included—faced a crisis of legitimacy.

———

Berger married Mařenka on a rainy Saturday in May of 1920. Štepánek was his best man.[46] Shortly thereafter Berger got on a train to Prague to work for a master carpenter in Karlín.[47] He had been considering the move for some time. His job in Todně was dangerous, Berger wrote in his diary, and did not include insurance. He could barely eke out a living on the twelve crowns per day that the village provided.[48] In Prague, the Czechoslovak Federation of Carpenters had, after a long strike, won wage increases for its members. Recently announced construction projects held out the promise of a decent wage. Berger's political views, and bluntness, also made him few friends in Todně. (He often camped out on the village square on Sundays, quietly taunting churchgoers returning from morning services as he read his newspaper.)[49] Not long before Berger's wedding, Todně's mayor (a "political idiot," according to Berger) informed him that the village would no longer employ him. "You're not a mayor, you're an ass," Berger allegedly told the mayor in response. Berger then accused the mayor of cheating him of the pay he was due. According to his diary entry, Berger ended the conversation with a threat: "If you start something, we'll be reading about it in the paper next week!"[50]

Berger's arrival in Prague was difficult, however. He rented an apartment in Vinohrady from a bourgeois Catholic who maintained a strict 7:00 p.m. curfew. There were long lines for bread, and the pub where he penned his diary entries often ran out of beer, thus reducing him to drinking water. It did not take long for Berger to consider moving on. Shortly after arriving in Prague he sent Mařenka a postcard of Charles Bridge and wrote that he might get work in the eastern city of Košice. He then wrote her another letter, saying that he would be sure to visit her, should that job pan out. Mařenka replied with a letter of her own, saying that she would never move to "horrible Slovakia," and that she had been looking forward to joining him in Prague, where they could make a life together. "I am angry at you," she wrote, words that she underlined three times. "The first letter from my wife," Berger wrote sardonically in his diary, before realizing how outlandish his plan was. He also confessed, to his diary, that leaving Todně just days after their wedding might have upset her.[51] He eventually found steady work and earned enough to send money home to his mother and Mařenka's family.[52] Soon thereafter, Mařenka joined Berger in Prague. They moved into an apartment in Podskalí, just below Vyšehrad. They would remain in Prague for the rest of their lives.

In Prague, Berger returned to many of the prewar political practices that had provided him with a sense of belonging. Now, however, he did so within the context of political upheaval and a growing rift within the Social Democrat Party. Five days after arriving in Prague, Berger went downtown to the People's House and bought a stack of newspapers.[53] He became a sporadic, and then dedicated reader, of the leftist *Rudé právo* (Red Right), whose first edition appeared shortly after radicals seized the People's House that autumn. He attended a number of public lectures, including one about the Russian Revolution.[54] He joined in protesting the opening of parliament, calling instead for Bolshevik-style action committees.[55] He and Mařenka met up with fellow construction workers on Wenceslas Square to protest military aid to Poland, which was at war with Bolshevik Russia.[56] Following a

December court ruling, police expelled leftists from the People's House. In response, radicals organized a general strike in which protesters seized factories, public buildings, and churches across the country. Masaryk's government imposed martial law in parts of Bohemia, Slovakia, and Subcarpathian Rus. Military courts tried and executed a number of protesters.[57] For many of their former supporters, the Social Democratic Party's refusal to support the general strike, along with their failure to condemn the crackdown, was the final straw. The divide between "rightists" and "leftists" had become insurmountable. In May 1921 leftists joined the Third International led by Bolshevik Russia.[58]

Berger did not participate in the protests surrounding the general strike, due in part to a painfully swollen right hand. He continued, however, to march and attend speeches organized by radical leftists. He joined a breakaway gymnastics organization and encouraged others to do the same. (The remaining Social Democratic gymnasts, he wrote with disdain, "blindly follow their leader, Medákoura, even though he pisses on their heads."[59]) His disgust with the Social Democratic Party, combined with hurt pride, also threatened to hasten rifts with his local carpenters' union. Berger had joined the union shortly after his arrival in Prague and, at the beginning of 1921, had run an unsuccessful campaign for secretary. During a meeting at a pub he suggested that the newly appointed secretary, a Social Democrat, could not be trusted with the union's strike fund. "Don't believe him, he's a Communist!" someone shouted. Berger then unleashed a tirade of insults, accusing the leadership of betraying its members and cozying up to the bourgeoisie. Later that evening, still seething, he penned a two-page manifesto that he planned to deliver at the next meeting. "Before this horrible war," one passage declared, "they sold us on the idea of a socialist revolution of the working class, and after the war, when the proletariat arrived at the goal to vanquish capitalism and create a humane society, they spoiled and crushed the idea. . . . They take us for a subdued class of dairy cows."[60] He never delivered the speech, although he showed it to a few like-minded members who joined him in creating their own, pub-based political club. His agitation continued during a protest on Shooter's Island in support of a group of locked-out carpenters. When one Social Democratic loyalist spoke, Berger claimed, the speaker's eyes remained focused on Prague Castle, and Masaryk's presidential offices, not on the workers in the audience. Few among the crowd had any "desire to listen to this schmaltzy speech by a right-winger. . . . The speech went over just as the bourgeoisie and the right-wingers had wished," he concluded.[61] Two days later the editors of the Czechoslovak Federation of Carpenters' newspaper appealed to their members to keep politics out of the union. They feared, rightfully, that growing divisions among Communists and Social Democrats would tear the organization apart.[62]

The union did not split, but the Social Democratic Party and most of its attendant organizations did. In October 1921, leftists founded the Communist Party of Czechoslovakia. Berger became a card-carrying member shortly thereafter. In the ensuing years the Communist Party of Czechoslovakia survived, and in some ways thrived, but the street-level radicalism that inspired its founding eventually faded. The number of strikes and protests in Czechoslovakia decreased following the violence of the general strike but spiked again in 1922 before fading away.[63] Economic stability played a role. Unemployment remained high after 1921, thanks to Finance Minister Alois Rašín's deflationary policies, yet those same policies had helped stave off the hyperinflation that plagued neighboring Germany, Poland, and Austria.[64] Police and the forces of order also reaffirmed their power. In 1923 a self-described anarcho-communist shot Rašin, who suffered for several months before dying. In response, the government passed the Law for the Protection of the Republic, which gave authorities wide discretion to crack down on anyone who threatened the republic. Police harassed Communist Party members; censors limited what *Rudé právo* could print.[65] Protests and marches continued to fill the streets of the city throughout the interwar period, but the threat of revolution had become less menacing.

As the violence and uncertainty of war faded, Czech middle-class imaginations reasserted themselves on Prague's cityscape, albeit in a radically different context. Powerful legacies from the past also shaped Prague as it emerged from World War I. From 1919 to 1937 the city had just one mayor, Karel Baxa, whose potent mixture of politics and xenophobia had gained him and his political party much notoriety before the war. Following the armistice, Baxa and his party benefited politically from popular anti-German and antisemitic violence. As that violence diminished, Baxa and city hall settled on realizing traditionally middle-class visions for the city. High-end shops, movie theaters, and hotels lined Wenceslas Square. A six-story, modern shoe store owned by the Czech magnate Tomáš Baťa opened on Wenceslas Square. All along the square, newly constructed passages led pedestrians to indoor arcades with even more shops. Streetcar lines extended throughout the city. The first traffic light was installed in 1929. The number of privately owned cars in Prague jumped from 2,669 in 1921 to 26,000 by the mid-1930s. Horse-drawn carriages, however, continued to deliver mail, coal, and milk to private homes.[66] The expansion of the city that had begun near the turn of the century also continued. It was driven largely by the need to coordinate public services so the city might become a European metropolis of note. In 1922 city leaders and their regional counterparts agreed to the creation of "Greater Prague," which incorporated suburbs such as Vinohrady and dozens of surrounding towns and villages. Seven hundred thousand people became citizens of Prague, which, almost overnight, became the sixth most populous city in Europe.[67]

Much political power in the city, however, resided in the hands of Czechoslovak leaders rather than city officials. They were eager to make Prague the capital of their new state. Bold expressions of their newfound political power soon dotted the city. Parliament sat in a former concert hall and museum, the Rudolfinum, just up the river from Charles Bridge. Government ministers occupied the baroque Kolowrat

Palace in the Lesser Town. After a temporary stay in the Clam-Gallas Palace near Old Town Square, the Finance Ministry appropriated a monastery in the Lesser Town, adding art deco touches to the baroque interior. Construction workers tore down adjacent buildings to make way for extension wings. In Podskalí, the demolition of older buildings created space for the Ministry of Health. In Vinohrady, the Ministry of Foreign Affairs established a publishing house dedicated to reminding the world of the new republic's strategic importance and inherent democratic qualities of its people.[68]

These coordinated efforts to propagate what Andrea Orzoff has called the "myth of Czechoslovakia" started with Masaryk and others during the war.[69] A key element of these attempts, both at home and abroad, involved the demonization of the Habsburg monarchy, which was now cast as a reactionary, repressive, and antinational regime. The heroes of their narrative were those most responsible for the founding of a democratic, tolerant Czechoslovakia. Powerful reminders of Emperor Francis Joseph, who ruled the monarchy from 1848 to 1916, disappeared from the cityscape. The main train station named in his honor became Woodrow Wilson Station; Emperor Francis Joseph Square became Republic Square. Signs for Legion Bridge replaced those honoring another former Habsburg emperor. In 1928 Masaryk laid the first stone for a crematorium on Vítkov Hill dedicated to former Legionnaires, whose exploits were also mythologized in popular literature.[70] In Prague, for the most part, Habsburg veterans such as Berger were ignored or forgotten.

Masaryk and his close allies also filled the media and the cityscape with powerful myths and narratives meant to legitimate the new state. In addition to celebrating the Czech nation's democratic characteristics, Masaryk called on his citizens to engage in consistent "small-scale work" that elevated the individual while raising national esteem. Small-scale work, he said, would become a source of national pride and cultivate a sense of responsibility for society and democracy. This work, with its incremental progressivism, was also an antidote to radical revolution, just as promises of liberal democracy gratified Western leaders eager to establish a geopolitical buffer zone in eastern Europe against Bolshevism. Other aspects of the Czechoslovak myth were grandiose, perhaps even high-handed. Czechoslovak leaders and prominent intellectuals fostered a cult of personality around "Papa" Masaryk, whose portrait adorned the country's schools, public buildings, and stamps. Prague Castle became the seat of the presidency, its president determined to transform the dilapidated complex into a "symbol of our national democratic ideals." His lead architect complemented a collage of preexisting historical styles with gardens, walkways, and obelisks. His intention was to evoke for pedestrians links to the past as well as monumental embodiments of the new democracy. The president's daughter, Alice Masaryková, who was also the director of the Czechoslovak Red Cross, encouraged architects to envision the Castle as an acropolis high above the city, hovering over the republic.[71]

These visions, however, effaced some less democratic aspects of the First Republic. Thanks to the 1920 constitution, Masaryk had accumulated extraordinary powers for the presidential office. Castle offices had wide-ranging powers to censor the media, so they were often able to shut down efforts to criticize both the office and his person. From the Castle, Masaryk could appoint and dismiss governments, which, combined with his prestige and position, allowed him to insert loyalists into cabinet positions. Masaryk even had his own intelligence service, and he used it more than once to spy on fellow politicians. He could rule directly in case of emergency.[72] Parliament remained under the firm control of five Czech political parties that often acted in unison with Masaryk's Castle—even though Czech parties represented just a little more than half of the country's population. In the city below the Castle and throughout the country, symbols of Czech nationalism infused both the built environment and people's daily lives. The Czech language predominated on street signs, postage stamps, and even passports. The Hussite slogan "Truth prevails" adorned the presidential standard.[73]

These visions also eliminated or simply ignored very real political and national fissures in the country. As the interwar period progressed, German and Slovak political movements gained increasing support in regions beyond Prague. As Ines Koeltzsch has convincingly argued, middle-class Praguers of various national leanings often sat next to each other in movie theaters. They mingled in the same downtown shops. Prague's Jews often played key roles in mediating cultural differences.[74] Still, anti-German, antisemitic demonstrations, including some that attacked theater owners for showing German movies, flared up during the interwar era and won headlines and the support of Mayor Baxa.[75] Prague's leaders also had good reason to worry about class fissures and class resentment. In 1920 nearly half (47 percent) of Greater Prague's inhabitants were workers, as defined by census takers.[76] Most still inhabited cramped apartments, a limited number of publicly funded housing projects aside. Families often squeezed into shoddy one-room rental apartments that lacked basic necessities. Along the city's peripheries, "makeshift colonies"—often disused railway cars made into homes or hastily built wooden shacks with tar roofs— appeared near factory complexes.[77] In Prague, as elsewhere throughout the country, a male worker was still far more likely to die of tuberculosis than his middle-class counterpart.[78]

Not surprisingly, then, the Communist Party enjoyed considerable support in Prague, especially beyond the city center. In the local elections of 1923, nearly 68,000 Praguers voted for Communist candidates, making it the third most popular party in the city. (The Social Democrats received only nine mandates, compared to the Communist Party's nineteen mandates that year.)[79] The Communists also garnered much support outside of Prague, especially in industrial cities and among the impoverished communities on the country's eastern periphery. In the 1925 elections for parliament, nearly a million women and men voted for Communists, more than any other party save (just barely) the conservative Agrarian Party. Despite their successes, the Communists' rivals managed to exclude the party from power.

Throughout the interwar period, not one of Prague's thirteen district majors (*starosty*) was a Communist. No Communist received a ministerial post at the federal level. Still, the party, aided by its widely read *Rudé právo* and many active members, remained a formidable presence—and threat—until the end of the republic.[80]

As one of just two legally tolerated Communist parties in central Europe, Czechoslovak Communists did more than participate in elections. Similar to other parties throughout the region, they created a subculture of their own, replete with their own organizations, relationships, and political practices. For Berger and other adherents, this world was equal to if not more meaningful than success at the ballot box. Like his counterparts throughout the city, Berger self-identified according to his craft or trade, but referred to himself as a worker, or member of the proletariat, when speaking about politics and his political party—labels that offered a sense of collective identity and also a sense of belonging.[81] Communist Party members tended to marry each other rather than members of other political parties. (Mařenka joined the party not long after Berger had.) Unlike Todně and most rural communities, Prague had a critical mass of fellow travelers with whom Berger could socialize and empathize. He met with fellow members of the Communist Party in local pubs. As before the war, he referred to fellow members of his party as "comrades," a bond that they shared in defiance of the rest of Czechoslovak society and political culture. He noted when comrades died or were arrested. He kept copious lists of people who left the party to join another.

Berger was also an active participant in the world of Communism.[82] He continued to be an avid reader of newspapers, first and foremost among them *Rudé právo*. In addition to purchasing newspapers and books, he contributed part of his hard-earned wages to various Communist Party charities such as Red Help, which aided families who had been affected by political persecution. (According to police records, courts in Prague convicted 119 Communist Party members in 1927, and 57 members lost their jobs.)[83] He and Mařenka went to lectures, concerts, film showings, and exhibitions. Avid theatergoers, they attended performances by well-known troupes and by local players staged in their neighborhood theater.[84] Mařenka danced the waltz at an annual workers' ball while Berger sat alone, enjoying his drink.[85] As their family grew to include three daughters—Máňa, Liba, and Věra— the couple included the children in various party events.

For Berger, these activities allowed him to re-create, albeit in a modified form, the sort of relationships and practices of belonging that he had enjoyed in Vienna. As a respected member of the Vyšehrad party district cell, he enjoyed a sense of dignity and belonging in the present as well. The political practices he embraced also had a familiar ring to them. Berger had been an active protester before the war, and now he took particular note of the number of demonstrations in Czechoslovak Prague. He participated in demonstrations of anger and solidarity following the arrests of Communists. He marched as part of electioneering efforts. In the 1930s, he and others took to the streets to demand aid during the Great Depression. They protested the Munich Olympics hosted by Nazi Germany. He faithfully inserted newspaper clippings about protests in Prague and beyond in his diary, replete with article summaries. Descriptions of protests and demonstrations are among his longest and most detailed entries.

Most meaningful for Berger, however, was the Communist Party's annual May Day parade through the city. After arriving in Prague, Berger faithfully attended every May Day parade organized by the party during the interwar period. Each of his May Day diary entries, similar to the event itself, had a ritualistic quality to them. The day began early in the morning, when the Vyšehrad Communists gathered somewhere in the neighborhood while Berger, Mařenka, and others distributed May Day leaflets to their comrades. To his great pride, Berger was often asked to carry the district's banner. The assembled group met up with other Communist cells near the Vltava before heading to Charles Square, where party members from throughout the city also gathered. A combined march then proceeded through the

A portion of Berger's diary from May 1920. The photograph, printed in the left-leaning *Rudé květy* (Red Flowers) and pasted here, depicts a demonstration on Old Town Square protesting the opening of parliament earlier in the month. Archiv hlavního města Prahy.

city center, culminating at Republic Square. There, under the gaze of armed police, the assembled listened to oratorical performances before dispersing. The next day Berger spent much of his time collecting various newspaper reports about May Day events in Prague and elsewhere in the world.

May Day, as Berger and other participants knew quite well, was full of intentionally potent symbolism. The press of bodies and shared act of walking, in rough unison, suggested solidarity and purpose. The parade itself portrayed an image of rising strength as small organized groups of Communists marched toward Charles Square. From there the assembled mass captured, if only for a brief moment, decidedly bourgeois public spaces such as Wenceslas Square and Na příkopě. Then they took over Republic Square itself, where participants sang songs and chanted slogans. Orators made strident political demands and often called for revolution. For a few hours on May 1 each year, the traditional order of things was turned upside down, provoking middle-class consternation and fear along the way. For most Communist leaders and their followers, May Day represented an opportunity to play out the narrative of Marxist-Leninist revolution while providing a real-time reminder of the party's political potency. May Day allowed Communists throughout the city to share a moment of global solidarity. The movement of so many bodies suggested mobilization toward a seemingly common cause.

Demonstrations, as the Communists knew well, served a number of purposes. In this respect, *manifestace,* the Czech word for demonstration used by Berger and *Rudé právo,* is perhaps more apt than its English-language counterpart. Drawing on its Latin root, *manifestace* is a derivative of "manifest," which nineteenth-century Czech lexicographers defined as a public statement intended to enlighten others and justify a political stance. *Manifestace* was thus a public, bodily manifestation of politics and political power.[86] Berger and his comrades were also taking part in a very modern political tradition. In walking, en masse, toward a shared destination—and as part of a shared ritual gathering—May Day parades and other demonstrations recalled religious pilgrimages as well as the coronation procession. The modern form and meaning of demonstrations, however, had arisen in tandem with the emergence of popular political activism in Europe. In 1789, as a prelude to the French Revolution, news of Jacques Necker's dismissal provoked demonstrations in which marchers carried busts of the deposed finance minister. Soon thereafter crowds stormed the Bastille.[87] Mass demonstrations and protests characterized the Chartist movement in England and the revolutions that swept across Europe in 1848, including in Prague. With the rise of mass politics within the Habsburg monarchy and throughout Europe, suffragettes, socialists, and others demanding a share of political power filled city squares near the turn of the century. Political parties, such as the Czech National Socialists, rallied their adherents into the streets during times of nationalist upheaval, often with dire consequences for Jews and Jewish property.[88] During the interwar period, Mussolini and Hitler mobilized thousands to participate in coordinated, often aesthetically attractive, demonstrations of political homogeneity, which included violence. With the leader playing the commanding role, these demonstrations were bodily expressions of the fascist state.

For Berger, the May Day events were also an emotional communal experience. Marchers sang workers' songs and shouted slogans in unison throughout the event. They shared an underlying fear of police repression, and possible violence. As photographs from the era attest, protesting bodies were not only in motion, they were often pressed together—quite different from late nineteenth-century practices, when Social Democratic protesters kept their distance. The effect of being part of a mass body, as Elias Canetti has suggested, was that the fear of touch dissolves into a feeling of collective oneness. Canetti writes, "Ideally, all are equal there; no distinctions count, not even that of sex. . . . The man pressed against him is the same as himself. He feels him as he feels himself. Suddenly it is as though everything were happening in one and the same body."[89] Berger's May Day was, however, a gendered experience. Mařenka marched with other women, young children in tow. Nor did every marcher fall into the crowd, or participate with the same fervor. Berger criticized fellow marchers who hung back from the others, searching for positions that allowed them "to avoid being seen by the bourgeoisie and thus not to anger their masters."[90]

May Day was also much more than a mass demonstration for Berger. It was a local experience, beginning with the morning gathering of neighborhood comrades at a local landmark, such as the U Kroka pub. After the speeches were over, he sometimes shared a beer with friends before going home for lunch. He and his family played ninepins with fellow Communists on May Day afternoons. Berger's long-standing obsession with his Social Democratic rivals played out in his May Day diary entries as well. His newspaper article summaries described same-day parades by Social Democrats and other political parties, often comparing the total number of participants of each parade. One May Day morning in 1932 he snuck a peek at the Social Democrats who were gathering in front of the Vyšehrad town hall, where he took note of familiar faces and did a count.[91] These were complicated moments. May Day parades also reminded him of his Social Democratic days in Vienna. A pamphlet produced for his first May Day event was among his most treasured possessions.[92] Berger did not refrain from criticizing the Communists' event. He consistently complained that Vyšehrad Communists were traditionally positioned near the end of the parade. On May Day 1938, much to Berger's chagrin, the Communists joined other Czechoslovak parties on Wenceslas Square in a show of unity against the threat of fascist Germany.[93] The year before, during that morning's meet-up in Vyšehrad, Berger refused to carry a banner of the republic that had been given to them.[94]

Equally meaningful to Berger were his participation in the Communist gymnastics club and his break from the Social Democratic gymnasts. In the spring of 1921, Berger excitedly read an announcement in *Rudé právo* proclaiming the formation of a splinter gymnastics club, dubbed the Federation of Workers Gymnastics Association. Shortly thereafter, he and thousands of others began frantically preparing for a mass gymnastics performance on the fields of Maniny northeast of the city center. While drawing upon central and eastern European gymnastics traditions, Czechoslovak leftist radicals also took inspiration from their Russian counterparts, who had embraced gymnastics as an alternative to bourgeois activities such as competitive sports. They dubbed their event the Spartakiad, a reference to the Thracian gladiator Spartacus who led an uprising against the Roman Republic and, in the words of the event's organizers, invoked images of the proletariat, social revolution, and physical education.[95]

Berger did not perform in the Spartakiad, which drew thousands of participants and observers from across the country, but he was deeply invested in the effort. In the weeks before the performance, he often rushed from work to Maniny, where he built stands for spectators and other performance facilities in his precious spare time. The tone of his diary, usually suffused with bitterness and cynicism, softened during these preparatory weeks as he extolled the pleasures of comradeship and self-sacrifice. Among the few photographs in Berger's collection is a postcard of Maniny's empty stands. On the back, Berger notes with pride his contribution and the name of a comrade with whom he worked. Other photographs of the Maniny grounds, clipped from the pages of *Rudé právo,* fill his diary. The Spartakiad took place in June, and it was a resounding success. Berger and the official accounts claimed that 100,000 people had attended. With pleasure, Berger pasted into his diary *Rudé právo*'s articles about the event as well as the official program, "Why We Are Communists."[96] He would later remember the day as one of the happiest of his life.

The federation, while smaller in numbers than its political rivals, continued to thrive. It held Spartakiads in Brno in 1922 and in Ostrava in 1925. It sent representatives to the international Spartakiad in the Soviet Union in 1927. Five years after its founding, Prague's federation had more members than any other Communist organization in the city. The organization published its own magazines, exercise pamphlets, and song sheets, even as it became enveloped within a larger Communist Party umbrella organization that included sports and tourist groups.[97] Czechoslovakia's authorities forbade the 1928 Spartakiad to go forward, but the federation managed to hold smaller summer performances throughout the interwar period. Berger and his daughters attended many such performances hosted by clubs in Prague. He took note, too, when the authorities forbade such events from being held. In 1933, out of work, he gratefully accepted twenty crowns from a fellow gymnast to take the train to a summer performance in nearby Kladno. As at Maniny, participants marched en masse toward exercise grounds, which were under police surveillance. Despite an official

The Spartakiad on Maniny, June 1921. Archiv hlavního města Prahy.

order forbidding children to take part in the event, two of Berger's daughters snuck off with others to do their own performance, without music. He deemed their mischievousness to be the most beautiful part of the performance. The day was a grand success for the workers' movement, he concluded, the scorching heat aside.[98]

Berger's participation in the Communist gymnastics movement suggests a number of similarities with street demonstrations. Mass gymnastics performances represented a peculiarly central and eastern European expression of political strength and solidarity. Like street demonstrations, they had their roots in the nineteenth century, specifically among German nationalists during the darkest days of the Napoleonic Wars. As the movement's founder, Friedrich Ludwig Jahn declared, collective physical exercises not only created bonds among its members dedicated to the nationalist cause. Their coordinated displays of earnest strength embodied the imagined nation.[99] Other nationalist movements throughout central and eastern Europe mimicked

Jahn's efforts. The most prominent of these were the many Sokol (Falcon) organizations that emerged among Slavic nationalists. In the Bohemian lands, the Sokol gymnastics association, also referred to as the "Czech national army," included more than 1,000 clubs and 119,000 members in 1912.[100] In 1918 Czech Sokolists often acted as forces of order and counterrevolution and enjoyed generous state support throughout the interwar period.

Similar to his participation in the May Day parade, Berger's relationship to the federation had a distinctly local, face-to-face character. Throughout the interwar period he remained an active member of the federation's Vyšehrad club, often inserting himself into financial decisions. He proudly helped to build the local chapter's own exercise complex along the river, just below the Vyšehrad fortifications, which opened in 1926, and he insisted that members participate in its upkeep. The fields included a clubhouse where members met, and where mothers could enjoy a respite while their children played outside. During spells in which he was out of work, Berger would simply spend an afternoon in the Vyšehrad clubhouse. His May Day afternoons playing ninepin bowling took place at the Vyšehrad exercise field. Gymnastics, as before World War I, provided Berger with a sense of purpose, a home of sorts where he socialized with like-minded comrades. He obtained a sense of belonging in an associational life framed by his political party. In a way, his life had come full circle, albeit as an older man and in a radically different context.

Berger was not alone in many of his sentiments. Film footage from the 1921 Spartakiad shows crowds of people, many of them having just arrived at Wilson Station, happily occupying entire city streets as they walked toward Maniny. Shots of well-dressed youth and adults performing coordinated motions mix with scenes of participants socializing in the crowded stands.[101] Rare, Communist-era testimonies, while also framed by ideological expectations, offer a complementary perspective. Others shared Berger's feelings about the federation. In April 1953 *Rudé právo,* still the flagship newspaper of the Communist Party, published a request that former members of the federation submit memories of their participation in the organization. More than one hundred people from across the country responded. The call was occasioned by the recent death of Klement Gottwald, who had assumed the leadership of the party in 1929 and later the Czechoslovak presidency, shortly after the 1948 Communist coup. Gottwald had joined the Social Democratic Party's gymnastics organization while a cabinetmaker in Vienna. After the war, living in southern Moravia, he spearheaded the founding of his local federation chapter and led their participation in the 1921 Spartakiad. He then became a prominent federation organizer in Slovakia, where he also became editor in chief of its magazine, *Spartakus*. From there Gottwald moved up the party ranks, eventually moving to Prague in 1926. His early experiences in the federation figured prominently in his later biographies. The federation and its eventual successor also made much of his early involvement.[102]

Thus, the implicit task behind the solicited contributions was, as the editors of *Rudé právo* no doubt knew well, to commemorate their recently deceased leader. Previous mythmaking around the early years of the federation, as well as the success of the first Spartakiad at Maniny, provided a framework and language for the contributions. Most entries, however, made little mention of Gottwald by name. They also diverged from the apparent directive in a number of ways. Some concentrated primarily on the building of their local organizations, financial matters, and a careful naming of people who participated in the federation's activities. Their primary intent, it seems, was to provide a historical record that, as *Rudé právo* had promised, would be preserved in the Archive of Physical Education and Sport. Many contributions developed themes found in Berger's diary: the role that the general strike played in their decision to break with the Social Democratic Party; efforts to encourage friends and comrades to follow them to join the federation; the impressive, quick work that members such as Berger did to construct the exercise site so quickly; and the sheer numbers of people who took part in the event. Many described how inspiring the event was to its participants, thus consolidating their break with the Social Democrats and their subsequent decision to join the Communist Party.

Many also spoke about the sense of belonging and political purpose that the federation provided them. Anna Hronková, a member of the Prague Košíře branch, called the federation "my second home" for the eleven years in which she was a member. She wrote that, decades later, she remained close to a few former members "who are dear to me, like sisters." She also stated that it was through the federation that she had made sense of crucial political events of the interwar period, such as the death of Lenin and furious attacks on Communists by the ruling parties. She marched with friends from the federation on May Day.[103] Similar to Berger, Stanislav Honek of Hradec Králové commented on how politics, the fight for socialism, and his participation in the federation activities constituted a combined effort to create a better society.[104] Gymnastics was also, similar to demonstrations, a way of claiming urban space while engaging in a coordinated, collective protest against the powers that be. One gymnast in the Prague district of Hloubětín recalled marching around their exercise hall for a half an hour before each practice, singing the leftist anthem "The Internationale." Nearly every time, he wrote, local police would bang their nightsticks against the window, demanding that they stop singing, but they always refused.[105] For many contributors, the Spartakiad on Maniny stood out in their memories, more than any other single event or experience from their time in the federation. Several recalled riding in specially commissioned trains to Prague and the impression that seeing so many bodies, from all over the country, had made on them.

———

For Berger, the interwar period was a time of relative, familiar predictability between two storms of violence and revolution—a time in which he re-created, in a vastly different context, much of the world he had known as a loyal Social Democrat in Vienna. Berger also experienced, of course, immense changes between the wars. He married and became a father to three daughters. Mařenka, so wary of the workers' movement in Vienna, was often at his side during party events and demonstrations—a change symptomatic of the workers' movement in general, which had largely excluded women before World War I. She also carved out her own political and public life. In 1929 Mařenka became a member of a workers' co-op, Včela (Bee), and joined their neighborhood shop's oversight committee.[106] (This local shop, part of workers' daily experience throughout the period, often served as the gathering point for the Vyšehrad district's May Day parade.) Several years later she served as the Communist Party's poll observer for their district.[107]

Following his mother's death in 1932, Berger continued his work as a carpenter. His assignments ranged from home repairs to construction of the Trade Fair Palace, a bulking functionalist structure in the Holešovice district. He helped construct a workers' colony on the outskirts of Žižkov from 1935 to 1936.[108] Berger and his family suffered through long spells without work during the Great Depression. He suffered injuries while on the job that also prevented him from working. Mařenka opened a newspaper stand on Wenceslas Square.

More broadly, the 1930s were a time of immense, and tragic, change for the Czechoslovak Communist Party and for the Czechoslovak Republic as well. In 1929, in a house not far from the fields of Maniny, Gottwald and other hard-line Moscow loyalists seized control of the Communist Party, replacing former Social Democrats of Berger's generation. Czechoslovak Communists volunteered to fight against fascist forces in Spain. Many Communists, along with members of the Jewish Community and a host of nongovernmental organizations, attempted to aid refugees from Hitler's Germany.[109] With Stalin's blessing the Czechoslovak Communists joined other political parties in forming a united political front against fascism. By 1938 the situation looked dire; Nazi Germany occupied Austria that spring, and as the summer turned to fall, Hitler demanded the annexation of the mostly German-speaking territories of Czechoslovakia. In Munich, Great Britain and France, along with Germany's ally Italy, acquiesced. Protesters stormed the streets of Prague in defense of the republic, but to no avail. Despite having mobilized the army to protect the country, Masaryk's successor, Edvard Beneš, ordered his troops to stand down. The republic fell. Amid an atmosphere of rising antisemitism, which took particular aim at German-speaking Jewish refugees, Beneš's successors took measures to purge Jews from certain professions. They criminalized the Communist Party and disbanded its organizations, including Berger's gymnastics club. Many Communist leaders, including Gottwald, fled to Moscow or other points abroad.[110]

The Czechoslovak Republic was also undone from within, in part thanks to several tragic ironies. Masaryk and others, by conflating notions of democracy with essentialist notions of the nation, unwittingly undermined the former. For many non-Czechs, the word "democracy," according to Peter Bugge, lacked meaning, "or it could stand for something not quite the same: ethnocracy."[111] In addition, while Masaryk and Czech parties maintained a stranglehold on power within Czechoslovakia they also, within limits, permitted a vast and vibrant array of political movements and positive political expressions. Czech Jewish and Zionist clubs, often based in Prague, served as expressions of various forms of Jewish self-identification.[112] Liberal-minded women organized to demand equal rights, as promised under the Constitution of the Czechoslovak Republic. Catholic activists in Moravia organized their own women's clubs, which had strong ties to the pro-Catholic Czechoslovak People's Party and its newspapers.[113] By 1936 1.4 million Czechoslovaks belonged to a gymnastics organization.[114] Yet many Czechoslovaks, Berger included, weaponized demonstrations and associations against a republic that they felt had disowned them. They actively sought to undermine the very republic that tolerated their existence. To the east, the Catholic gymnastics club Orol produced radicalized youth supportive of the Slovak People's Party and their calls for autonomy.[115] Along the peripheries of Bohemia and Moravia, Konrad Henlein's gymnastics organization formed the core of an increasingly powerful Sudeten German movement. By 1938, his party, secretly funded and supported by Nazi Germany, helped set in motion a series of crises that led to the Munich debacle.[116]

Six months after Munich, Wehrmacht troops marched into Prague, which became the capital of the Nazi-controlled Protectorate of Bohemia and Moravia. Nazi leaders ruthlessly dismantled what remained of the liberal democratic practices, institutions, and protections once enjoyed by interwar Praguers. Arrests and executions put an end to public demonstrations. Political parties and associations were either banned or forcibly integrated into state-sponsored institutions. The occupiers imposed strict censorship. A core of collaborationist journalists and others filled the media with propaganda intended to justify Nazi rule and mollify the population. Thanks to an expanding web of local informants, the Gestapo arrested both prominent political figures who had not fled abroad and everyday Praguers whose actions were deemed a threat to Nazi rule. Terror threatened Praguers and others in the Protectorate, especially following the assassination of the acting Reich protector, Reinhard Heydrich, by paratroopers trained by Beneš's Czechoslovak government-in-exile in London. Resistance groups loyal to Beneš, which had supplied London with intelligence while maintaining a brave propaganda campaign at home, were all but wiped out.[117]

People categorized as Roma, homosexuals, "antisocials," and others became objects of state terror and violence. For those whom the regime identified as Jews, public persecution proceeded, step-by-step, toward murder. In the first years of the occupation, public notices announced decrees prohibiting Jews from visiting movie theaters, swimming pools, and parks, as well as from riding in streetcars. These measures created, as Benjamin Frommer observes, a "ghetto without walls" enforced by Nazi leaders and local Praguers. The regime, along with everyday Germans and Czechs, stole Jewish businesses and property. Crucially, the Nazi authorities required Jews, as defined by the

Nuremberg Laws, to register with the local authorities. The first deportations began in 1941 as Praguers marked as Jews were gathered in the Trade Fair Palace before being marched to railway cars that took them to concentration camps. Today, the walls of the Pinkas Synagogue in Josefov are covered with the names of nearly 80,000 individuals murdered because Nazi officials had declared them to be "full Jews" or "Mischlinge."[118] Thanks to the bravery of local organizers, and with help from abroad, roughly 30,000 Jews managed to flee to other countries before the deportations had begun.[119] After the war, many members of Prague's greatly diminished Jewish Community consisted of emigrants from Slovakia and Subcarpathian Rus who had miraculously managed to survive Nazi terror.[120]

Drawing upon lists created before the invasion, Gestapo agents also set upon leading Communists as the occupation of Prague began. Many party members who had not fled abroad organized underground resistance cells. Similar to their counterparts who had been loyal to Beneš, they passed on intelligence to Moscow while they engaged in publishing underground literature, including editions of *Rudé právo*. Most Praguers, while living under a shroud of terror and fear, did not experience extreme forms of violence. Plans to "Germanize" half of the Protectorate's Czech population and deport the rest were put on hold. Industrial production within the Protectorate was crucial for the Nazi war effort. Instead, Nazi leaders "Germanized" many of Prague's street names. Following Heydrich's assassination, they goaded roughly 60,000 locals and leaders to participate in a public demonstration of loyalty to the regime on Old Town Square. A month later, they packed an estimated 200,000 people into Wenceslas Square for the same purpose. In the final years of the war, they adorned public spaces with banners and signs intended to rally Praguers to support Nazi Germany in its war against the Soviet Union.[121]

Although Berger and his family were members of the Communist Party, the Gestapo did not come for them.[122] Berger continued his carpentry work until 1942, when he officially retired. Before then he had been spending more and more time helping out at Mařenka's newspaper stand on Wenceslas Square. Thereafter, he spent most of his day there. Surrounded by newspapers, he spent much time reading collaborationist articles—paying particular attention to any mention of Communism, Stalin, or the Soviet Union. He also, remarkably, continued to write in his diary. This very act was fraught with danger. If found by the Gestapo, any compromising materials would have led to his arrest, and perhaps also to the arrest of Mařenka and his daughters. He risked being exposed to local informants and blackmail. Yet the pace of his writing continued unabated.

One possible reason was simply habit, and perhaps an obsessive compulsion to document his life. Before his death, Berger had amassed sixty-five volumes of material, most of which are now housed in the Prague City Archive. The majority of his collection consists of diary entries that focus on politics, his social life, work, family, and whatever he considered important. He also compiled eight volumes of political cartoons collected over the years. Another volume is a compendium of workers' songs that he transcribed. He kept a list of every job he had ever held and kept a separate volume dedicated to his yearly budgets. In his early diaries he listed every train he had taken, how long the journey was, and if the train had arrived on time. Under Nazi rule, he kept a running list of collaborators.[123] There is, of course, much that Berger left out. His diary entries never take the reader into his home. Moments of self-criticism or admissions of inadequacy are rare. Several diary entries obliquely mention anti-Jewish laws and regulations, without comment. He did not make note of the deportations.

Berger might also have been motivated by his desire to leave a historical record, even under Nazi rule. Each of his volumes is meticulously organized; diary collections contain helpful tables of contents. Around the turn of the century, publication of diaries for mass consumption had inspired "amateur" efforts across the continent—including, perhaps, those of Berger, an avid reader who often visited the Social Democratic Party library. Regardless of author, there is often an expectation among diarists, even if unconscious, that what they write will be read by others someday.[124] This was especially true of prominent politicians who wrote diaries and of many Jews who kept diaries as they faced the Holocaust.[125] It was also at least partially true of other diarists, including those from working-class backgrounds. In 1924 *Rudé právo* published reworked portions of Berger's World War I diaries.[126] Perhaps, too, writing for posterity was an act of dignity on the part of someone forced to endure the humiliations of relentless financial uncertainty and middle-class disdain.

Berger was also writing in the present. With the exception of a volume leading up to 1913 and portions rewritten for publication after World War I, his diary entries contain no hint of hindsight. Although he might have retranscribed some entries, there is no indication that he knows how the story will end, let alone what awaited him the next day. Unlike so many memoirs about the Nazi occupation, his entries during that period are not refracted through postwar memories and myths of resistance. His entries thus have a "real-time" quality, to borrow a phrase from the Holocaust diary historian Alexandra Garbarini. Throughout his diaries, Berger's entries have the feel of a chronicle, organized around dated entries, focused on summary and description. These entries sometimes then shift in authorial voice, where Berger offers up opinions, analysis, and choice words about his political enemies—all reflective of the moment in time he inhabited. Berger's diary entries also depict daily interactions and relationships, as well as his interpretation of the world, at specific moments in time.[127]

Berger's writing style and content also changed over time. In this respect, his entries during the Nazi occupation stand out. Unlike entries in his other volumes, they contain little about his life. Newspaper clippings in his diary, and his attendant commentary, consist of careful, often bland, descriptions of major events. Only hints of interior thought emerge, such as in his entry about the Nazi attack on the Soviet Union in June 1940. During this moment, which reenergized Czechoslovak

Communists throughout the Protectorate and beyond, Berger provided only detailed summaries of collaborationist newspaper propaganda. At one point, however, Berger's own voice reemerged as he
added a cautionary note: "In France they are arresting Communists."[128]
Most article summaries contain no commentary at all. The rhetorical
shift might have reflected a very real fear that his diary would fall into
the wrong hands. Alone, often in his newspaper stand, diary writing
might have given him something to do, a sense of purpose. His focus
on propaganda attacks against Communists and the Soviet Union reflect an old habit of reading oppositional newspapers and might also
have expressed a hope for the future. His summaries of collaborationist
articles, along with his list of collaborators, suggest dreams of revenge.
In sum, however, Berger's entries reflected an author who had become
a witness, but not a participant, in the world around him.

Near the end of the war, as Soviet troops pressed westward, Berger
and his diary entries became bolder. He began listening to Radio
Moscow. He managed to get access to illegal newspapers, including
some printed in English. In the pages of his diary, he also began to
imagine a world that would emerge after the war's end. Just as in the
last years of World War I, he became obsessed with the idea of revolution as he devoured information from disparate newspaper articles
that fed his hopes for revenge and the destruction of the vaguely defined bourgeoisie. He described Communist uprisings in Africa, Co-
lombia, and Portugal, as reported by Reuters and the *Daily Mail*. He
drew from a collaborationist article titled "Bolshevik Hyenas Suffo-
cating Romania" to describe the rise of Soviet influence there, happily
concluding in April 1945 that everything was being done according to
"Bolshevik Diktat."[129] He claimed that shortly after the Red Army's
liberation of Prešov, Slovakia, local Bolsheviks had quickly seized
power, arresting collaborators and nationalizing banks and large fac-

tories in an effort to present the Czechoslovak president-in-exile, Beneš, with a fait accompli. "Beneš's assurances that the future Czecho-Slovakia will not be a Bolshevik country," Berger declared gleefully, "now seem completely absurd."[130] While distrustful of Beneš, Berger approved of the Košice Program for a postwar government, which included the Communist Party. The Communists, he wrote, would not betray the revolution as the Social Democrats had after World War I. "The Czech bourgeoisie are not looking forward to the end [of the war]; they are quite aware that it will also be their end, and that 1945 will not be 1918. The Communists and a few reliable Social Democrats will be at the helm."[131] On May 1 he noted that 1945 would be the last year without a May Day celebration: "Next year, May Day will be mightily Communist."[132] Four days later, fighting broke out between the SS and armed Czechs near the city's radio station. The Prague Uprising had begun.

Just as before, the violence of war spilled into the postwar era, perhaps the bloodiest in the city's history.[133] For three days Praguers took up arms against their German occupiers, some of whom, particularly the SS, shot captured Czech fighters and used civilians as human shields in front of their Panzer tanks. By the time the Wehrmacht had retreated and Soviet troops had entered the city, more than 3,700 Czechs were dead. Over 230 people, including children, had been murdered outright. (The number of dead German soldiers and SS members is unknown. Many corpses were taken from the city and buried in mass graves.) The violence then focused on local Germans. Praguers burned Germans alive on the streets while hundreds looked on. Sick and wounded Germans were shot in hospitals. Armed insurgents and even nurses led Soviet troops to captured German women, who were then raped.[134] In the months following liberation, Czechoslovak soldiers, local Czechs, and others murdered between 19,000 and 30,000 Germans across the Bohemian lands. Germans, marked with white armbands, were gathered into camps, where they were subjected to more violence, which led to the death of thousands more. Roughly

5,000 Germans committed suicide.[135] Crowds had also set upon collaborators of various sorts shortly after liberation. Retribution trials, while remarkably thorough and bound by newly created laws, were swift. Their decisions could not be appealed. More people, Czechs and Germans, were executed following the retribution trials than during the entire Communist era.[136] While occasional exceptions were made for documented "antifascists," the postwar government, Communists included, then oversaw the expulsion to Germany of the vast majority of the country's Germans. In some cases, as Kateřina Čapková has demonstrated, the persecution of Jews continued as citizens and local officials identified them as "Germans."[137]

Prague and the Bohemian lands had become definitively "Czech," thanks in large part to the murders and violence from 1939 to 1947. A Communist revolution did not come to Prague, but the Communist Party enjoyed considerable influence within a newly constituted government under President Beneš. They also enjoyed remarkable popular support. In the elections of 1946, the Communists won 38 percent of the seats in parliament. In Prague, a *Rudé právo* editor became mayor and held the position until 1954.[138] Even among its coalition members, every party but one agreed on the need to build "socialism," however defined. All but one were united in their calls for a "national and social revolution."[139] Gottwald and Czechoslovak Communists proffered a peculiarly "Czechoslovak" road to socialism. They also benefited from their association with Czechoslovak Communist partisans and the Soviet Union, which had not signed the Munich Agreement and had, after much sacrifice, liberated much of the country. Just a month after the Prague Uprising, Soviet Tank no. 23 was installed atop a pedestal in the working-class neighborhood of Smíchov.[140] In 1947 Prague's city government renamed one of the main boulevards running through Holešovice and called it Partisan Street. Local groups, often on their own initiative but using state funds, erected small monuments to "fallen heroes," both local and Soviet.[141]

Berger, however, was slow to embrace the postwar Communist Party and to celebrate its newfound political power. He took note of the publication of the postwar first issue of *Rudé právo,* but he only occasionally read the newspaper. Paradoxically, he preferred reading the Social Democratic *Hlas lidu* (People's Voice), even as he continued to rant against the Social Democrats, mindful of their betrayal of the working classes during and after World War I. ("We can't trust those goddamn rogues," he wrote in June 1945.)[142] Soon after the arrival of Soviet troops he walked into the newly established archive of the Communist Party and donated thirty-two books, all of them published before 1925. (He later signed each one and wrote terse reminders to young readers that the books must be returned to the library.)[143] Two years later he had donated nearly three-fourths of his personal library. Was he turning his back on his past, hoping to influence young comrades, or was he seeking favor? Indeed, Berger's many donations to the Communist Party archive and library soon earned him a spot as the party's representative on a local preservation committee. At one meeting he demanded the destruction of a medieval church, allegedly the site of the city's first Slavic-language Mass. He then quit the committee, although it is possible that even fellow Communists had encouraged his departure.[144]

Most strikingly, Berger refused to rejoin with the Communist Party. His first entries on the subject appeared just weeks after the occupation's end, when Mařenka and his daughters asked him to attend a party function on Wenceslas Square. Berger refused, explaining: "I didn't attend because there will be horrible riffraff, scabs, profiteers; lots of people are joining the party to take advantage of the moment. If I become a member of the party I will have to say 'comrade' whenever I speak with a member instead of saying 'bastard.'"[145] Responding to a June 1945 article in the Czechoslovak Legionnaire daily *National Liberation* about the infamous collaborator Emanuel Moravec, Berger wrote: "We have more than enough of such bastards like Moravec in the Communist Party." They might have been able to "change colors," he continued, "but inside, their souls remain deceitful and traitorous, ever ready to betray the Communist Party with a stab in the back."[146] Almost a year later, in April 1946, Mařenka told him that the Prague section of the Communist Party now had 200,000 members. "Listen," Berger responded. "If I go into the party I will have to call every bastard a comrade. And for me that is a great nuisance."[147] As if to confirm his claims that opportunists and other bastards were supporting the Communists, someone stole a Communist banner, which Berger had secretly hidden during the occupation, from his apartment window. Berger then allegedly saw a neighbor, unnamed in the diary, waving the stolen banner at the 1946 May Day celebration.[148]

Numerous contemporary commentators also expressed concern that opportunists and collaborators had joined the Communist Party in order to hide their ignoble pasts or profit materially, or both. For Berger, their admission into the party proved especially disturbing, in part because they challenged his notions about what it meant to be a Communist and a comrade. Interwar Communists, as Berger recalled, had put comradeship first. They had dedicated political ideals. Berger's Communist Party, as he had imagined it, was one inhabited almost solely by workers. They had been united as political outsiders targeted by the First Republic's 1923 Law against Terror, and hounded by Czechoslovak police throughout the interwar period. The post–World War II Communist Party was, on the contrary, a mass party that included few interwar comrades. After World War II, party membership skyrocketed, reaching a million members in the Bohemian lands by April 1946. Only 2.4 percent had been members of the Communist Party before the war.[149] Upon witnessing the departure of Red Army tanks from Prague in November 1945, Berger despaired. His hopes for genuine revolution—and revenge upon the bourgeoisie—faded. Berger had now become skeptical of the Communist Party's decision to join a government put together by Beneš, a dreaded Czechoslovak National Socialist. This Communist Party hardly had the stuff to forge a revolution, he concluded.[150]

For Berger, now in his sixties, there was also an abiding sense that his generation was passing and that the party now belonged to younger generations. The same 1946 May Day on which he saw his stolen banner, Berger was overcome by sadness, cognizant of the many comrades who had not lived to see that day.[151] He often penned long entries about the passing of interwar Communists who had perished in concentration camps.[152] The spring 1947 deaths of Antonín Bouček, a prewar Social Democrat who became the editor of *Rudé právo* in 1921, and Franta Sauer, the celebrated leftist author responsible for the toppling of the Marian column in 1918, prompted long sessions of lamentation at the local pub.[153] Absences in the diary also suggest a nagging sense of impotence. Berger had muddled through the Protectorate, full of quiet unease. Even after liberation he only rarely wrote of the resistance, even the Communist resistance, and never mentioned the Czechoslovak Army. Was it, perhaps, because these heroes were younger men, full of the sort of vibrancy and sense of legitimacy that he had possessed after World War I? After 1945, Berger often referred to himself not as a Communist, but as an "old Communist."

The post–World War II Communist Party was also one that included an increasing number of women, among them Berger's three daughters. Mařenka, active before the war, became a leading functionary in the local Vyšehrad section of the Communist Party. Berger's entries about their participation in the party are strained, imbued with a mixture of pride and resignation. As he wrote on May 12, two days after liberation, "My wife and three daughters have joined the Communist Party. It is their duty." (Mařenka had been a veteran member since 1921. Two of his daughters had been members of a Communist youth group before the occupation.)[154] Early the following year, when Mařenka was in charge of organizing Lenten Carnival festivities for the Vyšehrad and Podskalí sections of the Communist Party, Berger complained, reminding her of all the cleaning up that would have to be done. His daughter Libuše responded that they were not concerned about that. "And you still aren't a member of the party?" she asked. "It's my affair," Berger responded curtly.[155]

Ironically, perhaps, Mařenka and his daughters partially succeeded in drawing Berger into the associational life of the party. Berger eventually joined the Lenten Carnival celebration. ("It was good fun, and there was enough hard liquor.")[156] He attended numerous public rallies, art exhibitions, and gatherings for party functionaries with the women in his life. Mařenka mediated Berger's relationship with the party in other ways as well. At one point, at Berger's suggestion, she prevented the appointment of an allegedly disloyal carpenter to the regional committee of the party.[157] Just as in 1905 and 1907, the thrill of elections and electioneering brought him more fully into party politics. He excitedly reported on his wife's efforts and on various political campaigns during the June 1946 elections, which represented a remarkable victory for the Communists. In addition to winning more parliament seats than any other party, he reported that the Communists had done extremely well in his neighborhood. The National Socialists won Vyšehrad with 3,470 votes, but the Communists received 2,513 votes in the district. During the First Republic they had never received more than 800 votes there.[158]

During the evening of the 1946 elections, Berger celebrated throughout the night with local party leaders, sleeping less than an hour. While disappointed that the Communist Party had not received a clear majority, his thoughts returned to the past. The National Socialists and Beneš, he noted, "must consider the Communists a true pain in the ass. This isn't 1918, when the socialists perpetrated a government of capitalists."[159] "Ach, comrades-workers!" he wrote, "what a shame that you didn't get to experience these last few days: May Day and today's election." He then listed the names of comrades who had passed away, adding, "you didn't live to see this victory as we have now, a victory that you worked for your entire lives."[160] Even these moments of satisfaction, tinged with sadness, could not, however, bring full reconciliation with the post-1945 party. When Berger finally relented in 1947 and joined the Communist Party, he returned to similar themes:

> Today I filled out an application to join the Communist
> Party. . . . How often have I been in quarrels in which comrades

reproach me, saying that I, an old worker and Bolshevik am not a member of the party. I don't want it to be any other way; on the other hand I live in times in which they chant words like "forward with youth" and have in their ranks a lot of bastards, scoundrels, and so on, and I am supposed to call them comrades and offer them my right hand. . . . I am no longer wide-shouldered enough to impose my will. We achieved important things in the workers' movement during the capitalist era, and now we must go.[161]

———

In February 1948, amid the heating up of the Cold War, Gottwald and the Communist Party seized power. They were unwittingly aided in their efforts by twelve non-Communist ministers who resigned to protest the Communist minister of interior's efforts to solidify his party's influence among the country's security police commissioners. The twelve ministers had expected President Beneš to refuse their resignations and call for new elections, but they were sorely disappointed. Instead, Gottwald rallied his supporters, demanding that the cabinet be constituted according to the Communists' wishes. Pro-Communist demonstrations swept across the country. Gottwald spoke to crowds that filled Old Town Square while other Praguers marched throughout the city. Armed industrial workers formed People's Militias. Local activists spontaneously arrested "class enemies" and other reactionary elements. Approximately 2.5 million people took part in a one-hour general strike.[162] Faced with an extraordinarily vibrant, at times violent, show of political strength, and with the threat of Soviet invasion hanging in the air, Beneš accepted his ministers' resignations and inserted Gottwald's men in their places.

Berger's entries during these tumultuous times are filled with clippings from various newspaper articles. He spent most of his days working at his newspaper stand, summarizing the major events of the

Pro-Communist demonstration on Old Town Square, February 1948. The banner reads, roughly, "Workers united for socialism." ČTK.

day for his diary. He continued to rant against non-Communist political parties, and especially the Social Democrats. Once again, he wrote, the Social Democrats, while claiming to be Marxists and speaking of revolution, have thrown their lot in with the bourgeois parties. He condemned, however, the "unseemly" Communist practice of publishing fake versions of the National Socialist newspapers, replete with misinformation and propaganda.[163] Shortly after the non-Communist ministers resigned, he walked down Wenceslas Square, noting that most Praguers seemed rather calm and even-tempered.[164] At night, various groups of Communist supporters marched through the city chanting pro-union slogans and "Long Live Gottwald's New

Government!"[165] A few days later Berger allegedly began to move on a small group of National Socialist protesters before a group of workers chased the interlopers from the square. During another stroll he found a Social Democratic leaflet and, on the back, wrote "historical flyer" and added five sentences describing how the party, just as during the First Republic, refused to destroy the capitalist system. He signed it "Vojtěch Berger, carpenter." (Berger did not mention what he did with the flyer thereafter.)[166] On the day of the general strike he walked to Charles Square and joined the protesters there. Several months later, on May Day, his wife and daughters marched, replete with banners, with the local Vyšehrad chapter of the Communist Party. Berger remained at his stand until he sold out of newspapers before joining the crowds on Wenceslas Square.[167]

Once outside the crowd, however, Berger's enthusiasm waned. He often returned to familiar themes in his diary. In the midst of the coup, he wrote, a young woman who allegedly had been a member of another political party before 1946 had been elected to the Communist Party's Vyšehrad section—yet another sign, he wrote, that no one wants anything to do with Communists from the interwar period. Occasional rants against opposing parties aside, his descriptions of the February coup were sterile and lacking in emotion. In the months that followed he took special note of the closing of non-Communist newspapers. In the ensuing years he continued to pen diary entries, many of them summaries of newspaper articles followed by skeptical commentary. While Berger eased into retirement other Praguers marched in carefully coordinated demonstrations and voted in rigged elections. They participated in party associations and read *Rudé právo*. They often had no other choice. One wonders if, as a young man, this is what Berger had had in mind.

4

COMMUNIST CITY

∞

IN JUNE 2018 I met Hana Frejková in her apartment, which is located on a hill above Smíchov not far from Klamovka Park. Books lined a wall that leads to a kitchen space. Opposite, an array of potted plants spilled out onto a balcony. I had brought flowers, of course. On the coffee table between us sat my tea and a large plate of poppyseed strudel. A few years earlier a dear friend and colleague had recommended that I read Frejková's book *Odd Roots* (*Divný kořeny*) and speak with the author. *Odd Roots,* as Frejková suggested to me several times, is neither a memoir nor a work of scholarship, even if it has elements of both. The book, published in 2007, drew upon three years of archival work that involved poring over documents created by the Communist secret police, and it was partly Frejková's effort to reconstruct her family's past. It was, she wrote, the culmination of her lifelong attempt to understand "who my parents were and what set them on such a miserable life path."[1] In the book she puzzles through her ethnic identity. She grew up speaking Czech, yet her parents grew up speaking German. Most of her father's family had been murdered by the Nazis for being Jews. *Odd Roots* is also an extended artistic essay about trauma and loss under Communism. In 1953, after months of torture, Frejková's father "confessed" to participating in a fictional plot to undermine Communist Czechoslovakia. He and ten others were executed following one of the most infamous show trials of the Stalinist era. The Communist authorities then expelled Frejková and her mother from the city.

Odd Roots, as well as Frejková's other writings, also relates the author's struggles to understand her relationship to society and to forge her own sense of belonging under a regime that had murdered her father. Frejková and her mother were eventually allowed to return to Prague, which was fast being refashioned as a socialist city imbued with the Communists' particular Czech national imaginations. Memorials and street names reflected a Czech national past reworked for the Communist present and future. Impressive, concrete examples of technological prowess and rational planning dotted the cityscape, part of a larger vision that promised social justice and a radical transformation of society. The regime mobilized large segments of the population, including thousands of workers in nearby factories, behind rationally constructed five-year plans. Many more participated in public events that embodied Communist visions, which were also meant as displays of loyalty to the regime. The secret police monitored Frejková, her mother, and countless others.

In this context, Frejková refashioned her relationship to society while creating her own sense of community and place. Following in her mother's footsteps, she pursued a successful career as a stage actress. In the theater Frejková found not just a home, but a place where she belonged. Acting, as she describes in *Odd Roots* and in a series of online articles published by *Theater News* (Divadelní noviny), constituted an attempt to create a "normal," meaningful life for herself in Communist Prague. It was also her way of feeling accepted by a city and society that had previously rejected her. In contrast to the rationalized planning and collectivist visions engaged in by the regime, Frejková and her fellow artists pursued small-scale, creative projects that forged their own notions of community and place. Along with other Praguers, they created their own sense of belonging within and in spite of a Communist regime that was determined to mold and coordinate their lives.

———————

"Dear comrades," Frejková's mother, Alžběta, wrote in a letter shortly after her husband's execution, "Today I have to tell my young daughter that her father was a traitor, that he betrayed our people. . . . I told her that she is not to blame—that children will like her when she shows them that she is a nice girl."[2] Shortly thereafter, Alžběta lost her job acting in the theater. "There was a vacuum around us in Prague," Frejková writes. Family friends, with one heroic exception, abandoned them. One good friend said that helping them might bring harm to his children. Others crossed the street when they saw Hana and her mother approaching on the sidewalk.[3] One day a black Tatra, the secret police car of choice, arrived at Hana's school. The driver took the girl and her mother northward, high into the mountains near the border with Germany, and eventually deposited them in an abandoned hut near the village of Janov. The Communist authorities seized the family's house. They made long lists of the family's belongings to be confiscated.[4]

Frejková had grown up in Prague, but she was born in London, in Middlesex Hospital, just before a German bomb fell on the facility's newborn ward.[5] Her father, Ludwig Freund, was a doctor's son from a German-speaking Jewish family in North Bohemia. He was a Communist activist before World War II, and one of the few economists of his time trained in Marxist thought. (He studied in Berlin and at the London School of Economics.) Shortly after the Munich Agreement he escaped to London, where the British government, wary of Freund's Communist credentials and German-speaking background, imprisoned him for a year on the Isle of Man. Upon his release, Freund's standing as an economist provided him with a number of opportunities while still in exile. He contributed to German-, Czech-, and English-language publications. He became an influential economic adviser within Eduard Beneš's government-in-exile, whose State Council added five Communist Party representatives following Nazi Germany's attack on the Soviet Union. Freund helped lead a group of Communist experts in London who charted the party's postwar economic policy and planning.[6]

Frejková's mother, who at the time went by the name Elisabeth, had grown up in Hamburg, Germany. She relocated to Prague during the interwar period to pursue a career in acting. After the Nazi seizure of power in Germany, she raised funds to support Communist refugees. She and Ludwig most likely met in one of the many cafés in the city where leftists gathered. A few months after Ludwig had fled Prague, Elisabeth also escaped to London, where she worked for the German-language BBC. Despite Elisabeth's apprehensions, the couple returned, with Frejková, to Prague after the war's end. Amid postwar expulsions and anti-German rhetoric, Ludwig Freund officially changed his name to the Czech-sounding Ludvík Frejka. Elisabeth changed her name to Alžběta. Despite Alžběta's then minimal understanding of the language, they spoke only Czech to Hana at home. Alžběta performed in various theaters throughout the city, often playing the role of German characters. In Prague, Frejka became one of the Communist Party's leading economists. After the 1948 Communist coup he worked directly under Klement Gottwald within the Office of the Presidency. He and his family moved from their apartment in Vinohrady to a villa in Bubeneč, a short walk from Prague Castle.[7]

Images of Gottwald at Prague Castle in *Rudé právo* cast the Communist leader as the rightful successor to the presidency. Propaganda newspapers recast the president as an expression of the party's will, which in turn conveyed the will of the working class. *Rudé právo* and other propaganda organs also fostered a leadership cult around Gottwald. Busts of Gottwald, "our first working-class president," could be found in offices throughout both the city and the country.[8] Echoing the efforts of nineteenth-century Social Democrats, Communist leaders also refashioned the national hero Jan Hus to suit their own purposes, portraying him as the representative of the "true" Czech nation, the toiling classes. In the Old Town, they began renovation work on the proto-Protestant preacher's Bethlehem Chapel. They also reappropriated the still-unfinished crematorium for the Czechoslovak Legionnaires, where in 1950 they unveiled a massive monument to Jan Žižka. Situated high atop Vítkov Hill, the site of a famed Hussite victory, the one-eyed military leader served as a reminder that violence must often accompany social change. The fact that Vítkov Hill lay at the edge of Žižkov, the working-class neighborhood named in Žižka's honor, only added to the monument's significance.[9] In 1949 plans were announced to build the world's largest statue of Stalin on the top of Letenská Plain, popularly known as Letná, overlooking the city. In February 1952 construction finally began on a monument. Not long thereafter the Soviet leader, followed by workers, a woman partisan, and other stock Communist figures— four Czechoslovaks on one side, four Soviets on the other—stood on a plinth fifteen meters high.[10]

During the Stalinist era, however, changes to the cityscape paled in comparison to the changes that the regime brought to the daily lives of Praguers and Czechoslovakians more broadly. Shortly after a government reorganization that further weakened municipal rule in Prague, the state confiscated much of the city's property. The centralized state nationalized all factories, regardless of the number of employees, and confiscated 43,000 smaller firms in the city.[11] The First Five-Year Plan, whose creators included Frejka and other leading economic experts, transformed a market economy into a planned one, replete with production quotas, set prices, and distribution plans. Trade unions became primarily organs of the state, as did newspapers and associations, all of which aimed to mobilize workers and others toward collective economic goals. Beyond Prague and other urban areas, efforts were made to strip farmers of their land and collectivize the pro-

Construction work on Stalin statue on Letná, 1954. ČTK.

duction of agriculture. In Prague, as US ambassador Ellis Briggs wrote in December 1951, the government was "announcing daily how many Ostrava mines are reaching targets, in which connection a bulletin board has been erected in Wenceslas Square near the museum, complete with little red stars lighted in the evening to show which mines are winning the production marathon."[12]

Upon seizing power, Communist leaders aggressively sought to eliminate human obstacles to their grand visions of a just, equal, and homogeneous society. Aided by the increasingly powerful secret police, they targeted "reactionaries," "saboteurs," and other alleged enemies in nearly every sector of society. After non-Communist political leaders assumed power, they quickly became targets of persecution, as did army officers and former members of the resistance, especially those with links to Beneš's London government. "Operation P" imprisoned or placed under house arrest thousands of prominent religious figures. In the face of resistance to collectivization efforts, "Operation K" targeted so-called rich farmers accused of sabotaging Communist efforts.[13] Secret police and other instruments of the state took particular aim at anyone deemed to have "bourgeois" or "petit bourgeois" backgrounds. The state subjected any individual who hindered its efforts to political terror and persecution. Many members of the working class as well as Nazi-era resistance fighters were targeted, whether they were guilty or the regime only imagined them to be.[14] Communist courts prosecuted roughly 90,000 Czechoslovaks for "political crimes" from 1948 to 1954. In the first four years of Communist rule the courts condemned 233 people to death. More than 20,000 others were sent to labor camps. In the infamous mines of Jáchymov, prisoners extracted plutonium for the Soviet Union.[15]

Show trials similar to those conducted during the Stalinist purges in the Soviet Union before World War II joined this repertoire of political terror. Early victims included prominent non-Communist political leaders such as Milada Horáková, but show trials reached deep into society as well. Between January and March 1951 alone the secret police and their collaborators in the justice system performed 480 local show trials of "class enemies" that took place across the country.[16] Even after Stalin's death in 1953 the regime staged show trials featuring "Slovak bourgeois-nationalists," "Trotskyites," army officers, and even members of the secret police. Most of these show trial victims were, perhaps surprisingly, well-placed within the Communist regime. One of Frejka's colleagues from his days in exile in London, Josef Goldmann, became the main target in a show trial of leading economists that ended in July of 1954. The most infamous show trial, conducted at the end of 1952, centered around the regime's second-most powerful man, Rudolf Slánský, who was accused of masterminding a fictional "anti-state conspiratorial center" along with thirteen other men whom *Rudé právo* described as "a gang of repugnant traitors."[17] Frejka's name occupied the third place on the docket.

Historians have long emphasized the unmistakable Soviet imprint on the Slánský trial, and for good reason. Slánský's arrest came only after Stalin's approval. Soviet advisers appear to have helped prepare the trial script. Soviet suspicions of anyone with ties to Western countries pervaded the trial. Many of the defendants had either worked in the foreign service or had formulated trade policy with Western countries. Frejka and six others on the docket had spent the wartime years in London.[18] Many defendants had middle-class backgrounds. Furthermore, Frejka made for an ideal victim in a trial designed to play on popular xenophobia. The prosecutor repeatedly declared that eleven of the fourteen defendants, including Frejka, were Jews with ties to Western Zionists and their capitalist coconspirators.[19] He often pointed out that several defendants had changed their German-language names to Czech ones. ("Ludvík Freund, alias Frejka"—oddly ignoring the fact that his first name, too, had once been a German one).[20] The prosecutor mocked another defendant, Bedřich Geminder, for speaking Czech badly.[21] The trial script blamed the economic troubles that Czechoslovakia faced in 1952 on overt sabotage and giveaways to the West by Frejka and others on the docket. They, of course, had done no such thing.

Shortly after his conviction Frejka wrote Gottwald a final letter: "In the last hour of his life, a man does not lie. I beg you, therefore, to believe what I am writing you. In any case, these lines will reach you after I am no more, so why would I write anything but the truth?"[22] He had he only admitted to the crimes, Frejka continued, out of a sense of duty to the working people and to the Communist Party—and at the insistence of his interrogators:

> When after four days I saw that you, Mr. President, regarded me as a saboteur and traitor and that this was the view of the

security personnel who, while my case was being investigated, represented the working people in my eyes, I decided that my ideas about myself and what I had wanted to do must have been subjectively wrong. From that day, believe me, Mr. President, I—who have been active in the working-class movement for thirty years—looked at myself honestly and mercilessly from the objective standpoint of the Czechoslovak working people and forced myself to see all of my activities through the eyes of the investigators; and, accordingly, I testified against myself as severely as possible the whole time.[23]

Several days later Frejka and the other condemned men were hanged in Prague's Pankrác prison. Their ashes were strewn along a road leading out of the city. Three months after Frejka's execution, Stalin died. Shortly after returning from Stalin's funeral, Gottwald died as well. Alžběta picked some flowers growing outside their Prague villa and, along with Hana, joined a massive procession of mourners walking toward Prague Castle. "Today," Frejková writes, "I believe that I was crying for my father. The atmosphere was truly monumental. I cried for that lost world and lost life."[24]

Just as the show trials of fictional enemies continued well after the deaths of Stalin and Gottwald, so did the persecution of Frejková and her mother. Expelled from Prague days after Stalin's funeral, they attempted to begin a new life in Janov. Their small brick home lay amid worn-down, abandoned buildings. Surrounded by damp air, they huddled in the kitchen for warmth. Hana's mother did her best to adapt to the situation. They bathed once a week in a wooden tub, where the warm water often lulled Hana to sleep. They adopted a small white dog that they named Lumpík. Hana found other moments of happiness, too—picking the first cherries to appear on the tree outside their house and washing clothes in the creek during the summer. Alžběta soon befriended a Sudeten German family who lived in a small wooden house nearby. Their daughter, Kristl, taught Hana how to gather wood. They often went hunting for mushrooms in the forest.[25]

Back in Prague, power and the mechanisms of power had begun to change, slowly, within the Communist Party. In February 1956 Stalin's successor, Nikita Khrushchev, denounced the cult of Stalin and the "excesses" that had characterized the Stalinist era. Within the Czechoslovak Communist Party, reformers became increasingly bolder in their challenges to hard-line Stalinists. The reformers, unlike their rivals in the party, sought to regain popular legitimacy and popular trust by imagining a socialism without the horrors of the Stalinist era. Thousands of political prisoners were quietly released. References to Stalin were stripped from factory names. In 1962 Prague's Stalin Avenue was renamed Vinohrady Avenue.[26] That same year, three separate blasts, using more than 2,000 pounds of explosives, reduced the Stalin monument on Letná to rubble. Only the plinth remained.[27] The need to reimagine Czechoslovak Communism, and perhaps a nagging sense of guilt, also led some Communist officials to establish commissions to investigate the persecutions of political enemies.[28] In the same year that the Stalin statue disappeared from Letná, officials returned Alžběta's Communist Party card, to her great satisfaction. Many of her friends congratulated her, Frejková recalled. The next year the Party Presidium ratified the Kolder Report, which condemned the Slánský trials as a fabrication. The same presidium then rehabilitated, in a purely juridical sense, its defendants, including Frejka. Hana and her mother were allowed to return to Prague.

For Frejková, their return to the city did not feel like a homecoming. She and her mother moved into a newly constructed apartment building "still surrounded by mud, without a telephone and without continuity to the past" not far from their former villa. Much in the city now seemed strange to Frejková. She feared stepping into an elevator, which this self-described girl from the village had never seen before.[29]

Frejková, however, spent much of her time over the next four years out-side the city. After several attempts she had been accepted to study at the Janáček Academy for Musical Arts in Brno. Upon graduation in 1967, Frejková, now twenty-two years old, began working for a theater in Karlovy Vary: "Suddenly I felt like an adult, full of hope and expec-tation."[30] Meanwhile, reformers in the party continued to gain ground. As Frejková was settling into a new life, the Czechoslovak Academy of Sciences hosted an international conference on Franz Kafka at a venue just outside the city. One of the last show trial victims, Eduard Goldstücker, co-organized the event, which represented the clearest at-tempt yet to break from the antisemitism of the Stalinist era. Other efforts included a subtler approach to Czechoslovak-Israeli relations and a tentative dialogue about the Holocaust in the media, especially in film.[31] Behind closed doors, Slovak Communists demanded more autonomy, which they obtained in 1968, while denouncing the past in-justices suffered by those accused of being "bourgeois Slovak nation-alists." Reformists called for persuasion instead of coercion. They de-manded democratization and decentralization of rule even as they reaffirmed the one-party state. More broadly, a discourse that focused on a more decent and humane socialism, and "humanness," emerged that challenged the rigid, inhumane Communist rule of the past.[32]

In the early months of 1968, reformers firmly gained the upper hand. They loosened the censorship laws in March, sparking a new open-ness heralded as the Prague Spring. Associations and clubs formed, and media of all sorts became remarkably free of control and diverse in their content and opinions. The new leader of the Communist Party, Alexander Dubček, boldly spoke about creating "socialism with a human face." Meanwhile, more conservative party leaders were quietly dismissed from their posts. Khrushchev's successor, Leonid Brezhnev, openly worried, however, about the loss of so many "good and sincere friends of the Soviet Union."[33] He and Communist leaders throughout the bloc wondered where the reforms might lead. Dubček and others affirmed their sincere commitment to socialism and to maintaining the central role of the Communist Party. Their critics in Czechoslovakia, but especially beyond its borders, condemned the reformists' efforts as scattered, unpredictable, and potentially destabilizing. Recent events in Czechoslovakia, they maintained, were the product of "counterrevolutionary elements" that threatened not just the integrity of the bloc but of other Communist regimes as well. Allies within the Warsaw Pact, the Communist bloc's answer to NATO, readied their forces.

On the night of August 20–21, 1968, Warsaw Pact tanks invaded Czechoslovakia, occupying Prague and much of the country. Frejková was living in Karlovy Vary at the time. After midnight a friend came into her bedroom and screamed: "Wake up, the Russians are here!" to which Frejková responded, "Such stupid jokes, let me sleep!" They walked outside to see tanks stationed around the city's main square, where people were running around excitedly, holding radio transistors next to their ears. Frejková and her friends donated blood to the local hospital—"just in case." Popular protests in Prague and throughout the country began immediately after the invasion and continued through the end of the year. In January 1969 Jan Palach, a student at Charles University, walked to the top of Wenceslas Square and lit himself on fire in protest; he died several days later. Frejková and her friends hid placards beneath their clothes and set off to attend his funeral.[34] That March roughly 150,000 people joined demonstrations and protests when the Czechoslovak hockey team, for the second time that month, defeated their Soviet counterparts at the world hockey championship. These protests, however, emboldened Soviet leaders and their allies to impose even stricter censorship laws and to finally oust Dubček. Tens of thousands of Soviet troops were stationed just outside of Prague, one of five bases scattered across the country. From Prague, conservatives in the Czechoslovak Communist Party, now led by the former show trial victim Gustáv Husák, instituted structural changes aimed at stabilizing the regime. Backed by Brezhnev and Warsaw Pact forces, they reasserted their position within the party and initiated a new era dubbed "Normalization," which suggested a return to the country's "normal" path to Communism and its "normal" relationship to the Soviet Union.[35]

As the Soviet newspaper *Pravda* reported shortly after the Warsaw Pact invasion, "rightist, anti-socialist forces" bore grave responsibility for misleading Czechoslovaks, for questioning the party and its leading role in all spheres of life. Soon thereafter, supporters of Normalization set upon these enemies. They fired the leading reformists in the party, and many leading intellectuals were arrested. The regime also pursued a number of small-scale show trials against those charged with having a nefarious influence over the population.[36] Hard-liners revived their anti-Zionist propaganda campaign, echoing many of the tropes from the Slánský trials. The secret police's "Operation Spider," which began in 1971, eventually surveilled and harassed about 20,000 people whom the regime considered to be Jewish. They especially targeted influential party members who supported the Communist reform movement. In Prague's Jewish community, leaders were required to collaborate with the regime in order to protect the very existence of their institutions and religious practices.[37] Years after the invasion, the city used confiscated Jewish gravestones to repave portions of Wenceslas Square.[38]

Hard-liners also moved aggressively to ensure loyalty within the party and acquiescence to their rule. Beginning in 1970, committees across the country began screening more than 1.5 million party members. More than a fifth of those screened either had their party memberships canceled or were expelled from the party outright. The consequences were not merely symbolic, as party membership could mean the difference between promotion or demotion and between keeping your job or losing it. The screenings especially targeted reformists and the cultural figures who supported them. The careers of well-known performers who had supported Dubček's reforms were cut short. Other professionals in the arts and humanities, as well as historians and other scholars in the social sciences, also lost their jobs. These humiliating exercises, as one historian has written, had the effect of ritualizing new forms of power and compliance. They educated everyone involved—screeners and screened—in a new political language to be used in public while offering a warning against making open, honest, and truthful statements.[39] They also signaled a new era of surveillance in the workplace. "Special branches" of the secret police were embedded in major enterprises and institutions. Any coworker might be an informant; anyone might be approached to provide information about a workplace.[40]

Work, and a person's livelihood more generally, were bargaining chips exploited by a regime that suffered from a lack of legitimacy. In the first half of 1969 alone more than 20,000 rank-and-file members voluntarily quit the Communist Party, Alžběta among them. The regime thus complemented state violence with promises of a distinctively socialist "good life" characterized by ample consumer goods, decent wages, and considerable leisure time. Working less, while being guaranteed employment, sweetened the deal. Promises of a socialist good life served a number of ideological aims. It was contrasted with the fast-paced, uncertain professional lives of those in the West. Yet the promise of the "good life" was also intended to foster a quiet acquiescence. Under Normalization, unlike during the Stalinist era, the regime typically prioritized apolitical behavior over political mobilization. Dishwashers, refrigerators, and bottles of Kofola—a Czechoslovak version of Coca-Cola—complemented police interrogations and the threat of job dismissal.[41]

———

It is important to remember, however, that the Communist regime's reach into society, into the lives of its inhabitants, was never total—even if that was its aim. We should be wary of words such as "resistance," "opposition," and "conformity," as well as "collaboration" and "compliance"—words that replicate the regime's worldview, and especially that of its secret police. These same words, along with the word "totalitarianism," also had their uses in the West. They justified Cold War–era critiques of Communist Eastern Europe that, ironically, employed the rhetorical logic of their ideological enemies. We need not adopt these words and the perspective that they imply. In his study of the late Communist Soviet Union, Alexei Yurchak writes that members of the Communist youth group Komsomol distinguished activities that were "pure pro forma" from those that entailed "work with meaning," or activities that they found meaningful and satisfying, even if they coincided with ideological goals and rhetoric.[42] Similar translations and reformulations happened throughout the Communist bloc, including in Prague. The regime may have shaped the contexts in which Praguers lived, but those same Praguers gave meaning to their own lives and actions. Their thoughts and practices were not simply understood as either coordinating with or resisting its efforts, as the regime might have it. Borrowing a metaphor from Jonathan Bolton, we might ask instead how Praguers inhabited various "worlds" that enveloped very human experiences, situations, and behaviors.[43] While not entirely distinct from the regime and its efforts, it was in these worlds that Praguers and others could create their own notions of community and place as well as a sense of belonging.

For Frejková, the theater constituted the most important world in which she created meaning for herself. From 1967 to 1970 she performed at the city theater in Karlovy Vary, a spa town west of Prague. Frejková then signed a contract to work at the avant-garde Maringotka Theater in Prague and moved back to the city. Three years later, in 1973, she signed a contract with the Jaroslav Průcha Theater in nearby Kladno. (Frejková remained in Prague, however, choosing to commute by car.) She interpreted her work in the theater as a means of rehabilitation and a break with her traumatic past. As Frejková later recalled, it often felt as if, because of her father's having been convicted and sentenced to death, all of society was against her. She had thus become a solitary figure who had to consciously fight isolation and alienation—

From left to right, Alena Hesounová, Milan Livora, and Hana Frejková in a publicity photo for Prague's Maringotka Theater, 1971. Olga Procházková and the Divadelní ústav.

to "make it" and to achieve, to the best of her ability, a decent life for herself.[44] For many years, theater provided that sense of acceptance. Walking the streets of the Old Town to work at the theater, Frejková felt that she was a "person like anyone else" who "finally . . . had the right to everything."[45] "I was going to the theater because I had to, because I had work there," she told me, but also because "for me it meant being a person of equal value, like everyone else."[46]

When asked if she had ever considered a career other than acting, Frejková's reply was clear: "No, never."[47] In this respect, she took after her mother, who, in addition to guiding Frejková into the theater, influenced the ways in which her daughter thought about the theater. Elisabeth Henke Warnholz was born to a well-to-do middle-class family in Hamburg, Germany, in 1907. As Frejková writes, a rebellious streak and an emerging passion for theater characterized her mother's early life. She had to leave one school, having insisted on wearing pants and having caused problems with her teachers. Elisabeth then enrolled in a college-track high school (*gymnasium*) in Essen, where she began studying theater in earnest. Upon graduating in 1927, she moved to Berlin to train in a private school led by the famed theater and film actress Ilke Grüning. A few years later Elisabeth received the Reinhardt Prize, given each year to the most promising graduate of a theater school in Germany. Her mentors then suggested that she seek work in Prague, where she could get good roles while building her reputation on the periphery of the German theater world.

In Prague, she enjoyed numerous professional successes. She obtained Czechoslovak citizenship and joined the Communist Party of Czechoslovakia. In addition to aiding refugees from Nazi Germany, she played a key role in bringing together Czech- and German-speaking actors for antifascist performances, including one attended by President Eduard Beneš. Her brief return to the theater after the war was cut short by Frejka's show trial, however. Following her expulsion with her daughter to Janov, Alžběta worked in various factories while Hana was at school. Upon their return to Prague and after Frejka's rehabilitation, Alžběta joined her daughter and enrolled at the well-regarded Janáček Academy of Musical Arts in Brno to study to become a director. ("It was a bit strange when my classmates pointed out that I was studying with my mom," Frejková writes.) Theater, Frejková suggested, was her mother's first passion, a love that had betrayed her. In the many years following her husband's death, Alžběta never obtained full-time work in the theater.[48]

Alžběta did, however, succeed in laying the groundwork for Hana's successes in the theater. In Janov, she encouraged her daughter to learn crucial skills, such as singing. While living in Janov, and despite great difficulty, Alžběta enrolled Hana in a music school in nearby Jablonec, where, three times per week, she studied piano and rhythm. Because they did not have a piano at home, Hana practiced once a week in a local pub among the tipsy regulars. At home she played silently on a piece of paper onto which her mother had drawn piano keys. Later, in high school, she performed with an amateur group in a local theater.[49] The play was *Students' Story,* based on a nineteenth-century novel by Alois Jirásek about student life and the virtues of embracing the Czech language, and not German, in all aspects of public life. Alžběta directed the performance.[50] In 1962, at the age of seventeen, Hana got a job as a lighting technician and played bit parts for a theater in nearby Most.[51] Alžběta attended Hana's performances in Most, as she did throughout Hana's career, often offering critical appraisals of her daughter's efforts. (During our last interview, Frejková visible bristled when this topic arose.) In Most, Hana befriended Emma Černá, a source of inspiration. "She was, for me, a star from Prague," Frejková writes. "Her whole existence, the way she held her herself, suggested how I might go from being a lighting technician to an actress."[52]

Her mother's stories about her own former acting career, albeit related only rarely, also allowed Frejková to imagine present and past connections to the acting world. Thanks to these accounts she conjured up visions of Prague as a vibrant city full of theaters. One actor's First Republic costumes reminded Frejková of her mother's stories about suitcases full of costumes and banter about dressing "as a civilian" while in public. Alžběta's accounts, as well as links to certain places and people, also complemented Frejková's nostalgic memories of a prewar past that she had never herself experienced. In Janov, when she met a well-regarded member of the prewar avant-garde with a Hungarian Jewish accent who had also been deported from Prague, Frejková was reminded of her mother, "a beautiful woman, an extraordinary combination of artist and Communist." In Most she learned to play solitaire from an actor who could easily have been mistaken for the famous interwar actor and playwright Jan Werich. In Karlovy Vary, the spa town famously visited by Johann Wolfgang von Goethe, classical music played in the outdoor amphitheater where Elisabeth had performed. Frejková remembered seeing there an older couple "dressed in the Austro-Hungarian style, a sort of aristocratic pair . . . [who]

wonderfully evoked the atmosphere of a lost time, an entirely different, non-socialist world."[53]

Frejková was good at acting, something that others acknowledged, and she enjoyed the work. She also reveled in the world of the theater and the characters who inhabited it. In Most, she marveled at the scene found in the women's fragrant dressing room, where actresses used makeup to create their own personal styles. Even while offstage, actors took on personalities that at times felt fantastical, and sometimes comical. Male actors flirted with her. In Karlovy Vary, one actor enjoyed drinking wine from Frejková's slipper into the wee hours of the morning. Another, in a more traditional approach, wrote Frejková love letters when he was not cursing during rehearsals or staying up all night playing ping-pong. The theater also provided opportunities for socializing and friendship. In Karlovy Vary, Frejková had friends all over town with whom she sat late into the night talking and drinking. In Prague, as a member of the Maringotka Theater, life was more hectic, bubbling with activity, chaos, and "many parties, faraway excursions, sleepless nights, [and] long discussions." On their way back from Kladno, she and her friends sometimes stopped at the airport, which was near Frejková's apartment, and stared in wonder as airplanes arrived from lands forbidden to them. More often, however, they went out for drinks with other theater artists or attended post-premiere parties that lasted until the morning and ended with coffee at a local café.[54]

The world of the theater remembered by Frejková was not a world unto its own. Higher-ups in the Communist bureaucracy could easily replace or fire directors and producers, as happened in several theaters where Frejková worked. The Jaroslav Průcha Theater suffered three directorial changes in the 1970s alone.[55] The Ministry of Culture paid the wages of the theater employees, and this, combined with the lingering presence of the secret police, gave the state considerable influence over the workings of the theater. Within those restrictions, however, there was room for a relative degree of autonomy. Each theater signed individual contracts with its actors for terms of anywhere from a year to a lifetime, thus giving them considerable leeway to assemble their own troupes. Theater directors and producers chose their own material. A season's program required approval from the Ministry of Culture. Still, theater directors and producers decided what to stage and how to stage it. Theater producers and directors also gamed the system. In the wake of the purges that followed the 1968 invasion many theater directors and producers simply "stepped back," allowing others officially to assume their posts while they, as "substitutes," continued their work behind the scenes. In other cases, the "cleansing" of theater leadership had the unintended consequence of bringing new talent into leadership positions.[56]

To its benefit, theater also inhabited a distinct niche within the Normalization-era media sector. Once a powerful site of political agitation, theaters suffered from declining attendance in the first decades of Communist rule. Stalinist-era productions were often predictable and dull, and they faced increasing competition from radio, television, and film. By the 1970s, theatergoers consisted mostly of students and members of the intelligentsia. Neither group was a prime target for state-sponsored propaganda efforts, which meant that theaters and theatergoers received less scrutiny. By the late 1970s, critics in Prague's leading theater magazine often deviated from the party line, providing theaters with varying, and sometimes refreshing, judgments and incentives.[57] Theater professionals, unlike their counterparts in television and film, also shared a nightly experience and perhaps a brief sense of community with theatergoers. Spectators laughed along with the actors and applauded at the end of performances. They often prolonged the shared experience by enjoying a glass a wine at the theater bar.[58]

Lesser-known theaters and so-called peripheral theaters outside of major cities like Prague often enjoyed an even greater degree of autonomy. As most theatergoers under Normalization knew, the most impressive and innovative performances were to be found in less obvious places. Puppet theaters and amateur theaters thrived, as did regional theaters in Gottwaldov (now Zlín), Cheb, and Uherské Hradiště. The troupe of the avant-garde Maringotka Theater where Frejková worked typically performed in locales on the outskirts of Prague, such as the Braník Theater, which was near the southern border of the city.[59] At one point they occupied the quiet basement of a restaurant in the Old Town. The Jaroslav Průcha Theater in Kladno, Frejková writes, was an especially successful peripheral theater. It had the additional advantage of being close to Prague and also being a stop-off point for travelers making their way to and from the city.[60]

Within these submerged and peripheral theater worlds, directors could take daring chances and engage in playful experimentation distinct from the main contours of the Normalization regime. Zuzana Kočová, a director at the Maringotka Theater, embraced the experimental movement of her time while also paying homage to the poeticism of her late husband, the avant-garde artist E. F. Burian. Kočová, whom Frejková describes as "a very persistent and tenacious woman," also put great effort into cultivating young theatergoers and providing space for young actors to perform.[61] At the Jaroslav Průcha Theater, which was shared by the towns of Kladno and Mláda Boleslav, the young Bulgarian director Nikolaj Georgijev staged experimental forms of improvisational theater. Frejková recalled their brief popularity: "When the theatergoers realized that that [play's] ending could be relatively untraditional—the princess rejected marriage with Honza because she didn't like him—and moreover that we could modify each performance, busloads of theatergoers and critics arrived from Prague."[62]

Less peripheral theaters and artists could pursue daring creative projects as well. In 1973 Prague's Jára Cimrman Theater staged a second premiere of *Akt: A Family Drama with Singing and Dancing,* which, similar to other performances by the troupe, began with a scholarly lecture about a forgotten Czech hero, Cimrman, his accomplishments, and his philosophy of externism. The second act was a reconstruction of one of Cimrman's works, which, in the original 1967 performance, included an officer of the secret police as a main character; in the 1973 performance he was a sexologist.[63] Leaders of the Jazz Section, officially part of the Communist Musicians' Union, consistently fought back official attempts to limit or halt their members' activities, often using the regime's own words and laws in self-defense. They provided professional training for up-and-coming musicians and created space for other creative activities, including book publishing.[64] Throughout the city, small clusters of intellectuals still met each other in cafés and apartments, albeit under the watchful eye of the secret police. Others, such as Václav Havel, an outspoken poet, playwright, and philosopher, relocated to the countryside. From his country house near the northern border, playfully nicknamed Hrádeček, or "the little Castle," Havel wrote a number of plays that earned him critical fame abroad. In 1975, on the easternmost outskirts of Prague, Havel staged *The Beggar's Opera,* a scathing critique of Normalization in Czechoslovakia and of the secret police. His wife Olga later described the performance as "the best theatrical night of her life." Nearly 300 guests were in attendance.[65]

Creative endeavors and the creation of community and place within different worlds were not, of course, limited to professional artists. Praguers decorated their apartments according to their own tastes and pursued various hobbies and interests. In fields and villages across the country young people met for impromptu, unsanctioned rock 'n' roll concerts, amateur theater performances, and "happenings," semi-structured theatrical events in which members of the audience became participants. Self-described tramps took to the woods, singing songs and observing escapist traditions that harked back to the interwar period.[66] On weekends other Praguers left the city for country homes, where they were freer to say and do as they liked, and to pursue long-held traditions such as gathering mushrooms. In fact, the *chata,* or country home, is one example of the ways in which the regime's efforts mingled with the existence of various worlds within society. Among Praguers, the popularity of the *chata* skyrocketed in the first years of

Normalization. By the 1980s, roughly two-thirds of Prague households either owned or had access to a *chata* and spent more than 100 days per year there. Communist leaders, albeit with some hesitancy, supported Praguers' escapes to their country homes in order to undermine the tramping movement, over which they had less control. Near-empty cities on the weekends reduced the likelihood of collective political action.[67]

———

The Normalization regime in Prague still attempted to shape society, and thus the larger world in which Praguers and other Czechoslovaks lived. It did not limit itself to silencing enemies and making efforts to realize, broadly speaking, the promises of the "good life." It was not bereft of imaginative powers or national imagination. Similar to their counterparts in Western Europe, Czechoslovak leaders embraced a common set of beliefs central to their rule, summarized by David Harvey as "the belief in linear progress, absolute truths, the rational planning of ideal social orders, and the standardization of knowledge and production" that became central to the postwar order on both sides of the Iron Curtain.[68] In Communist Czechoslovakia, however, such thinking not only formed the bedrock of political legitimacy, it was also most clearly expressed in Marxist-Leninist terms. This idea also blended nicely with Czech(oslovak) pride in the nation's educational system, engineering prowess, and technical expertise. This was especially true under Normalization, when "technological socialism" reached its apex.

Planners such as Frejka, along with five-year plans, best epitomized this strain of thought, even under Stalinism. Early planners, while at the mercy of powerful, at times unpredictable, party elites, set production targets, established wages and price controls, and determined how and where to develop certain sectors of the economy, often under the rubric of various five-year plans. The role of planners, and planning, would undergo a number of changes after Gottwald's death. The spontaneity and violence of the Stalinist era, along with taxing drives to mobilize the population and disappointing economic progress, spurred a counterreaction that prioritized reason, calculation, and technology as a means to a better future. Science (*věda*), as Doubravka Olšáková has written, became a central node of power centered around a rising number of experts and technocrats. It also informed and legitimized politics in the post-Stalinist era.[69] Amid the ideological battles of the 1960s, reformist experts imagined a variety of futures in which centralized planning mixed with local or individual decision making. Many of these experts, along with some reformist party leaders, reflected hopeful, pan-European expectations about the roles that technology and technocrats could play in creating a better society. Others—again in line with their counterparts throughout Europe—feared that humanness and humanity would fall victim to rational technocratic thinking that measured lives in purely statistical terms.[70]

Planning and the role of planners changed again under Normalization. In the years that followed the Warsaw Pact invasion, a number of leading reformists were either purged or forced into exile. "Consolidation," another keyword of the era, justified the reorganization of institutes and experts. Economic forecasters, for example, were "consolidated" within a cluster of government institutions and unified under the term *prognostika*.[71] Experts and technological socialism, rather than becoming the objects of Normalization purges, became even more central to Communist rule and to the legitimacy of the regime. Well-executed, centralized economic planning was key to creating a depoliticized society where Czechoslovaks would enjoy a socialist "good life" and abundant material goods in return for acquiescence. Technological socialism also matched up well with post-1968 desires among normalizers for economic and political order, and consolidation rather than instability, multiplicity, and radical change.[72] As Vítězslav Sommer writes of *prognostika* experts, they shared with the regime "the image of the socialist economy as one huge factory optimally managed by sophisticated planning technologies."[73]

It was in Prague, the capital of Communist Czechoslovakia, that power was concentrated, and from whence power and the plans to transform society emanated. In addition to being the seat of government and the party headquarters, Prague remained home to the thousands of civil servants who executed the government's will. Prague was home to the country's leading research institute, the Czechoslovak Academy of Sciences, which was founded just before Stalin's death. It was from Prague that scientific, rational efforts to transform society along Marxist-Leninist lines were often first put to paper. Planners also designated Prague's role within the national economy more broadly. By design, Prague's industries focused on foodstuffs, clothing, energy, construction, and construction materials.[74] Communist leaders and their experts either modernized factories in traditionally working-class neighborhoods or built new factories in the vast, open spaces along the city's peripheries. In Smíchov, the former Ringhoffer Plant manufactured more streetcars than did factories anywhere else in the world. A small number of its T-series streetcars, the only model used on city streets throughout the Eastern bloc, still clank along in Prague.[75]

The main tenets of technological socialism also informed the transformation of Prague's urban spaces. Urban planners had long dreamed of making Prague and other urban areas throughout Czechoslovakia into "socialist cities" characterized, as Kimberly Elman Zarecor observes, by a rational, logical infrastructure and system that prioritized efficiency and higher living standards. Unlike other governments, Communist regimes had a greater ability to transform the built environment, and thus the fabric of urban life more broadly, thanks to the elimination of real estate markets, state ownership of property, centralized planning, and a determined commitment to public housing.[76] Prague, in contrast to the emergent industrial cities in the borderlands previously inhabited by Sudeten Germans, was not, however, a relatively blank slate onto which Communist leaders could realize their ideological dreams.[77] Urban planners did not have free reign to realize their visions for the city and often came into conflict with political leaders and fellow experts. Local inhabitants, preservationists, and even Communist ideologues typically demanded that Prague's historic core be protected, even if some planners dreamed of leveling much of Žižkov and even nineteenth-century buildings in the city center.[78]

Thus, planners envisioned a historic core surrounded by a socialist city. Communist leaders greatly expanded the city outward, almost tripling its total area.[79] *Sídliště*, housing estates complete with their own parks, schools, cultural institutions, and public transportation stops, began to appear on the landscapes. Concrete, mass-produced *paneláky* (panel apartment buildings) characterized the housing estate, and for good reason. Improved housing for Prague's residents was a priority for Communist leaders and planners alike, as it had for leftist thinkers and others since the interwar period, when roughly half of working-class families lived in one-room apartments, often in unimaginable squalor.[80] Even as late as 1961, nearly one-third of Prague households shared a toilet with others; nearly half lacked their own space for washing up.[81] For many Praguers, *paneláky* provided, for the first time, the kind of decent, modern housing enjoyed by Prague's middling classes. Construction on a housing complex near Petřín Hill was completed in 1965. Work on Červený Vrch, the complex where Frejková and her mother eventually settled, began in 1960 and was completed in 1972. That same year workers began to erect Prague's largest housing estate, Jižní Město (South City). The first families moved there in 1976, and by 1991 its population was roughly 80,000. Various hotels and parks also appeared on the landscape surrounding the city center. Just south of Vyšehrad, near the newly modernized Podolí Waterworks, a massive swimming complex opened to the public.[82]

Planners and the Communist authorities also made a great effort to create a vast infrastructural network of water, gas, and telecommunications lines throughout the city. Massive tunnels shot through the landscape and bridges spanned its waterways. Other multilane highways spread out around the city. Near the center, a new thoroughfare followed the New Town's former wall along the top of Wenceslas Square,

Červený Vrch housing estate, circa 1970. Reproduced from a copy of Otakar Nový, *Architekti Praze* (Prague: Pražský projektový ústav, 1971), in the personal collection of Kimberly Elman Zarecor.

thus cutting off pedestrians from the National Museum. In 1974 Prague's first subway line, which connected the city's southern periphery to the center, opened to great fanfare. Part of the Prague Metro's line went through a tube situated along the bottom side of Klement Gottwald Bridge, a newly built six-lane concrete bridge in the Nusle district. Stops included the main train station and an entrance located under Wenceslas Square. The line's nine stops could be covered in only thirteen and a half minutes. The line was celebrated as a technological achievement and proof of the country's enduring loyalty to the Soviet Union, which provided the subway's cars and trained Prague's first subway drivers. Young women were hired to position themselves near subway escalators to assist pedestrians as they navigated escalators for the first time. Future subway lines and extensions were planned in coordination with urban designs for housing estates such as South City, which eventually had four subway stops of its own.[83]

Rational, scientific planning that sought to create an ordered and rational socialist society complemented efforts to realize various as-

Construction on the "A" subway line, 1979. ČTK / Jaroslav Sýbek.

pects of the socialist "good life." In the center of Prague, two modern department stores, Máj and Kotva, opened in 1975. Another of Prague's major industries was entertainment, especially movies and television, which promised, the regime hoped, to subtly inculcate the population with socialist ideals while providing a needed escape from everyday life.[84] Here, too, dreams that combined technology and the propaganda efforts of television took form on Prague's cityscape. Inspired, no doubt, by the Ostankino Tower (a television and radio tower in Moscow completed in 1967), in 1985 the Communist authorities began construction on their own massive television tower, destroying a section of a Jewish cemetery in the process. (Similar television towers loomed above just about every capital in Communist Eastern Europe, from Berlin to Riga.) Construction on Prague's bright white, needle-shaped tower high above Žižkov was not completed, however, until three years after the fall of Communism.[85]

Prague also became a stage for the Normalization regime's attempts to project its visions of socialism and an idealized socialist society. Each year, for example, May Day celebrations filled Wenceslas Square, except when the festivities were moved to Letná while the square's subway stations were under construction. This highly coordinated and controlled ritual not only recalled the history of the workers' movement in the Bohemian lands but also deployed symbols that linked the workers' movement to the nation while celebrating the regime's achievements.[86] No spectacle, however, was greater than Spartakiad, the successor to the mass gymnastics event first organized by the Communist Party in the interwar period. Under Communist rule, the first Spartakiad took place in 1955 and was held every five years thereafter with the exception of 1970, when the Warsaw Pact invasion had disrupted event planning. Participants traveled from across the country to the world's largest sports facility, Strahov Stadium, which had the capacity to accommodate 30,000 performers. Tens of thousands of spectators boarded special buses and streetcars, as well as a funicular, to watch the festivities inside this massive concrete structure located near Petřín Hill. Leading artists, musicians, choreographers, filmmakers, architects, and designers collaborated in planning the carefully coordinated, extremely costly spectacle.[87] As in the interwar period, the Spartakiad recalled nationalist performances dating back to the nineteenth century while reflecting a Communist version of Czech(oslovak) nationalism with its organized, collectivist notions of socialism. Under

Normalization, the performers' synchronous movements, apparently performed without direction, suggested a Communist society that was paradoxically obedient, vibrant, and sovereign. Performances evoked the courage of men and the motherhood of women, along with youthful exuberance, suggesting an unchanged world based on family, traditional gender roles, and nation.[88]

Plans, construction projects, and socialist spectacles, however, often masked a very different realty. In their studies, expert prognosticators consciously ignored glaring problems in society, such as drug use and crime. They often viewed society merely as an object of study, rather than as an interlocutor. They lacked the thoughtful, philosophically informed methods that characterized the 1960s.[89] Furthermore, women often faced discrimination in the workplace. They were paid lower wages than men. Many worked as nurses, shop assistants, and in other low-paying jobs traditionally reserved for women. They continued to shoulder the burden of childcare and remained largely excluded from leadership positions.[90] By the 1980s the economy in Prague, as throughout the Communist bloc, began to sputter as well. Consumer goods became less available, and grumbling grew louder. People could justify working less than necessary and engaging in small-scale corruption within the warped moral universe of Normalization: "We pretend to work and they pretend to pay us," as one joke went.

Economic sputtering aside, many Praguers also benefited materially from technological socialism and the effort to create a socialist city. Ladislav Urbánek, who became a director of Prague's public transportation system in 2012, began working for the subway system in 1976. His father was a railroad man. The work guaranteed Urbánek a much-desired apartment in Prague.[91] Work could also be a world in which Praguers and others not only found purpose but also created their own meanings. Petr Vostřez, one of the subway system's first drivers, fondly recalled the yearly ball that the Prague Metro held for its employees. He and his coworkers went to the theater together and often chatted over a beer at the pub. After the fall of Communism, Metro employees and retirees continued to meet annually.[92] Vostřez took great pride in his work, as did the firefighters interviewed for a study by Hana Bortlová-Vondráková. Coming to the aid of others and sometimes risking their lives in the process gave them a sense of meaning and purpose that existed outside of politics.[93] Nurses interviewed by Petra Schindler-Wisten also mentioned the sense of having a calling and a higher purpose in their narratives.[94] Others, including the visual artists interviewed by Lenka Krátka, found both meaning and a creative outlet, combined with the sense of a calling, within the structures of the regime.[95]

Similarly, as Paulina Bren has written, television shows might have been intended to depoliticize, but viewers found their own meanings in the stories on the screen. Even after the fall of Communism, viewers saw themselves, their loves, and their worries in television characters from the 1970s and 1980s.[96] Participants in the Spartakiad gave the event their own meanings and significance. According to Petr Roubal, many Spartakiad performers demanded that the 1990 event take place despite the fall of Communist rule the year before. Some maintained that they were carrying on a long-standing Czech, and Slavic, tradition. Canceling the Spartakiad, one gymnast wrote, would be akin to destroying the subway because of its associations with the Communist era. As another gymnast stated, she longed for the "wonderful feeling of belonging to a group of people" and wanted to feel "a part of broader society."[97] Indeed, the Spartakiad failed to inculcate socialist values, as the regime imagined it would. Although the Spartakiad drained critical state resources, its relative popularity and the regime's need for legitimacy meant that the event could not be abandoned. It had become a ritual in which, recalling Clifford Geertz, Roubal writes, "Power served pomp, not pomp power."[98]

———————

The notion of various worlds of experience and interpretation enjoying relative autonomy within Communist society should not be overstated.

The Communist regime and its secret police still had the power to penetrate these various worlds at will, and they often did. In 1973 the authorities shut down Kočova's Maringotka experimental theater. Georgijev's run at improvisation at the Jaroslav Průcha Theater came to an end shortly after it had achieved popular notoriety. In 1974 an informant (codenamed Andreas III) detailed for the secret police a March 19 performance at the theater. An actor allegedly slashed a portrait of Lenin with a knife during a performance. A second actor took down the portrait and tore up its remnants. The informant suggested that the original gash was an accident and was meant to be symbolic only. The second actor, Oldřich Vízner, in a moment of improvisation, made a deliberate decision to play along, tearing up what was left of the portrait. Secret police agents dug up information on Vízner (his brother had emigrated in 1969) and his wife and, through Andreas III and other agents, demanded statements from other members of the troupe and gathered more information. Frejková did not provide a statement. (The poster, before being torn, measured 607 × 426 mm. Agents conducted a chemical analysis of this important piece of evidence.) Vízner claimed that he was unaware that the poster depicted Lenin. The secret police informed the directorship of the theater and the Ministry of Culture. Vízner was warned that his duties included following the director's lead. If another "criminal act" took place, official proceedings against him would begin.[99]

The secret police were also well aware of Havel's production of *The Beggar's Opera* a year later, and retribution was even more brutal and swift. Actors were fired from their jobs, as were a number of university employees in attendance.[100] One of its organizers departed the Jára Cimrman Theater, where he had been stage director, in order to protect his colleagues.[101] The Communist government also took aim at members of the Czech artist underground, many of whom, in Bolton's description, shared a "primitivist" embrace of raw authenticity that rejected both the regime and high, civilized culture. (Scatological imaginations abounded.) In 1976 the arrest and trial of some of the underground's most prominent members inspired Havel and other persecuted intellectuals to launch a public protest. The scene had been set for a confrontation between the Normalization regime and those who came to be known as dissidents.[102]

In January 1977, Communist leaders were confronted with Charter 77, which emerged from a world of intellectuals who, while subsisting on translations, royalties from abroad, and reassigned work as stokers and other manual laborers, had maintained mutual friendships and a shared intellectual life in the shadow of political terror.[103] Originally signed by 241 individuals, the Charter demanded that Communist leaders adhere to promises to respect the human and civil rights embodied in the Helsinki Final Act signed by nearly every European country, the Soviet Union, the United States, and Canada in 1975. The Party Presidium launched a counterattack. They denounced the Charter as an "anti-state, counter-revolutionary document . . . prepared in collusion with foreign countries."[104] Writers, visual artists, composers, architects, singers, actors, and actresses were pressured to sign an "Anti-Charter," which denounced

> those who, in the unbridled pride of their narcissistic haughtiness, for selfish interests, or even for filthy lucre in various places all over the world . . . divorce and isolate themselves from their own people and its life and real interests and, with inexorable logic, become instruments of the anti-humanistic forces of imperialism and, in its service, the heralds of disruption and discord among nations.[105]

Secret police agents hounded and harassed the Chartists. Its leading spokesperson, Havel, was sentenced to six years in prison beginning in 1979.[106]

"With the Charter, things began to get chilly," Frejková writes. She knew a number of people who had signed the Charter, including two sons of Slánský trial victims with whom she had been in touch. Others in the world of theater were in contact with the Chartists, thus placing Frejková one or two degrees away from the dangerous world of dissent and underground literature. The decision not to sign the Charter weighed on her at a time when the traumas of her childhood enveloped her. "My guilt, instability, fears, and the foggy horrors of my childhood didn't allow it—I hadn't 'earned' the Charter. Also, against which injustice should I have protested? Against those, that I alone had unconsciously made possible? I went on, depressed."[107] Signing Charter 77 would almost certainly have meant losing her job, something that would have been an extraordinary sacrifice. "I would have died," she writes. "I didn't have a different life, a different life didn't exist [for me]."[108] Nor did she sign the Anti-Charter, despite being threatened and hounded by the authorities. Refusing to sign the Anti-Charter, as her colleagues in the theater knew all too well, could lead to being fired from your job, and worse. As a result, Frejková lived in fear of being thrown out of the theater, of losing her profession, the work that she lived for, uncertain "what would happen to me, to my body and mind, if they sacked me."[109]

The secret police harassed her nonetheless, and summoned her to their headquarters for interrogation. Agents had found Frejková's telephone number while conducting a raid on the apartment of Jan Šling, the son of another victim of the Slánský trials, Otto Šling. From there, as described by secret police documents, they constructed a web of connections linking Frejková to Czechoslovak émigrés, as well as to sons and daughters of other Slánský trial defendants. They pressed her about contacts abroad, especially in London. Although Frejková had been polite, the agents concluded that she had deliberately sought to avoid providing concrete information. She repeatedly spoke about her father's execution and the effect that it had had on her life. (Playing the role of the distraught, apolitical daughter of a Slánský trial victim was a deliberate strategy that she had planned in advance of the meeting, Frejková told me.)[110] Without being asked directly, but clearly reading their intent, Frejková refused to cooperate as an informant and asked to have nothing do to with the secret police. They paraphrased her as saying she did not want to have anything to do with politics, that she simply wanted to be left alone.[111]

The secret police nevertheless categorized Frejková as a "person of interest." An informant apparently living in her apartment building provided information for a follow-up report dated June 16, 1978. The informant described Frejková as a friendly, outgoing young woman with a good reputation in the building and as someone who enjoyed theater, music, and driving her Fiat 125 (license plate AT 33-94). She took care of her mother, a woman "with unstable nerves who had suffered from illness for many years." Traces of Stalinist-era antisemitism and other echoes of the trials ran through the report. It stated that Frejková's "notions regarding the Jewish question, as well as Zionism," were not known. The report also "confirmed" that her father had been "of Jewish origin" and had been condemned to death for "anti-state actions." His rehabilitation and the injustice of the trial were not mentioned. The report concluded that, while not an enemy of the state, Frejková had a "passive relationship" to the regime. Her neighbors considered her to be "nonpartisan," someone who neither attended meetings nor spoke about the politics of the Communist Party with her neighbors. She had not participated in the events of 1968–1969, the report incorrectly stated, and nothing from that era decorated her apartment.[112] Yet another report, dated November 1, 1978, detailed Frejková's conversations with a secret police informant, most likely someone she had trusted. The two had spoken about Frejková's friendly relationship with Goldstücker, the former ambassador to Israel who had been subjected to a show trial shortly after her father's execution, and his two daughters.[113]

———

Frejková has crafted two complimentary narratives of her life. One is the story of her life in the theater up to this point, as expressed in her online article for *Theater News*. A second runs through her book *Odd Roots*. Regarding the latter, Frejková has reminded me that her tale is about a solitary figure, a *solitér*, struggling through life. It is the story of a heroic effort to "be someone" born of individualist rigor and professional talent. It is also about being a damaged soul for many years and living a divided life—a secretly traumatized woman known best for her comedy roles. This account, based on a fascinating mixture of primary sources and personal memories, is told in hindsight. She knows how the story ends. She has reconstructed events and feelings while inhabiting a post-Communist world. While writing this chapter I have faced similar challenges, albeit from a different perspective in time and space, and with different purposes and methods. I paid careful attention to her words as I read them; when we met I tried to observe the customary practice in obtaining oral histories of asking open-ended questions. Rather than guide Frejková toward certain answers I let her tell her own story, which is, at its core, a tale of self and self-discovery. It is her life, after all. It is here, then, that her story, and this chapter finds its climax.

A few years before Charter 77, in 1975, Frejková began seeing an underground psychotherapist, driving 100 kilometers three times a week for visits.[114] (Coincidentally, her father's former secretary had visited the same therapist.) "I was moving on the peripheries of society, the only place where I was allowed to survive," she writes. "The feeling of guilt always clung to me, like pincers, and I never dared to claim anything for myself. Relations in our family were totally abnormal, our life was soaked with guilt that existed, relentlessly, under the surface and held us with totalitarian-like pincers." "I want to come to terms with this guilt," she continued, "I want to charge my parents and at the same time I want to vindicate them by narrating their lives, my life, how I became an individual who . . . has a right to be a member of society and have a place in the sun!"[115] The visits continued for many years, eventually leading Frejková to come to terms with the events from her past and with her father's life and death. These were trying times, she later wrote, yet "I slowly, but surely, found my place in society."[116] In the meantime she married and had a daughter while continuing to perform with the Jaroslav Průcha Theater. In 1986 she decided to give notice, somewhat unexpectedly, and without a clear plan for what was to come next. Then she became pregnant with her second daughter and attempted to create a new life.[117] Making new friends proved difficult, especially since people of her generation already had long-established relationships and friendships.[118] One day someone asked Frejková, a bit cynically perhaps, if she was happy. She answered, "Yes. . . . And only once I got home did it occur to me: what a miracle!"[119]

Frejková eventually returned to the theater, albeit in a different form and in a different community. In 1986 she auditioned to join a young, unofficial avant-garde troupe, the Free and United Directors (*Volné spojení režisérů*), in Prague. While at first wary of the newcomer, she wrote, they then softened and, incredulously, realized that "my soul was the same as theirs."[120] Belonging among the young avant-gardists required effort. She wore a hairstyle from the 1930s, one that her mother had also worn for a while, which made her look like "an old lady." Did these young people, she asked, really want to go to the pub with someone twice their age? It was demanding work as well, especially for a mother of two whose colleagues were young people with few family responsibilities. Frejková often spent her days caring for her children and her evenings rehearsing with her fellow avant-gardists. She slept only a few hours a day between these two commitments. She had to build new relationships and rely upon her past achievements to do so.[121]

Nor could she return to the world of theater to which she had once belonged. Having not performed for several years, she was considered "dead." In one instance, upon walking into a club frequented by members of an official theater, former colleagues and friends either ignored her or shifted uncomfortably. Frejková imagined how an outsider might have described the scene: "A relatively normal woman is standing right in the middle of a crowd of people, and suddenly small groups pull away from her . . . until she finds herself in a vacuum. I begin to smile. From a bird's-eye view, it looked as if I stank." Another sort of chasm had opened up between Frejková and acquaintances from her previous life, most of whom, understandably, did not comprehend her inner struggles. Actors, she wrote, are often driven by a desire to stand out, to be appreciated for being odd, different. She nevertheless sought out a "normal" existence, a "normal" life in society. "I had had enough of this extraordinariness," she concluded.[122]

At this point, the story of Communism in Czechoslovakia was also reaching its climax, although no one knew it at the time. For dissidents, these were some of their darkest days. During much of the 1980s, the 1960s generation of opposition intellectuals in Czechoslovakia, as in neighboring Poland, appeared to be scattered, beaten down. In 1983, after almost four years in prison, Havel was granted a compassionate release by the Communist authorities. His health had greatly deteriorated in prison and recovery was slow. Physically weakened, he endured bouts of depression, which he soothed with the help of sedatives. In April 1987 Havel published an essay in the underground magazine *Revolver Revue* titled "Stories and Totalitarianism," which his biographer Kieran Williams has described as "full of graveyard gloom."[123] He wrote that the regime had dispensed with "fiery utopia builders spreading discontent with their dreams of a better future." In their place, under the catchphrase "really existing socialism," they created a society in which there is "no hiding place, no reservation, where one is safe from the virus of nihilisation."[124] To make his point, Havel described a scene in the subway:

All you have to do, for example, is ride the subway escalators and observe the faces of people going in the opposite direction. This journey is a brief pause in the daily rat race, a sudden stoppage of life, a frozen moment which may reveal more about us than we know. Perhaps it is one of those legendary "moments of truth." In this situation, a person suddenly stands

outside of all relationships; he is in public, but alone with himself. The faces moving past are all strangely empty, strained,
almost lifeless, without hope, without longing, without desire.
The eyes are expressionless, dull.[125]

We now know, however, that the ground was shifting beneath Havel's
feet as he penned "Stories and Totalitarianism," bringing changes
that would eventually create the conditions for the possibility of revolution. Throughout the Communist Eastern bloc, the economic situation had begun to worsen. Shortages and other signs of a declining
economy threatened a regime that had staked its legitimacy on providing citizens with the socialist "good life." Another challenge to the
regime came in the person of Mikhail Gorbachev, a young(ish) reformer who became the Soviet general secretary in 1985. Under the
rubric of perestroika, Gorbachev called for economic reforms and an
end to corruption. Other efforts toward more openness, called glasnost,
promised a greater ability to speak freely in public, to publish and broadcast without censorship. Eventually, Gorbachev signaled the end of the
Brezhnev Doctrine, essentially nullifying the justification for the Warsaw
Pact invasion and making it clear that Soviet troops would not interfere
in domestic political affairs. Just as in the 1960s, rifts between conservatives and reformers developed within the Czechoslovak Communist
Party, often around questions regarding central, rationalized economic
planning and the "leading role of the party." These debates, as Michal
Pullmann has argued, further exposed the facade of Normalization and
its promise of the good life while splintering the discourse and fragile
ideological unity that held the party together. New discourses questioned
the "normality" and stability of the regime but also created space for
new expectations and demands.[126]

It did not help that Husák's eventual successor, the conservative-
leaning Miloš Jakeš, known for his odd, grammatically challenged
pronouncements, epitomized an aging leadership increasingly characterized by "incompetence, impotence, lack of direction, endemic cor-

ruption, and fear of change."[127] Other cracks in the facade appeared as well. A number of leading experts and enterprise managers called for reform. By 1987 there were limited efforts to decentralize the economy, such as by legalizing small-scale business enterprises. Sociologists and those working within the Prognostika Institute turned their attention to real-existing problems, rather than fanciful, statistically supported notions of an imagined present and future that ignored the reality of day-to-day struggles. By 1989 some, such as the young *prognostika* expert and future prime minister Miloš Zeman, declared that, in the economic interest of the country, the regime had to go. The longer the regime stayed in power, the deeper the economic hole, he predicted, thus condemning the country to "its new role as a backward country" that no revolution or democratic change could make better.[128]

Movements calling for reform and revolution also gained ground outside of the regime's institutions. By the mid-1980s, again as throughout much of Communist Eastern Europe, a younger generation began to complement, and sometimes surpass, the efforts of dissidents and other self-described opposition figures. In Prague and throughout the country, young people proved to be the driving forces behind all sorts of single-issue concerns, from environmental degradation to religious freedom, women's rights, and the threat of nuclear war. Official party bodies, such as the Socialist Union of Youth, quietly acted as an umbrella organization for various youth-led efforts and initiatives.[129] Czechoslovak youth published their own underground materials, such as the *Revolver Revue,* whose text and stunning graphic design they painstakingly produced at home.[130] They benefited from a loosening of censorship, new technologies, and access to information from abroad (the regime stopped jamming Radio Free Europe in 1988).[131] They in turn had allies within the "gray zones" of the party and state bureaucracy who supported change and eventually became some of the most influential voices in the revolution. They often shared, according to James Krapfl, a common ethos, a common call for "humanness" or "humanity" that echoed notions inherited from the reform Communists of the

1960s and ideas found in dissident writings. Principles such as non-violence and democracy complemented grander calls for human-ness at every level of administration. Calls for humanness rejected the Communist regime not "because it was socialist but because it was unresponsively bureaucratic and 'inhumane.'"[132]

These movements, often driven by youth, also coalesced on the streets of cities across the country. Prague became the main stage for popular protests in a story unfolding before people's eyes, at an unex-pectedly rapid rate, without a clear notion of how the story would end. Protesters met on Wenceslas Square on August 21, 1988, to mark the anniversary of the Warsaw Pact invasion. In January 1989, student activists and others organized a Palach Week of protests that were met with vicious reprisals by riot police. As summer turned to fall, Communist regimes negotiated their way out of power in Poland and Hungary. Other regimes, such as East Germany, teetered under the pressure of popular protests. On November 17, 1989, 1,500 riot po-lice viciously beat student protesters as they marched down National Boulevard (Národní třída). Rumors spread that one of the students, Martin Šmíd, had been killed. The rumors proved to be untrue, but they added to a sense of disgust that mobilized further protests throughout the country. Hundreds of thousands of people filled Wenceslas Square calling for the end of the regime. Havel, Dubček, and others spoke and received resounding rounds of applause as onlookers shook their keys, a signal for members of the regime to go.

Padraic Kenny has suggested that there was something carni-valesque about the events of 1989. Humor and absurdity mixed with the unmistakable notion that everything was being turned on its head. The theater and theatrics were also an unmistakable presence. In the years before 1989, theater directors had become more daring. Various alternative theaters, such as the avant-garde troupe to which Frejková belonged, staged productions in venues throughout the city.[133] Un-authorized publications and lectures complemented unofficial per-formances.[134] Beyond theater walls, students, actors, and singers per-

Actors onstage at Divadlo na Vinohradech, November 22, 1989. ČTK.

formed at protests and in town squares while others organized so-called happenings.[135] Underground cassette tapes were passed around throughout the country, including one by the actor Miloš Kopecký, who had a simple message for the country's leaders: "If the fate of socialism is as important for you as you always stress, you have an excellent opportunity to do something good for socialism: resign."[136] Just after the November 17 attack by riot police on National Boulevard, theaters across the city went on strike and opened their doors for public discussions. Students at the Academy of Performing Arts helped to mobilize other students. Onstage, performers joined others throughout the city and the country in calling for a general strike.

At the Činoherní Klub theater, Havel assembled dissidents and others opposed to the regime under an umbrella group called the Civic Forum. The Civic Forum's headquarters then moved to the basement of the Magic Lantern Theater, where they devised strategies to negotiate with an increasingly weakened Communist regime. They also

Václav Havel in the Činoherní Klub theater, November 19, 1989. ČTK / Petr Mazanec.

held news conferences in the theater and met with a select number of journalists. The young British commentator Timothy Garton Ash described being struck by "the speed, the improvisation, the merriness, and the absolutely central role of Václav Havel, who," he added, "was at once director, playwright, stage manager, and leading actor in this, his greatest play." Other "actors and performers" included "dissidents and students, Slovaks and a symbolic worker." Dubček, back from political exile in Slovakia, enjoyed top billing. Various *prognostika* experts, including another future prime minister, Václav Klaus, also played various roles. Finally, at 7:30 p.m. on November 24, word arrived that the entire leadership of the Communist Party had resigned. "Havel leaps to his feet, makes the V for Victory sign, and embraces Dubček," Ash wrote. "Someone brings them champagne. Havel raises his glass and says 'to a free Czechoslovakia!'"[137] In the ensuing days, demonstrations turned to celebrations on Wenceslas Square.

Frejková heard about the November demonstrations while at her cottage outside of Prague. Upon learning of the rumored death of Martin Šmíd, she and her family quickly packed their things and headed home to the city. (Šmid had been the son of a family friend.) She and other members of the Free and United Directors joined the protests on Wenceslas Square. Just after the Communist leaders resigned she was on Letná, along with her husband, their daughters Marianka and Josefinka, and tens of thousands of other Czechoslovak citizens. Marianka sat on her father's shoulders and Josefinka, despite having to stand in wet shoes, sang along as Jaroslav Hutka, a formerly exiled folksinger, performed onstage. "It was unbelievable, just now I have tears in my eyes," Frejková told me.[138] A few months later Frejková, the daughter of a man unjustly executed as a traitor to the nation and Communism, performed in *A Midsummer Night's Dream* in the newly opened gardens of Černín Palace, home to the Ministry of Foreign Affairs. The new foreign minister was Jiří Dienstbier, a former Chartist, whom Frejková had known before 1989.[139]

On New Year's Day 1990 Havel addressed the country on national television—not as a revolutionary dissident, but now as the country's new president with an office in the Castle. Sporting a gray tie and sitting in front of a sparsely filled bookcase, he delivered a speech that, at the beginning, was surprisingly somber, yet determined. As president, he promised, he would not lie to his countrymen about the current state of affairs or construct fanciful visions of the country and its people. Instead, Havel spoke about the "obsolete economy" and the lack of funding for education, and about environmental degradation and diminished life expectancy rates. He spoke of the country's "contaminated moral environment" born of a system that had left citizens selfish, parochial, and unable to think in terms of the common good: "Our main enemy today is our own bad traits. . . . The main struggle will have to be fought in this field."[140]

Havel also struck a hopeful, inspiring tone. The peaceful revolution of the past year had "shown the enormous human, moral, and spiritual potential and civic culture that had slumbered in our society under the enforced mask of apathy." These virtues, he continued, should be the basis for a democratic order that emphasized moral awareness and a sense of responsibility, words that echoed those of the interwar president Tomáš Masaryk. Havel then offered his own post-Communist vision for Czechoslovakia:

> You may ask what kind of republic I dream of. Let me reply: I dream of a republic independent, free, and democratic, of a republic economically prosperous and yet socially just; in short, of a humane republic which serves the individual and which therefore holds the hope that the individual will serve it in turn. Of a republic of well-rounded people, because without such [people] it is impossible to solve any of our problems, human, economic, ecological, social, or political.

As elections approached, he declared, "the important thing is that the winners will be the best of us, in the moral, civic, and professional sense, regardless of their political affiliations." He promised to ensure that the elections would be free and fair; to encourage mutual respect among Czechs and Slovaks; and to provide for the disadvantaged within society. He concluded by promising to recast the role of president. Unlike political elites of the past, he said, "I want to be a president who will speak less and work more. To be a president who . . . will always be present among his fellow citizens and listen to them well."[141]

Yet the rush of events led to the establishment of political parties that often sidelined former revolutionaries, parties often tainted by corruption and influenced by monied elites. As in most European systems, the presidency held very little practical power, as opposed to the prime minister, a position held for many years by Havel's archrival, Václav Klaus, a star economist turned neoliberal reformer who had found a place on the Magic Lantern's stage in 1989. Upon being re-elected in 1993, Havel announced that his role was not so much to take direct part in decision making but, through words, to "be felt in the background as a certain guarantee of the legitimacy of those deci-sions." His job, he continued, was to provoke thought and act as a "watchman of political culture."[142] He imagined a democracy of active citizens, a society enlivened and improved by civil society. Havel re-mained in office until 2003, when, in poor health, he retired to focus on writing. Several weeks later Klaus, who was also the leader of the country's largest conservative party, was elected president.

After 1989, Frejková's work, life, and visions of her own past com-bined in new ways. While Frejková was growing up, her parents were determined that she integrate fully into Communist Czechoslovak so-ciety. She said, "[They] never gave me a single chance to be anything other than a Czech." After 1989, however, she pursued searching ques-tions as to whether "I am a German, a Czech or a Jew . . . [and] ended with [the conclusion] that I am, simply put, a mix, that I am some-thing thrown together."[143] It was a role well suited for the time. Many former dissidents and others, eager to recall a past largely ignored by the Communist regime, slowly began to confront issues surrounding the Holocaust and the postwar expulsion of the Germans. Especially in Prague, literature, public markers, and tourist brochures often em-braced a nostalgic vision of a pre–World War II multicultural Prague of Czechs, Germans, and Jews.[144] Even though under Communism Frejková had only minimal contact with Prague's Jewish community, and with Jewish culture, she soon found herself performing at events organized by Jewish cultural leaders intended for locals and returning émigrés. She even learned Yiddish and performed concerts in Yiddish.

Similar to many artists, Frejková also had to adjust quickly to new freedoms as well as the demands of capitalism and diminishing state-sponsored support. On the advice of colleagues based in the West, she joined the actors' guild, which worked to help actors navigate the brave new world of entertainment in a free market economy. She soon hired an agent and began working solely as a freelancer, appearing in a number of television shows and films. Yet she also became convinced that work should not be a substitute for life or constitute her entire world, secure in the knowledge that "now I can remove the makeup after a performance." She savored moments when she left work and wandered through the Old Town, "enjoying the feeling that I am walking on these old, narrow streets and that a bit of me belonged here, too."[145]

5

GLOBAL CITY

ℚ☉

In February 2008, nineteen-year-old Duong Nguyen, a second-semester student at Prague's Metropolitan University, published her first blog post on Aktuálně.cz, one of the Czech Republic's first online news outlets. Nguyen's blog post, "The Dual Life of the Banana Children," was part manifesto, part self-reflection. She also asked some pressing questions on her post:

> They call us banana children—yellow skin and white core. And this creates a number of problems. . . . We have Vietnamese parents, many of us were born in Vietnam. We grew up, however, on the other side of the world. Are we still Vietnamese? Or are we characterized as such only by the color of our skin, and inside we're really Czechs?

Themes of duality, of in-betweenness, of struggles for a sense of belonging ran through this post and others that she typed out as spring turned to summer. "Because we live in two worlds, two cultures, that are quite different from one another, it's never boring," she wrote. "Whenever someone asks me where I feel at home, I never give a one-word answer," she concluded. "Nor do I know for whom I would cheer if, by some sports miracle, Vietnam and the Czech Republic were playing in the World Cup final."[1]

By 2008, nearly one out of every 100 Praguers belonged to the Vietnamese diaspora, yet Vietnamese Praguers barely figured in powerful imaginations of the city.[2] Václav Havel's nostalgic visions of Prague as the multicultural home of Czechs, Germans, and Jews largely ignored the Vietnamese, even though he did champion ethnic tolerance more broadly. Havel's archrival Václav Klaus held a competing vision, but he too took little notice of the Vietnamese in his midst. Klaus's vision, which became more and more predominant as the years passed, did much, however, to shape the world in which Nguyen and others of her generation came of age. Whereas Havel imagined a vibrant civil society defined by an active citizenry and pluralism, Klaus staked his claim on national visions that combined anti-Communism and the gospel of free market capitalism. He imagined a nation of largely apolitical Czechs, now free of Soviet domination and central planning, primed to realize their proclivities for hard work and economic prowess. These public stances belied a reality in which actual reforms moved slowly and Communist-era cronies benefited from privatization in Prague and elsewhere. Klaus also trafficked in the language of national provincialism, even as Prague, to the advantage of many of his followers, became more integrated into Europe and the wider global economy. After the end of Communism, Prague, more than ever, became a global city in which goods, money, and ideas flowed into and out of the nation's capital. People, too, flowed into and out of the city. Some stayed.

During that same period, Praguers such as Nguyen were also engaging in radically new practices of belonging. Nguyen and many of her peers created their own virtual spaces to meet, console each other, and debate. Unlike their parents, who gathered in large marketplaces and formed traditional, on-the-ground organizations, Nguyen's generation connected online—in the comment sections of blog posts, via email, and on social media. They met and mobilized online. They formed networks across space that led them to create "real" face-to-face gatherings and associations. Similar to second-generation migrants throughout Europe, Nguyen and her peers struggled with a sense of belonging in a nation-state that implied a national homogeneity that was racially coded. Nguyen's very presence, combined with her native Czech, her knowledge of Czech history and culture, and her "Czech" mannerisms, required her readers to ask a simple question. What does it mean to be Czech? Who should belong to the national community? Nguyen and her generation struggled with similar questions, asking how best to navigate their Czech and Vietnamese worlds. Nguyen and her cohort lived in a confusing, in-between world in which digital information and ideas flashed at lightning speed across vast internet networks within and beyond Prague. Amid the swirl, Nguyen typed on her keyboard as her world and the city she called home changed around her.

———

Nearly a century and a half after Czech-speaking liberals began to realize their visions of "golden, Slavic Prague," Czech leaders after the fall of Communism added their own layer of national coding to the cityscape. Particular emphasis was placed on transforming the socialist city into an anti-Communist one. The first step was to erase Communist heroes from the cityscape, part of a larger attempt to imagine the Communist era as an aberration in the natural flow of Czech national history. Communist-era monuments were quickly removed. Street names were changed. New national heroes and victims took their place. City leaders renamed the square in front of Charles University after Jan Palach, the student who burned himself alive to protest the 1968 Warsaw Pact invasion. They embedded a monument in the cobblestones on Wenceslas Square marking the spot where the self-immolation took place. A bronze depiction of hands raised in desperate protest appeared

The Memorial to the Victims of Communism below Petřín Hill shortly after its unveiling in 2002. ČTK / René Volfík.

on National Street to commemorate student marchers beaten by riot police in November 1989. Working with city hall, in 2002 the Confederation of Political Prisoners installed a series of all-male figures that fade into nothingness as the viewer's eye follows a set of stairs upward toward Petřín Hill. At the bottom of the stairs a bronze plaque with raw statistical information about imprisonments, exiles, and deaths under Communism completes Olbram Zoubek's chilling Memorial to the Victims of Communism.[3]

These efforts complemented a cascade of legislative acts that sought to distinguish the new regime from the old. They also sought justice for crimes of the past. In 1990 the government granted total rehabilitation to Communist political prisoners. Nearly all of the almost 9,000 employees of the Communist secret police were fired. A year later, over the vociferous protest of President Havel, the legislature passed a "lustration" law that, in theory, excluded Communist Party functionaries and former secret police officers from jobs in a number of public offices. Most controversial was the law threatening to "lustrate" people whom the Communist secret police had deemed as potential recruits, ex post facto allegations that often relied on sketchy documentary evidence and, in the end, were difficult to prove. A 1994 law returned property taken from individuals following the 1948 Communist coup, conveniently avoiding the question of returning property stolen during the Holocaust or seized during the postwar expulsion of Czechoslovakia's Germans.[4]

The break from the past, of course, was far from complete. The lustration law exempted candidates for the legislature and also Communist-era government ministers. Remnants of the Communist Party survived to contest elections following a number of organizational and name changes. The death penalty was abolished in 1990, but Pankrác prison remained in operation.[5] The Moscow metro stop in the traditionally working-class district of Smíchov was renamed Angel, which had been the station's commonly used name under Communism.[6] In the southwest of the city, officials changed the name of the Kosmonautů metro station to Háje ("Groves"). The nearby monument depicting two cosmonauts (one Soviet, one Czechoslovak) waving remained, however, as did other physical remains from Communist-era monuments scattered throughout the city.[7] One of the main thoroughfares from the city, Lenin Street, became Europe Street, but Moscow Street, located just beyond the city center, remained unchanged. Before 1948, Moscow Street had been named after František Palacký, except for a time under Nazi rule when it honored Otto von Bismarck.[8]

The Communist past also informed new Czech national imaginations and new political agendas. According to Kieran Williams, Prime Minister Klaus and his followers visualized "the Czech nation as Europeans naturally inclined to democracy, hard work, commerce, and self-reliance," characteristics envisioned in contrast to life under Normalization.[9] Their proclaimed faith in a relatively unhindered free market stood in stark contrast to the Communists' faith in a centrally controlled economy. Rapid privatization, Klaus and those around him proclaimed, would prevent the return of Communism.[10] In their rush to privatize state property and enterprises, however, Klaus and others presided over massive corruption and the concentration of wealth among a well-placed few. Ironically, former Communist elites translated their connections and knowledge into newfound fortune. Privatization schemes that enabled massive corruption were concocted, in part, by experts from the Communist era, including Klaus himself.[11] Privatization also fed into a larger culture of political corruption inherited from the Communist era. This corruption poisoned not only Klaus's Civic Democrats and their rivals, Miloš Zeman's Social Democrats, but also civil servants and officeholders in general. Transparency International's 2000 corruption index, based on worldwide surveys of international businesspeople, the public, and country experts, placed the Czech Republic in forty-second position, just ahead of Belarus. By 2008 its overall score had improved slightly, but its ranking had dropped to forty-fifth in the world.[12]

Throughout the 1990s, political rhetoric often contrasted with reality on the ground. Bluster aside, many reforms, such as the privatization of banks and the deregulation of prices, proceeded slowly, especially in comparison to neighboring Poland. Crucial economic, judicial, and legal reforms, which faced considerable obstacles from entrenched elites and cultures of corruption, were realized in good part due to incentives created by the European Union's accession process.[13] (The Czech Republic, along with seven other post-Communist countries, formally joined the European Union in 2004.) Claims about the Czech nation's innate democratic character also flew in the face of Klaus's behind-the-scenes machinations that, in 1993, split Czechoslovakia into the Czech Republic and Slovakia without a vote. A petition signed by 2.5 million citizens calling for a referendum on the question was simply ignored. The split with Slovakia concentrated Klaus's power, but for many people it also represented the logical culmination of Czech national history. Prague, they argued, had at last become the capital of a truly independent and ethnically homogeneous nation-state. Over time, Klaus and others trafficked in a provincial nationalism that mixed xenophobia with attacks on international institutions such as the European Union. Yet the reality was that Prague had become more integrated into Europe and the world than ever before, often to the gain of political elites who used such rhetoric in their campaigns.

Similar to capital cities throughout post-Communist Central Europe, Prague disproportionately benefited from its position as a legislative and financial center as well as a hub for trade, transportation, and ideas. By 1994 almost a third of the country's jobs in finance and insurance, and nearly three-quarters of its jobs in foreign trade, were located in Prague, which accounted for just 12 percent of the country's inhabitants.[14] Unemployment in Prague was far below the national average. Average gross domestic product (GDP) for the city was far above the national average.[15] The transformation of Prague's cityscape increasingly reflected its growing status as a global, increasingly prosperous capital. Ikea opened its first Prague store in 1991; by 2004 two enormous Ikea complexes had opened at opposite ends of the city. Together, the Ikea stores could have filled Wenceslas Square in its entirety.[16] Big-box stores opened near the end stops of subway lines and along highways that circled the city's peripheries. Near the center, one of Europe's largest shopping centers opened in 2001 just a few steps from Angel Station. It inhabited a space previously dominated by a Communist-era factory, which had, among other things, built streetcars for the Eastern bloc.[17] McDonald's and Starbucks complemented the arrival of multinational corporate outposts throughout the city. The French jeweler Cartier opened a boutique just off Old Town Square.

Prague's privileged economic position vis-á-vis the rest of the Czech Republic would remain unchallenged up to and throughout the 2008 economic crisis.[18] Much of this economic success was also thanks to tourism. "First things first," the 2007 edition of the *Rough Guide to Prague* began. "Prague is a beautiful city. With some six hundred years of architecture virtually untouched by natural disaster or war, few other cities, anywhere in Europe, look as good."[19] Renovations and colorful paint jobs, combined with the allure of inexpensive beer, transformed a previously gray historical center into a booming tourist destination. Hotels, guidebooks, and Prague's refurbished airport formed part of a larger capitalist structure designed to provide consumers with a particular set of experiences—walking, drinking, eating, or enjoying a concert. This infrastructure also positioned tourists to consume Prague's city center visually, to gaze at "must-see" sites.[20] In 2008 alone almost 500,000 people visited the Old Town City Hall.[21] Many more gazed at the astronomical clock on its southern exterior, often the starting point for a pilgrimage that followed the traditional processional route of kings from Old Town Square, across Charles Bridge, and up to Prague Castle. In 2011 approximately 5.1 million tourists came to Prague, which had a population of a little less than 1.2 million that year.[22]

After the fall of Communism the Czech Republic enjoyed low levels of income inequality—among the lowest levels in the world—yet the post-1989 economic gap between Prague and much of the rest of the country (especially former industrial regions) provoked considerable resentment outside the city. Within Prague, economic inequality and opportunity gaps accelerated after the fall of Communism. Young

Cartier boutique on Paris Street, just off Old Town Square, in 2008. ČTK / René Volfík.

English-speaking university graduates could most easily plug into the new economy. For pensioners and state employees left behind, however, real incomes dropped. Unemployed workers often had to seek out low-skill, low-paying jobs throughout the city such as kitchen work and cleaning services in hotels and restaurants in the city center.[23] This sort of transition proved especially difficult for former industrial workers. Once celebrated members of the relatively closed, secure economic system of Communism, many now suffered from post-Communist economic insecurity and diminished status.[24] Despite the promise of rent controls, elderly Praguers living in the city center were often forced to move, pressured out by ambitious property owners. Meager pensions did not go far in the city center.[25]

Migrants also filled low-paying economic positions created by post-Communist market capitalism, thus transforming the city further. Ukrainians, Mongolians, and Bulgarians offset labor shortages in factories and restaurants, as well as on constructions sites. In 1993 the Czech statistical office counted approximately 78,000 people with long-term and permanent-resident visas in the country. In 2008 the number peaked at roughly 439,000, or approximately 4 percent of the Czech Republic's total population.[26] In 2008 more than 141,000 registered foreigners, not counting asylum seekers and undocumented migrants, lived in the city—nearly one-third of the total number of registered foreigners in the country and one-tenth of the city's population.[27] Their labor underwrote an economic boom that Praguers enjoyed from 2000 to 2007, but at a cost. Employment contractors and dubious middlemen often charged high prices that left many migrant workers deep in debt. Unlike the city's Roma population, who have long been victims of vicious attacks and structural discrimination, the city's other ethnic communities received little attention from otherwise well-meaning locals and international human rights organizations.[28] Most migrants to Prague were both visible and invisible, there but not acknowledged as being there, except when singled out for racist abuse. Perhaps no other migrant group fits this description better than Prague's Vietnamese diaspora—a community intimately bound up with the city's Communist and post-Communist past.

———

Duong Nguyen was born in Vietnam and arrived in the Czech Republic in 1995, when she was just eight years old. Her family's connections to Czechoslovakia stretched back to the Communist period. Her father was born in 1951, the oldest of nine siblings, in Thanh Hoá-que, a city in the northwest of Vietnam, roughly 100 miles south of Hanoi. While still a teenager he was drafted into the army. After surviving his country's war he parlayed his status as a veteran and member of Vietnam's intelligentsia class to travel to Czechoslovakia in 1975. A quick study, he learned Czech and soon became a translator for Vietnamese student groups. Nguyen's mother was born in 1962 in Hanoi, the oldest of five children. Her father was at war for much of her childhood. Her mother, who secretly suffered from serious mental illness, was either working or in the hospital. Duong's mother, too, managed to travel to Czechoslovakia with a student group, where she met Duong's father while he was visiting a friend in her dormitory in northern Bohemia.[29] They fell in love. As Nguyen wrote, her mother became pregnant and, in her seventh month "got a burst of adrenaline . . . so the family moved back to Vietnam because they wanted to raise me as a Vietnamese."[30] Back in Hanoi, they hoped to make a good life for themselves. Their expectations were soon disappointed, however. As the oldest among their siblings, Duong's parents were pressured to help support their respective families, a pressure intensified by the assumption that Vietnamese who had lived abroad were well-off. Duong's father worked for a pittance at the Ministry of Education, and her mother worked in hotels, candy stores, and flower shops. Despite decent employment and party membership, they could barely support themselves while fulfilling obligations to the rest of the family.[31]

The couple then decided to return to the post-Communist Czech Republic, where they sold clothes, shoes, and other items in markets throughout eastern Bohemia. They often rose at 5:00 a.m. to head out to the markets. After they had achieved some initial success, someone broke the lock on a cart attached to their car, which sent them into debt. They started anew and, after many years selling goods from market stands, they managed to rent space for two shops and an apartment in the town of Třemošnice, east of Prague. In a room above one of the shops, Duong took care of the household and her newborn sister while also studying. She also helped out with the family business. Riding on her bike, she often ferried goods between the family shops, one located on the town square, the other near the bus station. Her parents, who worked long hours and over the weekends, also hired a Czech nanny, an elderly woman who resided in the building where she and her sister lived. As the years went on, the threesome visited sites throughout the region. They celebrated the Christmas holidays together. Duong and her sister took care of their nanny, their Czech grandmother, when she fell ill.[32]

Nguyen's family history is part of a larger story about migration during and after Communism. It is also a more complicated account than one that focuses solely on images of the Berlin Wall and armed border guards.[33] There was much truth in these images, of course. Throughout their rule, Communist regimes drew upon long-standing fears of discrimination and "white slavery" to warn against migration to the West. They used violence and the threat of violence to prevent labor and intellectual talent from fleeing abroad.[34] Still, between 1950 and 1989, nearly 500,000 Czechoslovak citizens emigrated from the country. They were escaping persecution, seeking economic opportunity, or both.[35] Migration went in other directions, too. Communists from across the European continent, including Hana Frejková's parents, arrived in Prague, eager to build socialism. Czechoslovak, East German, and Polish citizens could travel freely across shared borders beginning in the 1970s.[36] Beyond Europe, Communist Czechoslovakia fought a Cold War battle for hearts and minds. In the 1960s freedom fighters from Angola and South Africa studied at a military academy in Prague. Czechoslovak military experts traveled to Africa to advise liberation movements in Guinea-Bissau, Mozambique, Zimbabwe, and Namibia. Czechoslovakia also welcomed, often under the rubric of various friendship treaties, university students and technical experts from Cuba, Afghanistan, Libya, Iraq, Syria, and North Korea—countries that Czechoslovak students and experts traveled to as well.[37]

None of these international "friendships" was more developed or deeper than Czechoslovakia's relationship with Vietnam. Czechoslovakia established an embassy in Hanoi just months after the Democratic Republic of Vietnam obtained independence from French colonial rule in 1954. Over the next few decades, as Cold War tensions led to war on the Vietnamese peninsula, Czechoslovakia provided military assistance and loans as well as agricultural, transport, and other technical experts in support of Communist-led forces. Czechoslovakia also sent goods, such as condensed milk and paper, and equipment for hydroelectric plants, cement plants, and breweries. Czechoslovak medical personnel staffed the Vietnamese-Czechoslovak Friendship Hospital in Haiphong, which was completed in 1959.[38] This friendship also entailed welcoming Vietnamese to Czechoslovak institutions of higher education and integrating trainees and apprentice workers into Czechoslovak factories. By 1979 approximately 600 Vietnamese were studying at Czechoslovak universities and educational institutes, more than any other cohort of foreign students.[39] By that time, Communist Vietnam was in desperate need of outside support. The war had left 2 million dead. The American bombing campaign had destroyed more than 30 million acres of land. The massive out-migration that followed the fall of Saigon depleted the country of know-how and other valuable human resources. Vietnam's final split with Communist China, combined with the United States' successful efforts to isolate Vietnam economically, further contributed to making the country one of the poorest in the world.[40]

Czechoslovakia's efforts vis-à-vis Vietnam were, not surprisingly, part of a larger Communist project. The Soviet Union, East Germany, and Bulgaria had also signed "friendship treaties" with Vietnam. Together, these treaties helped the Soviet Union's foreign policy objectives while promoting a particular version of socialist internationalism and economic development among its non-Western allies. Vietnamese guest worker labor in Czechoslovakia was originally thought of in these terms, and also as a carefully coordinated means of foreign aid. Few

Czechoslovak officials believed that their country's economy would benefit from the influx of workers from Vietnam and other socialist allies such as Cuba or Mongolia. The Vietnamese government vetted and selected people to be assigned to positions in Czechoslovakia. Migrants often benefited from connections to the Vietnamese Communist Party or the government in general. Others had been celebrated as war heroes. In the 1980s roughly 300,000 unskilled Vietnamese workers traveled to Czechoslovakia and other "friendship treaty" signatories under expanded labor programs.[41]

These expanded labor programs, however, point to ways in which the Communist world was becoming increasingly entangled in the global capitalist economy. Saturday Vietnamese open-air markets offered Praguers and other Czechoslovaks hard-to-find goods, especially clothing, obtained from abroad. Czechoslovak leaders, increasingly desperate for consumer goods, came to believe that Vietnamese migrants could fill gaps in the Czechoslovak labor force, and thus hastened their arrival.[42] Direct flights connected Prague with airports in Hanoi and Ho Chi Minh City. Other Vietnamese already in the country, such as those graduating from Czechoslovak universities, were typically allowed to stay. For Vietnamese migrants, old and new, this was a privileged opportunity to experience "the West" and send wages back home to family members, even if the Vietnamese state took its own cut.[43] Vietnam's 1986 Đổi mới economic reforms further accelerated out-migration to Czechoslovakia. The Vietnamese state vigorously encouraged emigration for an economy partially fueled by remittances. These same reforms laid the groundwork for capitalist-style trade and commerce linking Vietnam with migrants abroad.[44]

Border restrictions loosened after the fall of Communism in Czechoslovakia allowed for another, much larger wave of Vietnamese migration. Soon Czechoslovak officials severed work contracts with many Vietnamese migrant workers and expelled them from workers' dorms. Lacking the proper paperwork, many were unable to find employment, and some returned to Vietnam. Unlike in the former East

Germany, however, Vietnamese migrants in Czechoslovakia were not strong-armed into leaving the country.[45] Many thus chose to remain. They in turn acted as a "pulling" force that brought family members and other Vietnamese to Czechoslovakia. By 2008 roughly 60,000 Vietnamese were living in the Czech Republic, and roughly a sixth of the Vietnamese migrant population lived in Prague.[46]

Many of these original migrants then orchestrated new roles for the Vietnamese community amid the rapid economic transformations of post-Communist Czechoslovakia. Vietnamese kiosks and open-air bazaars first established under Communism benefited from the emergence of relatively unregulated capitalism. Cross-national contacts and relationships forged during the Communist period also contributed to their success.[47] Post-Communist economic reforms created additional spaces for Vietnamese migrants. State-owned shops rapidly collapsed. Many traders, with the help of leading community members, filled the vacuum by establishing corner stores throughout the country. Others opened nail salons, dry cleaners, and Vietnamese restaurants.[48] Specialists (*dịch vụ*) helped new arrivals with visa questions, tax documents, and other dealings with Czech bureaucratic structures—all within a system that permitted relatively free movement of people and goods across the border.[49] The economic boom years from 2000 to 2008 saw another wave of Vietnamese migrants who typically worked for "old settler" businesses or arrived as guest workers recruited by employment agencies to work in Czech factories. Unlike their predecessors, second-wave migrants lacked powerful connections to the Vietnamese government and came from poorer families in the countryside. Thus, they often remained dependent on *dịch vụ* and "old settlers," not to mention unscrupulous recruitment agencies and "middlemen." Factory owners often underpaid them, taking advantage of the precarious visa status of these migrants and their desperate need to keep their jobs.[50] Similar to labor migrants across Europe, they become especially vulnerable once the economic boom was over.[51]

———————

In the fall of 2007 Nguyen enrolled in Prague's Metropolitan University, a recently established private institution located east of the city center. When she arrived from the countryside she initially relied on family friends who helped her move into her dormitory, but she quickly made friends at the university, some of whom had Vietnamese backgrounds. She met other second-generation Vietnamese students thanks to gatherings organized by Klub Hanoi, a local youth group. These newfound friends and acquaintances began discussing their experiences as children of Vietnamese migrants, as Czech-speaking Vietnamese who also felt "Czech." Shortly after the New Year, the editor of Aktuálně.cz invited Nguyen to write a blog. When she was growing up in Třemošnice Nguyen had a computer, and she corresponded with an English-speaking Vietnamese pen pal by email. But before coming to Prague she had never read a blog, let alone written one.[52]

"Names offer a simple point of entry into this muddle," Nguyen wrote in her first blog post on February 4, 2008. In order to avoid confusion and mispronunciation many Vietnamese kids took on Czech-sounding names, she explained. Sometimes their Vietnamese names remained a secret until the official graduation ceremony.[53] Among Czechs, Duong adopted the name Linda, which eventually became Lin. Some of her classmates, she joked, called her Lane, referring to the Korean-American character on the television show *Gilmore Girls*. She detested it, however, when they called her Ling, the "bitch" from *Ally McBeal*.[54] Another topic of conversation, she wrote, was language. Most Vietnamese kids, she claimed, were more comfortable using Czech. Surrounded by Czech language and Czech-speaking friends at school, most also spoke Vietnamese with their parents, watched Vietnamese television, and read Vietnamese newspapers. Others let it go, seeing Vietnamese as a punishment and as something unimportant. Czech, Vietnamese, and sometimes English words found their way into Nguyen's speech: "'Mẹ ơi, podáš mi cơm?' After hearing these words my mother no longer feels like handing me the bowl of rice, but to dump it on my head instead. I can't help it, though; languages mix and interweave within me like rice noodles."[55]

Themes of duality and mixture ran through Nguyen's blog posts. She described what Andrea Svobodová, in her dissertation on 1.5-generation (meaning those who, like Nguyen, arrived in the Czech Republic as children) and second-generation Vietnamese, termed a "transnational social space," a vast network of overlapping relationships and practices that, together, have disrupted singular notions of identity, culture, and place.[56] "We live in a double world, in two cultures that are quite different from one another, it's never boring for us," Nguyen wrote, recalling the horror on her grandparents' faces when she set the table with forks rather than chopsticks. During a school field trip she taught classmates to use chopsticks.[57] In another blog post about the Vietnamese New Year (Tết) she wrote about her decision to "flip the script" and celebrate Tết alongside Christmas "as I'm living in this multicultural world." Her sister greeted her in both Czech and Vietnamese. They and their parents sang Vietnamese songs and played karaoke. A Christmas tree stood in one corner of the living room, a peach tree in another. In the end, however, the world of Vietnam filled the day and the space. Scents from candles made in Vietnam filled the air. The food consisted of spring rolls and a traditional Tết dish, *bánh chung*. They told legends and stories while they cooked. The best food was left on the family altar, an invitation to ancestors. Outside, they burned fake money as an appeal to those same ancestors to protect the family financially through the next year. Lacking an extended family, they sat around a table for four, rather than participating in a celebration with dozens of loved ones. A laptop allowed them to speak virtually with relatives abroad, and channel VTV4 broadcast the celebrations in Vietnam. When her father saw that fireworks had been banned in Vietnam he set some off, enjoying a "moment of freedom" that caused the neighbors to think he had become senile. Nguyen clapped with joy.[58]

Nguyen's first blog post received nearly 15,000 hits in just a few months' time. Successive posts consistently topped 10,000. In March 2008 she published a wildly popular article in the online version of a leading newspaper, *Lidové noviny* (People's Newspaper).[59] She also inspired others to post online. Earlier that year four other young Vietnamese women bloggers began posting on iDnes, the online portal for the country's largest daily newspaper. All but one of the bloggers, a sixteen-year-old high school student, were university students in the Czech Republic. Along with Nguyen, they became brief internet sensations. By the time Nguyen had published her article in *Lidové noviny,* three of the Vietnamese women counted among the ten most popular bloggers on iDnes. The top spot went to Phuong Thuy Do Thi (aka Lenka), who received 17,000 hits.[60] In May two Vietnamese men bloggers also began to post on iDnes.[61]

Much of this success was because the blogs, written in Czech on mainstream websites, found a welcoming and curious audience beyond the Vietnamese community. As Lenka Tungová wrote in her senior honors thesis in communications and journalism that spring, the bloggers opened "the 'doors' to a previously closed Vietnamese community" and introduced Czechs to Vietnamese customs while debunking myths.[62] Vietnamese faces had been almost entirely absent from the media landscape. Precious few documentaries presented the Vietnamese community and its origins to television viewers.[63] Many Vietnamese shopkeepers spoke only halting Czech, unlike their more fluent children. As a result, few Czechs knew much about the Vietnamese with whom they interacted, even when they cared to know. Comment after comment on Nguyen's blog thanked her for providing a glimpse of her life. Nguyen also offered drama. She and the other bloggers wrestled with a number of everyday issues familiar to many in their generation, but in ways that were intimate yet still accessible to readers beyond the community. Most important, Nguyen and her generation gathered and mobilized in ways distinct from their elders, both in place and in form.

If there has been a center, or home, for the Vietnamese migrant community in Prague, it is Sapa, the site of an abandoned Communist-era meat and poultry-packing complex located on the southern outskirts of the city. Named after the northwest frontier town of Sa Pa, Vietnamese migrants first used the site's warehouses for the import and export of goods. Over time it has grown to become the largest open-air Vietnamese market in Prague and one of the largest in Europe. (Other large markets can be found at the An Dong Center in Malešice and the Holešovice Market. Both are located on the peripheries of the city in similarly large urban spaces abandoned during post-Communist urban planning and privatization.)[64] As it did in 2008, Sapa today serves as a central cultural hub for Prague's Vietnamese community, especially for new arrivals in the city. Many inhabit panel apartment complexes around Libuš.[65] *Dịch vụ* often work out of Sapa, as have those working for translation services and employment agencies. A Vietnamese-language school occupies space near the TourViet travel agency and a Vietnamese magazine and newspaper publisher. A gate to the market welcomes visitors in Vietnamese and Czech. Vietnamese-language signs and the sounds of Vietnamese being spoken predominate.

Founded in 1999, Sapa was a central node for various Vietnamese networks that stretched across the Czech Republic when Nguyen entered university. Well-to-do "original settlers" based in Sapa tested business opportunities throughout the country and were a crucial link in corner stores' supply chains. "Original settlers" also abounded in the Association of Vietnamese in the Czech Republic. Supported by the Vietnamese state, the organization's network extended from Sapa across the country. Local branches, replete with board members, enjoyed a certain authority over their communities. These same board members, elites in Sapa, and others organized a variety of events for their communities, including outings, ping-pong and soccer tournaments, and singing contests.[66] Several years before Nguyen began

Entrance gate to Sapa, 2009. "Welcome" is written in Vietnamese and Czech along its arch. ČTK / Milan Jaroš.

blogging, the Klub Hanoi youth group, which was based in Sapa, had established a website to promote on-the-ground events.[67] In 2004 they organized a concert at the Slavia football stadium in Vinohrady featuring performances by stars of the Vietnamese diaspora.[68] Its members also worked with local schools to educate teachers about Vietnamese culture and acted as translators during parent–teacher meetings.[69]

Vietnamese in Prague and beyond often met in Sapa, where they conducted business, socialized, and bought food for preparing home-cooked meals. They moved within spaces and structures established by "original settler" elites based largely in Sapa. Vietnamese families tended to live spatially isolated from one another. According to Tereza Freidingerová, Vietnamese communities in Germany, Slovakia, and Poland concentrated in big city neighborhoods. In Prague, however, "old settlers" often lived above their shops, which, in order to reduce mutual competition, were dispersed throughout the city. Vietnamese-owned shops were ubiquitous throughout the city, whether just a few steps from Charles Bridge or amid panel apartment clusters, but they seldom shared the same street or even neighborhood. Only rarely could one speak of a Vietnamese neighborhood; the concentration of migrant workers in Libuš was the exception, not the rule. The same pattern also held true in larger cities such as Brno. Other families, drawn by market forces, concentrated in towns bordering Germany and Austria. Still others scattered throughout the country where, similar to Nguyen's parents, they were sometimes the only Vietnamese family in town.[70]

The children of "original settlers" participated in Sapa-organized activities or met peers and family members there. They were also, naturally, geographically isolated from one another. As the children grew up, these conditions shaped their experiences, which differed significantly from those of their parents. Unlike their parents, Vietnamese children learned to read and write Czech fluently. Many of them spoke Vietnamese but could not read or write the language well. Vietnamese children had Czech friends and knew only a few, if any, classmates with similar backgrounds.[71] As was the case with Nguyen's parents, it was common for Vietnamese shop owners, who were required to work extremely long hours, to hire a "Czech grandma" to take care of their youngest children for stretches of time—relationships that many children of Vietnamese migrants maintain and treasure to this day.[72] Members of the Vietnamese diaspora's 1.5 generation and its second generation tended to be less attached to Vietnam. Their ties to family members in Vietnam were usually thinner. This was also true among kids who, at their parents' behest, had spent a year abroad with extended family in Vietnam.[73] Similar to many émigré kids across Europe, Vietnamese youth in the Czech Republic often found themselves betwixt and between—partially inhabiting the closed Vietnamese world of their parents as well as local variations of Czech society. They inhabited points in Vietnamese networks that crisscrossed the Czech

Republic and extended to Vietnam. They also enjoyed connections to Czech society that their parents did not.

In 2008 the preconditions came together for Nguyen and others to wrestle publicly with these tensions. As a member of the only Vietnamese family in Třemošnice, a town of 3,500, Nguyen always stood out, she later recalled. She was the only Vietnamese kid in elementary school. Everyone in the village knew her, and even strangers waved at her as if they were old acquaintances. A desire for anonymity was one reason that she chose to study in Prague. At the same time she yearned for Vietnamese friends, to see how they had fared, what their perspectives had been.[74] In this desire, she was anything but alone. Nguyen was part of a large generational cohort entering adulthood around 2007. In 2003 roughly 3,000 Vietnamese between the ages of fifteen and twenty-four lived in the Czech Republic; by 2007 the number had more than doubled to a little less than 7,000, or 40 percent of the Vietnamese population.[75] That same year the first significant wave of 1.5- and second-generation Vietnamese enrolled in institutions of higher education, especially in the University of Economics and Business (Vysoká škola ekonomická) and other institutions in Prague.[76] Vietnamese students fortunate enough to enter the university and to live in dorms far from their parents' homes could gather in greater numbers, and more often, than ever before in their lives. In 2007 more than half of the Czech Republic's population had become internet users, which in turn had the potential to further connect young Vietnamese within networks separate from the networks created by their parents' generation.[77] Virtual connections not only distinguished the 1.5 and second generation from their parents but also created the conditions for a generational revolt.

Nguyen's first blog post began with a disturbing scene in Sapa, "a place in Prague where our community gathers, a thick network of gossip and the latest information." She described sitting in a market booth with an auntie, meaning an acquaintance and woman of respect: "'Do you see her? That one with the tummy. She had started up with some Czech and now look, she's pregnant, so he left her,' my auntie commented nastily to me. . . . This is why my peers sometimes don't like walking through markets" such as Sapa.[78] Nguyen returned to this theme and expanded on it in posts that followed over the next few months. "I know from personal experience that news about a girl dating some boy spreads throughout our community terribly fast," but news of a Vietnamese dating a Czech spreads much faster, so fast that "famous physicists must rewrite all the textbooks in which the speed of light is defined."[79] Other news flashed across the network as well. "Information about whether or not you got into a college-track high school, if you passed your driver's license test the first time, if you're getting all As, spreads at lightning speed," she wrote in a post titled "Study, Study." "So a young person has to face constant pressure from his or her own family and from the whole community. It is a great responsibility for us."[80]

Nguyen also detailed injuries and embarrassment at the hands of the gossip network. It angered her, she wrote, to know that the aunties gossiped about the fact that she sometimes ate potatoes instead of rice, used a napkin, read Czech books, went to Czech movies, and had Czech friends. One auntie told her father, who visited Sapa every Saturday, that Nguyen dressed inappropriately in bright colors and should not study diplomacy; her own daughter dressed in gray and studied travel and tourism. The same auntie, whom she referred to by name, also criticized Nguyen for her choice of eyeglasses. In another instance, her parents, who still ran their shop in Třemošnice, learned of a bad grade before Nguyen could tell them. "You cannot imagine how any sort of failure is harped upon and discussed throughout the community," she wrote. "And God forbid if you get a B! I had the feeling that I had not fulfilled my responsibilities to my family, that I was not respecting the sacrifices [that they had made for me]." The aunties, she charged, were "constantly sticking their noses where they don't belong." At times, the pressure had proved unbearable. As Nguyen wrote, "I often wished that I had been born a bushman and lived my own, quiet life in some desert."[81]

Nguyen and the other Vietnamese bloggers distinguished themselves from their elders not just in the content of their writing but also in its form. They wrote exclusively in Czech, and they published in mainstream Czech media outlets. In choosing to blog, they adopted a literary form quite different from the magazine and newspaper articles published out of Sapa. "Blog" is a portmanteau, a blending of "web" and "log" that, in English, dates back to 1999. It entered, unchanged, into the Czech language shortly thereafter.[82] Like the log, the blog is a record of events and impressions as they happen, representing a moment in time rather than a story, such as memoir, structured around a beginning, middle, and end. In this respect, as *Slate* reporter and seasoned blogger Andrew Sullivan observed in 2008, the blog is more than a log, as in a ship's log, whose purpose is primarily to record events as they happen. Similar to the diary, he continued, the blog's main subject is the author herself: "You end up writing about yourself, since you are a relatively fixed point in this constant interaction with the ideas and facts of the exterior world." A blog also differs from a diary, but in other ways. Diarists might intend their work to be read by others, often after the writer's death. The diary might be a first draft for a future memoir or autobiography. The blog, however, is instantly public, accessible to anyone with internet access. Blog posts instantly publish private thoughts and experiences—and confessions—in this most public of platforms.[83] The blog, and internet posts and social media more generally, have also democratized publishing. In the Czech Republic, traditional publishers, whether Czech or Vietnamese, most likely would not have considered putting Nguyen's writing into print. Aktuálně.cz published her work, unfiltered and unedited.

Suddenly, Nguyen had an audience. Aktuálně.cz made her work instantly accessible to fellow 1.5- and second-generation Vietnamese as well as a larger, Czech audience, in Prague and beyond. Readers then distributed her work further via hyperlinks and hashtags. The comment section proved to be equally revolutionary. Similar to blog posts themselves, comments were public and spontaneous. At first, Aktuálně.cz published responses in the comment section instantaneously, without editing or filtering. Nguyen received much praise in her blog's comment sections. Czech commentators often simply thanked Nguyen for her insights into a community about which they knew very little. Czech and Vietnamese responses praised the beauty of her prose, the elegance with which she addressed difficult issues. They urged her to keep posting. Others commented that her blog posts were a welcome relief from the ugliness of the presidential campaign that was under way in early 2008. "I just hopped over here from a blog where they were arguing about the presidential election. Here there is calm and peace. You write really well. You have literary talent. Your blog is among the best," one wrote. "Your pleasant, lively posts show us that there is something better than politics. Thanks for the soft breeze of fresh air . . . from the heart," wrote another.[84] In the comment section, "Czech" and "Vietnamese" worlds (and words) intermingled, replicating the life described by Nguyen in her blog.

Nguyen's blog, along with those posted by her colleagues on iDnes, also sparked various online and offline conversations among 1.5- and second-generation Vietnamese. The comment sections acted as virtual meeting spaces for young Vietnamese readers dispersed throughout Prague and the Czech Republic. Here, online, they shared experiences and commiserated about common struggles. Choppy conversations in the comment section could also spill over into other digital and face-to-face conversations. Nguyen's blog post on dating Czechs prompted a number of reactions among her friends. One said that she would prefer to date an Englishman; another said that she would only marry a Vietnamese because he will remain with her out of a traditional duty to the family long after the initial flame of love has gone out. They agreed, however, that they were unlike "typical" Vietnamese women, always obeying the man of the house, doing all of the cooking and cleaning.[85]

The comment section could also be contentious and hurtful. Comments could be anonymous, and they remained on the screen long after the thought was transmitted through the keyboard. Xenophobic attacks often marred the comment section. Even with the help of emojis, postings lacked intonation, eye contact, the ability to gauge responses, yet were there for all to read. Commentators also struggled, as we still do, with questions of etiquette and decency. Trolling and hurtful attacks by Czechs and second-generation Vietnamese did real harm. The same post on dating, for example, included a comment in which one Vietnamese young man imagined a hierarchy of possible girlfriends: a "clean Vietnamese girl" who was born and raised in Vietnam; a Czech; and finally an "unclean Vietnamese girl" who grew up in the Czech Republic. Another commentator said that he would never date a girl who had dated a Czech.[86]

Nguyen's challenge to Vietnamese custom, and the patriarchal family, was just one point of contention. Perhaps most provocative, however, was her use of the term "banana children." Her first post intimated that it was a term of abuse deployed by her elders. A few months later she wrote that she had first heard the term in Sapa, from Martin Ryšavý, whose documentary film *Banana Children* was released in 2009. One of the film's first scenes features a conversation, over soup, in which one young man is explaining to his friend, in Czech, the meaning of the term: "Basically, it's that we look normal yellow but we act like Czechs, as Europeans." "Yeah, that's good, yeah," his friend replies. Later in the film, Ryšavý is talking to the two young men while enjoying a late-night meal somewhere in Vietnam. He explains that the term comes from the United States, where it was used to refer to Chinese Americans who had lost touch with their heritage.[87] Unlike other terms used by the Vietnamese community, "banana children" was specific to a generation and translated into Czech. *Việt xù* emerged as a term for Vietnamese living in Czechoslovakia / the Czech Republic, taken from a plural form of the word "Vietnamese" (*Vietnamců*). Vietnamese who lived abroad in general are referred to as *việt kiều*, a term that originally meant something akin to "sojourner" and contains positive and negative connotations. *Tây hòa* and *mất gốc* are different ways of referring to those who have lost their roots, betrayed their heritage. *Con lai* is a derogatory term meaning crossbreed, or a hybrid.[88]

Over time many younger Vietnamese have come to adopt the term "banana children," which, both in 2008 and now, is not understood as pejorative. (Indeed, like "queer," it might have been an abusive term that was appropriated and given a positive connotation by the original targets of abuse.) Its usage was not universally accepted, however. Other terms emerged in response to Nguyen's blog posts, each representing different claims about self and self-identification. "Yeah, banana girl, but more precisely Czech-Vietnamese. Got it? Cool, I'm glad," Phuong Thuy Do Thi wrote on her blog's home page. "I write from the perspective of a Czech-Vietnamese, not simply as a Vietnamese living in the Czech Lands. And to those who don't like it, well. . . . Yeah, you probably know what."[89] In her blog Trang Tran Thu called herself "an atypical typical Vietnamese" but disregarded the notion that there was much Czechness about her. "I'm a Vietnamese girl, truly Vietnamese, not at all Czech-Vietnamese."[90] One young woman said that she best resembled an egg: "Dark on the outside, and there is a sort of white layer, but the core is beautifully yellow. What about that? Everyone is something. And everyone has a different perspective on the world."[91] One friend commented on Nguyen's blog that after a hot summer she felt more like a baked potato, dark on the outside and yellow on the inside. The comment was part of an online conversation with Nguyen, played out in various comment sections, that became testy. As the comment string progressed, both seemed to agree that their disagreements should not be hashed out in public.[92]

These discussions, of course, spoke to questions of self, of working through feelings of living in a "transnational social space," of young women and men figuring out who they were as they reached adulthood. True to the discourse of the day, questions of "identity" mixed with ethnic markers. And as several commentators remarked, the blogs pointed to a particular moment in time when questions of identity had become especially pertinent and public for second-generation Vietnamese. One online summary of the blogs that emerged in 2008 stated that, in addition to giving readers a sense of the Vietnamese community in Czechia, Vietnamese culture, and Vietnam, they often tackled a common question: "Where does the generation of Vietnamese coming of age in the Czech Republic belong: are they more Vietnamese or Czech?"[93] As a piece in iDnes declared in March 2008, the popularity of three young women bloggers on their site showed "how their home country remains deep in their hearts yet also that they have a grateful and positive relationship with Czechia and the Czechs." In their "search for identity," the site continued, "there is a richness worthy of readers' attention."[94]

These assessments, however, masked another, darker side to the discussion. The very first comment on Nguyen's blog post about grades asked why the Roma were not more like the Vietnamese. The next comment said their genetic makeup doomed the Roma. The following comment said that Roma were originally nomads who, unlike Europeans and Asians, lacked the markings of civilization—"writing, history, philosophy, astronomy, mathematics, economics."[95] Ad hominem insults also marred the screen. One commentator, similar to Nguyen's "auntie" at Sapa, questioned her decision to attend a private university. A commentator named Quan, addressing Nguyen condescendingly as "Miss Duong," wrote:

And you call yourself a banana. Yellow on the outside and white on the inside? What kind of nonsense is that? You are yellow on the inside and shouldn't change that, and if you are right and have such a nice relationship with your parents then you can't be white on the inside. In the best case you are a mix of each, or in the worst cast the white part predominates and you forget your roots and your culture.

Later in the thread Quan intensified his attack, accusing her of writing the blog to please Czechs, of acting the same and having the same thoughts that they do, and preferring in her heart to be Czech rather than Vietnamese.[96]

Nguyen was not the only woman blogger to be the object of this and similar attacks, often made by men commentators. As Tungová commented at the time, the tensions that came with living in two worlds played out online. On the one hand, the bloggers had grown up as Czechs in a world that encouraged them to have their own opinions. On the other hand, as members of the Vietnamese community, they could be accused of forgetting their heritage and carrying out other acts of betrayal.[97] Some criticized the women for claiming to speak for an entire generation of Vietnamese. Others defended traditional gender roles while imposing their own, ethnically charged terms on the young women. Young men, in particular, attacked the women for bringing shame to their families, for betraying the Vietnamese community and culture. "I have read all of your articles and each time come to the same conclusion," one commentator wrote. "Apparently you are either ashamed of your heritage or of yourself. . . . I don't lead a double life. Nor do I feel like a banana or some other tropical fruit." Nguyen responded, with a touch of humor, defending her pride in her heritage, which was why she began blogging in the first place. "I'm sorry if the term 'banana' offends you. As for you, I personally see a nice cactus!"[98] Anonymous trolls also emailed Nguyen attacking the term "banana children" and accusing her of having lost her roots, of being "mất gốc."[99] She lost friends. Parents ordered their children to cut off ties with her.[100] One group began a blog dedicated to attacking her.[101] Offline, older, conservative members of the community attacked Nguyen and the young bloggers for revealing too much about the Vietnamese community, addressing troublesome topics that should not have been made public.[102] At times the pressure could be overwhelming. After apologizing for being too strident, and still being attacked online,

Phuong Thuy Do Thi posted a short piece entitled "Enough," which concluded: "Try, please, to take my articles as thoughts of a sixteen-year old girl who really does live in two separate worlds and truly doesn't have it easy. I am trying to find out who I really am."[103]

"Unfortunately I had not realized that Vietnamese really don't like to hear criticism," Nguyen wrote in a blog post titled "Not All Bananas Are Alike." She then made a joke about not paying closer attention to the lectures on international diplomacy at the university. "I, however, unfortunately (or thankfully) am in the habit of telling it like it is, without window dressing," something that has also provoked a fair share of criticism, she added. She then went on to admit that she might have been too critical of the aunties and should have spoken to them personally about how their actions bothered her. She added that she missed the "real" aunts she knew in Vietnam, who did not gossip but instead provided loving counsel and advice, "the kind of things that help us to find our 'roots.'" Her criticisms of some aspects of Vietnamese community and culture, Nguyen wrote, was not because she wanted to become a Czech or simply portray the Vietnamese in a bad light. "It's just that when you live in two parallel worlds you have some wonderful advantages as well as clear disadvantages."[104]

Nguyen then returned to a defense of her Vietnameseness, her sense of belonging to its culture and its history. Quoting one of her fellow bloggers in iDnes, "Vietnameseness is in the heart and need not be demonstrated, a person simply has to feel it." She took a swipe at the older generation and public demonstrations of Vietnameseness. She concluded by drawing a comparison between the "celebrated odes about Vietnam" and her own writing: "They are pathetic, almost entirely empty words that are foreign to me, and so you'll either feel the Vietnameseness in my articles, or not."[105] A follow-up post addressed attacks that she was ashamed to admit to the Vietnamese custom of eating dogs. Visiting a dog show with her friend, she mused about emotional attachment and meat, concluding that perhaps the Vietnamese custom of eating dogs should remain in Vietnam. "I would not like to hear of someone losing their dog because his Vietnamese neighbor ate him." And after three hours at the dog show, giggling much of the time, she became hungry, only to realize that only dog food was sold in the stalls in the exhibition hall. "Oh God, please, may I be born a dog in the next life. In Bohemia." She dedicated the essay to Kačenka, the top medal winner in the Yorkshire Terrier category.[106]

———

The attacks had taken their toll. Many years later, Nguyen and I spoke over coffee in the basement of AntHill, a Vietnamese café a few steps from the Náměstí míru streetcar stop. (Not long thereafter, the café went out of business amid the COVID crisis.) An art exhibit decorated the walls. I sat uncomfortably on a beautiful rug while Nguyen, now Nguyen Jirásková, sat across from me. Her daughter played with Nguyen's sister nearby. Twice the conversation circled back to 2008 and the critical, at times hateful attacks in her blog's comment sections. Both times her eyes became piercing, yet calm. In retrospect, she said, she had spent too much time thinking about the "haters," and less on the support that she was receiving from Czechs and Vietnamese. The experience was one reason, she wrote, she left for France in the fall of 2008. She spent the next academic year in Strasbourg thanks to a European Union student exchange program. Nguyen posted a few times on her blog over the next year and then stopped posting, as had most of the young Vietnamese women who began blogging in the spring of 2008.[107] Later in life she realized that she had been grappling with bipolar disorder, which she continues to battle to this day.[108] In 2013 she returned to blogging, eventually publishing, in 2017, *Banana Child: A Vietnamese Woman in the Czech Jungle*—the country's first Czech-language book by a Vietnamese author.[109] The hurtful memory of 2008 remained, however. "I've already lived through the media boom of 2008, and it's not what it's cracked up to be," Nguyen Jirásková posted on her public

Duong Nguyen Jirásková in Malešický Park, 2015. Photograph by Jan Žalský. Used by permission of Duong Nguyen Jirásková.

Facebook page in response to those who asked why she was not promoting the book more aggressively. Doing so, she wrote, "subconsciously leads to self-censorship and possible escapes to France."[110]

In the summer of 2008, Nguyen's blog posts softened in tone and tended toward the sentimental. Escaping Prague and traveling had also given her a different perspective on questions of belonging that she had written about earlier in the year. Over the summer she described a vacation to Vietnam, her "second home."[111] After enjoying the buzz of Hanoi, she and her father visited his hometown, Thanh Hoá-que, where her grandmother's house is still one of the oldest in town. Her father cooked a meal for the extended family. As the evening wore on, "glasses and plates rang out louder than Vietnamese cicadas." (She did, however, note that in a city where "bicycles, motorcycles and on rare occasions, luxury automobiles ride on new streets," there were still peasant farmers who worked sixteen-hour days in the rice paddies for just ten crowns a day.)[112] She titled her posts from Vietnam "In Search of [My] Roots and Quê, or a Return to the Village from Whence I Truly Come." Back in Europe, about to begin her study abroad in France, Nguyen recalled her struggles earlier in the year, when "every morning I prayed that the next morning would be just a smidgen better." In Vietnam, she wondered how she would adjust. "In the end I really didn't like leaving either place."[113] She described adventures with newly made friends in France.

Upon returning to Prague, Nguyen reconsidered her relationship with Sapa, where she found a sense of belonging and sense of pride. In one blog post she described walking through the market with her friend Slobodanka. Moving through Sapa, they surveyed the stalls, which sold "everything from pig tongues to fresh crabs to sweet-scented herbs grown in garden plots outside Sapa." Slobodanka, new to the market, ate her first *bún ngan,* a duck soup with noodles.[114] Nguyen also met Vietnamese friends in Sapa, which prompted her to consider generational differences in a new light. Their parents' generation, she wrote, grew up under a different ideology. As children they had lived different lives in Vietnam, which in turn informed their parenting styles. Still, Nguyen continued, she was thankful for the firm Vietnamese upbringing that her parents had provided her and her sister, and for the language classes provided by the Friends of Vietnam in the Czech Republic at Sapa. Having experienced the wider world, she wrote, she had now come "to know my country through the heart, rather than by compulsion."[115] She described Sapa as the heart of the community, where "we read our Vietnamese newspapers, go to Vietnamese barbers, eat our food, and purchase our ingredients." Nguyen now imagined Sapa as home, a safe space for her and other Vietnamese. "As long as we're inside Sapa, the world outside doesn't give us much thought."[116]

This was not entirely true, as Nguyen knew quite well. In November 2008, Czech Foreign Police conducted a massive raid on Sapa, using a helicopter, armored vehicles, and so-called Schengen buses designed to conduct document verifications. Police officials claimed to have arrested several people for improper documentation while also discovering a car full of weapons, drugs, and counterfeit knock-off goods—claims that many have disputed. The minister of the interior, a member of Klaus's Civic Democratic Party, said the raid was a response to an alleged rise in crimes committed by Vietnamese, words that played into a popular stereotype that linked the community with a nefarious "Vietmafia." Vietnamese students and others shot back, pointing out that 800 personnel had descended upon 400 traders, shopkeepers, and restaurateurs. Thirty children attending a school in Sapa were forced to remain outside in the freezing cold as police conducted their searches.[117] The timing was also suspect. The raid had taken place just fourteen days after the Czech government had suspended the issuance of visas from its embassy in Hanoi.[118] Earlier in November, a fire had ripped through Sapa, briefly capturing media attention throughout the country. Following the raid, a group of nearby residents organized a petition protesting the Vietnamese presence at Sapa, alleging that they had suffered ill effects on their health from the fire and that the well-being of the neighborhood had been endangered.[119]

Klaus's press secretary sought to distance the president from the brewing controversy. He called the raid megalomaniacal and without effect. He also criticized the visa decision.[120] "I don't get what the Czech cops are trying to do here. Look like Hollywood movie stars? Embarrassing," one student declared during a discussion forum in Prague at the University of Economics and Business. "Is it a crime to be Vietnamese? Is it a crime to exist together?" another student asked.[121] Blogging from France, Nguyen took aim at the minister of the interior,

Ivan Langer: "Please, how can Czech society be free of xenophobia when a member of the Czech government acts like this?" The current government is sinking, a commenter wrote on her blog. Now that anti-Communist rhetoric is no longer working, they have "fallen back on a tried and true recipe of populist regimes and are trying to feed the flames of xenophobia, nationalism, and hate."[122]

Few might have known much about the Vietnamese diaspora or thought much about its members before 1989, but the raw materials to mobilize racial hatred were there. Communist-era secret police often complained that Vietnamese, broadly speaking, lacked a proper work ethic. Others accused Vietnamese of hoarding valuable goods. Still more claimed that, in contrast to Cuban migrant workers or the Roma population, the Vietnamese were the model minority: hardworking and docile. In all cases, as Alena Alamgir writes, these visions were informed by high-school biology textbooks and other discourses that assumed the natural existence of races, each with its own characteristics.[123] These stereotypes, as well as condescending microaggressions, continued into the post-Communist era. Czechs often addressed Vietnamese using the informal pronoun (*ty*), used for close friends, family, and children, rather than the formal pronoun (*vy*), reserved for adults who are not close friends and family. The verbal effect was to discursively position Vietnamese as children, a common imperialist trope.[124] More overt and violent displays of racism became possible after 1989. One of the first skinhead groups that emerged after 1989 named themselves, with vicious irony, MY LAI—referring to the massacre perpetrated by US troops in 1968. "In 1991, I had [a] bad accident with racists, and I will never forget it," one man told Czech Radio in 2004. "We were at a bus stop, and some Czech people beat us up."[125] In 1999 one hate group's pamphlet made an all-too-familiar declaration: "We want to be a solid dam against the torrent [of] foreign hordes from Asia and Africa. We will not accept racial minorities that live from the blood and sweat of the native inhabitants, leeching from the hard work of our people."[126]

Throughout the Communist and post-Communist periods, many in the Vietnamese community attempted to avoid confrontation and to be as invisible as possible. The 2008 financial crisis, however, created the conditions for Vietnamese to become objects of political scapegoating and fearmongering. Across the country, GDP growth began a slide that continued until 2010.[127] In 2008 unemployment hovered around 5 percent across the country and at just 2 percent in Prague, but the economic downturn was noticeable.[128] Overnight stays in Prague leveled off, and roughly 90,000 fewer people visited the historical monuments under the care of the Prague Information Service than the year before. This downturn, combined with internal mismanagement, led the Prague Information Service to lay off one-fourth of its workforce. Renovation projects budgeted at 3.2 million crowns were put on hold.[129] In the Czech Republic and well beyond, economic downturn caused many to question the government's ruling elites and economic policies more generally. The ruling Civic Democrats were devastated in regional and Senate elections throughout 2008. In March 2009 the government fell following a no-confidence vote.

Economic recession and a tottering government created the conditions for another familiar trope: the Vietnamese as intertwined in illegality. The economic downturn had a particularly devastating effect on many in the Vietnamese community, especially among contract and guest workers, who were often the first to lose their jobs. According to state law, unemployed foreign workers had only sixty days to find work before facing deportation. Many simply left the country, often returning to Vietnam. Others obtained trade licenses, which gave them a better visa status.[130] The government's more restrictive visa policy, combined with a lack of employment opportunities and a corruption scandal in the Czech embassy, led to a dramatic drop in requests for long-term visas, from 10,000 in 2007 and 2008, respectively, to just 275 in 2009.[131]

While not a prominent topic in Czech media, stories about unemployed Vietnamese, and foreigners more generally, drew heavily upon themes such as illegal work, illegal immigration, illegal residency, and even unlawful activities such as drug smuggling.[132] Not surprisingly, these fears were vastly exaggerated, but they could be weaponized.[133] Czech (and Vietnamese) racist comments sullied Nguyen's blog posts from the beginning. They continued to appear even after Aktuálně. cz's editors announced their intention to remove offensive comments. "Yes, the Vietnamese are clever salesmen and quickly find a niche in the market," someone wrote in the comment section of Nguyen's spring 2008 post about Vietnamese cooking. "Not long ago they controlled the trade of heroin (in Brno, for example). Now their interest has shifted to the cultivation of quality marijuana."[134] The raid on Sapa played upon and legitimated many of these stereotypes.

The raid changed something else, too. Vietnamese students, fluent in Czech and armed with knowledge about Czech laws and norms, mobilized in protest. Specifically, six university students organized a petition under the rubric of the newly created Union of Vietnamese Students and Youth. They obtained more than 160 signatures. The petition alleged that police had used unnecessary force, wrestling to the ground and handcuffing waiters and others who were attempting to cooperate with the raid. Police entered the Buddhist temple, roughed up the priests, and dragged one of the most respected members of the community, an eighty-year-old woman, into the cold. There she waited, freezing, as did the elementary school children who had been forced from their classrooms. The entire raid, the petition stated, "appeared to be a politically motivated performance with excessive force that imposed collective guilt on those of Vietnamese ethnicity." They appealed to the rule of law, calling upon the Ministry of the Interior to launch an investigation.[135] In January the students met with the head of the Foreign Police and with several representatives of the Ministry of the Interior and Parliament.[136] Czech authorities showed little contrition at the meeting.

As one of the organizers later recalled, the attack on Sapa was just one instance of rising hatred aimed at the Vietnamese community as a whole. They had also been frustrated by their elders' failure to protest the raid. Official organizations claiming to speak for young and old Vietnamese alike had remained largely silent.[137] The protesters eventually formed their own association, Viet-Czech Friends, which aimed to improve relations and challenge misperceptions about the community at large.[138] Vietnamese students also obtained greater influence within the community and at Sapa. In the wake of the raid on Sapa, and amid growing tensions with the local community, Klub Hanoi organized an afternoon discussion that included the student protesters, the chairman of the Association of Vietnamese in the Czech Republic, the director of the Foreign Police, and local city leaders. The event, which took place at Klub Junior, several blocks from Sapa, included an evening of dancing and singing. The event ended with some remarks by a local political figure.[139] That same year Klub Hanoi obtained a prominent location in Sapa, something that Nguyen commented on in her blog while providing a link to their website.[140]

The protest against the raid marked a key moment in which second-generation Vietnamese mobilized in public, beyond the boundaries of the officially sanctioned community of their parents. They also mobilized in different ways from their parents. The student organizers, based at different institutions in Prague and throughout the Czech Republic, included their email addresses in the petition, which they posted as a Google Doc. In the petition, they supported their claims about abuse with links to online reporting by the popular Nova television network as well as the high-brow *Britské listy* (British Newspaper).[141] They found success promoting their efforts on sympathetic online news sites. "The Vietnamese are a modest nation, but this raid has provoked even us. We understand that the police must carry out their duties, but to thoughtlessly humiliate our people, to require pregnant women and small children to stand in the freezing cold on the streets, that goes too far," student Nguyen Son Tung told the online news site Týden.cz.[142] "As I have written in several articles, Sapa is for me and my fellow countrymen more than just a market," Nguyen posted from France—a post that included a link to the online petition. "But most of all it is a place, where one can feel 'at home.'" There have been other raids in the past, she wrote, and she had never heard of anything that would justify "a new raid policy that targets not just the guilty but also the innocent—the elderly, the sick, pregnant women, children—as apparently happened in Sapa."[143] As before, contrasting voices from the Vietnamese community emerged online. A rival online group, Viet Agent, questioned the students' legitimacy to speak for the Vietnamese community while warning that the students' approach might hinder integration rather than facilitate it.[144]

———

In many ways, Nguyen, her fellow bloggers, and the students who mobilized against the Sapa raid speak to a historic moment that has come to define our existence. By 2013 approximately three out of every ten inhabitants of the Czech Republic owned a smartphone,[145] and by 2015 4.2 million of the Czech Republic's population used Facebook at least once a month.[146] The rules of the game, and questions about online etiquette, were emerging as prominent concerns, and not just among Vietnamese youth in the Czech Republic. (Consider, for example, the public consternation about cyberbullying that emerged in the United States in 2008, the same year in which half of US households had obtained a smartphone.)[147] Trolls still despoil genuine attempts at conversations in comment sections across the internet. Some scholars warn that online interactions, especially email and texting, are not a substitute for face-to-face interaction. Online communication can be a detriment to thoughtful conversations, empathy, and genuine human connections. Online connections and interactive communities, such as those enabled by social media algorithms, have blinded us to alternative points of view, thus injuring democracy and the larger social fabric. Concerns about data privacy have been thrust into the public debate, and not just in the United States or the Czech Republic. Internet culture, some argue, has been overwhelmed by an obsession with status and self-promotion, to the profit of big tech.[148]

Returning to 2008, and Nguyen and her generation, might remind us that all is not lost, however. Blogging and other online posts, as mentioned above, provided a virtual space for authorial voices such as Nguyen's. Comments on their work could be instantaneous, if sometimes hurtful, but they also provoked public discussions that might otherwise have been difficult if not impossible. Vietnamese students such as Nguyen might have shared dormitories or met in cafés, but they and other second-generation youth were greatly dispersed geographically. Despite the harassment that Nguyen and others endured, other young Vietnamese women and men joined the blogosphere or created their own websites, many of which were publicized online by Klub Hanoi.[149] Online interactions have continued to create space and opportunity for twice marginalized members among first- and second-generation Vietnamese.

In some ways, then, the internet has much in common with the city, where, unlike smaller, on-the-ground communities, large numbers of diverse individuals can find each other. Again, there is a downside. White nationalists can also find each other online. It is easy to forget, however, the positive connections made possible by online platforms, connections that easily cross the boundaries of immediate communities or even the nation-state. Speaking of Subtle Asian Traits, an immensely popular global Facebook group she helped to found, Anne Gu, a teenager in Australia, commented: "We labeled the group as 'family,' so that's what the group's purpose is, to allow people to feel like they all belong to something." "Like nearly everyone we spoke with," Nicholas Wu and Karen Yuan wrote in *The Atlantic,* Gu was referring to "the loneliness of being a diasporic Asian, fitting in neither here nor there. Perhaps the explosion of this Facebook community was inevitable. People want to find their people."[150] "I am sixteen years old. I was born in Prague and have lived here my whole life. It is not my fault that I am a banana child. I find it rather sad that there are so many similar bananas walking this earth and I have nothing to do with them. I'm going to try and change that," one young woman commented, in red, yellow, and green type, on one of Nguyen's posts.[151]

The remarkable ability to interact instantly from anywhere in the country has also enabled face-to-face interactions. Young Vietnamese have turned away from the dating service run out of Sapa and toward a number of online sites. They have run food-related discussion forums and cooked in each other's homes. They have met in Vietnamese restaurants, which have become more prominent throughout Prague, and at cafés and other public spaces throughout the city.[152] Online connections have also led to the formation of on-the-ground clubs and organizations. Groups with a strong internet presence have led educational activities for Vietnamese of all ages. Web-savvy Vietnamese youth have organized celebrations of Vietnamese New Year as well as Czech holidays such as International Women's Day and St. Nicholas Day. They have organized summer coding camps and badminton and volleyball tournaments. A Facebook group for Vietnamese medical students emerged from evening meetings at a Vietnamese restaurant near Jiřího z Poděbrad.[153]

Here, too, Vietnamese youth have spoken to a larger moment in the history of the internet. As Harrison Rainie and Barry Wellman have recently argued, the internet has vastly accelerated the speed and ease with which we can tap others for information and mobilize. In particular, social media has allowed for "more ad hoc, open, and informal" networks that have largely replaced "bounded voluntary organizations." The argument deliberately questions claims that decreasing membership in traditional associations, such as bowling leagues, has led to a decline in civil society and democratic participation more broadly. The internet has also multiplied the number of people who, even if not close friends or family, compose an informal network capable of sharing information, providing mutual support, or advertising job opportunities.[154] In reality, of course, few online relationships lead to on-the-ground associations and political action, which makes such efforts by

Vietnamese youth all the more extraordinary. Havel, who died in 2011, would certainly have been proud of what they have accomplished.

It is difficult to imagine that the types of conversations Nguyen and other bloggers enjoyed would have had the same effect without the internet, given that they were so geographically dispersed. Nor is it possible to imagine Vietnamese students mobilizing against the raid on Sapa so quickly and effectively had they lacked access to the internet. So much of this differed from the ways that their parents had gathered and organized themselves, the ways in which they constituted their networks. "Original settlers" and others emphasized extended family networks that stretched back to Vietnam and were maintained via various forms of communication, as well as via remissions payments. From Sapa, a strict organizational structure with ties to the embassy linked members of the community across the country. Having few spaces of their own, Vietnamese youth went to the virtual world, and never left. These differences—between the virtual and "real," between generations—should not be exaggerated, however. Student mobilization against the Sapa raid was on the ground, too. Vietnamese groups and associations have met and continue to meet in physical spaces, face-to-face. The older generation also has adapted. The year before Nguyen began blogging, the Association of Vietnamese in the Czech Republic created its own youth organization, which, beginning in 2007, has held a soccer tournament in Prague's Strahov Stadium that has included participants from across the country.[155] The Association of Vietnamese in the Czech Republic eventually created its own website.[156] Since 2010 the Vietnamese government has maintained an online site containing legal information for Vietnamese abroad.[157]

Outreach beyond the Vietnamese community has also continued. This, too, has a prehistory. One of the stated goals of Klub Hanoi was to reach out to larger Czech society and provide information about their community and Vietnamese customs. As early as 2004, Nguyen participated in a workshop for Czech teachers about Vietnam and the

Vietnamese community in the Czech Republic. Recently, she spoke on similar themes at a Prague elementary school, as described on her Facebook page.[158] The three women bloggers who established Viet Food Friends worked from a belief that sharing a meal creates and deepens friendships while introducing others to Vietnamese culture. Begun in 2010, their website has included recipes along with maps of Vietnamese restaurants, bistros, and grocery stores throughout Prague.[159] Nguyen and other bloggers have found an increasingly wide audience. In 2016 Do Thu Trang, who began posting on iDnes in 2008, was nominated for the Czech equivalent of the Pulitzer Prize in the blogging category.[160] The filmmaker Diana Cam Van Nguyen's animated works about growing up in the Czech Republic have received considerable international acclaim. Her 2019 documentary *Apart* was screened at film festivals in London, Seoul, and Rotterdam, among others.[161]

Greater visibility has also been combined with a vibrant associational life. Viet Up, which relies heavily on various forms of social media, has taken on an especially prominent role in helping the community while reaching out to larger society. They have organized numerous events and activities for Vietnamese youth, including a yearly "Banánfest" held in Prague. Viet Up organizes lectures and other events for the general public. They have provided translators for Vietnamese parents who require translation services during teacher meetings. During the 2020 COVID-19 outbreak they sewed masks and provided various forms of aid.[162] They and other Vietnamese youth, along with the Viet Food Friends bloggers, have also offered guided tours to Sapa. Sapa has become a destination point for foodies of all sorts, the late Anthony Bourdain included.[163]

Vietnamese from various generations and with nongovernmental organizations have also mobilized to obtain legal rights. In 2013 a representative of the community gained a seat on the Government Council for National Minorities, which has provided opinions on laws that may affect minorities. It has also been responsible for the allocation of state

Viet Up banner photo from their Facebook page, 2020. Photograph by Danny Nguyen (Duc Anh Nguyen). Used by permission of Viet Up z.s.

funds to support minority languages and cultures. These funds have further buoyed Vietnamese associational life throughout the Czech Republic. Vietnamese activists and their supporters won this victory because they successfully argued that the Vietnamese constitute a "traditional community" whose members have inhabited the lands of the Czech Republic for a significant amount of time. It was also clear that, in addition to meeting the standard criteria of a minority, such as speaking a different language, the community was significantly large.[164] (Among the twelve recognized minorities, only the Slovak and Ukrainian communities, as measured in 2011, were larger.)[165] Furthermore, most Vietnamese, especially members of the second generation, were going to continue to call the Czech Republic their home. In 2014 the government permitted dual citizenship: for the first time, Vietnamese could apply for Czech citizenship without forfeiting their Vietnamese citizenship. The council's 2013 online description of the

Vietnamese community also included a long list of organizations, beginning with Klub Hanoi.[166]

Not all is well, of course. In more recent blog posts Nguyen has described instances of being the target of hate speech. Xenophobic remarks by President Miloš Zeman and others have affected her and others. "I feel a particular pressure that I really can't define," she commented in an interview. Previously she had defused racist comments with a combination of clever sarcasm and humor. These techniques, she said, now seem ineffective.[167] She is not alone, of course, and broader injustices remain. Vietnamese university graduates often face hiring discrimination and thus return to their parents' businesses. Others start businesses of their own. Many Vietnamese enter institutions of higher education only to drop out after a year or two. Large numbers of Vietnamese youth do not attend university at all, sometimes because they or their parents do not consider it worth the time and money. Such decisions reflect a strong sense of tradition and the responsibility to provide remittances. They also point to persistent generational divides. In Vietnam and abroad, family members have often pooled their resources to support the most talented among their children who, after receiving their degrees, have been expected to support the rest of the family. Many second-generation Vietnamese, however, possess a sense of "European individualism" that values independent initiative, success, and happiness, as opposed to an overriding sense of duty to family and the community. Meanwhile, girls are often burdened with housework while facing the same pressures to succeed in school that boys do.[168]

More than a decade after Nguyen posted her first blog post, themes of in-betweenness, of belonging neither here nor there, of being stuck, still run through the discourse of second-generation Vietnamese in Prague and beyond. "WHY then 'Banánfest' 👠👠👠?" Viet Up posted on their Facebook page before their 2018 festival. "Simply put, outwardly we appear to be Vietnamese ('yellow on the outside'), but [with regard to] character and thought we're somewhat more like Czechs ('white on the inside').)" (In 2016 the subtitle of the festival's name, "Not All Bananas Are Alike," was the same as the title of Nguyen's April 2008 blog post.)[169] For some, however, the term is imprecise or fails to capture their own feelings of belonging and sense of self. Efforts to make sense of their positionality, to find words to describe a sense of self and place, differ wildly, even if their dilemmas have much in common. "I feel more like a Czech, influenced by a Czech and Vietnamese upbringing, and I take the best from both, as I can," a twenty-two-year old who moved to the Czech Republic at the age of four told Tereza Freidingerová. "I feel at home here in Czechia, but I have roots in Vietnam and I don't want to forget that. It's the homeland of my parents and ancestors. It's a beautiful country, beautiful people. But I am bound to Czechia, to Prague." "Home," the young woman concluded, "for me isn't a country, but more like a place."[170] Renne Dang, a self-described Czech rapper with Vietnamese roots, sang the following in video he posted on YouTube:

> We don't want immigrants in ČR [Czech Republic]
> My Daddy was an immigrant, so you really don't want me
> And we don't want Viets in ČR.
>
> .   .   .   .
>
> I'm con lai, a banana kid, closed within the network.
> Home but in a foreign land.
> Con lai, I'm searching.
> Con lai, I'm searching.[171]

CONCLUSION

ഗ‍ൠ

The Stones of Old Town Square

IMAGINE A BOUND VOLUME of historic maps of Prague, similar in scale, organized according to date from the early nineteenth century to the present. Open the book and quickly flip the pages, as people did in the old days of cartoon animation. Most of Prague's fortifications fade away. Streets and buildings expand outward. Housing complexes appear where once there were only fields and villages. In the latter half of the nineteenth century, the language of the maps changes from German to Czech. Emperor Francis Bridge becomes Legion Bridge and then, after several other name changes, May Day Bridge, and then Legion Bridge again. Similar landmarks in the service of the Czech historical imagination and Czech political power appear in chronological succession: the Industrial Palace near Stromovka, the Žižka statue on Vítkov Hill, and the Monument to the Victims of Communism below Petřín Hill. Prague Castle is represented on every map, but a discerning eye can see, midway through our imaginary volume, the renovations, walkways, and gardens that appeared during Masaryk's interwar republic. We might even picture various Czechoslovak presidents attending to business within the Castle walls from the twentieth century to the present.

Now imagine being on Týnská Street, a curving alleyway a few steps away from Old Town Square. Embedded in the street is a small bronze plate, square-shaped and slightly scuffed. It reads, in Czech:

HERE LIVED BENJAMIN ROSENSTEIN
BORN 1886
DEPORTED 1942 TO TEREZÍN
MURDERED

Hundreds of other "stumbling stones" dot this city and other locales across Europe.[1] Rosenstein, an emigrant from Poland, obtained Czechoslovak citizenship in 1933, the same year that Hitler came to power. Before the war, he worked as a shoemaker. He lived on Týnská Street with his wife and three children. In 1942 the police arrested Rosenstein on nearby Masná Street for not wearing a yellow star identifying him as a Jew.[2] The Nazi authorities deported him in their belief that Jews had no place in Europe. They killed him in the Terezín concentration camp because they deemed it the best "solution" to their self-generated "problem." But Rosenstein belonged in Prague. Prague was his home.

Now, take a short walk from Rosenstein's apartment building to Old Town Square. The square is a stunningly refurbished location filled with "must-sees" that are recommended in every guidebook: a medieval clock tower, a baroque church, and nineteenth-century apartment buildings reminiscent of those found in Paris. Close by is the Marian column, a restored version of the monument torn down by anti-Habsburg protestors in 1918. A statue of Jan Hus and his followers, commissioned by Czech activists just before World War I, dominates the northeastern quadrant. The stones of Old Town Square have borne witness to world-shaking historical events such as the Communist seizure of power in 1948. They have also absorbed the footsteps of people like Rosenstein, who undoubtedly crossed this square many times in his life. What happens if, instead of focusing on the sights around us, we simply contemplate the stones beneath our feet? What happens if we imagine Rosenstein and the tens of thousands of Praguers who also walked here, their many differences aside?

Most of these pedestrians, similar to Rosenstein, have left behind few traces of their lives. Their walks across Old Town Square are almost never documented. In this respect, the characters whose stories have been told in this book, all writers engaged in various literary styles, belong to a select club. Karel Vladislav Zap preferred to stroll on Prague's islands and on paths on the outskirts of the city, but he, too, must have walked across these stones many times in his life—especially as he prepared his *Guide to Prague*. Egon Erwin Kisch is easier to place here. He grew up just around the corner, on Kozí Street. In one of his feuilletons he describes visiting the square with a friend during the annual Christmas market. He saw in the market's enchanting handmade toys and other crafts a gentle humanity that he also saw in so many of the people he encountered across the city.[3] Vojtěch Berger participated in several marches here. Many of the Carpenters' Union meetings he attended took place in a pub on Husova Street, a couple of blocks from the square.[4] In her memoir, Hana Frejková mentions walking across the square as she returned from work at the Maringotka Theater. The square has been a place to meet with friends, she told me, as well as a site of demonstrations. After the fall of Communism, she and other members of a musical trio performed Yiddish songs here.[5] Duong Nguyen Jirásková told me that in the summer of 2008 she was strolling through the city and chatting with a younger cousin who had plans to study in Great Britain. When they reached Old Town Square, Nguyen Jirásková advised her cousin to be herself and have fun. In 2019 Nguyen Jirásková visited the Christmas market for the first time with her husband and their newborn daughter. Following the temporary loosening of stay-at-home COVID-19 restrictions in the spring of 2020 she ventured onto the square, where she overheard a conversation littered with racist slurs.[6]

From our spot on Old Town Square, we might also imagine an entire city filled with individuals engaged in practices of belonging that have emerged over the centuries. Praguers continue to stroll along Petřín Hill, just as they did in Zap's time. Formal, middle-class salons may be a thing of the past, but Praguers still meet in each other's apartments to discuss politics, literature, and life. Other Praguers wander the streets alone, as Kisch did, enjoying the odd encounter with others in their shared city. Many more, undoubtedly, still meet in cafés and pubs, even if the cabaret is passé. Praguers still fill squares and parks with public demonstrations. Gymnastics organizations survive, but most people belong to other clubs and associations throughout the city, the majority of which have no affiliation with a political party. Praguers still perform in and attend the theater. They work together and engage in common artistic endeavors. They chat and converse with others while sitting in front of computer screens. Various online platforms, although they are increasingly commodified, still create communities whose participants can meet and mobilize in the world, just as Viet Up did as part of a vast, impressive relief effort during the COVID-19 outbreak. One wonders what practices of belonging will emerge in the years to come.

These practices of belonging need not be in opposition to national imaginations. In many cases, the two are intricately bound. It is important to remember that national imaginations are also a form of belonging—bounded communities whose numerous members will never see each other face-to-face. These imagined communities, while requiring much human effort and characterized by internal strife, are not going away. Nation-states predominate throughout the globe. Political leaders rely on national imagination for legitimacy, both at home and abroad. In the lands between Germany and Russia, as John Connelly writes, the "power of nationalist arguments to drive political imagination—indeed to create the space in which politics happens—is repeated in country after country" throughout the region's modern history. In addition to sharing a common investment in language, he continues, nationalisms here share a sense of precariousness. Such fears can be manipulated during times of crisis, including crises manufactured by powerful political leaders.[7]

Still, nationalist imaginations need not be so nefarious. In 2005, when asked by state television to vote for history's "greatest Czech," viewers chose Jára Cimrman, whose namesake theater has survived Normalization and the post-Communist era that followed. In addition to inventing yogurt, the telephone, dynamite, and the computerless internet, Cimrman founded a puppet theater in Paraguay and almost became the first man to reach the North Pole. Sadly, the organizers disqualified Cimrman because he is a fictional character, yet his fame lives on.[8] Cimrman's bust, or better said, the back of his head, adorns a building in the Michle suburb, marking the spot where the Czech hero allegedly enjoyed breakfast one day in 1901.[9] An asteroid orbiting the sun between Jupiter and Mars—this is true—bears his name.[10] Cimrman owes his popularity, in part, to his creators' playful mocking of Czech concerns about being a small nation with tenuous claims to historical significance. The ironic humor and sense of pride feel like an inside joke. Cimrman's plays, filled with puns and wordplay, are celebrations of the Czech language. His pearls of wisdom are part of today's lexicon throughout the Czech Republic.

According to Cimrman, "Sometimes a historic battle does more harm in a textbook than on the field of war." What he meant, as a well-regarded Cimrmanologist tells us during the perfunctory lecture that begins each play, is that history makers should do more than just consider the consequences of their actions in the present. They should time major events so as to make the memorization of dates and other historical facts easier for future schoolchildren. (The Habsburg emperor, he said, should have executed the *twenty-seven* rebellious Bohemian nobles—here on Old Town Square—on June 27, 1627, not on June 21, 1621.)[11] Ripped from its context, as so many Cimrmanisms are, this quotation might, however, be interpreted as a warning and a point of departure. In seeking an understanding of the past and condemning abuses, much can be gained from imagining history in ways that are decent and true. We need to understand the rise of nationalism, but we should not forget that it happened in tandem with people's individual needs to create a sense of belonging for themselves. What followed was the emergence of remarkable practices of belonging that exist to this day. In these practices, and the search for belonging that motivates them, we might see a common humanity. We might imagine ways in which this common humanity coexists with human difference and nationalism, and thus we might imagine a better future.

ABBREVIATIONS

ARCHIVES

ABS	Archiv bezpečnostních složek
AHMP	Archiv hlavního města Prahy
NA	Národní archiv
NKP	Národní knihovna Prahy
NM	Národní muzeum
PNP	Památník národního písemnictví

PUBLISHED PRIMARY SOURCES

A.cz	Aktuálně.cz
BD	Duong Nguyen Jirásková, *Banánové dítě: Vietnamka v české džungli* (Brno: BizBooks, 2017)
DK	Hana Frejková, *Divný kořeny* (Prague: Torst, 2007)
GWE	Egon Erwin Kisch, *Gesammelte Werke in Einzelausgaben,* vol. 2, part 1 (Berlin: Aufbau-Verlag, 1960)

PKHMP Karel Vladislav Zap, *Popsánj kr. hlawnjho města Prahy pro cizince i domácj* (Prague: W. Špinky, 1835)

PoP Karel Vladislav Zap, *Průwodce po Praze: Potřebná příruční kniha pro každého, kdo se s pamětnostmi českého hlawního města seznámiti chce* (Prague: Bedřich Krečmár, 1848)

NOTES

INTRODUCTION

1. Alois Jirásek, *Old Czech Legends,* trans. Maria K. Holeček (London: Forest Books, 1992), 13. The original version is in Alois Jirásek, *Staré pověsti české* (Prague: Jos. R. Vilímek, 1894).

2. *Prague Pocket Guide: Practical Tips for Visitors* (Prague: Prague City Tourism, 2017), https://www.prague.eu/file/edee/universal/download/brozury/praha-do-kapsy-2017/en.pdf.

3. Cathleen M. Guistino, *Tearing Down Prague's Jewish Town: Ghetto Clearance and the Legacy of Middle-Class Ethnic Politics around 1900* (Boulder, CO: East European Monographs, 2003).

4. Kimberly Elman Zarecor, *Manufacturing a Socialist Modernity: Housing in Czechoslovakia, 1945–1960* (Pittsburgh: University of Pittsburgh Press, 2011); Lukáš Beran and Vladislava Valchářová, eds., *Industrial Prague: Technical Buildings and Industrial Architecture in Prague; A Guide* (Prague: Czech Technical University, 2006), 146–147; "Nový Smíchov," Prague.eu—oficiální turistický portál Prahy, https://www.prague.eu/cs/objekt/mista/430/novy-smichov; and Lily M. Hoffman and Jiří Musil, "Culture Meets Commerce: Tourism in Postcommunist Prague," in *The Tourist City,* ed. Susan S. Fainstein and Dennis R. Judds (New Haven, CT: Yale University Press, 1999), 7–8.

5. My approach has taken particular inspiration from Robert Nemes, *Another Hungary: The Nineteenth-Century Provinces in Eight Lives* (Stanford, CA: Stanford University Press, 2016).

6. Lewis Mumford, *The City in History: Its Origins, Its Transformations, and Its Prospects* (New York: Harcourt Brace Jovanovich, 1961), esp. 82, 97–98.

7. Claude S. Fischer, "Toward a Subcultural Theory of Urbanism," *American Journal of Sociology* 80, no. 6 (1975): 1319–1341; Fischer, "The Subcultural Theory of Urbanism: A Twentieth-Year Assessment," *American Journal of Sociology* 101, no. 3 (1995): 543–577; and Paul Craven and Barry Wellman, "The Network City," *Sociological Inquiry* 43 (1973): 57–88.

8. Mark S. Granovetter, "The Strength of Weak Ties," *American Journal of Sociology* 78, no. 6 (May 1973): 1360–1380; Barry Wellman, "The Community Question: The Intimate Networks of East Yorkers," *American Journal of Sociology* 84, no. 4 (March 1979): 1201–1231. See also J. Clyde Mitchell, ed., *Social Networks in Urban Situations: Analyses of Personal Relationships in Central African Towns* (Manchester: Manchester University Press, 1969); Herbert Gans, *The Urban Villagers: Group and Class in the Life of Italian-Americans* (New York: Free Press, 1962); Carol B. Stack, *All Our Kin: Strategies for Survival in a Black Community* (New York: Harper and Row, 1975); and Melinda Blau and Karen L. Fingerman, *Consequential Strangers: The Power of People Who Don't Seem to Matter—But Really Do* (New York: W. W. Norton, 2009).

9. Edward S. Casey, *Getting Back into Place: Toward a Renewed Understanding of the Place-World* (Bloomington: Indiana University Press, 2009), 327, cited in David Seamon, "Lived Emplacement and the Locality of Being: A Return to Humanistic Geography?," in *Approaches to Human Geography*, ed. Stuart Aitken and Gill Valentine (London: Sage, 2006), 42. Or, as bell hooks has written: "Searching for a place to belong I make a list of what I will need to create firm ground. At the top of the list I write: 'I need to live where I can walk, I need to be able to walk to work, to the store, to a place where I can sit and drink tea in fellowship. Walking, I will establish my presence, as one who is claiming the earth, creating a sense of belonging, a culture of place." *Belonging: A Culture of Place* (New York: Routledge, 2008), 2.

10. Jane Jacobs, *The Death and Life of Great American Cities* (New York: Modern Library, 2011), 65–71, quotation on 66.

11. Angelo Maria Ripellino, *Magic Prague*, trans. Michael Henry Heim (Berkeley: University of California Press, 1994); Peter Demetz, *Prague in Black and Gold: Scenes from the Life of a European City* (New York: Hill and Wang, 1997); Derek Sayer, *Prague, Capital of the Twentieth Century: A Surrealist History* (Princeton, NJ: Princeton University Press, 2013).

12. For thoughtful essays on the concept of belonging and on the scholarly literature on belonging, see Marco Antonisch, "Searching for Belonging: An Analytical Framework," *Geography Compass* 4, no. 6 (2010): 644–659; and Tuuli Lähdesmäki et al., "Fluidity and Flexibility of 'Belonging': Uses of the Concept in Contemporary Research," *Acta Sociologica* 59, no. 3 (2016): 233–247.

13. See, for example, John T. Cacioppo and William Patrick, *Loneliness: Human Nature and the Need for Social Connection* (New York: W. W. Norton, 2008).

14. A. H. Maslow, *Toward a Psychology of Being* (New York: Van Nostrand, 1968); Roy F. Baumeister and Mark R. Leary, "The Need to Belong: Desire for Interpersonal Attachments as a Fundamental Human Motivation," *Psychological Bulletin* 117, no. 3 (1995): 497–529, quotation on 497.

15. As Linn Miller writes, "Belonging is a state of being from which well-being is derived; a relation that makes us feel good about our being and our being-in-the-world; a relation that is fitting, right or correct. This being the case, a minimum conception of belonging might be understood as standing in correct relation to one's community, one's history, and one's locality." He goes on to describe "correct relation," here drawing on Søren Kierkegaard, as "the quintessential mode of being human—a mode of being in which all aspects of the self, as human, are perfectly integrated—a mode of being in which we are as we ought to be: fully ourselves." Miller, "Belonging to Country: A Philosophical Anthropology," *Journal of Australian Studies* 27, no. 76 (2003): 215–223, quotation on 218. See also Vanessa May, "Self, Belonging, and Social Change," *Sociology* 45, no. 3 (2011): 363–378, esp. 369, 375; and Julia Bennett, "Researching the Intangible: A Qualitative Phenomenological Study of the Everyday Practices of Belonging," *Sociological Research Online* 19, no. 11 (2013), https://www.socresonline.org.uk/19/1/10.html.

16. See, for example, Jan Plamper, *The History of Emotions: An Introduction* (Oxford: Oxford University Press, 2015); and Ute Frevert, ed., *Emotional Lexicons: Continuity and Change in the Vocabulary of Feeling 1700–2000* (Oxford: Oxford University Press, 2014).

17. *Oxford English Dictionary Online,* s.v. "belong (v.)," http://www.oed.com /view/Entry/17506?rskey=glblng&result=1&isAdvanced=false.

18. Montserrat Guibernau, *Belonging: Solidarity and Division in Modern Societies* (Cambridge: Polity Press, 2013), esp. 1–6, 26–49, quotation on 4.

19. Marshall Berman, *All That Is Solid Melts into Air: The Experience of Modernity* (New York: Simon and Schuster, 1981).

20. Benedict R. Anderson, *Imagined Communities: Reflections on the Origin and Spread of Nationalism* (London: Verso, 2016), 6.

21. Richard Kearney, *Poetics of Imagining: Modern to Post-modern* (New York: Fordham University Press, 1998), 241.

22. Much of my thinking on this matter has been influenced by Vladimír Macura's essay "Prague," in *The Mystifications of a Nation: "The Potato Bug" and Other Essays on Czech Culture,* trans. Hana Pichová and Craig Cravens (Madison: University of Wisconsin Press, 2010), 35–49.

23. Göran Therborn, *Cities of Power: The Urban, the National, the Popular, the Global* (London: Verso, 2017), 12. On the spatial exercise of power in capital cities, see also Michael Minkenberg, *Power and Architecture: The Construction of Capitals and the Politics of Space* (New York: Berghahn Books, 2014); and Lawrence J. Vale, *Architecture, Power, and National Identity* (New Haven, CT: Yale University Press, 1992).

24. Cynthia Paces, *Prague Panoramas: National Memory and Sacred Space in the Twentieth Century* (Pittsburgh: University of Pittsburgh Press, 2009).

25. Jakub S. Beneš, *Workers and Nationalism: Czech and German Social Democracy in Habsburg Austria, 1890–1918* (Oxford: Oxford University Press, 2017), esp. 133–134.

26. Tara Zahra, *Kidnapped Souls: National Indifference and the Battle for Children in the Bohemian Lands, 1900–1948* (Ithaca, NY: Cornell University Press, 2008); Zahra, "Imagined Noncommunities: National Indifference as a Category of Analysis," *Slavic Review* 69, no. 1 (2010): 93–119; and Pieter Judson, *Guardians of the Nation: Activists on the Language Frontier of Imperial Austria* (Cambridge, MA: Harvard University Press, 2006). See also Karl F. Bahm, "Beyond the Bourgeoisie: Rethinking Nation, Culture, and Modernity in Nineteenth-Century Central Europe," *Austrian History Yearbook* 29 (1998): 19–35; Jeremy King, *Budweisers into Czechs and Germans: A Local History of Bohemian Politics, 1848–1948* (Princeton, NJ: Princeton University Press, 2002); Eagle Glassheim, *Noble Nationalists: The Transformation of the Bohemian Aristocracy* (Cambridge, MA: Harvard University Press, 2005); Robert Nemes, "Obstacles to Nationalization on the Hungarian-Romanian Language Frontier," *Austrian History Yearbook* 43 (2012): 28–44; and Pamela Ballinger, "History's 'Illegibles': National Indeterminacy in Istria," *Austrian History Yearbook* 33 (2012): 116–137. For an example of "national indifference" beyond the Habsburg monarchy, see James E. Bjork, *Neither German nor Pole: Catholicism and National Indifference in a Central European Borderland* (Ann Arbor: University of Michigan Press, 2008).

27. See, for example, Alon Confino, *A World without Jews: The Nazi Imagination from Persecution to Genocide* (New Haven, CT: Yale University Press, 2014).

28. On storyworlds and shared acts of imagination, see Stefan Arvidsson, Jakub S. Beneš, and Anja Kirsch, "Introduction: Socialist Imaginations," in *Socialist Imaginations: Utopias, Myths, and the Masses,* ed. Stefan Arvidsson, Jakub S. Beneš, and Anja Kirsch (London: Routledge, 2019), esp. 1–2 and 6–7. See also Lucia Traut and Annette Wilke, "Einleitung," in *Religion—Imagination—Ästhetik: Vorstellungs- und Sinneswelten in Religion und Kultur,* ed. Lucia Traut and Annette Wilke (Göttingen: Vandenhoeck & Ruprecht, 2015), 17–73, esp.

22 for a discussion of shared imaginary spaces and their concept of an "imagination collective." See also C. V. Wedgewood, "The Sense of the Past," in *Historians on History*, ed. John Tosh (Harlow, UK: Pearson Longman, 2009), 33.

29. R. G. Collingwood, *The Idea of History*, ed. Jan van der Dussen (Oxford: Clarendon Press, 1993). Collingwood thought little of biography, calling it a "spectacle of such bodily life and its vicissitudes," yet a study that reenacts, in the mind's eye, an individual life was central to his idea of historical scholarship, even if the lives of "great men" were his foremost concern. Collingwood, *The Idea of History*, 304.

30. Richard Rorty, "The Fire of Life," *Poetry* 191, no. 2 (November 2007): 129–131, quotation on 191. See also Rorty, *Philosophy as Cultural Politics*, Philosophical Papers, vol. 4 (Cambridge: Cambridge University Press, 2007), 105–119. For an interpretation, see Ulf Schulenberg, *Romanticism and Pragmatism: Richard Rorty and the Idea of a Poeticized Culture* (New York: Palgrave Macmillan, 2015).

31. Kearney, *Poetics of Imagining*, 241.

1. GERMAN CITY

Note: Translations of quotations in this book are the author's unless otherwise indicated.

1. Pavel Bělina, ed., *Dějiny Prahy: Od sloučení pražských měst v roce 1784 do současnosti* (Prague: Paseka, 1997), 70; Karel Vladislav Zap, *Průvodce po Praze: Potřebná příruční kniha pro každého, kdo se s pamětnostmi českého hlawního města seznámiti chce* (Prague: Bedřich Krečmár 1848), 51 (hereafter *PoP*).

2. Edgar Theodor Havránek, *Neznámá Praha*, 2 vols. (Prague: Paseka, 2004), 1:27; Wilhelm Ferdinand Bischoff, *Reise durch die Königreiche Sachsen und Böhmen in den Jahren 1822 und 1823* (Leipzig: Hartmann, 1825), 139. On the experience of entering a walled city more generally, see Daniel Jütte, "Entering a City: On a Lost Early Modern Practice," *Urban History* 41, no. 2 (2014): 204–227.

3. August Franz Wenzel Griesel, *Neustes Gemälde von Prag* (Prague: J. G. Calve'schen Buchhandlumg, 1823), 73.

4. Bělina, *Dějiny Prahy*, 15–17; Josef Janáček, *Malé dějiny Prahy* (Prague: Panorama, 1983), 243–244; Jitka Lněničková, *České země v době předbřeznové, 1792–1848* (Prague: Libri, 1999), 60–62.

5. On Jewish shops and house rentals just beyond the borders of the Jewish Town, see Cathleen M. Giustino, *Tearing Down Prague's Jewish Town: Ghetto Clearance and the Legacy of Middle-Class Ethnic Politics around 1900* (Boulder, CO: East European Monographs, 2003), 162.

6. Milan Hlavačka, *Cestování v éře dostavníku: Všední den na středoevropských cestách* (Prague: Argo, 1998), 23–28.

7. Emanuel Poche, *Prahou krok za krokem: Uměleckohistorický průvodce městem* (Prague: Orbis, 1958), 23–28.

8. Franz Klutschak, *Der Führer durch Prag* (Prague: Gottlieb Haase Söhne, 1845), 133.

9. Bělina, *Dějiny Prahy,* 24; Ludmila Kárníková, *Vývoj obyvatelstva v českých zemích 1754–1914* (Prague: Nakl. Československé akademie věd, 1965), 105, 107.

10. Griesel, *Neustes Gemälde von Prag,* 66; Karel Vladislav Zap, *Popsánj kr. hlawnjho města Prahy pro cizince i domácj* (Prague: W. Špinky, 1835), 250 (hereafter *PKHMP*).

11. Jiří Štaif, *Obezřetná elita: Česká společnost mezi tradicí a revolucí 1830–1851* (Prague: Dokořán, 2005), 72. I am consciously using the term "middling classes" to capture the socioeconomic diversity within the strata of society existing between the aristocracy on the one hand and the peasantry and laborers on the other. I use "middle-class" as an adjective when referring to commonly accepted values and sociability practices or to a specific population within the middling classes. For a thoughtful discussion of the term "middle class," see Jürgen Kocka, "The Middle Class in Europe," *Journal of Modern History* 67, no. 4 (December 1995): 783–810.

12. Lněničková, *České země v době předbřeznové, 1792–1848,* 254–255.

13. Griesel, *Neustes Gemälde von Prag,* 68.

14. Stanley Pech, *The Czech Revolution of 1848* (Chapel Hill: University of North Carolina Press, 1969), 9–12; Bělina, *Dějiny Prahy,* 22.

15. John Connelly, *From Peoples into Nations: A History of Eastern Europe* (Princeton, NJ: Princeton University Press, 2020), 61.

16. On the popularity of Prague as a destination for Germans, see Peter Demetz, *Prague in Black and Gold: Scenes from a Life of a Central European City* (New York: Hill and Wang, 1997), 272–274, and the voluminous quotations from various German travel writers in Julius Max Schottky, *Prag, wie es war und wie es ist: Nach Aktenstücken und den besten Quellenschriften geschildert,* 2 vols. (Prague: J. G. Calve'sche Buchhandlung, 1831), 1:10–33. A number of German-speaking British travelers ventured off the Grand Tour to visit Prague as well. Peter Bugge, "'Something in the View Which Makes You Linger': Bohemia and Bohemians in British Travel Writing, 1836–1857," *Central Europe* 7, no. 1 (May 2009): 3–29.

17. Demetz, *Prague in Black and Gold,* 272–273, quotation on 273. See also Jindřich Toman, "Making Sense of a Ruin: Nineteenth-Century Gentile Images of the Old Jewish Cemetery in Prague," *Bohemia* 52, no. 1 (2012): 108–122.

18. Stephan Oettermann, *The Panorama: History of a Mass Medium* (New York: Zone Books, 1997), 7. Soon thereafter, Oettermann writes, the word came

to mean a "survey" or "overview" of "a particular field of knowledge, such as art, literature, or history."

19. Karl Baedeker, *Handbuch für Reisende durch Deutschland und den oesterreichischen Kaiserstaat* (Coblenz: Karl Baedeker, 1842), 190. See also Ludwig Lange, *Prag und seine nächsten Umgebungen in malerischen Original-Ansichten nach der Natur* (Darmstadt: Gustav Georg Lange, 1841), 3–4.

20. Jaroslaus Schaller, *Beschreibung der königlichen Haupt- und Residenzstadt Prag: Sammt allen darinn befindlichen sehenwürdigen Merkwürdigkeiten* (Prague: Gaspar Widtmann, 1820), 3.

21. Vincy Schwarz, *Město vidím veliké: Cizinci o Praze* (Prague: Fr. Borový, 1940), 172.

22. J. G. Kohl, *Austria, Vienna, Prague, Hungary, Bohemia, and the Danube: Galicia, Styria, Moravia, Bukovina and the Military Frontier* (London: Chapman and Hall, 1844), 16.

23. Mack Walker, *German Home Towns: Community, State, and General Estate, 1648–1871* (Ithaca, NY: Cornell University Press, 1971), 322–328.

24. Bischoff, *Reise durch die Königreiche Sachsen und Böhmen*, 138. See also "Der Wanderer," *Wiener Zeitschrift* (1815), quoted in Schottky, *Prag, wie es war und wie es ist*, 1:12–13.

25. Karel Vladislav Zap to Antonin Zap, December 30, 1831, fond Karel Vladislav Zap, Památník národního písemnictví (hereafter PNP).

26. "Karel Vladislav Zap," *Národní listy* 3, no. 2 (January 1871): 2; "Zap, Karel Vladislav," in *Ottův slovník naučný: Illustrovaná encyklopædie obecných vědomostí*, 28 vols. (Prague: J. Otto, 1888–1909), 27:430–432; Vladimír Forst, Luboš Merhaut, and Jiří Opelík, *Lexikon české literatury: Osobnosti, díla, instituce* (Prague: Academia, 1985); and Karel Hynek Mácha, *May*, trans. Marcela Sulak (Prague: Twisted Spoon Press, 2010), 123.

27. Zap, *PKHMP*; J. K. Chmelenský, "Literatura česká," *Časopis českého Museum* 9, no. 1 (1835): 113. Zap's 1835 topography also received mention in Josef Wacláv Justin Michl, *Auplný literturnj létopis, čili, obraz slowesnosti Slowanůw nářečj českého w Čechách, na Morawě, w Uhřjch atd., od léta 1825 až do léta 1837¼* (Prague: J. W. J. Michl, 1839), 163; and *Časopis českého Museum* 9, no. 1 (1835): 130.

28. Josef Kunský, *Čeští cestovatelé*, 2 vols. (Prague: Orbis, 1961), 1:344.

29. Karel Vladislav Zap, *Zrcadlo života na východní Ewropě*, 3 vols. (Prague: Jan Bohumír Calve, 1843–1844). See also Kunský, *Čeští cestovatelé*, 1:345; Derek Sayer, *The Coasts of Bohemia: A Czech History* (Princeton, NJ: Princeton University Press, 1998), 129; and Irena Štepanová, "Obrazy a zrcadla: Etnografika a slavika v díle manželů Zapových," *Český lid* 93 (2006), 138–143.

30. "Proslov," *Pautník: Časopis obrázkový pro každého* 1 (1846): 1.

31. Karel Vladislav Zap, *Pomněnky na Prahu: Popsání nejpřednějších památností tohoto hlavního města* (Prague: Bedřich Krečmár, 1845).

32. In the course of my research I have been unable to locate a first edition of Zap's *Guide*. Thus, this chapter will rely on the second edition: Zap, *PoP.* Publication of the 1847 edition was announced in the winter edition of *Časopis českého Museum* 21, no. 4 (1847): 465. Just before the revolution, the same journal announced the publication of the 1848 edition. See *Časopis českého Museum* 22, no. 3 (1848): 324. During the intervening period Zap's publisher released his chapter on the Hradčany district of Prague, probably in the last months of 1847, even though the publication date suggests otherwise. K. V. Zap, *Popsání král. hradu, chrámu sv. Wita a všech ostatních památnosti na Hradčanech w Praze* (Prague: Bedřich Krečmar, 1848); *Časopis českého Museum* 21, no. 6 (1847): 673. The precise publication date of the German translation is unclear. Given the fact that the German translation makes no mention of the revolution we might assume that it was published before or shortly after March 1848. Karel Vladislav Zap, *Wegweiser durch Prag: Ein nothwendiges Handbuch für Fremde, die sich mit den Merkwürdigkeiten der böhmischen Hautpstadt bekannt zu machen wünschen*, trans. L. Ritter von Rittersberg (Prague: Friedrich Kretzschmar, 1848).

33. Peter Brock, *The Slovak National Awakening: An Essay in the Intellectual History of East Central Europe* (Toronto: University of Toronto Press, 1976), 29–33.

34. *Kwěty* 15, no. 156 (1847): 1; and *Kwěty* 15, no. 1 (1848): 1. After 1848 the journal's banner simply stated that it was a journal for the nation.

35. Wendy Bracewell, "Travels through the Slav World," in *Under Eastern Eyes: A Comparative Introduction to East European Travel Writing on Europe*, ed. Wendy Bracewell and Alex Drace-Francis (Budapest: Central European Press, 2008), 147–195, esp. 158–159; Štaif, *Obezřetná elita*, 134–143. On pan-Slavism more generally, see Hans Kohn, *Pan-Slavism: Its History and Ideology* (New York: Vintage Books, 1960).

36. Štaif, *Obezřetná elita*, 30–49; Jiří Kořalka, *František Palacký (1798–1876): Der Historiker der Tschechen im österreichischen Vielvölkerstaat* (Vienna: Verlag der Österreichischen Akademie der Wissenschaften, 2007), 106–107. On the centrality of language, see Peter Bugge, "Czech Nation-Building: National Self-Perception and Politics 1780–1914" (PhD diss., University of Aarhus, 1994), 25–37; Vladimír Macura, *Znamení zrodu: České národní obrození jako kulturní typ* (Jinočany: H & H, 1995); and Hugh LeCaine Agnew, *The Czechs and the Lands of the Bohemian Crown* (Stanford, CA: Hoover Institution Press, 2004), 100, 110–116.

37. Sayer, *The Coasts of Bohemia*, 82.

38. Peter Bugge, "The Czech World of Vladimír Macura," in Vladimír Macura, *The Mystifications of the Nation: The "Potato Bug" and Other Essays on Czech Culture*, trans. Hana Píchová and Craig Cravens (Madison: University of Wisconsin Press, 2010), xxiii.

39. Štaif, *Obezřetná elita*, 99, 101.

40. Miroslav Hroch, *Social Preconditions of National Revival in Europe: A Comparative Analysis of the Social Composition of Patriotic Groups among the Smaller European Nations* (Cambridge: Cambridge University Press, 1985), 38, table 2. See also Sayer, *The Coasts of Bohemia*, 80–81.

41. Piotr Wandycz, *The Price of Freedom: A History of East Central Europe from the Middle Ages to the Present* (London: Routledge, 1992), 145.

42. "Wýtah k aučtů Českého museum týkajících se příjmů a wydání Matice české roku 1846," *Časopis českého Museum* 21, no. 6, suppl. (1847): 16.

43. *Časopis českého Museum* 20, no. 3 (1846): 399.

44. On Honorata Zapová, see Edvard Jelínek, *Honorata z Wiśniowských Zapová: Zápisky z rodinné korrespondence a vlasteneckých vzpomínek* (Prague: J. Otto, 1894); Zofia Tarajło-Lipowska, "Snahy o sblížení národů na salónní půdě: Honorata z Wiśniowskich-Zapová a český salon," in *Salony v české kultuře 19. století*, ed. Helena Lorenzová and Taťána Petrasová (Prague: Koniash Latin Press, 1999), 108–115; Zofia Tarajło-Lipowska, "Pod rouškou spořádaného manželství aneb smutný případ Honoraty Zapové," in *Sex a tabu v české kultuře 19. století*, ed. Václav Petrbok (Prague: Academia, 1999), 104–113; Štepanová, "Obrazy a zrcadla," 137–151; and Dáša Frančíková, *Women as Essential Citizens in the Czech National Movement: The Making of Modern Czech Community* (Lanham, MD: Lexington Books, 2017).

45. Michael Henry Heim, *The Russian Journey of Karel Havlíček Borovský* (Munich: O. Sagner, 1979), 59.

46. Karel Vladislav Zap to Antonin Zap, August 26, 1942, fond Karel Vladislav Zap, PNP; Karel Vladislav Zap to Antonin Zap, June 27, 1844, fond Karel Vladislav Zap, PNP.

47. Karel Vladislav Zap to Honorata Zapová, February 20, 1840, fond Karel Vladislav Zap, PNP.

48. Karel Vladislav Zap to Honorata Zapová, June 1, 1839, fond Karel Vladislav Zap, PNP; Karel Vladislav Zap to Honorata Zapová, July 28, 1839, fond Karel Vladislav Zap, PNP.

49. Karel Vladislav Zap to Antonin Zap, August 26, 1842, fond Karel Vladislav Zap, PNP.

50. Karel Vladislav Zap to Antonin Zap, [n.d.; early 1843(?)], fond Karel Vladislav Zap, PNP.

51. Karel Vladislav Zap to Antonin Zap, November 3, 1843, fond Karel Vladislav Zap, PNP.

52. Karel Vladislav Zap to Antonin Zap, June 27, 1844, fond Karel Vladislav Zap, PNP. Zap's worries about his income predated the birth of his children, too. See, for example, Karel Vladislav Zap to Františka Zapová, January 16, 1838, fond Karel Vladislav Zap, PNP; Karel Vladislav Zap to Honorata Zapová, May 1, 1840, fond Karel Vladislav Zap, PNP.

53. Karel Vladislav Zap to Antonin Zap, June 27, 1844, fond Karel Vladislav Zap, PNP. See also Karel Vladislav Zap to Honorata Zapová, January 15, 1840, fond Karel Vladislav Zap, PNP.

54. Karel Vladislav Zap to Antonin Zap, May 19, 1843, fond Karel Vladislav Zap, PNP.

55. Karel Vladislav Zap to Antonin Zap, June 27, 1844, fond Karel Vladislav Zap, PNP.

56. Karel Vladislav Zap to Honorata Zapová, May 1, 1840, fond Karel Vladislav Zap, PNP.

57. Přehled ročních příjmů a vydání za léta 1831–1851, fond Karel Vladislav Zap, PNP.

58. Tarajło-Lipowska, "Snahy o sblížení národů na salónní půdě," 115.

59. Jelínek, *Honorata z Wiśniowských Zapová*, 55.

60. Václav Vladivoj Tomek, *Paměti z mého žiwota*, 2 vols. (Prague: W komissi u F. Řiwnáče, 1904–1905), 1:215, 231, 217.

61. Karl Vladslav Zap to Honorata Zapová, May 1, 1840, fond Karel Vladislav Zap, PNP.

62. Jelínek, *Honorata z Wiśniowských Zapová*, 54.

63. Jelínek, *Honorata z Wiśniowských Zapová*, 48.

64. Jelínek, *Honorata z Wiśniowských Zapová*, 49. Years later, in an advice piece about female friendships, Zapová cautioned readers against forming friendships with women from large cities. They have too many so-called friends, she wrote, and were thus generally only able to form superficial relationships. Frančíková, *Women as Essential Citizens in the Czech National Movement*, 42.

65. Jelínek, *Honorata z Wiśniowských Zapová*, 52.

66. Griesel, *Neuestes Gemälde von Prag*, 114–115.

67. Rebecca Solnit, *Wanderlust: A History of Walking* (New York: Viking, 2000), 85.

68. Wolfgang Kaschuba, "Die Fußreise: Von Arbeitswanderung zur bürgerlichen Bildungsbewegung," in *Reisekultur: Von der Pilgerfahrt zum modernen Tourismus*, ed. Hermann Bausinger, Klaus Beyrer, and Gottfried Korff (Munich: C. H. Beck, 1991), 165–173, quotation on 168.

69. Zap, *Zrcadlo života na wýchodni Ewropě*, vol. 3.

70. Bracewell, "Travels through the Slav World," 172.

71. Milada Součková, *The Czech Romantics* (The Hague: Mouton, 1958); Albert Pražák, *Karel Hynek Mácha* (Prague: Školni nakl., 1936); and Jan Čáka, *Poutník Mácha* (Příbram: Knihkupectví Mária Olšanská, 2006).

72. Holm Sundhaussen, *Der Einfluss der Herderschen Ideen auf die Nationsbildung bei den Völkern der Habsburger Monarchie* (Munich: R. Oldenbourg, 1973); Lonnie Johnson, *Central Europe: Enemies, Neighbors, Friends* (New York: Oxford University Press, 2011), 124–135.

73. Jozef Miloslav Hurban, *Cesta Slováka ku bratrům slavenským na Moravě a v Čechách* (Žilina-Košice: Nakl. Slovenského východu, 1929 [1841]), 65.

74. Zap, *Zrcadlo života na wýchodni Ewropě*, 3:25.

75. Hurban, *Cesta Slováka ku bratrům slavenským*, 11, quoted in Vladimír Macura, "Vlak jako symbol 19. století," in *Osudový vlak: Sborník příspěvků stejnojmenné vědecké konference k 150. výročí příjezdu prvního vlaku do Prahy*, ed. Rudolf Pohl (Prague: Nezávislý novinář (III), 1995), 59–60. On the ways that train travel transformed Europeans' conception of time and space while also creating new, often disturbing ways of perceiving the world, see Wolfgang Schivelbusch, *The Railway Journey: The Industrialization of Time and Space in the 19th Century* (Berkeley: University of California Press, 1986), esp. 9–15, 33–44; and Chad Bryant, "Into an Uncertain Future: Railroads and Vormärz Liberalism in Brno, Vienna, and Prague," *Austrian History Yearbook* 40 (2009): 183–201.

76. Zap, *PKHMP*, 203.

77. Schottky, *Prag, wie es war und wie es ist*, 1:77.

78. Zap, *PoP*, 2.

79. Zap, *PoP*, ii.

80. Vladimír Macura, "Where Is My Home?," in Macura, *The Mystifications of the Nation*, 3–7. The editors' translation of "Where Is My Home?" is on pp. 3–4.

81. Macura, *The Mystifications of the Nation*, 35–46, quotation on 41.

82. Zap, *PKHMP*, i.

83. Tomek, *Paměti z mého žiwota*, 1:26.

84. Jaroslaus Schaller, *Beschreibung der königlichen Haupt- und Residenzstadt Prag: Sammt allen darinn sehenswürdigen Merkwürdigkeiten*, 4 vols. (Prague: Franz Gerzabeck, 1794–1797).

85. Zap, *PoP*, 55, 230.

86. Zap, *PoP*, 55–56, quotation on 56.

87. See, for example, Deborah Epstein Nord, *Walking the Victorian Streets: Women, Representation, and the City* (Ithaca, NY: Cornell University Press,

1995), 19–48; Joseph A. Amato, *On Foot: A History of Walking* (New York: New York University Press, 2004), 153–178; and Alison O'Byrne, "The Art of Walking in London: Representing Urban Pedestrianism in the Early Nineteenth Century," *Romanticism* 14 (2008): 94–107.

88. Hayden Lorimer, "Walking: New Forms and Spaces for Studies of Pedestrianism," in *Geographies of Mobilities: Practices, Spaces, Subjects*, ed. Tim Cresswell and Peter Merriman (Burlington, VT: Ashgate, 2011), 20.

89. Karel Vladislav Zap to Honorata Zapová, April 6, 1839, fond Karel Vladislav Zap, PNP.

90. Tomek, *Paměti z mého žiwota*, 1:215, 231, 217.

91. Sebastian Willibald Schiessler, *Prag und seine Umgebungen: Ein Taschenbuch für Fremde und Einheimische*, vol. 1 (Prague: K. W. Enders, 1812), 12.

92. Griesel, *Neustes Gemälde von Prag*, 75.

93. Virgil Nemoianu, *The Taming of Romanticism: European Literature and the Age of Biedermeier* (Cambridge, MA: Harvard University Press, 1984), 11.

94. Lněničková, *České země v době předbřeznové, 1792–1848*, 255–256.

95. David L. Cooper, *Creating the Nation: Identity and Aesthetics in Early Nineteenth-Century Russia and Bohemia* (DeKalb: Northern Illinois University Press, 2010), 73.

96. Schaller, *Beschreibung der königlichen Haupt- und Residenzstadt Prag* (1820 ed.), 11, 51.

97. Adolph Schmidl, *Reisehandbuch durch das Königreich Böhmen, Mähren, Schlesien, Galizien, die Bukowina und nach Jassy* (Vienna: Carl Gerold, 1836), 40.

98. On the emerging middle-class practice of strolling and the cult of nature in Prague, see Lněničková, *České země v době předbřeznové, 1792–1848*, 271; Michaela Marek, *Kunst und Identitätspolitik: Architektur und Bildkünste im Prozess der tschechischen Nationsbildung* (Cologne: Böhlau, 2004), 24–32. On the phenomenon more generally, see Gudrun M. König, *Eine Kulturgeschichte des Spazierganges: Spuren einer bürgerlichen Praktik 1780 bis 1850* (Vienna: Böhlau, 1996); Amato, *On Foot*, 71–124; Robin Jarvis, *Romantic Writing and Pedestrian Travel* (Houndmills, UK: Macmillan, 1997); and Jeffrey C. Robinson, *The Walk: Notes on a Romantic Image* (Norman, IL: Dalkey Archive Press, 2006), esp. 70–77.

99. Zap, *PoP*, 297–298, 299–300, 302–304.

100. Zap, *PKHMP*.

101. Schmidl, *Reisehandbuch durch das Königreich Böhmen*, 40–41.

102. Schaller, *Beschreibung der königlichen Haupt- und Residenzstadt Prag* (1820 ed.), 67–68.

103. Constantin von Wurzbach, *Biographisches Lexikon des Kaiserthums Oesterreich*, 60 vols. (Vienna: K. K. Hof- und Staatsdruckerie, 1857), 2:241–242; Olga Bašeová, Ladislav Neubert, and Milada Vilímková, eds., *Pražské zahrady* (Prague: Panorama, 1991), 86. See also Robert Rotenberg, "Biedermeier Gardens in Vienna and the Self-Fashioning of Middle-Class Identities," in *Gardens, City Life, and Culture: A World Tour*, ed. Michel Conan and Chen Whangheng (Washington, DC: Dumbarton Oaks Trustees for Harvard University, 2008), 115–116.

104. John Murray, *A Handbook for Travelers in Southern Germany* (London: John Murray, 1843), 398, 176. See also Schmidl, *Reisehandbuch durch das Königreich Böhmen*, 41.

105. Schottky, *Prag, wie es war und wie es ist*, 1:23.

106. Rudolph E. von Jenny, *Handbuch für Reisende in dem oesterreichischen Kaiserstaate* (Vienna: Anton Doll, 1823), 431; Zap, *PKHMP,* 198–199; Murray, *A Handbook for Travelers in Southern Germany*, 328; Baedeker, *Handbuch für Reisende durch Deutschland*, 195; Zap, *PoP,* 53.

107. Washington Irving, "Prague, Saturday June 13, 1823, letter to Miss Emily Foster," in *The Life and Letters of Washington Irving*, 4 vols., ed. Pierre M. Irving (New York: G. P. Putnam, 1864), 4:402–403.

108. Griesel, *Neustes Gemälde von Prag,* 110.

109. Zap, *PKHMP,* 204–206; Schmidl, *Reisehandbuch durch das Königreich Böhmen*, 41–42.

110. Sabine Krebber, *Der Spaziergang in der Kunst: Eine Untersuchung des Motives in der Kunst des 18. und 19. Jahrhunderts* (Frankfurt am Main: Peter Lang, 1990), 26–29, 93–97.

111. Griesel, *Neustes Gemälde von Prag,* 110.

112. Griesel, *Neustes Gemälde von Prag,* 72–73.

113. Zap, *PoP,* 293; Schmidl, *Reisehandbuch durch das Königreich Böhmen*, 42.

114. Schottky, *Prag, wie es war und wie es ist*, 1:14n1.

115. Kárníková, *Vývoj obyvatelstva v českých zemích 1754–1914,* 105.

116. Zap, *PoP,* 285–286, quotation on 286.

117. Zap, *PoP,* 130–131.

118. Anon., *Die Unruhen in Böhmen: Ein Wort zu seiner Zeit* (Leipzig(?): Ph. Relam, 1845), 3; Anon., *Prag und die Prager: Aus den Papieren eines Lebendig-Todten* (Leipzig: Reclam, 1845), 69. See also Josef V. Polišenský, *Aristocrats and the Crowd in the Revolutionary Year 1848: A Contribution to the History of Revolution and Counter-Revolution in Austria* (Albany: State University of New York Press, 1980).

119. Toman, "Making Sense of a Ruin."

120. Zap, *PoP*, 52–53. On the ordinance, see Giustino, *Tearing Down Prague's Jewish Town*, 163.

121. Zap, *PoP*, 25.

122. Zap, *PoP*, 47.

123. On the Slavic Congress and Zap's role in it, see John Erickson, "The Preparatory Committee of the Slav Congress," in *The Czech Renascence of the Nineteenth Century*, ed. Peter Brock and H. Gordon Skilling (Toronto: University of Toronto Press, 1970): 176–201; and Václav Žáček, *Slovanský sjezd v Praze roku 1848: Sbírka dokumentů* (Prague: Československá akademie věd, 1958), esp. 135, 358–361. For elites distancing themselves from radicals as well as a description of events in Prague during the 1848 revolution more broadly, see Demetz, *Prague in Black and Gold*, 296–300; Pech, *The Czech Revolution of 1848*, esp. 47–78, 139–162; and Štaif, *Obezřetná elita*, 203–213, 255–268.

124. Honorata Zapová to Karel Vladislav Zap, June 17, 1848, fond Karel Vladislav Zap, PNP. She composed the letter after escaping the city.

125. Demetz, *Prague in Black and Gold*, 298–299.

126. Jelínek, *Honorata z Wiśniowských Zapová*, 66, 86.

127. *Průvodčí po Praze a okolí města: S plánem Prahy a popsáním nejvíce vynikajících památností historických, budov a ústavů veřejných* (Prague: Karel Bellmann, 1883), 82.

128. *Knappův průvodce po Praze a okolí* (Karlín: M. Knapp, 1900), 33.

2. CZECH CITY

1. Egon Erwin Kisch, "Der Clamsche Garten," *Bohemia*, August 7, 1910, 1. Reprinted in Kisch, *Gesammelte Werke in Einzelausgaben*, vol. 2, part 1 (Berlin: Aufbau-Verlag, 1960), 7–11 (hereafter *GWE*).

2. Gary B. Cohen, *The Politics of Ethnic Survival: Germans in Prague, 1861–1914* (West Lafayette, IN: Purdue University Press, 2006), 111.

3. Specifically, according to the 1900 census, 45 percent of Prague's self-declared Jews marked "German" as their language of everyday use. Ten years earlier, self-declared German speakers made up almost three-quarters of the city's Jewish population. Cohen, *The Politics of Ethnic Survival*, 76, table 3 / 3.

4. Pieter M. Judson, *The Habsburg Empire: A New History* (Cambridge, MA: Harvard University Press, 2016). See also "An Imperial Dynamo? CEH Forum on Pieter Judson's *The Habsburg Empire: A New History*," *Central European History* 50, no. 2 (2017): 236–259.

5. Jeremy King, *Budweisers into Czechs and Germans: A Local History of Bohemian Politics, 1848–1948* (Princeton, NJ: Princeton University Press, 2002); Pieter M. Judson, *Guardians of the Nation: Activists on the Language Frontiers of Imperial Austria* (Cambridge, MA: Harvard University Press, 2006); Tara Zahra, *Kidnapped Souls: National Indifference and the Battle for Children in the Bohemian Lands, 1900–1948* (Ithaca, NY: Cornell University Press, 2008).

6. Cohen, *The Politics of Ethnic Survival*, 92–93.

7. Cathleen M. Giustino, *Tearing Down Prague's Jewish Town: Ghetto Clearance and the Legacy of Middle-Class Ethnic Politics around 1900* (Boulder, CO: East European Monographs, 2003), 30, table 2.1, 42, 44.

8. On the restrictions imposed on women, see Katherine David, "Czech Feminists and Nationalism in the Late Habsburg Monarchy: The 'First in Austria,'" *Journal of Women's History* 3, no. 2 (Fall 1991): 27, 36–38.

9. The 1900 census reported that only 6 percent of those in the Austrian half of the monarchy who claimed Czech as their language of everyday life were illiterate. Only 8 percent of declared German speakers could not read. Hillel Kieval, *Languages of Community: The Jewish Experience in the Czech Lands* (Berkeley: University of California Press, 2000), 13. See also Otto Urban, *České a slovenské dějiny do roku 1918* (Prague: Aleš Skřivan, 2000), 257.

10. Derek Sayer, *The Coasts of Bohemia: A Czech History* (Princeton, NJ: Princeton University Press, 1998), 94.

11. Gary B. Cohen, *Education and Middle-Class Society in Imperial Austria, 1848–1918* (West Lafayette, IN: Purdue University Press, 1996), 184.

12. Catherine Albrecht, "The Rhetoric of Economic Nationalism in the Boycott Campaigns of the Late Habsburg Monarchy," *Austrian History Yearbook* 23 (2001): 58–60.

13. The term "professional nationalist" was first coined by Jan Křen. See his *Die Konfliktgemeinschaft Tschechen und Deutsche 1780–1918* (Munich: Oldenbourg, 1996).

14. See, for example, Svatopluk Čech, "Praha," in *Verše o Praze*, ed. Jaroslav Seifert (Československý spisovatel: Prague, 1962), 24. On funerals, see Marek Nekula, "Prague Funerals: How Czech National Symbols Conquered and Defended Public Space," in *Rites of Place: Public Commemoration in Russia and Eastern Europe*, ed. Julie Buckler and Emily D. Johnson (Evanston, IL: Northwestern University Press, 2013), 35–57.

15. Claire Nolte, "Celebrating Slavic Prague: Festivals and the Urban Environment, 1891–1912," *Bohemia: Zeitschrift für Geschichte und Kultur der böhmischen Länder* 52, no. 1 (2012): 40–41.

16. Zdeněk Hojda and Jiří Pokorný, *Pomníky a zapomníky* (Prague: Paseka, 1996). See also Cynthia Paces, *Prague Panoramas: National Memory and Sacred Space in the Twentieth Century* (Pittsburgh: University of Pittsburgh Press, 2009), 56–69; Nolte, "Celebrating Slavic Prague," 41, 50; Petr Wittich, "Sochařství," in *Praha národního probuzení: Čtvero knih o Praze; Architektura, sochařství, malířství, užité umění,* ed. Emanuel Poche (Prague: Panorama, 1980), 205–278, esp. 243; and Marek Nekula, "Die deutsche Walhalla und der tschechische Slavín," in *Brücken: Germanistisches Jahrbuch Tschechien-Slowakei* 9–10 (2003): 87–106.

17. Marek Nekula, "Die nationale Kodierung des öffentliches Raums in Prag," in *Praha-Prag 1900–1945: Literaturstadt zweier Spracher,* ed. Peter Becher and Anna Knechtel (Passau: Stutz, 2010), 63–88; Marek Nekula, *Franz Kafka and His Prague Contexts: Studies in Language and Literature* (Prague: Karolinum Press, 2016), 211–213.

18. Paces, *Prague Panoramas,* 56–73. See also Michaela Marek, *Kunst und Identitätspolitik: Architektur und Bildkünste im Prozess der tschechischen Nationsbildung* (Cologne: Böhlau, 2004).

19. Thomas Ort, *Art and Life in Modernist Prague: Karel Čapek and His Generation, 1911–1938* (New York: Palgrave Macmillan, 2013), 31–60.

20. In this respect, Prague had much in common with other east-central European cities. See, for example, Nathaniel D. Wood, *Becoming Metropolitan: Urban Selfhood and the Making of Modern Cracow* (Dekalb: Northern Illinois University Press, 2010).

21. Nolte, "Celebrating Slavic Prague," 44–45; Giustino, *Tearing Down Prague's Jewish Town,* 66–67, quotation on 67. German organizers had been part of the original event planning before they decided to boycott the event, meaning that the jubilee's success counted solely as a modern Czech success. See Catherine Albrecht, "Pride in Production: The Jubilee Exhibition of 1891 and Economic Competition between Czechs and Germans in Bohemia," *Austrian History Yearbook* 24 (1993): 101–118.

22. Pavel Bělina and Jan Vlk, *Dějiny Prahy: Od sloučení Pražských měst v roce 1784 do současnosti* (Prague: Paseka, 1998), 178, 181.

23. Bělina and Vlk, *Dějiny Prahy,* 2:183.

24. Giustino, *Tearing Down Prague's Jewish Town,* 3.

25. Giustino, *Tearing Down Prague's Jewish Town,* 75–77.

26. Ota Konrád and Rudolf Kučera, *Cesty z apokalypsy: Fyzické násilí v pádu a obnově střední Evropy 1914–1922* (Prague: Academia, 2018), 103.

27. Cohen, *The Politics of Ethnic Survival,* 95.

28. Nolte, "Celebrating Slavic Prague," 18.

29. Bělina and Vlk, *Dějiny Prahy,* 2:188.

30. Michal Frankl, Martina Niedhammer, and Ines Koeltzsch, "Umstrittene Gleichberechtigung: Juden in den böhmischen Ländern zwischen 1861 und 1917," in *Zwischen Prag und Nikolsburg: Jüdisches Leben in den böhmischen Ländern,* ed. Kateřina Čapková and Hillel Kieval (Munich: Collegium Carolinum, 2020), 167. See also Ines Koeltzsch, *Geteilte Kulturen: Eine Geschichte der tschechisch-jüdisch-deutschen Beziehungen in Prag (1918–1938)* (Munich: Oldenbourg, 2012), 362.

31. On the long history of the term "golden Prague," see Hana Svatošová, "'Zlatá slovanská Praha': Slovanství ve slovech a skutcích pražské obecní samosprávy 1800–1914," in *"Slavme slavně slávu Slávóv slavných": Slovanství a česká kultura 19. století,* ed. Zdeněk Hojda, Marta Ottlová, and Roman Prahl (Prague: KLP, 2006), 160–171.

32. Giustino, *Tearing Down Prague's Jewish Town,* 124.

33. Frankl, Niedhammer, and Koeltzsch, "Umstrittene Gleichberechtigung," 167–168.

34. Giustino, *Tearing Down Prague's Jewish Town,* 100–101, 107, 140–142; Frankl, Niedhammer, and Koeltzsch, "Umstrittene Gleichberechtigung," 169–171.

35. Cohen, *The Politics of Ethnic Survival,* 67, 270–271.

36. Egon Erwin Kisch, "Familiäres, allzu Familiäres," in *GWE,* 323–326.

37. Cohen, *The Politics of Ethnic Survival,* 61, 83, 80.

38. Egon Erwin Kisch, *Briefe an den Bruder Paul und an die Mutter 1905–1936,* ed. Josef Poláček and Fritz Hofmann (Berlin: Aufbau-Verlag, 1978), June 17, 1911, 46, and an undated letter from Paul excerpted on 425.

39. Cohen, *The Politics of Ethnic Survival,* 76. On the Jewish experience in Bohemia more generally, see Hillel J. Kieval, *The Making of Czech Jewry: National Conflict and Jewish Society in Bohemia, 1870–1918* (New York: Oxford University Press, 1988); Frankl, Niedhammer, and Koeltzsch, "Umstrittene Gleichberechtigung,"159–208; and Malachi H. Hacohen, *Jacob & Esau: Jewish European History between Nation and Empire* (Cambridge: Cambridge University Press, 2019), 279–331.

40. Kieval, *The Making of Czech Jewry,* 7.

41. Kieval, *The Making of Czech Jewry,* 6.

42. Cohen, *The Politics of Ethnic Survival,* 178.

43. Egon Erwin Kisch, "Arrestgebäude," in *GWE,* 181–184; Kisch, "Dragotin Podravič," in *GWE,* 260–267.

44. Kisch, *Briefe an den Bruder Paul,* November 18, 1905, 10. See also Paul's original letter in *Briefe an den Bruder Paul,* 417.

45. Kisch, *Briefe an den Bruder Paul,* November 18, 1905, 10.

46. Kisch, *Briefe an den Bruder Paul,* November 18, 1905, 10.

47. Danica Kozlová and Jiří Tomáš, *Egon Ervín Kisch* (Prague: Horizont, 1984), 19, 23.

48. [Egon Erwin Kisch], "In der Strafanstalt," *Bohemia,* November 26, 1907, 3–4. Kisch also sold this feuilleton to the well-respected *Illustriertes Weiner Extrablatt.* Kisch, *Briefe an den Bruder Paul,* November 27, 1907, 21.

49. Kisch, *Briefe an den Bruder Paul,* April 30, 1908, 425.

50. Kisch, *Briefe an den Bruder Paul,* April 30, 1908, 425.

51. Friedrich Lenger, *European Cities in the Modern Era, 1850–1914* (Leiden: Brill, 2012), 235–236. See also the essays in *Zločin a trest v české kultuře 19. století: Sborník příspěvků z 30. ročníku sympozia k problematice 19. století, Plzeň 25.–27. února 2010,* ed. Lucie Peisertová (Prague: Academia, 2011).

52. Konrád and Kučera, *Cesty z apokalypsy,* 103–109. See also Scott Spector, *Violent Sensations: Sex, Crime, and Utopia in Vienna and Berlin, 1860–1914* (Chicago: University of Chicago Press, 2016); Jakub Machek, *Počátky populární kultury v českých zemích: Tištěná média a velkoměstská kultura kolem roku 1900* (Příbram: Pistorius & Olšanská, 2017), 74–110.

53. *Týdenní zpráva statistické kanceláře hlav. města Prahy a spojených obcí* (Prague: Statistická kancelář, 1910); *Týdenní zpráva statistické kanceláře hlav. města Prahy a spojených obcí* (Prague: Statistická kancelář, 1911). In 1909 and 1910, 3,589 Prague citizens died of pulmonary tuberculosis. Reports of the disease, not surprisingly, were concentrated in working-class districts such as Žižkov. I thank Elisa Moore for compiling these statistics. Throughout Europe, serious crimes such as homicide were more common in the countryside. In Berlin "some twenty homicide a year took place around the turn of the century, half of them infanticides." Lenger, *European Cities in the Modern Era,* 235.

54. Bělina and Vlk, *Dějiny Prahy,* 2:190.

55. [Kisch], "In der Strafanstalt," 3.

56. [Kisch], "In der Strafanstalt," 3.

57. Kisch's "Prague Forays" column ran until April 2, 1911. He republished material from these columns in *Aus Prager Gassen und Nächten* (Prague: A. Haase, 1912). In subsequent years he published *Prager Kinder* (Prague: A. Haase, 1913) and *Die Abenteuer in Prag* (Vienna: Ed. Strache, 1920). In both cases the texts replicate the style, genre, and length of his original "Prague Forays" column. The pieces in the 1920 book appear to include texts written before, during, and after the war. Of the handful that I discuss here, all seem

to have been written before 1914. All three of these collections have been re-printed in *GWE*, from which I cite in these endnotes.

58. Egon Erwin Kisch, "Eine Nacht im Asyl für Obdachlose," in *GWE*, 51.

59. Egon Erwin Kisch, "Die Wirtschaft in der Fišpanka," in *GWE*, 304.

60. Egon Erwin Kisch, "Volksküchen," in *GWE*, 118–119.

61. Egon Erwin Kisch, "Die Zwangsarbeitsanstalt auf dem Hradschin," in *GWE*, 80–84.

62. Egon Erwin Kisch, "In der Wärmestube," in *GWE*, 195.

63. Kisch, "Volksküchen," 119.

64. Kisch, "In der Wärmestube," 195–200.

65. Kisch, "Eine Nacht im Asyl für Obdachlose," 51–59.

66. Kisch, "Die Zwangsarbeitsanstalt auf dem Hradschin," 80–81.

67. Kisch, "Die Zwangsarbeitsanstalt auf dem Hradschin," 84.

68. Egon Erwin Kisch, "Dramaturgy of the Flea Theater," in *Egon Erwin Kisch, the Raging Reporter: A Bio-Anthology*, ed. and trans. Harold B. Segel (West Lafayette, IN: Purdue University Press, 1997), 127.

69. Egon Erwin Kisch, "Bei 'Antouschek,' dem Wasenmeister," in *GWE*, 68–73.

70. Kisch, "Die Zwangsarbeitsanstalt auf dem Hradschin," 81.

71. Czech lessons were mandatory in Prague's German schools when Kisch was growing up. The reverse was true as well. Nekula, *Franz Kafka and His Prague Contexts*, 140.

72. Egon Erwin Kisch, *Pražské obrázky* (Prague: A. Svěcený, 1913), 80.

73. Karl Hans Strobl, "Aus Prager Gassen und Nächten," *Bohemia*, January 7, 1912, 1. See also Kisch, *Briefe an den Bruder Paul*, 550.

74. Strobl, "Aus Prager Gassen und Nächten," 2.

75. Reprinted in Kisch, *Briefe an den Bruder Paul*, 357.

76. Kisch, *Briefe an den Bruder Paul*, 357.

77. Egon Erwin Kisch, "Alt-Prager Mensurlokale," in *GWE*, 185–189.

78. Egon Erwin Kisch, "Die Gifthütte," in *GWE*, 149–153.

79. Cohen, *The Politics of Ethnic Survival*, 117.

80. Nekula, *Franz Kafka and His Prague Contexts*, 72–73.

81. Cohen, *The Politics of Ethnic Survival*, 118. On the percentage of German speakers in 1890, see Cohen, *The Politics of Ethnic Survival*, 70–71, table 3/1.

82. Cohen, *The Politics of Ethnic Survival*, quotation on 282, statistic on 279.

83. Cohen, *The Politics of Ethnic Survival*, 281.

84. See Kieval, *The Making of Czech Jewry*.

85. Cohen, *The Politics of Ethnic Survival*, 90.

86. Carl E. Schorske, "Politics in a New Key: An Austrian Triptych," *Journal of Modern History* 39, no. 4 (1967): 344–386, quotation on 345. See also Schorske, *Fin-de-Siècle Vienna: Politics and Culture* (New York: Vintage Books, 1981).

87. Hillel Kieval, "Nationalism and Antisemitism," in *Living with Antisemitism: Modern Jewish Responses*, ed. Jehuda Reinharz (Hanover, NH: Published for Brandeis University Press by University Press of New England, 1987), 216–217.

88. The same logic with regard to *Volksgeist* and *Volkssprache* lay behind some Zionist thinking, which also emerged as a political force at this time. Nekula, *Franz Kafka and His Prague Contexts*, 115–117.

89. Cohen, *The Politics of Ethnic Survival*, 175.

90. Nancy M. Wingfield, *Flag Wars and Stone Saints: How the Bohemian Lands Became Czech* (Cambridge, MA: Harvard University Press, 2007), 71–72. See also Martin Joachim Wein, *History of the Jews in the Bohemian Lands* (Leiden: Brill, 2016), 38–39; and Michal Frankl, "Emancipace od židů," in *Český antisemitismus na konci 19. století*, ed. Michal Frankl (Prague: Paseka, 2007), 111–150.

91. Gary B. Cohen, "Cultural Crossings in Prague, 1900: Scenes from Late Imperial Austria," *Austrian History Yearbook* 45 (2014): 1–30.

92. Koeltzsch, *Geteilte Kulturen*, 331.

93. Katherine David-Fox, "Prague-Vienna, Prague-Berlin: The Hidden Geography of Czech Modernism," *Slavic Review* 59, no 4 (2000): 735–760.

94. Cohen, "Cultural Crossings in Prague, 1900," 3.

95. Scott Spector, *Prague Territories: National Conflict and Cultural Innovation in Franz Kafka's Fin de Siècle* (Berkeley: University of California Press, 2000), esp. 19–20, 236.

96. Noah Isenberg, *Between Redemption and Doom: The Strains of German-Jewish Modernism* (Lincoln: University of Nebraska Press, 1999), 22, cited in Alfred Thomas, *Prague Palimpsest: Writing, Memory, and the City* (Chicago: University of Chicago Press, 2010), 78, 20. In the latter quote Isenberg translates "Einsamkeit" as "alienation," but the word construction suggests something akin to the state of being alone. "Einsamkeit" is typically translated as "loneliness."

97. Georg Gimpl, *Weil der Boden selbst hier brennt: Aus dem Prager Salon der Berta Fanta, 1865–1918* (Furth im Wald: Vitalis, 2001); Wilma A. Iggers, *Women of Prague: Ethnic Diversity and Social Change from the Eighteenth Century to the Present* (New York: Berghahn Books, 1995), 142–163.

98. Isenberg, *Between Redemption and Doom*, 40. See also Nekula, *Franz Kafka and His Prague Contexts*, 37–70.

99. Jiří Vlasák, *Název pomůcky: Kavárna ARCO* (Prague: Archiv hlavního města Prahy, 2011), i.

100. Vlasák, *Název pomůcky,* i.

101. Bernard Michel, *Praha: Město evropské avantgardy: 1895–1928* (Prague: Argo, 2010), 70; Nekula, *Franz Kafka and His Prague Contexts,* 170.

102. Katja Garlof, "Judaism and Zionism," in *Franz Kafka in Context,* ed. Carolin Duttlinger (Cambridge: Cambridge University Press, 2018), 209.

103. Michel, *Praha,* 76.

104. Kozlová and Tomáš, *Egon Ervín Kisch,* 19, 23.

105. "Von Feilbietungen, Auktionshallen und Von Chabrus," in *GWE,* 128–129.

106. Herbert Lederer, "The Vienna Coffee House: History and Cultural Significance," in *The Thinking Space: The Café as a Cultural Institution in Paris, Italy and Vienna,* ed. Leona Rittner and W. Scott Haine (Farnham, UK: Taylor and Francis, 2013), 25–32. See also Gábor Gyáni, *Identity and the Urban Experience: Fin-de-Siècle Budapest,* trans. Thomas J. DeKornfeld (Boulder, CO: Social Science Monographs, 2004), 106–109.

107. Jürgen Habermas, *The Structural Transformation of the Public Sphere: An Inquiry into a Category of Bourgeois Society* (Cambridge, MA: MIT Press, 1989).

108. Vlasák, *Název pomůcky,* i.

109. Michel, *Praha,* 71.

110. Kozlová and Tomáš, *Egon Ervín Kisch,* 23.

111. On the cabaret, see Rosemary Wakeman, *A Modern History of European Cities, 1815 to the Present* (London: Bloomsbury Academic, 2020), 179–181; Käthe Springer, "Theater und Cabaret im Wien der Jahrhundertwende," in *Vienna 1900: Art, Life, and Culture,* ed. Christian Brandstätter (New York: Vendome Press, 2006), 309–320; Lisa Appignanesi, *The Cabaret* (New Haven, CT: Yale University Press, 2004); and Harold B. Segel, *Turn-of-the-Century Cabaret* (New York: Columbia University Press, 1987).

112. Egon Erwin Kisch, "Zitate von Montmartre," in *GWE,* 524–528.

113. *Montmartre 1912* (Prague: Waltner, 1912), 36.

114. Kisch, "Zitate von Montmartre," 524–528, quotation on 526.

115. *Montmartre 1912,* quotations on 20, 36.

116. *Montmartre 1912,* 35.

117. Egon Erwin Kisch, "In the Omnibus on the Night of the Murder," in Segel, *Egon Erwin Kisch, the Raging Reporter,* 123–124. Similarly, while visiting a people's kitchen, Kisch left two spoonfuls of soup in his bowl, and spoke to a girl collecting the dishes as if she were a waitress: "'You can take the dish,'

I say, 'I'm not eating any more.' The girl puzzled over this wastefulness." Kisch, "Volksküchen," 110.

118. The pub, of course, has its own history in Prague, and in Europe, as a site for gathering, especially among the lower classes. See, for example, Vladimír Novotný, *Hospody a pivo v české společnosti* (Prague: Academia, 1997).

119. Kisch, "Eine Nacht im Asyl für Obdachlose," 57.

120. Egon Erwin Kisch, "Volksküchen," in *GWE*, 118.

121. Kisch, "In der Wärmestube," 195–200.

122. Kisch, "Eine Nacht im Asyl für Obdachlose," 59.

123. Kisch, "Volksküchen," 118.

124. Max Brod, *Der Prager Kreis* (Stuttgart: W. Kohlhammer, 1966), 191, quoted and translated in Segel, *Egon Erwin Kisch, the Raging Reporter,* 14.

125. Segel, *Egon Erwin Kisch, the Raging Reporter,* 15. See, however, Marcus G. Patka, "'Mädschenhirt' und Galegtoni': Zum Thema 'Prostitution' im Werk von Egon Erwin Kisch," *Österreich in Geschichte und Literatur (mit Geographie)* 54, no. 3 (2010): 234–244. On prostitution more broadly, see Nancy M. Wingfield, *The World of Prostitution in Late Imperial Austria* (Oxford: Oxford University Press, 2017).

126. Jakub Beneš, *Workers and Nationalism: Czech and German Social Democracy in Habsburg Austria, 1890–1918* (Oxford: Oxford University Press, 2017), 18–99.

127. See, for example, Kisch, *Briefe an den Bruder Paul,* January 25, 1906, 420.

128. Pavel Eisner, "Tonka, oder E. E. K.'s glückhafte Flucht," *Prager Presse,* April 6, 1930, [n.p.]; Egon Erwin Kisch, Výstřižky: Soubor výstřižků z let 1910–1929 k biografii E. E. Kische, inv. č. 4085–4176, PNP. In a strict sense, the Jewish ghetto had disappeared long before Kisch was born, as Marek Nekula rightly points out (Nekula, *Franz Kafka and His Prague Contexts,* 201–202, 40–49). For Eisner's notion of the "ghetto" and its influence on readings of Kafka and other members of the Prague Circle during the Cold War, see Veronika Tuckerová, "Reading Kafka in Prague: The Reception of Franz Kafka between the East and the West during the Cold War" (PhD diss., Columbia University, 2012).

129. Linda Clarke, *Building Capitalism: Historical Change and the Labour Process in the Production of the Built Environment* (London: Taylor and Francis, 2011), 114–117.

130. Zap, *PoP,* 56.

131. Bělina and Vlk, *Dějiny Prahy,* 2:194.

132. Bělina and Vlk, *Dějiny Prahy,* 2:191. In addition, horse-carriage stands could not be established in front of shops that sold food. Bělina and Vlk, *Dějiny Prahy,* 2:191.

133. Bělina and Vlk, *Dějiny Prahy,* 2:191.

134. Kisch, "Der Mann mit der Strassenspritze," 47.

135. Vanessa R. Schwartz, *Spectacular Realities: Early Mass Culture in Fin-de-Siècle Paris* (Berkeley: University of California Press, 1998).

136. Judith R. Walkowitz, *City of Dreadful Delight: Narratives of Sexual Danger in Late-Victorian London* (Chicago: University of Chicago Press, 1992).

137. Egon Erwin Kisch, "Typen der Strasse," in *GWE,* 510.

138. Karla Huebner, "Prague Flânerie from Neruda to Nezval," in *The Flâneur Abroad: Historical and International Perspectives,* ed. Richard Wrigley (Newcastle upon Tyne, UK: Cambridge Scholars Publisher, 2014), 281–297.

139. Franz Kafka, "The Sudden Walk," in *The Complete Stories,* ed. Nahum N. Glatzer (New York: Schocken Books, 1971), 397. Kafka also enjoyed walking the city. Similar to many other German speakers, one of his favored routes began at Charles Bridge and ended at the Castle. Nekula, *Franz Kafka and His Prague Contexts,* 21. See also Huebner, "Prague Flânerie," 287.

140. Andrei Bely, *Petersburg,* trans. John Elsworth (London: Pushkin Press, 2009 [1913]); James Joyce, *Ulysses* (New York: Vintage Books, 1961 [1922]).

141. Edgar Allan Poe, *Tales of Mystery and Imagination* (London: Hodder & Stoughton, 1912), 102.

142. Herman Scheffauer, "The City without Night: Berlin 'twixt Dusk and Dawn," *Pall Mall Magazine* 53 (1913–1914): 284.

143. Charles Baudelaire, *The Painter of Modern Life and Other Essays,* ed. and trans. Jonathan Mayne (London: Phaidon Press, 1995), 9.

144. Wolfgang Schivelbusch, *The Railway Journey: The Industrialization of Time and Space in the Nineteenth Century* (Berkeley: University of California Press, 2014), 150–170.

145. George Simmel, "The Metropolis and Mental Life," in *The Sociology of Georg Simmel,* ed. Kurt H. Wolff (New York: Free Press, 1964), 409–424, quotations from 409, 410, 411.

146. Robert Alter, *Imagined Cities: Urban Experience and the Language of the Novel* (New Haven, CT: Yale University Press, 2005), 10, cited in Angeliki Sioli, "Walking in Andrei Bely's Petersburg: Active Perception and Embodied Experience of the City," in *Walking Histories 1800–1914,* ed. Chad Bryant, Arthur Burns, and Paul Readman (London: Palgrave Macmillan, 2016), 271.

147. Walter Benjamin, "On Some Motifs in Baudelaire," in *Illuminations,* trans. Harry Zohn (New York: Schocken Books 1969), 155–200.

148. *Týdenní zpráva statistické kanceláře král. hlav. města Prahy a spojených obcí,* no. 52, (Prague: Statistická kancelář, 1911), 3.

149. Moritz Heyne, *Deutsches Wörterbuch,* 3 vols. (Leipzig: S. Hirzel, 1906), 3:868; Günther Drosdowski, ed., *Duden: Das große Wörterbuch der deutschen Sprache in acht Bänden,* 8 vols. (Mannheim: Dudenverlag, 1995), 7:3285. Several book titles then circulating in fin-de-siècle Prague give a sense of these overlapping meanings of the word: *Auf Java und Sumatra: Streifzüge und Forschungsreisen im Lande der Malaien; Steifzüge durch biblische Flora; Streifzüge durch die neueste englische Literatur; Streifzüge durch die Theorie und Praxis der Arbeiterbewegung; Streifzüge durch die Tierwelt;* and *Streifzüge durch die Welt der Grossstadtkinder: Lebensbilder und Gedankengänge für den Anschauungsunterricht in Stadtschulen.*

150. Josef V. Sterzinger, ed., *Německočeský slovník = Deutschböhmisches Wörterbuch,* 2 vols. (Prague: J. Otto, 1893–1895), 2:130 suggests "nájezd, vpád" as the closest Czech-language equivalent of "Streifzug." See, however, František Kretz, *Toulky po spišské stolici: Cestopisné vzpomníky na Slovensko* (Uherské hradiště: Spisovatelé, 1907); and Theodore Roosevelt, *Lovecké toulky po východní Africe,* trans. Václav Chabr (Prague: Česká grafická unie, 1921). For the contemporary definition of "toulka," see Josef Fronek, *Velký anglicko-český, česko-anglický slovník = Comprehensive English-Czech, Czech-English Dictionary* (Voznice: Leda, 2007), 1305.

151. When they walked into the pub that enjoyed a record ten-year run on the list, Kisch immediately spotted two soldiers. "Konsignation über verbotene Lokale," in *GWE,* 478–492.

152. Schorske, *Fin-de-siècle Vienna,* 9.

153. Egon Erwin Kisch, "Café Kandelaber," in *GWE,* 34–37.

154. Egon Erwin Kisch, "Die Gemeindetruhe,"in *GWE,* 12–15.

155. Egon Erwin Kisch, "Der Mann mit der Strassenspritze," in *GWE,* 47–50.

156. Egon Erwin Kisch, "Bei 'Antouschek,' dem Wasenmeister, in *GWE,* 68–73.

157. Kisch, "Typen der Strasse," 510–516.

158. Kisch, "Typen der Strasse," 510.

159. Egon Erwin Kisch, "Prags Erwachen," in *GWE,* 191.

160. Kisch, "Dramaturgy of the Flea Theater," 136.

161. Egon Erwin Kisch, "The Chief of the Prague Detectives," in Segel, *Egon Erwin Kisch, the Raging Reporter,* 120.

162. Egon Erwin Kisch, "Die Schnapsbutike als Gelddepot," in *GWE,* 236–239.

163. Kisch, "Typen der Strasse," 511–512.

164. Kisch, "Dramaturgy of the Flea Theater," 129.

165. Kisch, "The Chief of the Prague Detectives."

166. Egon Erwin Kisch, "Begegnung in London," in *GWE*, 299–303.

167. Kisch, "Dramaturgy of the Flea Theater," 127.

168. Kisch, "Zitate von Montmartre," 524.

169. Kisch, "Konsignation über verbotene Lokale," 308.

170. Gustav Meyrink, *The Golem* (Sawtry, UK: Dedalus, 1995).

171. Kisch, "Café Kandelaber," 37.

172. Kisch seems to have had a few essays in mind, among them Pavel Körber and Frant. K. (František Karel) Hejda, "Chabrus," in *Praha ve dne v noci: Zajímavosti a zvláštnosti ze života staré a nové Prahy*, 2 vols. (Prague: P. Körber, 1902) 2:197–212.

173. Egon Erwin Kisch, "Von Feilbietungen, Auktionshallen und vom Chabrus," in *GWE*, 128–137.

174. Elisabeth Susanne Schmidt, "Egon Erwin Kisch als vermittelnde Instanz zwischen Deutschen und Tschechen in Prag?," in *Im Einzelschicksal die Weltgeschichte: Egon Erwin Kisch und seine literarischen Reportagen*, ed. Viera Glosíková, Sina Meissgeier, and Ilse Nagelschmidt (Berlin: Frank & Timme, 2016), 79.

175. Melinda Blau and Karen L. Fingerman, *Consequential Strangers: The Power of People Who Don't Seem to Matter—But Really Do* (New York: W. W. Norton, 2009).

176. Kisch, *Briefe an den Bruder Paul*, November 1, 1910, 37.

177. Kozlová and Tomáš, *Egon Erwin Kisch*, 23.

178. Kisch, *Briefe an den Bruder Paul*, November 1, 1910, 25.

179. Kisch, *Briefe an den Bruder Paul*, November 16, 1911, 58.

180. Egon Erwin Kisch, *Der Mädchenhirt* (Berlin: Erich Riess, 1914).

181. Egon Erwin Kisch, *Soldat im Prager Korps* (Leipzig: Verlag der K. Andréschen Buchhandlung, 1922), 76–77, 220–222. On Kisch's experience on the front, see Kevin J. Hoeper, "Combat and Convergence: Fighting the First World War in an Austro-Hungarian Infantry Regiment" (MA thesis, University of North Carolina at Chapel Hill, 2018).

3. REVOLUTION CITY

1. Vojtěch Berger, inv. č. 9, 117, Archiv hlavního města Prahy (hereafter AHMP).

2. Most analyses of working-class diaries are primarily concerned with investigating notions of class and nation. See, for example, Tyler Edward Stovall, *Paris and the Spirit of 1919: Consumer Struggles, Transnationalism, and Revolution* (Cambridge: Cambridge University Press, 2012); Reginald Zelnik, ed., *A Radical Worker in Tsarist Russia: The Autobiography of Semën Ivanovich Kanatchikov* (Stanford, CA: Stanford University Press, 1986). For a fascinating study of the other concerns that informed workers' lives, see Carolyn Stedman, *An Everyday Life of the English Working Class: Work, Self, and Sociability in the Early Nineteenth Century* (Cambridge: Cambridge University Press, 2013).

3. Vojtěch Berger, inv. č. 7, 1–29, AHMP; Vojtěch Berger, inv. č. 68, 3–16, AHMP.

4. Vojtěch Berger, inv. č. 68, 16–37, AHMP; Vojtěch Berger, inv. č. 62, 3, AHMP.

5. Vojtěch Berger, inv. č. 67, AHMP.

6. Vojtěch Berger, inv. č. 7, 1, AHMP.

7. Vojtěch Berger, inv. č. 7, 8, AHMP.

8. Jakub Beneš, *Workers and Nationalism: Czech and German Social Democracy in Habsburg Austria, 1890–1918* (Oxford: Oxford University Press, 2017), 7–8, 23–28; Wolfgang Maderthaner, "Victor Adler und die Politik der Symbole: Zum Entwurf einer 'poetischen Politik,'" in *Österreichs politische Symbole*, ed. Norbert Leser and Manfred Wagner (Vienna: Böhlau, 1994), 759–776. On the prewar world of Austrian Social Democracy, see Lukáš Fasora, *Dělník a měšťan: Vývoj jejich vzájemných vztahů na příkladu šesti moravských měst 1870–1914* (Brno: Centrum pro studium demokracie a kultury, 2010).

9. Vojtěch Berger, inv. č. 7, 43, AHMP.

10. Vojtěch Berger, inv. č. 7, 79, AHMP.

11. Vojtěch Berger, inv. č. 8, 5, AHMP.

12. Quotation from Vojtěch Berger, inv. č. 7, 27, AHMP.

13. Vojtěch Berger, inv. č. 7, 28, AHMP.

14. Otto Urban, *České a slovenské dějiny do roku 1918* (Prague: Svoboda, 1991), 557, cited in Beneš, *Workers and Nationalism*, 8.

15. Vojtěch Berger, inv. č. 7, 8–9, AHMP.

16. Vojtěch Berger, inv. č. 7, AHMP.

17. Vojtěch Berger, inv. č. 62, 3, AHMP; Vojtěch Berger, inv. č. 62, 4, AHMP.

18. Vojtěch Berger, inv. č. 62, 8, AHMP.

19. Vojtěch Berger, inv. č. 62, 11–13, AHMP.

20. Anatol Schmied-Kowarzik, "War Losses (Austria-Hungary)," in *1914–1918 Online: International Encyclopedia of the First World War*, ed. Ute Daniel,

Peter Gatrell, Oliver Janz, Heather Jones, Jennifer Keene, Alan Kramer, and Bill Nasson, issued by Freie Universität Berlin, https://encyclopedia.1914-1918 -online.net/article/war_losses_austria-hungary; Antoine Prost, "War Losses," in *1914–1918 Online*, ed. Daniel et al., https://encyclopedia.1914-1918-online.net /article/war_losses.

21. Jan Ciglbauer, *Vojáci Švejkova pluku: Vzpomínky vojáků z Chotýčan na Velkou válku; Osvobození jihočeského pohraničí v roce 1918; Pohřbívání vojáků na Českobudějovicku* (Prague: Nakladatelství Brigadýr, 2016), 10. My thanks to Kevin Hoeper for pointing me to this citation.

22. Vojtěch Berger, inv. č. 62, 53, AHMP.

23. Vojtěch Berger, inv. č. 62, 55, AHMP.

24. Vojtěch Berger, inv. č. 62, 70, AHMP.

25. Vojtěch Berger, inv. č. 8, 39, AHMP; Vojtěch Berger, inv. č. 9, 58, AHMP.

26. Vojtěch Berger, inv. č. 8, 96–97, AHMP.

27. Vojtěch Berger, inv. č. 62, 62, AHMP.

28. Beneš, *Workers and Nationalism*, 173–238.

29. Vojtěch Berger, inv. č. 62, 16, AHMP.

30. Mark Cornwall, "News, Rumour, and the Control of Information in Austria-Hungary, 1914–1918," *History* 77, no. 249 (February 1992): 50–65, esp. 59. See also Bernhard Rosenberger, *Zeitungen als Kriegstreiber? Die Rolle der Presse im Vorfeld des Ersten Weltkriegs* (Cologne: Böhlau, 1998).

31. Vojtěch Berger, inv. č. 9, 2, AHMP.

32. Cornwall, "News, Rumour, and the Control of Information," 51–52; John Robertson, "Calamitous Methods of Compulsion: Labor, War, and Revolution in a Habsburg Industrial District, 1906–1919" (PhD diss., University of North Carolina at Chapel Hill, 2014), esp. 18, 176–178.

33. Rudolf Kučera, *Rationed Life: Science, Everyday Life and Working-Class Politics in the Bohemian Lands, 1914–1918* (New York: Berghahn Books, 2016), 12–56, esp. 35, 40–43. On the army, the rule of law, and the collapse of the Habsburg monarchy more generally, see John Deak and Jonathan E. Gumz, "How to Break a State: The Habsburg Monarchy's Internal War, 1914–1918," *American Historical Review* 122, no. 4 (October 2017): 1105–1136.

34. Kučera, *Rationed Life*, 136–137. See also Peter Heumos, "'Kartoffeln her oder es gibt eine Revolution': Hungerkrawalle, Streiks und Massenproteste in den böhmischen Ländern 1914–1918," in *Der Erste Weltkrieg und die Beziehungen zwischen Tschechen, Slowaken und Deutschen*, ed. Hans Mommsen, Dušan Kováč, and Jiří Malíř (Essen: Klartext, 2001), 255–286.

35. Kučera, *Rationed Life*, 152–153.

36. Zdeněk Kárník, *Socialisté na rozcestí: Habsburk, Masaryk či Šmeral* (Prague: Carolinum, 1996), esp. 273.

37. Mary Heimann, *Czechoslovakia: The State That Failed* (New Haven, CT: Yale University Press, 2009), 38–43.

38. Zdeněk Karník, *České země v eře první republiky (1918–1938)*, vol. 1: *Vznik, budování a zláta léta republiky (1918–1929)* (Prague: Libri, 2000), 63–76, cited in Rudolf Kučera, "Exploiting Victory, Sinking into Defeat: Uniformed Violence in the Creation of the New Order in Czechoslovakia and Austria, 1918–1922," *Journal of Modern History* 88, no. 4 (2016): 833.

39. Kučera, "Exploiting Victory, Sinking into Defeat," 835, 847. On the continuation of violence after World War I elsewhere in Europe, see Robert Gerwarth, *The Vanquished: Why the First World War Failed to End, 1917–1923* (London: Allen Lane, 2016); and Joachim von Puttkamer, "Collapse and Restoration: Politics and the Strains of War in Eastern Europe," in *Legacies of Violence: Eastern Europe's First World War*, ed. Jochen Böhler, Włodzimierz Borodziej, and Joachim von Puttkamer (Munich: Oldenbourg, 2014), 9–24.

40. Cynthia Paces, *Prague Panoramas: National Memory and Sacred Space in the Twentieth Century* (Pittsburgh: University of Pittsburgh Press, 2009), 87–92.

41. Michal Frankl and Miloslav Szabó, *Budování státu bez antisemitismu? Násilí, diskurz loajality a vznik Československa* (Prague: Lidové noviny, 2015).

42. Kučera, "Exploiting Victory, Sinking into Defeat," 844.

43. Ondřej Houska, interview with Rudolf Kučera, "Koronavirus? Češi už zažili epidemii, při které v Praze došly rakve: Velké nákazy jen málokdy dokážou změnit svět, říká historik," *Hospodářské noviny*, March 20, 2020, https://archiv.ihned.cz/c7-66738010-0isaa-84c73450676adb1.

44. Heumos, "'Kartoffeln her oder es gibt eine Revolution,'" 89.

45. Paces, *Prague Panoramas*, 90.

46. Vojtěch Berger, inv. č. 9, 85–86, AHMP.

47. Vojtěch Berger, inv. č. 68, 39, AHMP.

48. Vojtěch Berger, inv. č. 9, 79, AHMP.

49. Vojtěch Berger, inv. č. 21, 180, AHMP.

50. Vojtěch Berger, inv. č. 9, 80, AHMP.

51. Vojtěch Berger, inv. č. 9, 87–88, AHMP.

52. Vojtěch Berger, inv. č. 9, 113, AHMP.

53. Vojtěch Berger, inv. č. 9, 88, AHMP.

54. Vojtěch Berger, inv. č. 9, 123, AHMP.

55. Vojtěch Berger, inv. č. 9, 90, AHMP.

56. Vojtěch Berger, inv. č. 9, 113, AHMP.

57. Heimann, *Czechoslovakia*, 70; Peter Demetz, *Prague in Black and Gold: Scenes from a Life of a Central European City* (New York: Hill and Wang, 1997), 341; Kučera, "Exploiting Victory, Sinking into Defeat," 836.

58. Demetz, *Prague in Black and Gold*, 341.

59. Vojtěch Berger, inv. č. 21, 205, AHMP.

60. Vojtěch Berger, inv. č. 9, 11, AHMP.

61. Vojtěch Berger, inv. č. 21, 206–207, AHMP.

62. Vojtěch Berger, inv. č. 9, 20, AHMP.

63. Heumos, "'Kartoffeln her oder es gibt eine Revolution,'" 89.

64. Joseph Rothschild, *East Central Europe between the Two World Wars* (Seattle: University of Washington Press, 1974), 106–107.

65. Giovanni Capoccia, "Legislative Responses against Extremism: The 'Protection of Democracy' in the First Czechoslovak Republic (1920–1938)," *East European Politics and Societies* 16, no. 3 (2002): 691–738.

66. Václav Ledvinka and Jiří Pešek, *Praha* (Prague: Lidové noviny, 2000), 585, 582.

67. Demetz, *Prague in Black and Gold*, 344. See also Jiří Pešek, *Od aglomerace k velkoměstu: Praha a středoevropské metropole 1850–1920* (Prague: Scriptorium, 1999).

68. Ledvinka and Pešek, *Praha*, 584; Jaroslava Musilová, *Z historie budov Ministerstva financí* (Prague: Ministerstvo financí ČR, 2013), 1–2; and Andrea Orzoff, *Battle for the Castle: The Myth of Czechoslovakia in Europe, 1914–1948* (New York: Oxford University Press, 2009), 3.

69. Orzoff, *Battle for the Castle*.

70. Paces, *Prague Panoramas*, 171–172; Claire Morelon, "State Legitimacy and Continuity between the Habsburg Empire and Czechoslovakia: The 1918 Transition in Prague," in *Embers of Empire: Continuity and Rupture in the Habsburg Successor States after 1918*, ed. Paul B. Miller and Claire Morelon (New York: Berghahn Books, 2019), 45–46; Robert Pynsent, "The Literary Representations of the Czechoslovak 'Legions' in Russia," in *Czechoslovakia in a Nationalist and Fascist Europe 1918–1948*, ed. Mark Cornwall and R. J. W. Evans (Oxford: Oxford University Press, 2007), 63–88; and Martin Zückert, "Der erste Weltkrieg in der tschechischen Geschichtsschreibung, 1918–1938," in *Geschichtsschreibung zu den böhmischen Ländern in 20. Jarhhundert*, ed. Christiane Brenner, K. Erik Franzen, Peter Haslinger, and Robert Luft (Munich: Oldenbourg, 2006), 61–75. Approved Legionnaires also received special state benefits, such as land and preferential treatment within the civil service. Ivan Šedivý, "Legionářská republika? K systému legionářského zákonodárství a sociální péče v meziválečné ČSR," *Historie a vojenství: Časopis Historického ústavu Armády ČR* 1 (2002): 158–184; Radka Šuštrová, "The Struggle

for Respect: The State, WWI Veterans and Social Welfare Policy in Interwar Czechoslovakia," *Zeitgeschichte* 47, no. 1 (2020): 115–116.

71. Bruce R. Berglund, *Castle and Cathedral in Modern Prague: Longing for the Sacred in a Skeptical Age* (Budapest: Central European University Press, 2017), quotation on 8; Zdeněk Lukeš, Dajman Prelovšek, and Tomáš Valena, eds., *Josip Plečnik: An Architect of Prague Castle* (Prague: Prague Castle Administration, 1997).

72. Gregory Campbell, "Empty Pedestals?," *Slavic Review* 44, no. 1 (1985): 12. See also Antonín Klimek, *Boj o Hrad*, vol. 1, *Hrad a Pětka: Vnitropolitický vývoj Československa 1918–1926 na půdorysu zápasu o prezidentské nástupnictví* (Buková u Příbramě: TK, 2017); Peter Bugge, "Czech Democracy—Paragon or Parody," in *Phasen und Formen der Transformation in der Tschechoslowakei: Vorträge der Tagung des Collegium Carolinum in Bad Wiessee vom 23. bis 26. November 2000* (Munich: Carolinum, 2002), esp. 15.

73. Heimann, *Czechoslovakia*, 68.

74. Ines Koeltzsch, *Geteilte Kulturen: Eine Geschichte der tschechisch-jüdisch-deutschen Beziehungen in Prag (1918–1938)* (Munich: Oldenbourg, 2012), 270–288.

75. Nancy M. Wingfield, *Flag Wars and Stone Saints: How the Bohemian Lands Became Czech* (Cambridge, MA: Harvard University Press, 2007), 199–230.

76. Stanislav Holubec, *Lidé periferie: Sociální postavení a každodennost pražského dělnictva v meziválečné době* (Pilsen: Západočeská univerzita v Plzni, 2009), 27n57.

77. Holubec, *Lidé periferie*, 131–144; Vanda Tůmová, *Pražské nouzové kolonie* (Prague: Ústav pro etnografii a folkloristiku ČSAV, 1971).

78. Stanislav Holubec, "Between Scarcity and Modernity: Working Class Families in Prague in the Interwar Period," *Hungarian Historical Review* 3, no. 1 (2014): 186–187.

79. Ledvinka and Pešek, *Praha*, 573.

80. Ledvinka and Pešek, *Praha*, 573; Jiří Maňak, "Proměna dělnické strany v organizaci moci: Problematika dělnického charakteru KSČ v letech 1945–1953 ve světle stranické statistiky," in *Bolševismus, komunismus, a radikalní socialismus v Československu*, vol. 1, ed. Zdeněk Kárník and Michal Kopeček (Prague: Dokořán, 2003), esp. 158.

81. Holubec, "Between Scarcity and Modernity," 177.

82. For a larger discussion of this peculiar Communist milieu in Prague, see Holubec, *Lidé periferie*, 206–220.

83. Vojtěch Berger, inv. č. 69, n.p., AHMP; Holubec, *Lidé periferie*, 218.

84. See, for example, Vojtěch Berger, inv. č. 11, 78, AHMP; Vojtěch Berger, inv. č. 12, 188, AHMP.

85. Vojtěch Berger, inv. č. 11, 75–76, AHMP.

86. František Ladislav Rieger and Jakub Malý, *Malý slovník naučný,* 12 vols. (Prague: I. L. Kober, 1890), 5:89.

87. On the origins of the street protest, see George Rudé, *The Crowd in History: A Study of Popular Disturbances in France and England, 1730–1848* (London: Lawrence and Wishart, 1981), 241, 243.

88. Michal Frankl, "Emancipace od židů," in *Český antisemitismus na konci 19. století,* ed. Michal Frankl (Prague: Paseka, 2007), 111–150; Martin Joachim Wein, *History of the Jews in the Bohemian Lands* (Leiden: Brill, 2016), 46–60; and Wingfield, *Flag Wars and Stone Saints,* esp. 71–72.

89. Kučera, *Rationed Life,* 149–150, with remarks on Canetti on 149. Quotation from Elias Canetti, *Crowds and Power* (New York: Viking Press, 1962), 15–16.

90. Vojtěch Berger, inv. č. 14, 9, AHMP.

91. Vojtěch Berger, inv. č. 14, 8, AHMP.

92. Vojtěch Berger, inv. č. 7, 8–9, AHMP.

93. Vojtěch Berger, inv. č. 15, 252–253, AHMP.

94. Vojtěch Berger, inv. č. 15, 205, AHMP.

95. Petr Roubal, "Politics of Gymnastics: Mass Gymnastic Displays under Communism in Central and Eastern Europe," *Body & Society* 9, no. 2 (2003): 7.

96. Vojtěch Berger, inv. č. 21, 205, AHMP.

97. Holubec, *Lidé periferie,* 210, 207.

98. Vojtěch Berger, inv. č. 14, 25, AHMP.

99. Roubal, "Politics of Gymnastics," 4.

100. Claire E. Nolte, *The Sokol in the Czech Lands to 1914: Training for the Nation* (New York: Palgrave, 2002), 31, 185.

101. "Tělocvičné dny Federace dělnických tělocvič. jednot v Praze VII na Maninách, 1921," Národní filmový archiv, published online by European Film Gateway, https://vimeopro.com/narodnifilmovyarchiv/efg/video/151398419.

102. See, for example, Vilém Mucha, *Dějiny dělnické tělovýchovy v Československu,* 2 vols. (Prague: Orbis, 1955).

103. Archiv tělesné výchovy a sportu, Federace dělnických tělocvičných jednot (no box number or inv. č), Anna Hronková, Praha Košíře, April 14, 1953, Národní muzeum (hereafter NM).

104. Archiv tělesné výchovy a sportu, Federace dělnických tělocvičných jednot (no box number or inv. č), Stanislav Honek, Hradec Králové, n.d., NM.

105. Holubec, *Lidé periferie,* 217.

106. Vojtěch Berger, inv. č. 12, 281, AHMP.

107. Vojtěch Berger, inv. č. 14, 61, AHMP.

108. Vojtěch Berger, inv. č. 68, 53–54, AHMP; Vojtěch Berger, inv. č. 2, Photograph 05ab, "Nouzová kolonie 1935–1936 na křížku u kapslovny na Žižkově," AHMP.

109. On refugees, see Kateřina Čapková and Michal Frankl, *Nejisté útočiště: Československo a uprchlíci před nacismem 1933–1938* (Prague: Paseka, 2008).

110. Benjamin Frommer, "Der Holocaust in Böhmen und Mähren," in *Zwischen Prag und Nikolsburg: Jüdisches Leben in den böhmischen Ländern,* ed. Kateřina Čapková and Hillel Kieval (Munich: Collegium Carolinum, 2020), 269–274; Jan Rataj, *O autoritativni národní stát: Ideologické proměny české politiky v druhé republice 1938–1939* (Prague: Karolinum, 1997), esp. 115–118.

111. Peter Bugge, "A Nation Allied with History: Czech Ideas of Democracy, 1890–1948," in *Democracy in Modern Europe: A Conceptual History,* ed. Jussi Kurunmäki, Jeppe Nevers, and Henk te Velde (New York: Berghahn Books, 2017), 230.

112. Kateřina Čapková, *Czechs, Germans, Jews? National Identity and the Jews of Bohemia* (Oxford: Berghahn Books, 2012). See also Ines Koeltzsch, Michal Frankl, and Martina Niedhammer, "Plöztlich Tschechoslowaken, 1917–1938," in Čapková and Kieval, *Zwischen Prag und Nikolsburg,* 209–264.

113. Jana Burešová, "Společensko-politická aktivita a veřejná činnost žen za první Československé Republiky (1918–1938)," in *Československo 1918–1938,* vol. 2, *Osudy demokracie ve střední Evropě,* ed. Josef Harna, Jaroslav Valenta, and Emil Voráček (Prague: Historický ústav, 1999), 393–400. See also Melissa Feinberg, *Elusive Equality: Gender, Citizenship, and the Limits of Democracy in Czechoslovakia, 1918–1950* (Pittsburgh: University of Pittsburgh Press, 2006).

114. *Statistická příručka Československé Republiky* (London: Československé ministerstvo zahraničních věci, informační oddělení, 194?), 156–157.

115. Thomas Lorman, *The Making of the Slovak People's Party: Religion, Nationalism and the Culture War in Early 20th-Century Europe* (London: Bloomsbury Academic, 2019), 197–198; James Mace Ward, *Priest, Politician, Collaborator: Jozef Tiso and the Making of Fascist Slovakia* (Ithaca, NY: Cornell University Press, 2013), esp. 67–68, 73–75.

116. Mark Cornwall, *The Devil's Wall: The Nationalist Youth Mission of Heinz Rutha* (Cambridge, MA: Harvard University Press, 2012).

117. Chad Bryant, *Prague in Black: Nazi Rule and Czech Nationalism* (Cambridge, MA: Harvard University Press, 2007).

118. Frommer, "Der Holocaust," 280–309. See also Wolf Gruner, *Die Judenverfolgung im Protektorat Böhmen und Mähren: Lokale Initiativen, Zentrale*

Entscheidungen, Jüdische Antworten 1939–1945 (Göttingen: Wallstein Verlag, 2016); and Peter J. Stein, *A Boy's Journey: From Nazi-Occupied Prague to Freedom in America* (Chapel Hill, NC: Lystra Books and Literary Services, 2019).

119. Laura E. Brade, "Networks of Escape: Jewish Flight from the Bohemian Lands, 1938–1941" (PhD diss., University of North Carolina at Chapel Hill, 2017), 1.

120. Kateřina Čapková, "Peripherie und Zentrum: Juden in den Böhmischen Ländern von 1945 bis in die Gegenwart," in Čapková and Kieval, *Zwischen Prag und Nikolsburg,* 323–327.

121. Bryant, *Prague in Black.* On the demonstrations of loyalty, see Radka Šustrová, "Ve jménu Říše a českého národa: Veřejné manifestace po atentátu na Reinharda Heydricha," *Paměť a dějiny: Revue pro studium totalitních režimů* 6, no. 2 (2012): 52.

122. Shortly after the Munich Agreement, Berger was fined 20 crowns for illegally selling newspapers without a proper license. This was the only police report he appears to have generated. Fond PŘ II—EO, Policejní ředitelství Praha II—evidence obyvatelstva, Sign.: Berger, Vojtěch 1882, Národní archiv (hereafter NA).

123. Jan Schwaller, *Vojtěch Berger, 1901–1965: Inventáře a katalogy Archivu hlavního města Prahy* (Prague: Archiv hlavního města Prahy, 2004). This remarkable collection was donated to the Prague City Archive in 1985. Berger's collection of songs is located in a different archive: Soukromá knihovna tesaře Vojty Bergera, Písně: Kramářské a politické, Kniha II, PNP.

124. Gustav René Hocke, *Das europaische Tagebuch* (Wiesbaden: Limes, 1978). The question of audience and editing for an audience is effectively discussed in Lynn Z. Bloom, "'I Write for Myself and Strangers': Private Diaries and Public Documents," in *Inscribing the Daily: Critical Essays on Women's Diaries,* ed. Cynthia Anne Huff (Amherst: University of Massachusetts Press, 1996), 23–37.

125. See, for example, Joseph Goebbels, *Die Tagebücher von Joseph Goebbels: Aufzeichnungen 1923–1941,* ed. Elke Frölich, 9 vols. (Munich: K. G. Saur, 1998–2006); Galezzo Ciano, *The Ciano Diaries, 1939–1943: The Complete, Unabridged Diaries of Count Galeazzo Ciano, Italian Minister for Foreign Affairs, 1936–1943,* ed. Hugh Gibson (New York: Doubleday, 1946); "Daily Entries of Hersh Wasser," ed. J. Kermish, *Yad Vashem Studies* 15 (1983): 201–282; and *Scroll of Agony: The Warsaw Diary of Chaim A. Kaplan,* ed. and trans. A. I. Katsh (New York: Collier Books, 1981). For an excellent bibliography of Holocaust diaries and works that interpret these diaries, see "Diaries," United States Holocaust Memorial Museum, https://www.ushmm.org/collections/bibliography/diaries.

126. Vojtěch Berger, inv. č. 9, 140, AHMP.

127. Alexandra Garbarini, *Numbered Days: Diaries and the Holocaust* (New Haven, CT: Yale University Press, 2006), 18. See also Steven E. Kagle, *American Diary Literature, 1620–1799* (Boston: Twayne, 1979); Peter Fritzsche, *The Turbulent World of Franz Göll: An Ordinary Berliner Writes the Twentieth Century* (Cambridge, MA: Harvard University Press, 2011); and Allison Somogyi, "The Bitter End: Jewish Life and Survival in Budapest Under the Arrow Cross Regime, October 1944–February 1945" (PhD diss., University of North Carolina at Chapel Hill, 2019).

128. Vojtěch Berger, inv. č. 16, 122, AHMP.

129. Vojtěch Berger, inv. č. 16, 266–277, AHMP, quotation on 272.

130. Vojtěch Berger, inv. č. 16, 266, AHMP.

131. Vojtěch Berger, inv. č. 16, 269, AHMP.

132. Vojtěch Berger, inv. č. 16, 273, AHMP.

133. Matěj Spurný, "Dlouhý stín pětačtyřicátého: Pilíře legitimity a sebeporozumění české společnosti (1945–2015)" (paper presented at the "Liberation, Transformation, Revolution: Central Europe in 1945 in an Interdisciplinary Perspective" conference, Prague, November 2015).

134. Eagle Glassheim, "The Mechanics of Ethnic Cleansing: The Expulsion of the Germans from Czechoslovakia, 1945–1947," in *Redrawing Nations: Ethnic Cleansing in East-Central Europe, 1944–1948*, ed. Philipp Ther and Ana Siljak (Lanham, MD: Rowman and Littlefield, 2001), esp. 200–201; Tomáš Staněk, *Verfolgung 1945: Die Stellung der Deutschen in Böhmen, Mähren und Schlesien (Ausserhalb der Lager und Gefängnisse)* (Vienna: Böhlau, 2003), esp. 94–97.

135. Ida Weidenhofferová, ed., *Konfliktní společenství, katastrofa, uvolnění: Náčrt výkladu německo-českých dějin od 19. století* (Prague: Ústav mezinárodních vztahů, 1996), 29–30.

136. Benjamin Frommer, *National Cleansing: Retribution against Nazi Collaborators in Postwar Czechoslovakia* (Cambridge: Cambridge University Press, 2005), 3.

137. Kateřina Čapková, "Between Expulsion and Rescue: The Transports for German-Speaking Jews of Czechoslovakia in 1946," *Holocaust and Genocide Studies* 32, no. 1 (2018): 66–92. See also Jan Láníček, "What Did It Mean to Be Loyal? Jewish Survivors in Post-War Czechoslovakia in a Comparative Perspective," *Australian Journal of Politics and History* 60, no. 3 (2014): 384–404.

138. Joseph Rothschild, *Return to Diversity: A Political History of East Central Europe since World War II* (New York: Oxford University Press, 2008),

91; Ledvinka and Pešek, *Praha,* 635; Kevin McDermott, *Communist Czechoslovakia, 1945–89: A Political and Social History* (London: Palgrave Macmillan, 2015), 37.

139. Bradley F. Abrams, *The Struggle for the Soul of the Nation: Czech Culture and the Rise of Communism* (Lanham, MD: Rowman and Littlefield, 2004), 9–38. See also Christiane Brenner, *"Zwischen Ost und West": Tschechische politische Diskurse 1945–1948* (Munich: Oldenbourg, 2009).

140. Marie Koldinská and Ivan Šedivý, "Smíchovský tank: Jsem zvláštní pomník, a já to vím," *Dějiny a současnost* 27 no. 1 (2005): 10.

141. Nancy M. Wingfield, "The Politics of Memory: Constructing National Identity in the Czech Lands, 1945–1948," *East European Politics and Societies* 14, no. 2 (2000): 263.

142. Vojtěch Berger, inv. č. 16, 284, AHMP.

143. Vojtěch Berger, inv. č. 16, 275, 278, AHMP.

144. Vojtěch Berger, inv. č. 16, 289, 297, AHMP.

145. Vojtěch Berger, inv. č. 16, 275, AHMP.

146. Vojtěch Berger, inv. č. 16, 283–284, AHMP.

147. Vojtěch Berger, inv. č. 16, 318, AHMP.

148. Vojtěch Berger, inv. č. 16, 298, 319, AHMP.

149. Maňak, "Proměna dělnické strany v organizaci moci," 160.

150. Vojtěch Berger, inv. č. 16, 301, AHMP.

151. Vojtěch Berger, inv. č. 16, 319, AHMP.

152. See, for example, Vojtěch Berger, inv. č. 16, 305, AHMP.

153. Vojtěch Berger, inv. č. 16, 372, AHMP; Vojtěch Berger, inv. č. 17, 1–5, AHMP.

154. Vojtěch Berger, inv. č. 16, 275, AHMP.

155. Vojtěch Berger, inv. č. 16, 309, AHMP.

156. Vojtěch Berger, inv. č. 16, 309, AHMP.

157. Vojtěch Berger, inv. č. 16, 291, AHMP.

158. Vojtěch Berger, inv. č. 16, 342, AHMP.

159. Vojtěch Berger, inv. č. 16, 347, AHMP.

160. Vojtěch Berger, inv. č. 16, 342, AHMP.

161. Vojtěch Berger, inv. č. 17, 20, AHMP.

162. McDermott, *Communist Czechoslovakia, 1945–89,* 56–57.

163. Vojtěch Berger, inv. č. 17, 90, AHMP.

164. Vojtěch Berger, inv. č. 17, 85, AHMP.

165. Vojtěch Berger, inv. č. 17, 85, AHMP.

166. Vojtěch Berger, inv. č. 17, 89, AHMP.

167. Vojtěch Berger, inv. č. 17, 139, AHMP.

4. COMMUNIST CITY

1. Hana Frejková, *Divný kořeny* (Prague: Torst, 2007), 8 (hereafter *DK*).

2. Frejková, *DK*, 119.

3. Frejková, *DK*, 96.

4. Frejková, *DK*, 73–75.

5. Frejková, *DK*, 8–9; Frejková, June 18, 2018 interview.

6. "Frejka, Ludvík," *Biografický slovník*, Historický ústav AV ČR, http://biography.hiu.cas.cz/Personal/index.php/FREJKA_Ludv%C3%ADK_15.1.1904-3.12.1952; František J. Kolář, "Vzpomínky na komunistu Ludvíka Frejku," *Příspěvky k dějinám KSČ* 2 (1965): 283–296; Ludvík Frejka file, MNB-5, část 1, 92–102, Archiv bezpečnostních složek (hereafter ABS). On the lack of Marxist-trained economists in Czechoslovakia, see Jiří Kosta, "Die tschechische Wirtschaftswissenschaft von 1945 bis 1990," *Bohemia* 36 (1995), esp. 378–379.

7. Frejková, *DK*, 32–35, 47–52; Frejková, June 18, 2018 interview; and Ludvík Frejka file, MNB-5, část 1, 97–102, 106, 119, 161, 260, ABS.

8. Nancy M. Wingfield, "The Politics of Memory: Constructing National Identity in the Czech Lands, 1945–1948," *East European Politics and Societies* 14, no. 2 (2000): 262.

9. Cynthia Paces, *Prague Panorama: National Memory and Sacred Space in the Twentieth Century* (Pittsburgh: University of Pittsburgh Press, 2009), 170–209; see also Michal Kopeček, "Čeští komunističtí intelektuálové a 'národní cesta k socialismu,'" *Soudobé dějiny* 1–2 (2016): 77–117.

10. Hana Píchová, *The Case of the Missing Statue: A Historical and Literary Study of the Stalin Monument in Prague* (Řevnice: Arbor vitae, 2014), 9, 21–38, 53–93, 81.

11. Václav Ledvinka and Jiří Pešek, *Praha* (Prague: Lidové noviny, 2000), 640.

12. Records of the Foreign Service Posts of the Department of State, US Embassy, Czechoslovakia, box 23: 1950–1952; 670.5—VOA, Briggs to SecState, December 7, 1951, report #442, 2, National Archives (College Park, Maryland), Record Group 84.

13. Kevin McDermott, *Communist Czechoslovakia, 1945–89: A Political and Social History* (London: Palgrave Macmillan, 2015), 68.

14. On the rise, composition, and methods of the secret police in Communist Czechoslovakia, see Molly Pucci, *Security Empire: The Secret Police in Communist Eastern Europe* (New Haven, CT: Yale University Press, 2020), 77–117, 197–250. The secret police also acted as agents provocateurs, as they did in Eastern Moravia where they rounded up former partisans who expressed grievances against the Communist regime. See Mira Markham,

"Světlana: Partisans and Power in Postwar Czechoslovakia," *Contemporary European History* 30, no. 1 (2021): 16–31.

15. McDermott, *Communist Czechoslovakia, 1945–89,* 65; Karel Kaplan and Vladimír Pacl, *Tajný prostor Jáchymov* (České Budějovice: K. Klub, 1993).

16. Pucci, *Security Empire,* 241.

17. Quotation from "Spravidelný trest," *Rudé právo,* November 28, 1952, 1. On the docket, see "Rozsudek nad vedením protistátního spikleneckého centra v čele s R. Slánským," *Rudé právo,* November 28, 1952, 1; and *Proceedings of the Trials of Slánský, et al, in Prague, Czechoslovakia, November 20–27 as Broadcast by the Czechoslovak Home Service* (n.p., n.d), 1.

18. Jan Gerber, *Ein Prozess in Prag: Das Volk gegen Rudolf Slánský und Genossen* (Göttingen: Vandenhoeck & Ruprecht, 2016), 57, 220.

19. The Jewishness of the defendants, and the role of antisemitism in the trial more broadly, is thoughtfully explored in *A Trial in Prague,* directed by Zuzuna Justman (Teaneck, NJ: Ergo Media, 2001), DVD.

20. *Proceedings of the Trials of Slanský,* 116.

21. Gerber, *Ein Prozess in Prag,* 229, 226, 227.

22. Jiří Pelikán, ed., *The Czechoslovak Political Trials, 1950–1954: The Suppressed Report of the Dubček Government's Commission of Inquiry* (Stanford, CA: Stanford University Press, 1971), 113.

23. Pelikán, *The Czechoslovak Political Trials, 1950–1954,* 128–129. See also Johann Wolfgang Brügel, "Die dunklen Jahre der Tschechoslowakei—Der 'Piller-Bericht' über Schauprozesse und Justizmorde," *Osteuropa* 2 (1971): 102; and Frejková, *DK,* 136.

24. Frejková, *DK,* 95–96.

25. Frejková, *DK,* 96–98.

26. Ledvinka and Pešek, *Praha,* 642.

27. Pichová, *The Case of the Missing Statue,* 110–115.

28. McDermott, *Communist Czechoslovakia, 1945–89,* 100.

29. Frejková, *DK,* 127.

30. Hana Frejková, "Ohlédnutí," *Divadelní noviny* 28, no. 15 (2019), https://www.divadelni-noviny.cz/author/hana-frejkova.

31. Gerber, *Ein Prozess in Prag,* 21.

32. McDermott, *Communist Czechoslovakia, 1945–89,* 106–111, 121–127, 132–124.

33. McDermott, *Communist Czechoslovakia, 1945–89,* 130.

34. Frejková, "Ohlédnutí."

35. Jonathan Bolton, *Worlds of Dissent: Charter 77, the Plastic People of the Universe, and Czech Culture under Communism* (Cambridge, MA: Harvard University Press, 2012), 52–56. See also Kieran Williams, *The Prague Spring*

and Its Aftermath: Czechoslovak Politics, 1968–1970 (Cambridge: Cambridge University Press, 1997), esp. 39–60 for a discussion of Normalization. On Husák, see Michal Macháček, *Gustáv Husák* (Prague: Vyšehrad, 2017).

36. McDermott, *Communist Czechoslovakia, 1945–89*, 154, 159.

37. Kateřina Čapková, "Peripherie und Zentrum: Juden in den Böhmischen Ländern von 1945 bis in die Gegenwart," in *Zwischen Prag und Nikolsburg: Jüdisches Leben in den böhmischen Ländern*, ed. Kateřina Čapková and Hillel Kieval (Munich: Collegium Carolinum, 2020), 167. See also Ines Koeltzsch, *Geteilte Kulturen: Eine Geschichte der tschechisch-jüdisch-deutschen Beziehungen in Prag (1918–1938)* (Munich: Oldenbourg, 2012), 363; Hedviga Novotná, "Diskurzivní rámce vztahu k židům (antisemitismu) v období tzv. normalizace," in *Podoby antisemitismu v Čechách a na Slovensku ve 20. a 21. století*, ed. Monika Vrzgulová and Hana Kubátová (Prague: Karolinum, 2016), 157–176; and Jacob A. Labendz, "Re-negotiating Czechoslovakia: The State and the Jews in Communist Central Europe; The Czech Lands, 1945–1990" (PhD diss., Washington University in St. Louis, 2014).

38. Robert Tait, "Prague Revamp Reveals Jewish Gravestones Used to Pave Streets," *The Guardian*, May 5, 2020, https://www.theguardian.com/world/2020/may/05/prague-revamp-reveals-jewish-gravestones-used-to-pave-streets.

39. Bolton, *Worlds of Dissent*, 59–66.

40. McDermott, *Communist Czechoslovakia, 1945–89*, 166.

41. Paulina Bren and Mary Neuberger, referring specifically to the promise of consumerism, have referred to this bargain as a "social contract" in *Communism Unwrapped: Consumption in Cold War Eastern Europe* (New York: Oxford University Press, 2012), 12. See also Paulina Bren, *The Greengrocer and His TV: The Culture of Communism after the 1968 Prague Spring* (Ithaca, NY: Cornell University Press, 2010); and Michal Pullmann, "'Ruhige Arbeit' und die Einhegung der Gewalt: Ideologie und gesellschaftlicher Konsens in der spätsozialistischen Tschechoslowakei," in *Ordnung und Sicherheit, Devianz und Kriminalität im Staatssozialismus: Tschechoslowakei und DDR 1948 / 49–1989*, ed. Volker Zimmermann and Michal Pullmann (Göttingen: Vandenhoeck Ruprecht, 2014), 39–56. In one important respect, then, Communist Czechoslovakia shared similarities with Western Europe in that it was a welfare state whose political legitimacy rested on the ability to provide its citizens with economic and social security. Jakub Rákosník, *Sovětizace sociálního státu: Lidově demokratický režim a sociální práva občanů v Československu, 1945–1960* (Prague: Filozofická fakulta Univerzity Karlovy, 2009). See also Tomasz Inglot, *Welfare States in East Central Europe, 1919–2004* (Cambridge: Cambridge University Press, 2008); and Konrad H. Jarausch, "Care and

Coercion: The GDR as Welfare Dictatorship," in *Dictatorship as Experience: Towards a Socio-Cultural History of the GDR,* ed. Konrad H. Jarausch (Oxford: Berghahn Books, 1999), 47–72.

42. Alexei Yurchak, *Everything Was Forever, until It Was No More: The Last Soviet Generation* (Princeton, NJ: Princeton University Press, 2006), 93.

43. Bolton, *Worlds of Dissent,* esp. 13–14.

44. Frejková, June 18, 2018 interview.

45. Frejková, *DK,* 174.

46. Frejková, June 29, 2019 interview.

47. Frejková, June 29, 2019 interview.

48. Frejková, *DK,* esp. 143.

49. Frejková, *DK,* 98–99, 122.

50. Frejková, June 29, 2019 interview.

51. Frejková, "Ohlédnutí."

52. Frejková, "Ohlédnutí."

53. Frejková, "Ohlédnutí."

54. Frejková, "Ohlédnutí."

55. Vladimír Just, *Divadlo v totalitním systému: Příběh českého divadla (1945–1989) nejen v datech a souvislostech* (Prague: Academia, 2010), 107.

56. Just, *Divadlo v totalitním systému,* 106, 107.

57. Just, *Divadlo v totalitním systému,* 113.

58. For an insightful discussion of the theater spectator's encounter with theatrical events and the shared experiences of theater, see Susan Bennett, *Theatre Audiences* (London: Routledge, 1997).

59. Just, *Divadlo v totalitním systému,* 366.

60. Frejková, "Ohlédnutí."

61. Frejková, "Ohlédnutí"; "Maringotka," *Česká divadelní encyklopedie,* 2015, http://encyklopedie.idu.cz/index.php/Maringotka.

62. Frejková, "Ohlédnuti."

63. Jára da Cimrman and Zdeněk Svěrák, *Akt (rodinné drama se zpěvy a tanci)* (Prague: Paseka, 1992); "50 let Divadlo Járy Cimrmana," Divadlo Járy Cimrmana, https://www.cimrman.at/list.php?l=4.

64. Peter Bugge, "Normalization and the Limits of the Law: The Case of the Czech Jazz Section," *East European Politics and Societies* 22, no. 2 (2008): 282–318, quotations on 283.

65. Kieran Williams, *Václav Havel* (London: Reaktion Books, 2016), 109.

66. Bolton, *Worlds of Dissent,* 115–151; Just, *Divadlo v totalitním systému,* 114; Pavlína Morganová, *Czech Action Art: Happenings, Actions, Events, Land Art, Body Art and Performance Art behind the Iron Curtain* (Prague:

Karolinum, 2014); and Jan Pohunek, *Století tramping / A Century of Tramping* (Prague: Národní muzeum, 2018).

67. Paulina Bren, "Weekend Getaways: The Chata, the Tramp, and the Politics of Private Life in post-1968 Czechoslovakia," in *Socialist Spaces: Sites of Everyday Life in the Eastern Bloc*, ed. David Crowley and Susan E. Reid (Oxford: Berg, 2002), 123–140, esp. 124.

68. Eagle Glassheim, *Cleansing the Czechoslovak Borderlands: Migration, Environment, and Health in the Former Sudetenland* (Pittsburgh: University of Pittsburgh Press, 2016), quotation on 8; See also Matěj Spurný, *Making the Most of Tomorrow: A Laboratory of Socialist Modernity in Czechoslovakia* (Prague: Karolinum, 2019), esp. 9–10.

69. Doubravka Olšáková, "Im globalen Netzwerk? Die Planung der wissenschaftlichtechnischen Entwicklung der Tschechoslowakei von der Sowjetisierung bis zu den ersten Integrationsversuchen in den sozialistischen Block," *Bohemia: Zeitschrift für Geschichte und Kultur der böhmischen Länder* 57, no. 1 (2017): 25–54. See also the introduction to Vítězslav Sommer, Matěj Spurný, and Jaromír Mrňka, eds., *Řídit socialismus jako firmu: Technokratické vládnutí v Československu, 1956–1989* (Prague: Ústav pro soudobé dějiny, 2019), 5–13; and Martin Schulze Wessel and Christiane Brenner, eds., *Zukunftsvortellung und Staatliche Planung im Sozialismus: Die Tschechoslowakei im ostmitteleuropäischen Kontext 1945–1989* (Munich: Oldenbourg, 2010).

70. Matěj Spurný, Doubravka Olšáková, Vítězslav Sommer, and Jiří Janáč, "'Technokratischer Sozialismus' in der Tschechoslowakei," *Bohemia: Zeitschrift für Geschichte und Kultur der böhmischen Länder* 57, no. 1 (2017): 22. See also Vítězslav Sommer, "Forecasting the Post-Socialist Future: Prognostika in Late Socialist Czechoslovakia, 1970–1989," in *The Struggle for the Long-Term in Transnational Science and Politics: Forging the Future*, ed. Jenny Andersson and Eglė Rindzevičiūtė (New York: Routledge, 2015), 147; and McDermott, *Communist Czechoslovakia, 1945–89*, 109.

71. Sommer, "Forecasting the Post-Socialist Future," 153.

72. Spurný et al., "'Technokratischer Sozialismus' in der Tschechoslowakei," 14.

73. Sommer, "Forecasting the Post-Socialist Future," 153.

74. Ledvinka and Pešek, *Praha*, 640, 665.

75. Lukáš Beran and Vladislava Valchářová, eds., *Industrial Prague: Technical Buildings and Industrial Architecture in Prague; A Guide* (Prague: Czech Technical University, 2006), 146–147.

76. Kimberly Elman Zarecor, "What Was So Socialist about the Socialist City? Second World Urbanity in Europe," *Journal of Urban History* 44, no. 1 (January 2018): 98, 100. See also David M. Smith, "The Socialist City," in *Cities*

after Socialism: Urban and Regional Change and Conflict in Post-Socialist Societies, ed. Gregory D. Andrusz, Michael Harloe, and Iván Szelényi (Oxford: Blackwell, 1996), 72.

77. Eagle Glassheim, "Ethnic Cleansing, Communism, and Environmental Devastation in Czechoslovakia's Borderlands, 1945–1989," *Journal of Modern History* 78, no. 1 (March 2006): 65–92; Glassheim, *Cleansing the Czechoslovak Borderlands*; and Matěj Spurný, *Making the Most of Tomorrow: A Laboratory of Socialist Modernity in Czechoslovakia* (Prague: Karolinum, 2019).

78. Petr Roubal, "Krize urbanistické moderny v socialismu," *Soudobé dějiny* 3 (2017): 335–360; Matěj Spurný, "Věda a plan až do obýváku: Městské plánování a proměna bydlení v Československu (1955–1980)," in Sommer, Spurný, and Mrňka, *Řídit socialismus jako firmu*, 138–174.

79. Ctibor Rybár, *Prague: Guide, Information, Facts* (Prague: Olympia, 1979), 67.

80. Stanislav Holubec, *Lidé periferie: Sociální postavení a každodennost pražského dělnictva v meziválečné době* (Pilsen: Západočeská univerzita v Plzni, 2009), 121–123.

81. Roubal, "Krize urbanistické moderny v socialismu," 345.

82. Ledvinka and Pešek, *Praha*, 669; Jana Barvíková, "Jak se žije na Jižním Městě z pohledu 'Husákových dětí,'" *Sociální studia* 3 (2010): 62–63. See also Kimberly Elman Zarecor, *Manufacturing a Socialist Modernity: Housing in Czechoslovakia, 1945–1960* (Pittsburgh: University of Pittsburgh Press, 2011).

83. Miroslav Šmejkal, ed., *Metro v Praze: Stavba československo-sovětské spolupráce; Aktualita k zahájení provozu na 1. úseku pražského metra* (Prague: Nadas, 1974); Bohumil Moravec et al., *Pražské metro, stavba československo-sovětské spolupráce* (Praha: Orbis, 1974); Josef Škorpil, *Pražské metro: Čtvrtá dimenze velkoměsta: Historie, výstavba, provoz* (Praha: Panorama, 1990); Rybár, *Prague*, 51; and Ledvinka and Pešek, *Praha*, 672.

84. Spurný et al., "'Technokratischer Sozialismus' in der Tschechoslowakei," 14; Bren, *The Greengrocer and His TV*.

85. Rosemary Wakeman, *A Modern History of European Cities: 1815 to the Present* (London: Bloomsbury Academic, 2020), 303.

86. Jana Ratajová, "Pražské májové oslavy 1948–1989: Příspěvek k dějinám komunistické propagandy," *Kuděj: Časopis pro kulturní dějiny* 2, no. 1 (2000): 51–64.

87. Petr Roubal, *Spartakiads: The Politics of Physical Culture in Communist Czechoslovakia* (Prague: Karolinum Press, 2019), 81, 11.

88. Roubal, *Spartakiads*, 11–16, quotation on 11.

89. Vítězslav Sommer, "Social Sciences and 'Socialist Life Style' in Czechoslovakia 1968–1989" (CSEEES Visegrad presentation, University of North Carolina at Chapel Hill, April 2019); Sommer, "Zkoumání budoucnosti socialismu: 'Vědeckotechnická revoluce' a prognostika v reformě a 'konsolidaci,'" in Sommer, Spurný, and Mrňka, *Řídit socialismus jako firmu,* esp. 80–81.

90. Sharon L. Wolchik, "The Status of Women in a Socialist Order: Czechoslovakia 1948–1978," *Slavic Review* 38, no 4 (1979): 583–602; Martin Franc, "O ženách za pultem," in *Příběhy (ne)obyčejných profesí: Česká společnost v období tzv. normalizace a transformace,* ed. Miroslav Vaněk and Lenka Krátká (Prague: Karolinum, 2014), 381–418.

91. Ladislav Urbánek, interviewed by the author and Veronika Pehe, July 23, 2012.

92. Petr Vostřez, interviewed by the author and Veronika Pehe, July 16, 2012.

93. Hana Bortlová-Vondráková, "'Co jste hasiči, co jste dělali . . .': Proměny a konstanty jedné profese," in Vaněk and Krátká, *Příběhy (ne)obyčejných profesí,* 19–72. Bortlová-Vondráková interviewed twenty firefighters, who, with two exceptions, began work in the first half of the 1970s.

94. Petra Schindler-Wisten, "Sonda do života zdravotních sester v období tzv. normalizace a transformace," in Vaněk and Krátká, *Příběhy (ne)obyčejných profesí,* 419–460.

95. See, for example, Lenka Krátka, "Chránit se své tužky a štětce: Proměny podmínek života a práce lidí kteří se věnují výtvarnému umění," in Vaněk and Krátká, *Příběhy (ne)obyčejných profesí,* 319–352.

96. Bren, *The Greengrocer and His TV.*

97. Roubal, *Spartakiads,* 355–360, quotation on 359–360.

98. Roubal, *Spartakiads,* 363, 23. Geertz's quotation is from his *Negara: The Theatre State in Nineteenth-Century Bali* (Princeton, NJ: Princeton University Press, 1980), 13.

99. Oldřich Vízner file, sign. KR-638275 MV, 138–139, 181, 49, ABS.

100. Williams, *Václav Havel,* 109–110.

101. "50 let Divadlo Járy Cimrmana."

102. Bolton, *Worlds of Dissent,* 115–151.

103. Bolton, *Worlds of Dissent,* esp. 72–114.

104. McDermott, *Communist Czechoslovakia, 1945–89,* 177. On the number of signatories, see Bolton, *Worlds of Dissent,* 312n18.

105. "For New Creative Deeds in the Name of Socialism and Peace," in *Charta 77 1977–1989: Od morální k demokratické revoluci,* ed. Vilém Prečan

(Scheinfeld-Schwarzenberg: Středisko nezávislé literatury, 1990), 35–38, quotation on 37.

106. McDermott, *Communist Czechoslovakia, 1945–89*, 177.

107. Frejková, *DK*, 131.

108. Frejková, *DK*, 131; Frejková, "Ohlédnutí."

109. Frejková, "Ohlédnutí."

110. Frejková, June 29, 2019 interview.

111. Frejková file, sign. KR-769019 MV, April 28, 1978, 3, ABS.

112. Frejková file, sign. KR-769019 MV, June 26, 1978, 1, ABS.

113. Frejková file, sign. KR-769019 MV, November 1, 1978, 1–2, ABS.

114. Frejková, *DK*, 138; Frejková, June 29, 2019 interview. For a fascinating look at the regime's vague toleration of psychotherapy and the peripheral status of its practitioners, see Adéla Gjuričová, "Proměna socialistického člověka v liberální individuum? Pyschoterapie v Československu po roce 1968," in *Architekti dlouhé změny: Expertní kořeny postsocialismu v Československu,* ed. Michal Kopeček (Prague: Argo, 2019), 185–216.

115. Frejková, *DK*, 137.

116. Frejková, "Ohlédnuti."

117. Frejková, *DK*, 140.

118. Frejková, *DK*, 173.

119. Frejková, *DK*, 139.

120. Frejková, *DK*, 140.

121. Frejková, *DK*, 140–141.

122. Frejková, *DK*, 141.

123. Williams, *Václav Havel,* 140.

124. Havel, "Stories and Totalitarianism," *Index on Censorship* 17, no. 3 (1988), 15. The original Czech version was published in *Revolver Revue* in April 1987.

125. Havel, "Stories and Totalitarianism," 20–21.

126. Michal Pullmann, "The Demise of the Communist Regime in Czechoslovakia, 1987–1989: A Socioeconomic Perspective," in *The 1989 Revolutions in Central and Eastern Europe: From Communism to Pluralism,* ed. Kevin McDermott and Matthew Stibbe (Manchester: Manchester University Press, 2013), 155.

127. McDermott, *Communist Czechoslovakia, 1945–89,* 188.

128. "Miloš Zeman—prognostik (Znovu89)," posted by Český rozhlas (Czech Radio) on February 12, 2014, https://www.youtube.com/watch?v=iq145cqXch4.

129. McDermott, *Communist Czechoslovakia, 1945–89,* 190.

130. Beata Parkanová and Alexandra Škampová, "Revolver Revue," Česká televize, 2010, https://www.ceskatelevize.cz/porady/10290259112-revolver-re vue/21057223070/.

131. McDermott, *Communist Czechoslovakia, 1945–89*, 186.

132. James Krapfl, *Revolution with a Human Face: Politics, Culture, and Community in Czechoslovakia, 1989–1992* (Ithaca, NY: Cornell University Press, 2013), esp. 7.

133. Just, *Divadlo v totalitním systému*, 114–131.

134. McDermott, *Communist Czechoslovakia, 1945–89*, 184.

135. Pavlína Morganová, *A Walk through Prague: Actions, Performances, Happenings 1949–1989* (Prague: The Academy of Fine Arts in Prague, VVP AVU Research Center, 2017).

136. Pullmann, "The Demise of the Communist Regime in Czechoslovakia, 1987–1989," 162.

137. Timothy Garton Ash, "The Revolution of the Magic Lantern," *New York Review of Books* 36, no. 21 (January 18, 1990): 42–51.

138. Frejková, June 18, 2018 interview.

139. Frejková, June 18, 2018 interview.

140. Václav Havel, "New Year's Address," in *Open Letters: Selected Writings, 1965–1990*, trans. and ed. Paul Wilson (New York: Knopf, 1991), 390, 391, 395.

141. Havel, "New Year's Address," 392, 396.

142. Williams, *Václav Havel*, 167.

143. Frejková, *DK*, 171.

144. For an excellent summary, see Koeltzsch, *Geteilte Kulturen*, 1–17.

145. Frejková, *DK*, 174.

5. GLOBAL CITY

1. Duong Nguyen, "Dvojí život banánových dětí," Aktuálně.cz (hereafter A.cz), February 4, 2008, http://blog.aktualne.cz/blogy/nguyen-thi-thuy-duong .php?itemid=2602.

2. Luděk Sýkora et al., "Vztahy mezi majoritou, vienamskou menšinou a dalšími národnostními skupinami v MČ Praha-Libuš," Univerzita Karlova v Praze, Přírodovědecká fakulta katedra sociální geografie a regionálního rozvoje / Centrum pro výzkum měst a regionů, https://aa.ecn.cz/img_upload/22 4c0704b7b7746e8a07df9a8b20c098/vztahy-mezi-majoritou-a-vietnamskou -mensinou-v-mc-praha-libus-2014.pdf.

3. Cynthia Paces, *Prague Panoramas: National Memory and Sacred Space in the Twentieth Century* (Pittsburgh: University of Pittsburgh Press, 2009), 252.

4. Michal Kopeček, "In Search of 'National Memory': The Politics of History, Nostalgia and the Historiography of Communism in the Czech Republic and East Central Europe," in *Past in the Making: Historical Revisionism in Central Europe after 1989,* ed. Michal Kopeček (Budapest: Central European University Press, 2008), 4; Kieran Williams, "A Scorecard for Czech Lustration," *Central European Review* 1, no 19 (November 1, 1999), http://www.ce-review.org/99/19/williams19.html. As Françoise Mayer argues, a variety of competing memories of the past also emerged in this context, including those constructed by former and current Communist leaders, former members of the "gray zone," former dissidents, former political prisoners, and former State Security (*Státní bezpečnost*) agents and other "collaborators." Mayer, *Češi a jejich komunismus: Paměť a politická identita* (Prague: Argo, 2009), 52–80. Efforts by government-sponsored institutions and citizen associations to foster anti-Communist, Czech nationalist memories continued well into the 2000s, despite the challenges posed by forgetting, nostalgia, and an increasing plurality of views about the Communist past. See Vítězslav Sommer, "Cesta ze slepé uličky 'třetího odboje': Koncepty rezistence a studium socialistické diktatury v Československu," *Soudobé dějiny* 1 (2012): 9–36; and Veronika Pehe, "Authenticating the Past: Archives, Secret Police and Heroism in Contemporary Czech Representations of Socialism," in *Perceptions of Society in Communist Europe: Regime Archives and Popular Opinion,* ed. Muriel Blaive (London: Bloomsbury Academic, 2019), 207–222.

5. On the death penalty, see Otakar Liška et al., *Vykonané tresty smrti: Československo 1918–1989* (Prague: Úřad dokumentace a vyšetřování zločinů komunismu, 2000).

6. Vladimír Macura, "Metro," in *The Mystifications of a Nation: "The Potato Bug" and Other Essays on Czech Culture,* trans. Hana Pichová and Craig Cravens (Madison: University of Wisconsin Press, 2010), 73–84, esp. 80.

7. "Sousoší Kosmonautů," https://www.hrady.cz/index.php?OID=4784; "Kosmonauti / Praha—Haje, CZ—Occupational Monuments on Waymarking .com," http://www.waymarking.com/waymarks/WMEERC_Kosmonauti _Praha_Haje_CZ; and Andrea Svitáková, "Kosmonauti: Sousoší dvou stojících kosmonautů Vladimíra Remka a Alexeje Gubareva v Praze 11," http://www .socharstvi.info/realizace/kosmonauti/.

8. Marka Lašťovky, ed., *Pražský uličník: Encyklopedia názvu pražských veřejných prostranství,* 3 vols. (Prague: Libri, 1997), 1:468. See also Zdeněk Hojda and Jiří Pokorný, *Pomníky a zapomníky* (Prague: Paseka, 1996). For a discussion of Communist-era monuments in Eastern Europe more broadly, see John Czaplicka, Nida M. Gelazis, and Blair A. Ruble, eds., *Cities after the*

Fall of Communism: Reshaping Cultural Landscapes and European Identity (Washington, DC: Woodrow Wilson Center Press, 2009).

9. Kieran Williams, "National Myths in the New Czech Liberalism," in *Myths and Nationhood,* ed. Geoffrey Hosking and George Schöpflin (New York: Routledge, 1997), 134. See also Michal Kopeček and Piotr Wciślik, "Introduction: Towards an Intellectual History of Post-Socialism," in *Thinking through Transition: Liberal Democracy, Authoritarian Pasts, and Intellectual History in East Central Europe after 1989,* ed. Michal Kopeček and Piotr Wciślik (Budapest: CEU Press, 2015), 1–38.

10. Petr Roubal, "Anti-Communism of the Future: Czech Post-Dissident Neoconservaties in Post-Communist Transformation," in Kopeček and Wciślik, *Thinking through Transition,* 171–200.

11. Economic experts were just one constellation of Communist-era experts who adapted and thrived in the post-1989 era. See Michal Kopeček, ed., *Architekti dlouhé změny: Expertní kořeny postsocialismu v Československu* (Prague: Argo, 2019).

12. In 2000 the survey included ninety countries. First, and thus perceived as least corrupt, was Finland, and last was Nigeria. The 2008 survey included 180 countries. First was Denmark and last was Somalia. Transparency International, "Corruption Perceptions Index 2000," https://www.transparency.org/research/cpi/cpi_2000/0; Transparency International, "Corruption Perceptions Index 2008," https://www.transparency.org/research/cpi/cpi_2008/0. As Freedom House declared in 2002, "corruption in the Czech Republic has long passed the stage of unrelated bribes to government officials" to something that "exists on a national scale as a sophisticated enterprise that is parallel with public service." Adrian Karanycky, Alexander Motyl, and Amanda Schnetzer, eds., *Nations in Transit 2001* (New Brunswick, NJ: Transaction Publishers for Freedom House, 2001), 166, cited in Jeffrey M. Jordan, "Patronage and Corruption in the Czech Republic," *SAIS Review* 22, no. 2 (Summer / Fall 2002): 21.

13. Wade Jacoby, *The Enlargement of the European Union and NATO: Ordering from the Menu in Central Europe* (Cambridge: Cambridge University Press, 2004); Milada Anna Vachudova, *Europe Undivided: Democracy, Leverage, and Integration after Communism* (Oxford: Oxford University Press, 2005); and Rachel A. Epstein, *In Pursuit of Liberalism: International Institutions in Postcommunist Europe* (Baltimore: Johns Hopkins University Press, 2008).

14. Martin Horak, *Governing the Post-Communist City: Institutions and Democratic Development in Prague* (Toronto: University of Toronto Press,

2007), 37. Similar developments took place in most Central European capitals. See Philipp Ther, *Europe since 1989: A History*, trans. Charlotte Hughes-Kreutzmüller (Princeton, NJ: Princeton University Press, 2016).

15. Horak, *Governing the Post-Communist City*, 38.

16. "O Ikea Group," https://www.ikea.com/ms/cs_CZ/about_ikea/facts _and_figures/ikea_group_stores/czech_republic.html.

17. Lukáš Beran and Vladislava Valchářová, eds., *Industrial Prague: Technical Buildings and Industrial Architecture in Prague; A Guide* (Prague: Czech Technical University, 2006), 146–147; "Nový Smíchov," https://www.prague.eu /cs/objekt/mista/430/novy-smichov. For a depiction of the neighborhood around Angel Station before gentrification, see Jáchym Topol, *Angel Station*, trans. Alex Zucker (Victoria, TX: Dalkey Archive Press, 2017).

18. Ther, *Europe since 1989*, 161–208.

19. On the other hand, *The Rough Guide* also acknowledged the effects of increasing prices and rents in the center on locals: "Some argue that over-zealous restoration has turned central Prague into a theme park, that the arrival of multinationals has made Prague like every other city." Rob Humphreys, *The Rough Guide to Prague* (London: Rough Guide, 2008), 4.

20. On the tourist gaze and tourism as consumption, see John Urry, *The Tourist Gaze* (London: Sage, 2002).

21. Pražská informační služba, "Výroční zpráva 2008," 8, https://www .praguecitytourism.cz/file/edee/cs/annual-reports/vz-2008.pdf.

22. Veronika Dumbrovská and Dana Fialová, "Tourist Intensity in Capital Cities in Central Europe: Comparative Analysis of Tourism in Prague, Vienna and Budapest," *Czech Journal of Tourism* 3, no. 1 (2014): 14, fig. 4, and 11, fig. 1.

23. Luděk Sýkora, "Processes of Socio-spatial Differentiation in Postcommunist Prague," *Housing Studies* 14, no. 5 (1999): 690, table 5.

24. Lily M. Hoffman and Jiří Musil, "Prague, Tourism, and the Postindustrial City," Great Cities Institute working paper, May 2009, 18.

25. Sýkora, "Processes of Socio-spatial Differentiation," 693.

26. Tereza Blahoutová, "An Overview of the Migration Policies and Trends— Czech Republic," migrationonline.cz, February 4, 2013, https://migrationonline .cz/en/an-overview-of-the-migration-policies-and-trends#_ftnref1. On the Czech Republic's population in 2008, see Czech Statistical Office, "Population Change—Year 2008," March 13, 2009, https://www.czso.cz/csu/czso/ari /population-change-year-2008-vscwxcfmhk.

27. "27-1. Selected Indicators on Areas (NUTS 2): 2008," in Czech Statistical Office, *Statistical Yearbook of the Czech Republic*, 2009, https://www

.czso.cz/csu/czso/statistical-yearbook-of-the-czech-republic-2009
-wprjf5u1ll. In 2008 Prague's population was approximately 1.2 million.

28. For an overview, see Celia Donert, *The Rights of the Roma: The Struggles for Citizenship in Postwar Czechoslovakia* (Cambridge: Cambridge University Press, 2017).

29. Interview with Duong Nguyen Jirásková, June 19, 2019.

30. Duong Nguyen Thi Thuy, "Banánové děti v české džungli," Lidovky.cz, March 28, 2008, https://www.lidovky.cz/domov/bananove-deti-v-ceske-dzungli .A080328_144645_ln_domov_glu.

31. Interview with Duong Nguyen Jirásková, June 19, 2019.

32. Interview with Duong Nguyen Jirásková, June 19, 2019.

33. A point well made in Christina Schwenkel, "Rethinking Asian Mobilities," *Critical Asian Studies* 46, no. 2 (2014): 235–258.

34. Tara Zahra, *The Great Departure: Mass Migration from Eastern Europe and the Making of the Free World* (New York: W. W. Norton, 2016), 217–254.

35. Dušan Drbohlav, "The Czech Republic: From Liberal Policy to EU Membership," *Migration Policy Institute Newsletter,* August 1, 2005, https://www .migrationpolicy.org/article/czech-republic-liberal-policy-eu-membership/. See also Zahra, *The Great Departure.*

36. Mark Keck-Szajbel, "A Cultural Shift in the 1970s: 'Texas' Jeans, Taboos, and Transnational Tourism," *East European Politics and Societies* 29, no. 1 (February 2015): 212–225; Michal Skalski, "Unequal Friendship: Economic and Social Differences across the Polish-East German Border, 1972–1980" (MA thesis, University of North Carolina at Chapel Hill, 2016).

37. Petr Zídek and Karl Sieber, "Československo a subsaharská Afrika v letech 1948–1989," Shrnutí výsledků vědeckého projektu MZV RM, March 28, 2004, https://www.mzv.cz/file/16676/RM._03._28._04.pdf, 1; Petr Zídek and Karl Sieber, *Československo a subsaharská Afrika v letech 1948–1989* (Prague: Ústav mezinárodních vztahů, 2007); and Vladislav Günter, "Imigrace do Československa a Česka po druhé světové válce," in *Migrace: Historie a současnost,* ed. Zdeněk Uherek, Šárka Ošťádlová, Věra Honusková, and Vladislav Günter (Ostrava: PANT, 2016), 69–70. For a literary account of an African-Czech experience in Communist Czechoslovakia, see Tomáš Zmeškal, *Životopis černobílého jehněte* (Prague: Torst, 2009).

38. Alena Alamgir, "Socialist Internationalism at Work: Changes in the Czechoslovak-Vietnamese Labor Exchange Program, 1967–1989" (PhD diss., Rutgers University, 2014), 51–66. The hospital, which remains in operation, still flies the Czech flag. BỆNH VIỆN HỮU NGHỊ VIỆT TIỆP, http://www .viettiephospital.vn/.

39. Alamgir, "Socialist Internationalism at Work," 63.

40. Alamgir, "Socialist Internationalism at Work," 64; Christopher E. Goscha, *Vietnam: A New History* (New York: Basic Books, 2016), 372–399.

41. Schwenkel, "Rethinking Asian Mobilities," esp. 239.

42. Alamgir, "Socialist Internationalism at Work."

43. Tereza Freidingerová, *Vietnamci v Česku a ve světě: Migrační a adaptační tendence* (Prague: Sociologické nakladatelství, 2014), 30–31, 41–56.

44. Freidingerová, *Vietnamci v Česku a ve světě*, 41–42; Goscha, *Vietnam*, 399–400. See also Ivan V. Small, *Currencies of Imagination: Channeling Money and Chasing Mobility in Vietnam* (Ithaca, NY: Cornell University Press, 2018).

45. Freidingerová, *Vietnamci v Česku a ve světě*, 67; Schwenkel, "Rethinking Asian Mobilities," 252.

46. Sýkora et al., "Vztahy mezi majoritou," 6.

47. On bazaars and kiosks, see Gertrud Hüwelmeier, "Post-socialist Bazaars: Diversity, Solidarity and Conflict in the Marketplace," *Laboratorium* 5, no. 1 (2013): 42–66; Freidingerová, *Vietnamci v Česku a ve světě*, 106; and Ther, *Europe since 1989*, 167–174.

48. Andrea Svobodová and Eva Janská, "Identity Development among Youth of Vietnamese Descent in the Czech Republic," in *Contested Childhoods: Growing up in Migrancy*, ed. M. L. Seeberg and E. M. Goździak (New York: Springer, 2017), 124.

49. Freidingerová, *Vietnamci v Česku a ve světě*, 30.

50. Freidingerová, *Vietnamci v Česku a ve světě*, 75–80, 100–102; Michal Krebs and Eva Pechová, *Vietnamese Workers in Czech Factories: Research Report* (Prague: La Strada Czech Republic, 2009[?]), 21–28.

51. On the opening of the new "labor frontier" in Central and Eastern Europe more generally, see Stephen Castles, Hein de Haas, and Mark J. Miller, *The Age of Migration: International Population Movements in the Modern World*, 5th ed. (New York: Guilford Press, 2014), 103.

52. Interview with Duong Nguyen Jirásková, June 19, 2019.

53. Nguyen, "Dvojí život banánových dětí."

54. Duong Nguyen, "Banánové děti v české džungli," Lidovky.cz, March 28, 2008, https://www.lidovky.cz/domov/bananove-deti-v-ceske-dzungli.A080328 _144645_ln_domov_glu.

55. Nguyen, "Banánové děti v české džungli."

56. Andrea Svobodová, "Vietnam vzdálený i blízký: Potomci Vietnamců v Česku z pohledu teorie transnacionalismu" (PhD diss., Charles University, 2007).

57. Nguyen, "Dvojí život banánových dětí."

58. Duong Nguyen, "Jak jsme oslavili náš Nový rok," A.cz, February 10, 2008, http://blog.aktualne.cz/blogy/nguyen-thi-thuy-duong.php?itemid=2649 #more.

59. Lenka Tungová, "'Vạn Xuân'—Deset tisíc jar: Vietnamský časopis v Čechách" (Honors thesis, Charles University, 2008), 53; Nguyen, "Banánové děti v české džungli."

60. "Vietnamská dívka okouzlila čtenáře blogu iDnes.cz," iDnes.cz, March 13, 2008, https://info.blog.idnes.cz/blog.aspx?c=28303&setver=touch.

61. Šárka Martínková / Šimečková, "Blogerky a blogeři made in Czech & Vietnam," Klub Hanoi, July 11, 2008, http://sea-l.cz/cs/clanky/posts/blogerky -a-blogeri-made-in-czechvietnam/.

62. Tungová, "'Vạn Xuân'—Deset tisíc jar," 53–55.

63. See, for example, the 2004 documentary Cizinci u nás: Vietnamci [Foreigners among us: The Vietnamese], which was produced in cooperation with the human rights organization People in Need, https://www.ceskatelevize .cz/porady/1141180245-cizinci-u-nas/. In 2007 a popular cooking program, Boys in Action, visited "one of our Vietnamese fellow citizens." "Kluci v akci: Vietnamská domácí kuchyně," M. Froyda, Česká televize, Prague, 2007, https://www.ceskatelevize.cz/porady/10084897100-kluci-v-akci/20756 2221900027/.

64. Tereza Freidingerová and Andrea Svobodová, "Sapa in Prague: A Gate for the Vietnamese into Czech Society. Or Vice Versa?," V4 Revue, now viewable at https://www.academia.edu/20220917/2015_Sapa_in_Prague_A_gate _for_the_Vietnamese_into_the_Czech_society_Or_vice_versa_Visegrad _Revue_; Ezra Rawitsch, "Seeing Sapa: Reading a Transnational Marketplace in the Post-socialist Cityscape," Urban People / Lidé města 22, no. 2 (2020): 159–197.

65. Luděk Sýkora, Klára Fiedlerová, Tereza Freidingerová, Andrea Svobodová, and Dita Čermáková, "Soužití v městské čtvrti: Majorita a Vietnamci v Praze-Libuši," Sociologický časopis / Czech Sociological Review 4 (2016): 475–503.

66. Freidingerová, Vietnamci v Česku a ve světě, 92, 97.

67. On the history of Klub Hanoi, see Šárka Martínková / Šimečková, "13 let Klubu Hanoi v kostce," July 7, 2015, http://sea-l.cz/cs/clanky/posts/13-let -klubu-hanoi-v-kostce/. In 2018 the group created a new website took on a new name, "South-East Asia—Liaison," at a new web address: http://sea-l.cz/cs/. Not all of the original Klub Hanoi blog posts migrated to this site, however.

68. P. K., "Špičky vietnamského zpěvu v Praze," Klub Hanoi, September 14, 2004, http://sea-l.cz/cs/clanky/posts/spicky-vietnamskeho-zpevu-v-praze/.

69. Interview with Duong Nguyen Jirásková, June 19, 2019.

70. Freidingerová, *Vietnamci v Česku a ve světě*, 235. See also Freidingerová and Svobodová, "Sapa in Prague"; Sýkora et al., "Soužiti v městské čtvrti."

71. Freidingerová, *Vietnamci v Česku a ve světě*, esp. 235.

72. Adéle Souralová, "Children of Vietnamese Parents Brought Up by Czech Nannies: Reconstructing and Redefining Family Ties," in *Gender and Migration: Critical Issues and Policy Implications*, ed. Sibel Safi and Seref Kavak (London: London Centre for Social Studies, 2014), 48–56. See also Svobodová, "Vietnam vzdálený i blízký," 82–84; Do Thu Trang, "České babičky: Ženy, které pomáhaly vychovávat celou generaci mladých Vietnamců," Lidovky.cz, January 16, 2019, https://www.lidovky.cz/lide/asi-jatka-ceske-babicky-zeny-ktere -pomahaly-vychovavat-celou-generaci-mladych-vietnamcu.A190103_202217 _lide_ssu; and Martin Ryšavý, *Banánové děti*, MILD production c/o Grant-Produk, Jílové u Prahy, 2009.

73. Freidingerová, *Vietnamci v Česku a ve světě*, 98–100.

74. Duong Nguyen Jirásková, *Banánové dítě: Vietnamka v české džungli* (Brno: BizBooks, 2017), 40, 41 (hereafter *BD*).

75. Freidingerová, *Vietnamci v Česku a ve světě*, 85–86, table 4.3, 86.

76. Tungová, "'Vạn Xuân'—Deset tisíc jar," appendix #2, 86.

77. While lower than the United States at the time, the percentage of Czech internet users equaled the number of internet users in the United States in 2011 and has either equaled or surpassed the United States since then. World Bank Group, "Individuals Using the Internet (% of Population)," https://data .worldbank.org/indicator/IT.NET.USER.ZS?locations=CZ.

78. Nguyen, "Dvojí život banánových dětí." See also Nguyen Jirásková, *BD*, 40.

79. Nguyen, "Mami, chodím s Čechem," A.cz, March 17, 2008, http://blog .aktualne.cz/blogy/nguyen-thi-thuy-duong.php?itemid=2945.

80. Nguyen, "Se učit, se učit," A.cz, http://blog.aktualne.cz/blogy/nguyen -thi-thuy-duong.php?itemid=2779.

81. Nguyen, "Banánové děti v české džungli."

82. *OED Online, s.v.* "blog (*n.*)," June 2019, https://www-oed-com.libproxy .lib.unc.edu/view/Entry/256732?rskey=kxoOHh&result=1&isAdvanced =false.

83. Andrew Sullivan, "Why I Blog," *The Atlantic*, November 2008, https://www .theatlantic.com/magazine/archive/2008/11/why-i-blog/307060/.

84. Nguyen, "Jak jsme oslavili náš Nový rok."

85. Nguyen, "Banánové děti v české džungli."

86. Nguyen, "Banánové děti v české džungli."

87. Rýšavý, *Banánové děti*.

88. Freidingerová, *Vietnmaci v Česku a ve světě*, 27–28.

89. Phuong Thuy Do Thi, iDnes.cz, [n.d.], dothi.blog.iDnes.cz, accessed via https://web.archive.org.

90. Martínková / Šimečková, "Blogerky."

91. Comment section in Nguyen, "Banánové děti v české džungli."

92. Nguyen, "Dvojí život banánových dětí."

93. Martínková / Šimečková, "Blogerky."

94. "Vietnamská dívka okouzlila čtenáře blogu iDnes.cz."

95. Nguyen, "Se učit, se učit."

96. Nguyen, "Dvojí život banánových dětí."

97. Tungová, "'Vạn Xuân'—Deset tisíc jar," 54.

98. Nguyen, "Dvojí život banánových dětí."

99. Nguyen Jirásková, *BD*, 38–39.

100. Nguyen Jirásková, *BD*, 38; interview with Duong Nguyen Jirásková, June 19, 2019.

101. Interview with Duong Nguyen Jirásková, June 19, 2019.

102. Tungová, "'Vạn Xuân'—Deset tisíc jar," 54.

103. Phuong Thuy Do Thi, "Tak dost!," iDnes.cz, March 10, 2008, http://dothi.blog.idnes.cz:80/c/28063/Tak-dost.html, accessed via https://web.archive.org.

104. Nguyen, "Není banán jako banán," A.cz, April 29, 2008, http://blog.aktualne.cz/blogy/nguyen-thi-thuy-duong.php?itemid=3307#more.

105. Nguyen, "Není banán jako banán."

106. Nguyen, "Jedí Vietnamci psy?," A.cz, April 9, 2008, http://blog.aktualne.cz/blogy/nguyen-thi-thuy-duong.php?itemid=3140.

107. Interview with Duong Nguyen Jirásková, June 14, 2018. See also Nguyen Jirásková, *BD*, 38–45.

108. Duong Nguyen Jirásková, email correspondence with the author, July 4, 2020. Nguyen Jirásková requested that I mention her diagnosis in this book because, as she wrote me, "my therapy includes sharing, writing, [and] speaking about it."

109. Nguyen Jirásková, *BD*. In 2009 Lan Pham Thi published an autobiographical account of growing up in Písek amid economic struggles and local corruption, a story that begins with a nighttime encounter with skinheads. The author was celebrated as the first member of the Vietnamese community to write a Czech-language book, entitled *Bílej kůň, žlutej drak* (White horse, golden dragon). The book received much critical acclaim and won several book prizes. The true author, however, turned out to be Jan Cempírek, who does not have

Vietnamese roots. He said he had written the book to bring attention to the problematic relations between the Vietnamese community and the wider Czech community. In an interview with *Lidové noviny* he chided publishers for not printing books written by Vietnamese authors, pointing out that "the internet is full of blogs by Vietnamese authors, some very well-crafted, and yet none have found a publisher willing [to] provide opportunity and space for Vietnamese literary talent." Years later Cempírek offered advice and encouragement to Nguyen Jirásková as she wrote *Banana Child*. Jan Cempírek, *Bílej kůň, žlutej drak* (Prague: Knižní klub, 2009); see also Marek Kerles, "Mohu potvrdit, tu knihu jsem napsal, přiznava Cempírek," Lidovky.cz, November 30, 2009, https://www.lidovky.cz/kultura/mohu-potvrdit-tu-knihu-jsem -napsal-priznava-cempirek.A091129_215357_ln_kultura_tsh.

110. Nguyen Jirásková added too that she had other priorities, beginning with responsibilities toward her family. Duong Nguyen Jirásková, Facebook, September 19, 2018, https://www.facebook.com/duong.jiraskova.

111. Nguyen, "Hledání kořenů," A.cz, July 11, 2008, http://blog.aktualne.cz /blogy/nguyen-thi-thuy-duong.php?itemid=3941.

112. Nguyen, "Quê aneb návrat do vesnice, odkud opravdu jsem," A.cz, July 16, 2008, http://blog.aktualne.cz/blogy/nguyen-thi-thuy-duong.php?itemid =3994.

113. Nguyen, "Můj multikulturní strom," A.cz, September 17, 2008, http:// blog.aktualne.cz/blogy/nguyen-thi-thuy-duong.php?itemid=4589.

114. Nguyen, "Do Vietnamu za pár desetikorun? Žádný problém!," A.cz, August 13, 2009, http://blog.aktualne.cz/blogy/nguyen-thi-thuy-duong.php ?itemid=7324.

115. Nguyen, "Nakažena francouzským virem: Vlastenectvím," A.cz, May 21, 2009, http://blog.aktualne.cz/blogy/nguyen-thi-thuy-duong.php?itemid=6637.

116. Nguyen, "Do Vietnamu za pár desetikorun?" See also Nguyen, "Kam za pravou chutí a vůní Vietnamu?," A.cz, May 23, 2008, http://blog.aktualne .cz/blogy/nguyen-thi-thuy-duong.php?itemid=3528.

117. "Policisté prohledávali libušskou tržnici," Lidovky.cz, November 22, 2008, https://www.lidovky.cz/domov/policiste-prohledavali-libusskou-trznici.A081122 _130156_ln_domov_tma; and "Vietnamci: Chovali se k nám nehumánně," Lidovky.cz, November 24, 2008, https://www.lidovky.cz/domov/vietnamci-chovali -se-k-nam-nehumanne.A081124_180503_ln_praha_mtr.

118. Hana Čápová, "Česko proti Vietnamcům," Lidovky.cz, November 24, 2008, https://www.lidovky.cz/domov/cesko-proti-vietnamcum.A081124_084306 _ln_domov_mel.

119. "Pražané sepisují petici proti vietnamské tržnici," Týden.cz, November 26, 2008, https://www.tyden.cz/rubriky/domaci/prazane-sepisuji-petici-proti-vietnamske-trznici_92330.html.

120. "Hrad kritizuje zásah policie ve velkotržnici a blokaci víz Vietnamcům," iDnes.cz, November 30, 2008, https://www.idnes.cz/zpravy/domaci/hrad-kritizuje-zasah-policie-ve-velkotrznici-a-blokaci-viz-vietnamcum.A081130_204538_domaci_adb; "Podle policie vietnamskou tržnici Sapa nikdo úmyslně nezapálil," Česká televize, January 14, 2009, https://ct24.ceskatelevize.cz/regiony/1426122-podle-policie-vietnamskou-trznici-sapa-nikdo-umyslne-nezapalil.

121. Čápová, "Česko proti Vietnamcům."

122. Nguyen, "Ministře Langře: Vysvětlete, proč na nás posíláte transportéry!," A.cz, December 3, 2008, http://blog.aktualne.cz/blogy/nguyen-thi-thuy-duong.php?itemid=5250.

123. Alena K. Alamgir, "Race Is Elsewhere: State Socialist Ideology and the Racialisation of Vietnamese Workers in Czechoslovakia," Race and Class 54, no. 4 (2013): 67–85.

124. Alamgir, "Race Is Elsewhere."

125. Rob Cameron, "A Glimpse at Prague's Secretive Vietnamese Community," Radio Praha, https://www.radio.cz/en/section/talking/a-glimpse-at-pragues-secretive-vietnamese-community.

126. Miroslav Mareš, "Přistěhovalectví a krajní pravice v ČR," Středoevropské politické studie 3, no. 3 (2001), https://journals.muni.cz/cepsr/article/view/3866. For Eastern Europe more generally, see Sabrina P Ramet, ed., The Radical Right in Central and Eastern Europe since 1989 (University Park: Pennsylvania State University Press, 1999).

127. Ther, Europe since 1989, 217.

128. Organisation for Economic Co-operation and Development (OECD), International Migration Outlook 2009 (Paris: OECD Publishing, 2009), doi.org/10.1787/migr_outlook-2009-en, fig. 1.2, 16. Unemployment hovered around 5 percent throughout 2008, lower than any of its neighbors as well as the OECD average. By the end of the year Slovakia's unemployment rate was almost 10 percent; Germany, Poland, and Hungary each had unemployment rates around 8 percent. Ther, Europe since 1989, 178, fig. 6.4. Prague's unemployment rate rose to a little more than 4 percent in 2010. One reason for this low unemployment, Ther suggests, was that Prague's high housing prices prevented many job seekers from moving to the city.

129. Pražská informační služba, "Výroční zpráva 2008," 1, 15.

130. In response, the government passed a law, effective in 2011, making it more difficult to obtain a trade license. Two years of residence was required

before candidates could declare "self-employment" as their purpose of residence. Organisation for Economic Co-operation and Development (OECD), *International Migration Outlook 2012* (Paris: OECD Publishing, 2012), 222, doi .org/10.1787/migr_outlook-2012-en.

131. Freidingerová, *Vietnmaci v Česku a ve světě*, 79.

132. Člověk v tísni, "Mediální analýza: Téma nelegalní migrace v českých tištěných mediích," migraceonline.cz, January 22, 2008, https://migraceonline.cz /cz/e-knihovna/medialni-analyza-tema-nelegalni-migrace-v-ceskych -tistenych-mediich; Lenka Šafránková Pavlíčková, "Otevření Pandořiny skříňky: Mediální obraz cizinců pracujících v ČR," migraceonline.cz, July 28, 2009, https://migraceonline.cz/cz/e-knihovna/otevreni-pandoriny-skrinky-medialni -obraz-cizincu-pracujicich-v-cr.

133. Eva Pechová, *Migrace z Vietnamu do České republiky v kontextu problematiky obchodu s lidmi a vykořisťování* (Prague: La Strada Česká republika, 2007), 31. See also *Zlaté ručičky vietnamské*, the 2011 state-owned television documentary that stoked Czech fears about Vietnamese competition and illegality. According to the documentary, in the immediate post-Communist era Vietnamese stalls and stores grew "like mushrooms after the rain." *Zlaté ručičky vietnamské*, https://www.ceskatelevize.cz/porady/1100627928-ta-nase -povaha-ceska/411235100011010-zlate-rucicky-vietnamske/.

134. Nguyen, "Kam za pravou chutí a vůní Vietnamu?," A.cz, May 23, 2008, http://blog.aktualne.cz/blogy/nguyen-thi-thuy-duong.php?itemid=3528.

135. Svaz vietnamských studentů a mládeže v ČR, "Petice proti způsobu provedení zásahu policie ČR ve velkoobchodním centru SAPA dne 22.11.2008," Týden.cz, November 22, 2008, https://www.tyden.cz/priloha/petice-sapa-studenti -492eb04472e90.pdf.

136. Tereza Rejšková, "'Vadilo nám, že se nikdo z Vietnamců neozval': Rozhovor s Hien Tran Thu," migraceonline.cz, March 17, 2009, https://aa.ecn.cz /img_upload/224c0704b7b7746e8a07df9a8b20c098/TRejskova_RozhovorHien TranThu.pdf. See also Ryšavý, *Banánové děti*.

137. Rejšková, "Vadilo nám, že se nikdo z Vietnamců neozval.'"

138. Trang Tran Thu, "Petice vietnamských studentů—začátek bez konce," iDnes.cz, March 14, 2009, http://www.cerme.cz/media/cerme/ukazka_stud _mat/04/Prilohy/petice.pdf.

139. "Vietnamci očima Čechů, Češi očima Vietnamců," Klub Hanoi, May 26, 2009, http://klubhanoi.cz/view.php?cisloclanku=2009052601, accessed via https://web.archive.org.

140. Sýkora et al., "Vztahy mezi majoritou," 20; Nguyen, "Do Vietnamu za pár desetikorun?"

141. Svaz vietnamských studentů a mládeže v ČR, "Petice proti způsobu provedení zásahu policie ČR ve velkoobchodním centru SAPA dne 22.11 .2008," Týden.cz, [n.d.], https://www.tyden.cz/priloha/petice-sapa-studenti -492eb04472e90.pdf; "Velké razie na trhovce v Libuši i Holešovicích: Zadrženo 44 lidí," TN.cz, November 22, 2008, https://tn.nova.cz/clanek/zpravy /regionalni/na-trznici-v-prazske-libusi-vypukla-razie.html; Milan Daniel, "Apelplac v tržnici SAPA," *Britské listy*, November 23, 2008, https://legacy.blisty.cz /art/43916.html. See also Ladislav Vaindl, "Proti pražské razii protestují i Vietnmaci z Plzně," Deník.cz, November 29, 2008, https://www.denik.cz/z _domova/vietnamci_petice_razie20081129.html.

142. Helena Stinglová, "Vietnamští student sepsali petici proti razii v Sapě," Týden.cz, November 28, 2008, https://www.tyden.cz/rubriky/domaci /vietnamsti-studenti-sepsali-petici-proti-razii-v-sape_92795.html. See also, for example, Čapová, "Česko proti Vietnamcům," and Veronika Rodriguez, "Vietnamci: Policejní zásah byl nepřiměřný," A.cz, November 25, 2008, https:// zpravy.aktualne.cz/domaci/vietnamci-policejni-zasah-byl-neprimereny /r~i:article:623054/?redirected=1551195220.

143. Nguyen, "Ministře Langře."

144. Trang Tran Thu, "Petice vietnamských studentů—začátek bez konce."

145. "Number of Smartphone Users in the Czech Republic from 2013 to 2019 (in Millions)," *Statista*, August 31, 2015, https://www.statista.com/statistics /494605/smartphone-users-in-czech-republic/.

146. J. Johnson, "Forecast of Facebook User Numbers in the Czech Republic from 2015 to 2022," *Statista*, February 14, 2020, https://www.statista.com/statistics /568761/forecast-of-facebook-user-numbers-in-the-czech-republic/.

147. See, for example, Rachel Dretzin and John Maggio, "Growing Up Online," a Frontline Co-Production with Ark Media, LLC, WGBH Boston, 2008.

148. See, for example, Sherry Turkle, *Reclaiming Conversation: The Power of Talk in a Digital Age* (New York: Penguin, 2015); Shoshana Zuboff, *The Age of Surveillance Capitalism: The Fight for a Human Future at the New Frontier of Power* (New York: PublicAffairs, 2019); and Alice E. Marwick, *Status Update: Celebrity, Publicity, and Branding in the Social Media Age* (New Haven, CT: Yale University Press, 2013).

149. "Odkazy," Klub Hanoi, http://www.klubhanoi.cz/showpage.php?name =odkazy&rsindexpage=0, accessed via https://web.archive.org.

150. Nicholas Wu and Karen Yuan, "The Meme-ifcation of Asianness," *The Atlantic*, December 27, 2018, https://www.theatlantic.com/technology/archive /2018/12/the-asian-identity-according-to-subtle-asian-traits/579037/.

151. Comment section in Nguyen, "Banánové děti v české džungli."

152. Until 2017, Viet Food Friends was one of the most well known of these online sites for discussing food. http://www.vietfoodfriends.cz/. Before its closing, the AntHill Café was also a popular site for gathering. AntHill Café, Facebook, https://www.facebook.com/anthillcafe/.

153. See, for example, Vietsport, Facebook, https://www.facebook.com /vietsport.for.all/.

154. Harrison Rainie and Barry Wellman, *Networked: The New Social Operating System* (Cambridge, MA: MIT Press, 2012), esp. 21–58

155. Tereza Freidingerová and Ming Ngoc Mai, "Občanská angažovanost druhé generace Vietnamců: Nová vlna spolkové činnosti?," in *Kamenné instituce národnostních menšin a role samospráv při jejich podpoře: Sborník příspěvků z konference konané v Praze* (Prague: Magistrát hlavního města Prahy a dům národnostních menšin, O. P. S., 2018), 98; Ryšavý, *Banánové děti*.

156. The organization, however, no longer exists and the site has been taken down. Svaz Vietnamců v České republice home page, http://www.hnvn.cz/, accessed via https://web.archive.org.

157. Freidingerová, *Vietnamci v Česku a ve světě*, 74.

158. Duong Nguyen Jirásková, LinkedIn, https://www.linkedin.com/in /doimoiduong/en; Duong Nguyen Jirásková, Facebook, January 3, 2019, https://www.facebook.com/duong.jiraskova.

159. Viet Food Friends, http://www.vietfoodfriends.cz/.

160. Ivan Motýl, "Kdo je nejlepší bloger? Možná Vietnamka Do Thu Trang," Týden.cz, March 20, 2016, https://www.tyden.cz/rubriky/kultura/literatura/kdo -je-nelepsi-bloger-v-cesku-mozna-vietnamka-do-thu-trang_376759.html.

161. Diana Cam Van Nguyen, Vimeo, https://vimeo.com/user24889256.

162. Viet Up, home page, http://vietup.cz/; Viet Up, Facebook page, https://www .facebook.com/vietup.org/; and "Banán fest," Facebook events page, https://www .facebook.com/events/316031655447892/. For an excellent analysis of 1.5- and second-generation Vietnamese organizations and their aims, see Freidingerová and Mai, "Občanská angažovanost druhé generace Vietnamců."

163. Sapa trip, Facebook page, https://www.facebook.com/prahasapa/; Anthony Bourdain, "No Reservations: Prague" (New York: Zero Point Zero Production, 2010). See, however, Sapamapa, home page, http://www.sapamapa.cz/.

164. Sylva Reznik, "Defining National Minority under Czech Law," *Journal on Ethnopolitics and Minority Issues in Europe* 17, no. 2 (2018): 1–16, quotation on 9.

165. "Vietnamese Community Granted Minority Status in Czech Republic," Tn.cz, July 8, 2013, http://www.thanhniennews.com/politics/vietnamese -community-granted-minority-status-in-czech-republic-1947.html.

166. "Vietnamská národní menšina," Vláda ČR, July 16, 2013, https://www.vlada.cz/cz/ppov/rnm/mensiny/vietnamska-mensina-108870/.

167. Zita Senková, "Přepis: Jak to vidí Duong Nguyen Jirásková," *Český rozhlas*, July 11, 2018, https://dvojka.rozhlas.cz/prepis-jak-vidi-duong-nguyen-jiraskova-11-cervence-2018-7577408.

168. Freidingerová, *Vietnamci v Česku a ve světě*, 99, 88.

169. "Banán fest."

170. Freidingerová, *Vietnamci v Česku a ve světě*, 80.

171. Renne Dang, "Con lai," from the album of the same name, 2016, https://www.youtube.com/watch?v=GspsXLUxlrU. See also the interview with Dang in "Jsme banánové děti," A.cz, https://magazin.aktualne.cz/jsme-bananove-deti/r~7daad216f68411eaa6f6ac1f6b220ee8/.

CONCLUSION

1. "Stumbling stones" (in German, *Stolpersteine*) are the brainchild of the Hamburg artist Gunter Demnig, who now heads a team that researches, designs, and places these individualized monuments to those who perished in the Holocaust and to other victims of Nazi rule. Kristen Harjes, "Stumbling Stones: Holocaust Memorials, National Identity, and Democratic Inclusion in Berlin," *German Politics and Society* 23, no. 1 (2005): 138–151; Matthew Cook and Derek H. Alderman, "Public Memory and Empathy in Gunter Demnig's Stolpersteine," in *Global Perspectives on the Holocaust: History, Identity, Legacy*, ed. Nancy E. Rupprecht and Wendy Koenig (Newcastle upon Tyne: Cambridge Scholars Publishing, 2015), 321–348. As stumbling stones are the products of local efforts, there is no centralized organization in Prague that tracks their placement. See, however, the crowdsourcing project "Map of Prague's Stolpersteine / kamenů zmizelých Praha," https://www.mapotic.com/stolpersteine-praha, and "Stolpersteine Prague," https://www.facebook.com/stolpersteineprague.

2. Rosenstein's citizenship papers, his arrest report from 1942, and a police report, in Czech, from the summer of 1939 can be found in Policejní ředitelství Praha, 1941–1950, R, Rosenstein Benjamin, sign. R 2022 / 6, NA. All of these documents have been digitized and reproduced at "Benjamin Rosenstein," Holocaust.cz, https://www.holocaust.cz/en/database-of-victims/victim/118788-benjamin-rosenstein/.

3. Vojtěch Berger, inv. č. 21, 187–188, 196, 201–202, AHMP.

4. Egon Erwin Kisch, "Weihnachtsmarkt," in *GWE*, 95–99.

5. Hana Frejková, *DK,* 174; email correspondence with Hana Frejková, May 13, 2020; Skype interview with Hana Frejková, May 20, 2020.

6. Duong Nguyen Jirásková, WhatsApp interview with the author, May 15, 2020; email correspondence with Hana Frejková, May 21, 2020; Duong Nguyen Jirásková, Facebook, May 14, 2020, https://www.facebook.com/duong.jiraskova.

7. John Connelly, *From Peoples into Nations: A History of Eastern Europe* (Princeton, NJ: Princeton University Press, 2020), 21.

8. "Ze života génia," *Cimrmanův zpravodaj,* February 4, 2016, http://www.cimrman.at/list.php?l=8; Craig S. Smith, "Feeling Short of Real Heroes, Thus Fond of a Fake One," *New York Times,* May 17, 2007, http://www.nytimes.com/2007/05/17/world/europe/17pilsen.html?ref=craigssmith.

9. "CIMRMAN Jára da—Na domě čp.400 v Čapkově ulici 13 Praha 4 Michle," *Pamětní desky v Praze,* https://www.pametni-desky-v-praze.cz/products/cimrman-jara-da-/.

10. "7796 Járacimrman (1996 BG)," in *Solar System Dynamics,* NASA Jet Propulsion Laboratory, California Institute of Technology, https://ssd.jpl.nasa.gov/sbdb.cgi?sstr=7796; Lutz D. Schmadel, *Dictionary of Minor Planet Names,* 2 vols. (Berlin: Springer, 2012), 1:600.

11. Ladislav Smoljak and Zdeněk Svěrák, "Blaník," https://cimrman-smoljak-sverak.blogspot.com/2019/05/blanik.html.

ACKNOWLEDGMENTS

While I take full responsibility for the contents of this book, the idea to write about Prague was not mine. That initial spark was provided by Kathleen McDermott, my patient and erudite editor. Nor was it my idea to organize the book around individuals. John Connelly, who has continued to offer sage advice years after my PhD graduation, deserves credit for that. I also came to meet the main characters in the book thanks to colleagues and friends. A probing discussion with Pieter Judson about early nineteenth-century train travel led me to Karel Vladislav Zap. It was thanks to Alena Šimůnková that I knew where to find him. The thought to include Egon Erwin Kisch occurred to me while reading an article by Gary Cohen, who kindly offered comments on Chapter 2. Veronika Knotková, who has taught me so much about Prague's history, first suggested that I include her archival "superstar" Vojtěch Berger in the book. Fellow Bergerologists Jakub Beneš and Rudolf Kučera read earlier versions of Chapter 3 and helped me decipher some the diarist's most colorful language. Kateřina Čapková, the eminent historian referred to at the beginning of Chapter 4, first put me in touch with Hana Frejková. Tereza Freidingerová kindly met a stranger at Mama Café to offer a one-hour introductory tutorial on the Vietnamese community. At the end of our meeting, she advised me to reach out to Duong Nguyen Jirásková. Benjamin Frommer suggested yet another character, an occultist turned Nazi informant who, unfortunately, did not make the final cut, perhaps for obvious reasons. Ben's thoughts on some of my early drafts, and our many conversations about things Czech, have had a powerful influence on this book, however. I am especially grateful to Hana Frejková and Duong Nguyen Jirásková for our lively conversations and for trusting me with their lives.

The hard work of writing this book began and ended thanks to the generous support of two local institutions: The National Humanities Center (NHC), where I was a Delmas Foundation Fellow, and the Institute for the Arts and Humanities (IAH) at the University of North Carolina (UNC)–Chapel Hill, where I was an Edith L. Bernstein Fellow. During my tenure at the NHC, Mia Bay, Jared Farmer, and Ellen Stroud kindly read early drafts and pushed me to engage a wider audience. The IAH provided the time, mental space, and intellectual spark needed to finish the book. I particularly want to thank our spin-off writing group—Kia Caldwell, Maggie Cao, Elizabeth Havice, and Lauren Leve—for their discipline, critical encouragement, and comradery in the final months of the book's preparation. Early research for another project, conducted thanks to an American Council of Learned Societies Fellowship, which I held with coauthors Kateřina Čapková and Diana Dumitru, found its way into Chapter 4 as well.

Many others read all or part of the book in its various iterations: Karen Auerbach, Andrea Bohlman, Laura Brade, Emily Burrill, Oskar Czendze, James Patrick Daughton, Kathleen DuVal, Thea Favaloro, Dáša Frančíková, Erik Gellman, Kevin Hoeper, Andrew Kapinos, Ines Koeltzsch, Max Lazar, Mira Markham, Kaarin Michaelsen, Robert Nemes, Caroline Nilsen, Conor O'Dwyer, Susan Pennybacker, Zora Piskačová, Donald J. Raleigh, George Severs, Michal Skalski, Logan Smith, Jason Scott Smith, Larissa Stiglich, Milada Anna Vachudova, and Leah Valtin-Erwin. Some of the people mentioned above also attended a truly invigorating and heartening manuscript workshop hosted by the UNC–Chapel Hill Department of History and the IAH.

Ebony Johnson, Lisa Lindsay, Tommie Watson, and many others made it happen. I am eternally grateful to the workshop's lead commentators, Cynthia Paces and Tara Zahra, who shaped the manuscript at a crucial moment. Harvard University Press's two anonymous peer reviewers, clearly generous scholars both, did the same. My coeditors and dear colleagues Arthur Burns and Paul Readman focused my thinking about walking, often as we walked. Two UNC undergraduate students, Caroline Gladd and Paige Kemper, not only helped with research but provided perhaps the most trenchant and valuable critiques of my prose.

Still more colleagues and friends kindly offered comments on conference papers and other public presentations of my work over the years. Others invited me to speak about Prague. Still others contributed to this book simply by listening patiently to my rambles, answering my seemingly endless questions, or simply helping me figure something out. Those colleagues make up a long, yet admittedly partial, list: Vivian Bickford-Smith, Muriel Blaive, Petr Brod, Marek Čaněk, Holly Case, Sarah Cramsey, Michael Dean, Jiří "Marta" Dvořák, Sonja Dvořáková, Rachel Epstein, Barbara Falk, Melissa Feinberg, Michal Frankl, Anna Grzymala-Busse, Randall Hansen, Miloš Hořejš, Jessie Barton Hronešová, Petra James, Kristina Juergensmeyer, Petr Kalač, Padraic Kenney, Kateřina Králová, Lloyd Kramer, Hana Kubátová, Jonathan Kwan, Christian Lentz, Marián Lózi, Lucie Malá, Jill Massino, Louise McReynolds, Zsolt Nagy, Robert Nemes, Norman Naimark, Marek Nekula, Gillian O'Brien, Finola O'Kane, Andrea Orzoff, Thomas Ort, Max Owre, Jiří Pehe, Veronika Pehe, Hana Pichová, Markian Prokopovych, Molly Pucci, Ezra Rawitsch, Dominique Reill, Martin Rhodes, John Robertson, Eli Rubin, Christina Schwenkel, Radka Šuštrová, Rosemary Sweet, Jindřich Toman, Sylvia Tomášková, Veronika Tuckerová, Alexander Vari, Stephanie Weismann, Larry Wolff, Nathan Wood, Veronika Zajaková, and Kimberly Elman Zarecor (who also kindly provided the image of the Červený Vrch housing complex).

This list does not include the many people who have participated in events at UNC–Chapel Hill over the years. Their scholarship, and our conversations, have had a lasting impact on my work as well. I am especially grateful to those who have participated in our Czech and Slovak Studies Workshops as well as our conference on 1968 in Poland and Czechoslovakia. The Center for Slavic, Eurasian, and East European Studies; the Center for European Studies; the Carolina Center for Jewish Studies; the Department of History; the Department of Germanic & Slavic Literatures and Languages; the Department of Music; Global Relations; the IAH; and other units on campus have, in various ways, made these conversations possible. Here I would like to make special mention of the Visegrad Fund, which brought Ota Konrád, Michal Kopeček, Lucia Najslová, Petr Roubal, and Vítěžlav Sommer to our campus and classrooms, as well as some of the scholars already mentioned above. Thank you, too, to Adnan Džumhur, Kathleen Shanahan Lindner, Donald J. Raleigh, Graeme Robertson, John Stephens, and Kathryn Ulrich for helping to make it all happen. I have also benefited immensely from events and workshops with colleagues at Kings College London, all part of a larger collaboration between our two universities that owes much to the determined efforts of Katie Bowler Young and Melissa McMurray. Martin Doyle gave it to me straight during our conversations at a nearby university. A Bohemistika Grant from the Masaryk Institute and Archive provided space and conversations for me to sharpen my thoughts. The idea to make belonging the central theme of the book hit me while sitting alone in a small apartment in Bremen, Germany, after a short walk back from a truly bizarre hotel bar. I was in Bremen as a visiting scholar thanks to Sarah Lemmen and Martina Winkler, who also commented helpfully on my earlier work.

The book is the sum effort of much more than edits and ideas, of course. Veronika Pehe will be happy to know that I made use of materials obtained during our aborted project on Prague's subway system. Malcolm Swanston crafted the book's maps. Gabe Moss created other maps that have informed my writing and appear regularly in my public talks about Prague. At UNC–Chapel Hill, Sharon Anderson, Joyce Loftin, and Jennifer Parker made sure that I got where I needed to go, and much more. Michaela Lenčéšová and Elisa Moore tracked down facts and documents on my behalf. Kirill Tolpygo deserves enormous credit for creating one of the premiere Slavic and East European library collections in the country. Elaine L. Westbrooks, vice provost of UNC Libraries, personally rescued a crucial book for me during the COVID-19 shutdown. I also relied on the kind help of knowledgeable archivists such as Zora Damová, Pavlína Fúrová, Danuše Hrazdirová, Veronika Knotková, Naděžda Macurová, and Denisa Šťastná—many of whom also located images that appear in this book. Kathleen Drummy, Stephanie Vyce, and a host of others at Harvard University Press, and John Donohue at Westchester Publishing Services, made the book real. Peter Stein, a good friend and Holocaust survivor, has often visited my classes to speak about his boyhood experiences in Nazi-occupied Prague. He and his wife Michelle have shown me, and so many others, how history, biography, and empathy can serve the greater good. The previous pages, I hope, reflect many of the values nurtured at the family dinner table outside of McKeesport, Pennsylvania. Thank you, Mom and Dad.

Milada, Lukas, and Dominik made every trip to Prague together a wonderful adventure. Lukas and Dom also deserve much credit for venturing out, alone, to fact-check some of the sites and observations mentioned the book. The four of us are extremely grateful to Eliška Haasová, Ahn Duh Nguyen and her family, Kateřina (Kačka) Pei-kerová, Lydie Šilarová, Petra Stibalová, Jiří Trunda, Hana Zapadlová, and everyone at the Čekárna Café for welcoming us to their neighborhood just below Vyšehrad over the years. We have also been blessed with friends who have made those adventures fun, meaningful, and enlightening. They include, in no particular order: Joel, Liz, and Sevan; Kateřina; Jana, Bryan, Janek, and Anuška; Thea, Jiří, and Isabella;

Katka, Jakub, David, Zuzana, Adam, and Hana; Lenka, Honza, Ben, and Beata; Marek and Luba; Conor, Ingrid, and Declan; Lenka, Petr, Jáchym, and Elen; David, Tina, Sofia, and Šimon; and Jitka, Michal, Sára, Matýsek, Josefínka, and Justýnka. I am not a Praguer. I do, however, have a deep affection and a humble respect for the city. Thank you all.

INDEX

Note: Page numbers in *italics* indicate figures.